Rebellion in Black and White

Rebellion in Black and White

Southern Student Activism in the 1960s

Edited by
ROBERT COHEN AND
DAVID J. SNYDER

Foreword by DAN T. CARTER

The Johns Hopkins University Press
Baltimore

© 2013 The Johns Hopkins University Press
All rights reserved. Published 2013
Printed in the United States of America on acid-free paper

2   4   6   8   9   7   5   3   1

The Johns Hopkins University Press
2715 North Charles Street
Baltimore, Maryland 21218-4363
www.press.jhu.edu

Library of Congress Cataloging-in-Publication Data

Rebellion in Black and White: Southern student activism in the 1960s /
Edited by Robert Cohen and David J. Snyder ;
Foreword by Dan T. Carter.
pages   cm
Includes bibliographical references and index.
ISBN 978-1-4214-0849-1 (hdbk. : alk. paper) — ISBN 978-1-4214-0850-7 (pbk. : alk. paper) —
ISBN 978-1-4214-0851-4 (electronic) — ISBN 1-4214-0849-X (hdbk. : alk. paper) —
ISBN 1-4214-0850-3 (pbk. : alk. paper) — ISBN 1-4214-0851-1 (electronic)
1. Student movements—Southern States—History—20th century. 2. College students—
Political activity—Southern States—History—20th century. 3. Civil rights movements—Southern
States—History—20th century. 4. Whites—Southern States—History—20th century. 5. African
Americans—Civil rights—History—20th century. 6. Southern States—Race relations.
I. Cohen, Robert, 1955 May 21– editor of compilation.
LA229.R385 2013
371.8'1—dc23   2012027074

A catalog record for this book is available from the British Library.

*Special discounts are available for bulk purchases of this book. For more information, please contact
Special Sales at 410-516-6936 or specialsales@press.jhu.edu.*

The Johns Hopkins University Press uses environmentally friendly book materials, including recycled
text paper that is composed of at least 30 percent post-consumer waste, whenever possible.

CONTENTS

Deep South Campus Memories and the World the Sixties Made

DAN T. CARTER

Fifty years later, it is still difficult to grasp the cultural and political transformation of student life in the 1960s. In the 30 March 1959 issue of *Life* magazine, a full-page photograph showcased the latest college fad: 22 students crammed into a telephone booth in an attempt to break the Guinness world record, which had been held by a South African university. A decade later, a dozen photos in *Life*—including a Pulitzer Prize winner—featured triumphant black students with bandoliers of ammunition as they marched out of a Cornell University administration building, their rifles and shotguns held high.[1]

But that was in the North. In many ways, the essays in this book have been a revelation to me, as I suspect they will be to many readers. The images of militant protests during the sixties on the Berkeley, Madison, Columbia, and Cornell university campuses may be nearly as familiar as the photographs of black and white northerners (and some white southerners) participating in civil rights marches and demonstrations. But the writers in this collection tell us stories we haven't heard before: of hippie coffeehouses and countercultural neighborhoods scattered around predominantly white southern colleges and universities, even demonstrations and riots by their students against police brutality, the repression of free speech, and *in loco parentis* restrictions by academic administrators. It seems so "un–white southern." As one bemused University of Alabama professor wrote after he watched the violent demonstrations at his school in May 1970, "It's like finding marijuana in your grandmother's jewelry box."[2]

There was no marijuana in grandmother's jewelry box when I transferred to the University of South Carolina in 1960. It was a parochial institution with fewer than six thousand students, all of them white and most of them from South Carolina.

1. *Life,* 2 May 1969, vol. 66, 20–27.
2. From Gary S. Sprayberry, chapter 6 in this volume.

Five years earlier, history professor Dan Hollis, who would become my under-graduate thesis adviser, complained about the openly anti-intellectual attitudes of most students, who seemed far more interested in football games and weekend beer parties than in politics or indeed in ideas of any kind. That was not an alto-gether accurate assessment. During the 1950s, the campus newspaper, *The Game-cock,* became the home of a small group of future journalists who sometimes dis-sented from the region's massive resistance to racial change. But Hollis's evaluation was not far off the mark; the campus was conservative to the core.

For the mostly middle-class students, fraternities and sororities, as the main entrée into future social and business relationships, dominated campus life. The proportion of women students had grown to one-third of all students by the end of the 1950s. Training to be primary or secondary school teachers remained the most popular major of Carolina coeds with, according to a campus newspaper columnist, a secondary major in capturing a husband. If so, they were handi-capped in this landscape of repressed but testosterone-charged 18- to 22-year-old men. The dean of women forbade female students from donning slacks or shorts of any kind outside the women's quadrangle, and skirts and dresses had to be worn below the knee. (Although there was no official dress code for male students, most still wore coats and ties to classes.)

Gender roles, to use contemporary terminology, remained traditional, to say the least. There were a number of beauty contests, with Carolina coeds seek-ing to be named Miss Garnet and Black (the school's colors) or to be crowned homecoming queen, but none could quite match the Sigma Chi's annual Derby Day celebration. Before a raucous crowd of mostly male students, sorority girls donned high heels, short-shorts, and tight blouses before putting paper bags over their heads and strutting across the stage for the honor of being crowned Miss Venus. The only seditious activity of the decade occurred in 1955, when as many as a thousand male students staged panty raids (or "lingerie raids," as University officials discreetly described them).[3]

When I signed up for classes at USC in September 1960, the registration desks were piled high with "gift packs" courtesy of Roger Milliken, the Spartanburg textile magnate who had jump-started the modern Republican Party in South Carolina. Later in life, Milliken wanted to be remembered for his role in supporting the 1964 integration of his Spartanburg alma mater, Wofford College. In the 1950s, how-ever, the longtime John Birch Society supporter had made a national reputation

3. Henry H. Lesesne, *A History of the University of South Carolina, 1940–2000* (Colum-bia: Univ. of South Carolina Press, 2001), 108.

for busting unions by closing his Darlington, South Carolina, mill in 1956 after workers voted to unionize. Packed neatly next to the toiletry articles—toothbrush, toothpaste, deodorant, shampoo—was a copy of J. Edgar Hoover's paranoid anti-communist screed, *Masters of Deceit* (1958), and an anti-union pamphlet published by the National Right to Work Committee. Although I wrote a suitably indignant letter of protest to *The Gamecock,* I quickly learned that most students at Carolina, like other southern campuses, could not have cared less. They were instinctively conservative in their racial and economic attitudes and—as Dan Hollis had said—far more interested in the location of the best weekend keg party than either politics or race relations.

During my two years as a reporter for the Florence *Morning News,* from 1958 to 1960, I had come to identify, at least intellectually, with the emerging civil rights struggle and a variety of liberal positions, but I initially found few students who shared my interests. After I wrote a letter to *The Gamecock* expressing the scandalous view that labor unions were not necessarily advance agents of the Communist Party, Hayes Mizell, a first-year history graduate student, tracked me down. Hayes introduced me to Charles Joyner, Selden Smith, and the handful of campus liberals who recruited new members to their ranks with the diligence of embattled missionaries.

As Marcia Synnott notes in her essay in this collection, I was one of the students who formed the South Carolina Student Council on Human Relations in 1961. The first meetings brought together black and white students from colleges and universities in Columbia. Under the guidance of Alice Spearman and Libby Ledeen, we expanded our membership to include students from around the state. In seminars in the basement of the Methodist Church's Lady Street headquarters; in workshops at the Penn Center on St. Helena's Island; at the Dorchester, Georgia, civil rights training center; and at the famous Highlander Folk School, I came to know a remarkable group of young men and women who were in the vanguard of the nonviolent civil rights struggle.

Even though we were extraordinarily cautious by the standards of the late 1960s, there were unpleasant consequences. Hayes Mizell and Charles Joyner lost their teaching fellowships, and members of the legislature darkly warned that "radical students" would be expelled if they challenged the state's segregation laws.

Still, I suffered few consequences. I never took part in civil rights direct action beyond a voter registration drive in a black neighborhood of Columbia, and the only violence I encountered came at a USC football game in 1961 when three members of Kappa Alpha dragged me out of my seat and shoved me down the concrete stairs of the old Carolina Stadium after I refused to stand for the USC band's rendition of "Dixie." While activist friends such as John Lewis and Bob

Zellner were getting their heads cracked by Alabama's finest, I had to sit in the dean's office and listen to his plaintive concern that my civil rights activities might "embarrass" the university. The closest I came to a brush with the law was when an agent from the South Carolina Law Enforcement Division visited my father and warned him that I was consorting with "known communist racial agitators."

My father ignored him. He already suspected that I was consorting with "known communist racial agitators."

If fewer than three dozen students from the university joined our group, looking back I can see the first tentative signs of change. In the fall of 1961, South Carolina State Representative Albert Watson (soon to be Sixth District Congressman Albert Watson) reserved a large auditorium in the campus student center, the Russell House, for a showing of the House Un-American Activities Committee film *Operation Abolition*. The documentary portrayed the raucous May 1960 anti-HUAC demonstrations at San Francisco's City Hall by Berkeley and Stanford students as the latest chapter in the effort of red agents and their gullible "pinko" dupes to communize America. Watson, a fanatical anticommunist and segregationist, had repeatedly expressed his fear that left-wing faculty members at Carolina were luring students into their web of anti-Americanism. With a warning to be on the watch for subtle procommunist propaganda, Watson introduced the film to a crowd of more than two hundred USC students.

When the discussion period opened, however, the questions were hardly what Watson had expected. Was he aware that the scenes were edited totally out of sequence or that the film clip of one communist activist depicted as leading the students actually came from footage of a communist demonstration in 1950? Did it concern him that reporters from both San Francisco newspapers had documented dozens of factual errors in the film and had found no evidence that students were inspired, led, or controlled by members of the Communist Party? And why had the *Christian Century* and the Catholic weekly *America* condemned the film as a distortion of events in San Francisco?

Increasingly angry, Watson cut off the questioning and slammed his hand on the rostrum: "The communists are out to cut our throats!" he yelled. "And I say we cut theirs first!" It hardly evoked the response he was expecting; several students openly laughed. As Watson stalked from the auditorium, I called out, "If you want to see the truth, come across the hall!" All but a handful of students marched to a nearby room where an ad hoc group of activists showed *Operation Correction*, the ACLU's documentary rebuttal to the HUAC film. As a number of these essays point out, segregationists had carefully nurtured the argument that integration was a communist plot unleashed on a peaceful and racially harmonious region. A willingness to consider the possibility that student protest was not prima facie evidence of communist direction hardly reflected a revolutionary shift, but—in retrospect—the bemused response of many of my fellow students to Watson's table-pounding brand of anticommunism reflected a subtle shrinking of Cold War orthodoxy.

Still, it's important to get the chronology straight. Reading these essays, I realize that, as a college student from 1958 to 1962, I missed out on the full cultural upheavals of the 1960s, with its promise of liberation through easy sex, drugs, and rock and roll. Sex? I grew up in the 1950s. The only drugs I sampled at the University of South Carolina were "blue bennies" (Benzedrine) obtained at the local truck stop to help me through all-night study sessions. While I sang along with the new folk movement and collected LPs by the likes of Pete Seeger, Joan Baez, and Odetta, I had no use for rock and roll. If you wanted to listen to something besides classical music, I kept asking myself, why would anyone prefer Elvis Presley, Chuck Berry, or Little Richard to *real* musical artists such as John Lewis and the Modern Jazz Quartet, Bill Evans, Charlie Byrd, J. J. Johnson, Art Blakey, and Miles Davis?

In the fall of 1962, I began graduate study at the University of Wisconsin. In comparison with the University of South Carolina, Wisconsin was an intellectually lively and politically engaged campus with civil rights as the galvanizing force for social change among black students and white supporters. Civil rights activists and other prominent political figures regularly spoke on campus; I first heard George Wallace in 1963 when he gave a turgid lecture on states' rights to a critical, but polite, audience. I took diplomatic history from an avowed Marxist, William Appleman Williams, but there were no calls to the barricades in his or any other classes. (Williams's most admiring comments seemed to be reserved for President Herbert Hoover.) In the fall of 1963, I recall reading with great interest about the demonstrations by predominantly white Berkeley students against the discriminatory hiring practices of a number of San Francisco businesses. I found these developments encouraging but exotic. In short, I detected little foreshadowing of the broad student unrest and political upheavals that would soon grip the campus.

Ironically, there was more campus political activism on the Chapel Hill campus of the University of North Carolina, to which I transferred in the fall of 1964. I arrived there in the wake of the previous year's large-scale student protests against racial segregation in Chapel Hill's restaurants and motels. (Police arrested dozens of students; several received stiff prison sentences, gaining their release only when they promised to leave the state.)

Although the Civil Rights Act of 1964 brought about the integration of local businesses, student activism expanded in protest against the state's 1963 Speaker

Ban Law, which barred from the campus all "known communists" as well as those who had invoked the Fifth Amendment in federal, state, or local investigations of "subversive activities." After the newly organized chapter of Students for a Democratic Society invited the communist historian Herbert Aptheker, university officials barred Aptheker from speaking on campus. In a decorous piece of political theater negotiated with university officials and carefully choreographed for television cameras and news reporters, I joined over a thousand students on the quadrangle to listen to Aptheker as he stood five feet away on the public sidewalk of Chapel Hill's East Franklin Street.

The student movement seemed to explode in 1964 and 1965. If the rise of a more free-spirited student culture, the growing campus resistance to *in loco parentis,* and the political impact of the civil rights movement laid the foundations for student rebellion, the war in Vietnam sent students to the street in far greater numbers. In May 1964, several hundred demonstrators in half a dozen American cities peacefully marched to protest the nation's growing involvement in Vietnam; the Free Speech Movement erupted on the Berkeley campus that same fall. At that time there were fewer than 30,000 American "advisers" in Vietnam. By the fall of 1965 there were 185,000 soldiers, sailors, and marines engaged in increasingly lethal combat. In 1966 that number increased to nearly 400,000, and male students were clinging to their II-S student draft deferments, well aware that, with graduation (or academic failure) they might well join the ranks of the 8,000 dead and 30,000 wounded. As the war escalated, so did the level of political activism on college campuses. It is not cynicism to recall Samuel Johnson's pithy line: "When a man knows he is to be hanged in a fortnight, it concentrates his mind wonderfully." The prospect of being sent halfway around the world to die in the jungles of Vietnam was scarcely more comforting.

As a married graduate student from a rural area of South Carolina with a disproportionately small number of young men claiming student deferment status, I was relatively safe from the draft. But the war was driven home to me in the summer of 1966 as I taught summer school at East Carolina University. When the head of UNC's graduate program recommended me for the position, I saw it as a great opportunity. I would be able to establish some teaching experience for my curriculum vitae, and East Carolina was prepared to furnish a free dorm room, a meal card, and the munificent sum of $2,400 for only five weeks of teaching, the same amount as my annual UNC graduate stipend. No one had bothered to tell me that, in this, my first teaching assignment, I would have 16 hours of new class preparation per week. Nor was I prepared for the fact that many of my students were taking my U.S. History and World Civilization courses after ending their first year on academic probation. With the typical zealotry of the first-year teacher, I graded my midterms with slashing red marks, exclamation points of sarcastic disbelief, and dozens of Fs.

I don't remember his name, but I can still recall the face of the withdrawn (and rather overweight) student who came in to see me the day after I returned the papers. He said that he wanted to know how to improve his grade from F to C. In reality his visit was to remind me that he was on the verge of academic suspension and that a failing grade would lead to his immediate induction into the army. His older brother, he told me, was already fighting in Vietnam. As I looked out at my class the next day, I reminded myself that my job was to teach my courses and then evaluate the performance of my students as fairly as I could. Still, however melodramatic it may sound, I never have forgotten turning in those final grades, looking at the list of students with "F" beside their names, and asking myself: what if one of these young men—most of them only three or four years younger than me—dies in Vietnam because they confused Charlemagne with Pepin the Short?

By the time I began my first teaching appointment at the University of Maryland in 1967, the campus was alive with student protests. In 1968, as the first faculty member to offer a course in "Negro History"—quickly changed to "Black History"—I struggled to navigate through the sometimes angry reactions of newly radicalized black students. (At the end of my first lecture, a distressed black student walked past me and said, very loudly, to one of his friends, "My God, he's not only a honky, he's a cracker, too.") Protests demanding greater student rights paralleled, and sometimes combined with, antiwar marches and sit-ins. Twice I made the journey to Upper Marlboro, Maryland, to testify on behalf of teaching assistants arrested for taking part in campus sit-ins. Only 20 miles southeast of the university, the small county seat seemed closer to Mississippi than suburban Washington, and the right-wing county prosecutor and presiding judge disagreed only over who was the more detestable: ungrateful student hooligans or their left-wing academic advisers.

But my time at the University of Maryland proved only prologue to 1969, when I returned to the University of Wisconsin as a young visiting associate professor. The campus I remembered from my time in the early 1960s had become a war zone, with student marches, demonstrations, and almost continuous strikes: attacking job recruitment by Dow Chemical for making napalm for use in Vietnam, calling for a halt to ROTC on campus, demanding a union for student teaching assistants. Much of that year is a collage of memories: a striking graduate student spitting on me after I reluctantly crossed the teaching assistants' picket line to go to my class; holding a wet handkerchief to my face as I walked through billows of tear gas lobbed into crowds of demonstrating students by nervous National Guardsmen; and pausing before beginning one of my lectures on twentieth-century radicalism to allow time for bandana-wearing undergraduates to march in and arrange themselves on the floor in front of the raised speaker's platform. (There were over four hundred students in the class.)

Perhaps most memorable was the surreal conversation I had with one of my teaching assistants just before I testified on his behalf after he was charged with the felonious destruction of public property. I found it difficult to imagine this gentle and soft-spoken young man jaywalking, let alone committing a felony. "Professor Carter," he said as he knelt down next to me. "I really appreciate you speaking up for me, but I do need to tell you that they have a series of photographs of me setting fire to a Madison city police car."

Despite all of my misgivings about what I believed to be the undisciplined—even anarchic—behavior I encountered, I never again felt so fully engaged with students who seemed to be asking fundamental questions about domestic and foreign policy and their responsibility to speak and act to bring about a different, and more humane, America. These essays remind us that, although that upsurge of student activism may have been greater elsewhere in the country, it touched a generation of southern students. Some may now look back with embarrassment on what they see as their youthful indiscretions; for others it shaped their outlook for the remainder of their adult lives.

There is no doubt that the sixties remains the great divide of the twentieth century. If the civil rights and antiwar movements as well as the broader cultural revolution resonated in different ways across the nation, north and south, how much really changed? Certainly there were transformations. First civil rights, then feminism, gay rights—later gay, lesbian, bisexual, transgendered rights—all grew out of the sixties. And in many ways, the "youth culture" of the sixties has come to play a far greater role over the last half-century. The 1950s now seems another country.

But there was more than youthful rebellion and personal liberation involved in the sixties. However naive the emotionalism (and sometimes self-righteousness) of the idealism, there was a vision of change that went beyond that self-liberation. Many students of the 1960s (and the 1970s) imagined an America that would reject the warrior state and create a more just society, what leaders of the civil rights movement had come to call the "Beloved Community."

In 1967, during my first year of teaching at the University of Maryland, I was in the library looking for primary sources that would give my students some insight into the passion and intensity of earlier generations, and I stumbled across a reissued edition of Walter Lippmann's 1915 classic of optimistic progressivism,

Drift and Mastery. Lippmann explained how a "fear economy" had paralyzed civic activism during World War I. By making voters fearful of losing their jobs, fearful that their welfare in old age would not be secured, fearful that their children would lack opportunity, they became, in language that smacked of the nineteenth century, a "servile and dreaming race," clinging desperately to a precarious niche.

Lippmann, like many of his fellow progressives, confidently looked forward to the day when our nation would be "intelligent enough to have made destitution impossible, when it secures opportunity to every child, when it establishes for every human being a minimum of comfort below which he cannot sink." At that point, he wrote, "Every issue will not be fought as if life depended upon it, and mankind will have emerged from a fear economy."[4] Even when I acknowledged in my teaching the heedless optimism of Lippmann and his fellow progressives, it was a reading that seemed part of an earlier intellectual tradition that had re-emerged in the 1960s.

Perhaps it is the cynicism of age that leads me to conclude that the 1960s began a "freedom revolution" in the larger society—and among students—but quickly lost this earlier search for a more humane reconstruction of America. In his essay in this volume, Nicholas Meriwether evocatively describes the Columbia, South Carolina, "hippie" emporium, The Joyful Alternative. As he notes, founder Dale Bailes sought to build a distinctive southern counterculture by self-consciously looking backward to progressive elements in southern history. His great passion was introducing readers to intellectually challenging books by southern writers and poets and stocking his shop with traditional regional crafts like corncob pipes—even if they were designed for toking rather than traditional smoking. As Bailes acknowledged, however, drug paraphernalia were what financed the Joyful—"a lot more people were getting stoned than were reading."[5]

Ideas are important. Beginning in the 1970s, it was the ideologues of the New Right who seemed to be brimming with inventiveness. They dismissed the creativity and the concrete accomplishments of the 1960s, skillfully turning them into a caricature of "rapist-coddlers and flag burners and pornography purveyors and other elitists who were out of touch with 'mainstream American values.'"[6] Blended with the powerful forces of racial backlash, the dogma of government incompetence, and the promise of a free-market utopia, the new narrative fueled the conservative backlash of the 1980s and 1990s.

4. *Drift and Mastery* (New York: Henry Holt and Company, 1914), 248.
5. From Nicholas G. Meriwether, chapter 9 in this volume.
6. George Packer, *Blood of the Liberals* (New York: Farrar, Straus, and Giroux, 2000), 333.

As the new conservatism of Ronald Reagan and his heirs skillfully fueled the growing hostility toward government policies that benefited the most vulnerable members of our society, veterans of the protest movements of the 1960s were among the most forceful critics of the domestic and foreign policies of the Reagan administration. But there had always been a tension between the assertive individualism of the decade—"Do your own thing!"—and the communitarian idealism that had shaped so much of that rebellion. And with the slogan, "the personal is political," identity politics—Black Power, feminism, gay rights (eventually)—became a political battleground; too often the result was a reversal of the slogan: the political became personal, emphasizing differences over a faltering common vision.

Writing in the *Harvard Crimson* in the late 1980s, undergraduate Lisa Taggart insisted that there was a continuity of purpose in the student activism of her generation, but she acknowledged that it was much more fragmented and skeptical of broad change. Students were likely to be involved in discrete and generally nonconfrontational activities: distributing petitions for divestment of South African stocks, tutoring students in minority neighborhoods, running campus educational programs against sexism and homophobia. After talking with students around the country, she concluded that most did not want to establish a national network of student activism; they believed that "a more effective way to work for political change is to focus on local issues and local change."[7]

Ultimately, the loss of confidence in collective action through government that had formed the foundation for the New Deal, the civil rights legislation of the 1960s, and Lyndon Johnson's Great Society was not restricted to conservatives. As the pollsters discovered in their surveys of "trust in government," a growing number of self-identified liberals had lost that faith as well.[8]

At the risk of making the study of history utilitarian, how important is it to look back at the student rebellions of the sixties? Student life is inherently transient; one class disappears, and another arrives on campus with a fading connection to the issues and experiences of those who have graduated. The first thing to recognize is that the decade may have reshaped our ways of thinking, but it cannot serve as any roadmap for the present or the future. Historian Gordon Wood has described the ways in which the Founding Fathers looked to republican antiquity to "help shape their values and justify their institutions." But the ideas of the past,

7. "The Times They Have Changed," *Harvard Crimson*, 27 May 1988.
8. "Fewer Are Angry at Government, But Discontent Remains High," http://people -press.org/2011/03/03/section–1-attitudes-about-government/, accessed 26 June 2012.

he argued, then and now, have only a limited impact on the present: "What really *determines* thought are the events of the participants' present, their immediate interests and emotional needs, their present experience."[9]

College students today live in a different world from that of the generation that came to maturity in the 1950s and 1960s. I entered the Florence County extension program of the University of South Carolina in 1958. My tuition bill for the year was $276 ($2,107 in today's dollars). USC's 2012 tuition is more than $10,000. As a white male university graduate, I never worried about finding a job or a achieving a reasonably secure economic future. If the Cold War still raged, by the 1980s it had become background noise for most of us. As a college student I had listened to Pete Seeger's rendition of "Little Boxes," with its sarcastic description of suburbia where the doctors, lawyers, and business executives living in their "ticky-tacky" little boxes all had gone to university, played golf, had pretty children who went to summer camp, and then sent them to university so that they could be put in the same little boxes.[10] For undergraduates in today's insecure postindustrial world, often graduating with crushing student loans, the security of little boxes must seem appealing rather than something to be scorned—especially if the ticky-tacky houses can escape foreclosure.

At the same time, the path to a more humane and just America seems far more daunting to this generation than it was for the students of the 1960s. In the "fear society" bemoaned by Walter Lippmann, how is it possible even to imagine changing a dysfunctional political system surrounded by shallow media outlets that seem to reward slogan-wielding ideologues, the more simple-minded the better? Bull Connor and Lyndon Johnson proved to be easier targets than faceless hedge fund managers, a globalized labor market, or the challenge of dealing with global warming when half of the American people believe that it is not a serious problem.[11]

As a member of a generation with at least one foot in the 1960s, I believe that we have failed to challenge the conservative vision of an America that demands little more from its citizens than the reckless exercise of self-interest. Unless we are once again willing to imagine in new ways a nation in which the dignity and worth of every person are more than an empty slogan, this is the world our children and our children's children will inherit.

---

9. Gordon S. Wood, *The Idea of America: Reflections on the Birth of the United States* (New York: Penguin, 2011), 77.

10. Words and music by Malvina Reynolds, copyright 1962, Schroder Music Company.

11. "Americans' Global Warming Concerns Continue to Drop," www.gallup.com/poll/126560/americans-global-warming-concerns-continue-drop.aspx, accessed 24 Sept. 2011.

Still, it is worth remembering that authentic political movements have often emerged when least expected. If, as Gordon Wood says, each generation must find its own way, there is still something to be learned from those students of the sixties who struggled to liberate themselves and to create an America that demands something greater from us all.

This book would not exist were it not for the Vietnam-era antiwar protesters whose history, after decades of neglect, sparked the convening of a major historical conference on southern student activism in the 1960s, which in turn generated many of the essays in *Rebellion in Black and White*. The "Student Activism, Southern Style" conference was held at the University of South Carolina in 2010 to mark the fortieth anniversary of the takeover of the Russell House, the campus student union building, by students protesting the Kent State massacre and the U.S. invasion of Cambodia. Like most of the southern campus demonstrations portrayed in *Rebellion in Black and White*, the Russell House takeover has failed to make it into the northern-centered histories of 1960s America, but it was an event that made headlines across the Palmetto State. The National Guard and state police were mobilized; tear gas, used to disperse unruly crowds, wafted into dormitories and drove students into the waiting arms of the police; dozens were arrested or suspended; Governor McNair declared a state of emergency. The Russell House occupation, when viewed together with the Orangeburg massacre of 1968, calls into question some persistent regional tropes: that outside agitators were responsible for campus unrest; that South Carolina's embrace of civil rights was peaceful; that southern students are polite and genteel.

Although southern historians are finally beginning to recognize the Russell House occupation, perhaps the best-known account of the occupation is a fictionalized version, which appeared in acclaimed South Carolina author Pat Conroy's *Beach Music*, a low-country coming-of-age novel. Conroy depicts the Russell House takeover as an irrational detonation of youthful exuberance. His southern college students were unknowing victims of a mad time, entering into that "slippery, rampaging decade" obliged to guard their "soft underbellies" against "inspection or slaughter." Unlike Conroy's naive protester-victims, however, the participants in the Russell House takeover, like all the student activists depicted in the following pages, were conscious agents of democratic change in a region massively resistant to that change. Conroy's fictitious account represents his deeply personal coming to terms with the period his narrator remembers as "the silliest and stupidest of times," but the South Carolina protest followed a logic repeated at campuses across the South. While Conroy imagines a "spontaneous riot that had neither purpose nor leadership," the University of South Carolina protests actually emerged against a backdrop of profound institutional change as the university was transformed from a parochial Jim Crow school into a racially integrated cosmopolitan university and major international research center. South Carolina students, ending their regional isolation, were influenced by powerful national trends: resistance to *in loco parentis* rules, the civil rights and antiwar movements, and the rise of the counterculture.

The veterans of the Russell House takeover continue to resist being erased from history, much as they resisted war, racism, and political repression in their student days. Brett Bursey, perhaps the most prominent of the University of South Carolina's student radicals in the 1960s, was persecuted and jailed. Yet he maintains his independent-mindedness and activism to this day, proudly championing progressive causes in a deeply conservative region. Vickie Eslinger, who recalls pounding on the trunk of the squad car that took Bursey to jail for his role in the Russell House takeover, later stood up as lead plaintiff in a suit against the discriminatory page-hiring practices of the state legislature; Eslinger is now one of the leading civil rights attorneys in Columbia. Another prominent local attorney, Luther Battiste III, traces his public career to his early activist days at the University of South Carolina when he served as campaign manager for Harry Walker, the university's first African American student body president.

At the "Student Activism, Southern Style" conference, Bursey, Eslinger, and Battiste recounted how their work as student activists shaped their lives and careers. We would like to thank them for their role in "Student Activism, Southern Style" and also extend our thanks to other sixties-era movement veterans who shared their memories of the southern freedom struggle: Connie Curry, Tom Gardner, Tom Hayden, Chuck McDew, Martha Noonan, and Cleveland Sellers. Their powerful stories helped to inspire this book. We are also grateful to the historians and other scholars who came to Carolina from across the nation to present fresh research on student activism in the South. Much as we might like to, we cannot with complete veracity represent the conference as a successful act of closure, a binding of old wounds, and a recognition that new narratives have been embraced to replace the old. When the local newspaper, *The State,* covered the conference, including Hayden taking in a Gamecocks baseball game as a guest of university president Harris Pastides, fiery protests complaining about the university hosting such notorious radicals filled the online comments section of the story.

Such sentiments call to mind Faulkner's line: "The past is never dead. It's not even past."

We express our gratitude to our colleagues in academic units across and beyond the University of South Carolina campus who came together to support and host the conference. These include the University of South Carolina's Department of History, the Honors College, First Year Experience, the Department of Political Science, the Office of the Provost, the Department of English, the Office of Research and Graduate Education, the College of Education, the Institute for African American Research, the Museum of Education, Women's and Gender Studies, the Department of Educational Leadership and Policies, and the Russell House Bookstore. Generous sponsorship came from the Humanities Council of South Carolina, the Western Carolina University Department of History, the Western Carolina University Office of the Dean, the Western Carolina University Provost, and the Peace History Society.

For their assistance at various stages of the conference and this anthology project, we thank Dan Carter, Ray Farabee, Lacy Ford, Kent Germany, Lawrence Glickman, Gael Graham, Carrie Hoefferle, Chaz Joyner, Craig Kridel, Dan Littlefield, Nick Meriwether, Hayes Mizell, Kate Shelton and Jim Twitty, Marjorie Spruill, Doyle Stevick, Pat Sullivan, Tom Terrill, Celia Tisdale, and Merll Truesdale. Special thanks to (now former) University of South Carolina students Katherine Jernigan and John Warren, who embody the best traditions of the engaged southern student. We are also deeply grateful to the historians who could not make it to the conference but who agreed to contribute essays to this book. Robert Cohen would like to thank Leon Litwack for sparking his interest in southern history and to thank Robert P. Moses, Charlayne Hunter-Gault, Walter Stovall, Calvin Trillin, Tom Gardner, Tom Hayden, Chuck McDew, Martha Noonan, Sue Thrasher, Lee Frissell, George Ware, and Floyd M. Hammack for discussing with him both their experiences in the freedom struggle in the deep South and their views of the southern campus scene of the 1960s. Finally, we thank our editor at the Johns Hopkins University Press, Jackie Wehmueller, for her wise advice and strong support, which helped make this book possible.

We want to thank all those student activists who gave so much of themselves to build a democratic South in the "long sixties." The book is dedicated to the students who lost their lives in that struggle as well as those nonstudents who fell with them. These students are listed with their college or university and affiliation and the years of their deaths; those listed together lost their lives together. It is our hope that historians will honor their memory by teaching about the history of the southern struggle for social justice and racial equality and that students of the twenty-first century will carry on the work of building a new South.

DEDICATION

In memory of those killed in the student struggle for social justice and racial equality in the South:

Henry Hezekiah Dee, Charles Eddie Moore, Alcorn A&M (1964)
James Earl Chaney, Andrew Goodman, Queens College, and
    Michael Henry Schwerner, Columbia University (1964)
Samuel Leamon Younge Jr., Tuskegee Institute (1966)
Samuel Ephesians Hammond Jr., Delano Herman Middleton, and
    Henry Ezekial Smith, South Carolina State College (1968)
Willie Ernest Grimes, North Carolina, A&T (1969)
Phillip Lafayette Gibbs and James Earl Green, Jackson State College (1970)
Denver Smith and Leonard Brown, Southern University (1972)

Rebellion in Black and White

Prophetic Minority versus Recalcitrant Majority

Southern Student Dissent and the Struggle for Progressive Change in the 1960s

ROBERT COHEN

Readers accustomed to thinking about America today as divided into blue (liberal Democratic) and red (conservative Republican) states—with the South shaded a deep crimson, as the heartland of conservatism—are in for a big surprise in the pages that follow. These essays attest that, on both black and white college campuses south of the Mason-Dixon line, there was, in the 1960s, considerable liberal and radical ferment and a southern New Left that was active enough—as Gregg Michel's essay attests—to generate fear, espionage, and dirty tricks by the FBI, segregationist state and local police, and their confederates. Southern student activists championed such progressive causes as racial integration, gender equality, birth control, an end to the Vietnam War, student rights, labor's right to organize, the introduction of Black Studies departments, and greater African American student and faculty representation and power on campus. These activists were vocal, well organized, and often courageous in standing up for their principles, even though this initially proved unpopular in a region famed for its conservatism. Southern student organizers during the "long sixties"—an era of reformist and radical ferment that extended into the early 1970s—deployed a range of tactics from polite petitioning to mass protest, including civil disobedience. And the southern campus rebellion transcended politics, also encompassing the counterculture and support for greater personal freedom, alternative lifestyles, and sexual liberation.[1]

Even before African American student activists from North Carolina A&T College launched the sit-in movement against Jim Crow lunch counters in February 1960, a small group of dissident southern students sought ways to undermine racial segregation. Erica Whittington's chapter shows that, from the late 1950s to the mid-1960s, southern student activists affiliated with the National Student

Association brought black and white students together for human relations seminars, hosting interracial conversations that were deep, candid, and moving because they broke so radically with the segregated social relations of the Jim Crow South. These interracial gatherings forged lifelong friendships and changed the lives of participants, some of whom would go on to play leading roles in the sit-in movement, the Student Nonviolent Coordinating Committee, and other organizations and movements for racial equality. Whittington's regional study is complemented by Marcia Synnott's chapter on human relations organizers in South Carolina. Synnott finds that while South Carolina's sit-in movement was weaker than in such movement centers as Atlanta or Nashville, the human relations veterans helped make up for this by promoting public support of peaceful accommodation to racial integration—which, she suggests, contributed to South Carolina's desegregation process often (but not always—as the Orangeburg massacre attests) being less polarized and violent than its counterparts in other deep South states, such as Alabama and Mississippi.

Southern student protest will never be fully understood until historically black colleges and universities (HBCUs) are more widely recognized as major sources of dissent. Too often, white America's historical memory (embodied, for example, in U.S. history textbooks and in book-length histories of the 1960s) slights or ignores the black colleges. This is a key reason why when one reads about the history of violent suppression of campus dissent, the first image that appears is white and northern: John Filo's Pulitzer Prize–winning photo from Kent State University, showing the teenage Mary Ann Vecchio grieving over the body of Jeffrey Miller, one of the 4 students fatally shot (9 were wounded) by National Guardsmen during protests on 4 May 1970 against the U.S. invasion of Cambodia.[2] But cumulatively, the death toll from such violent suppression of student protest was actually higher on the South's historically black campuses, with 3 dead and 27 wounded in 1968 at South Carolina State College in Orangeburg after a protest against a Jim Crow bowling alley; one student killed and another wounded at North Carolina A&T in 1969, as police used guns and an armored personnel carrier to quell racially charged student protests in Greensboro; 2 students killed and 12 wounded by police gunfire at Jackson State College in Mississippi in protests growing out of clashes with racist white motorists in 1970; and 2 students killed by sheriff's deputies dispersing a student takeover of the administration building at Southern University in Baton Rouge, Louisiana, in 1972.[3]

When we begin to focus on the HBCUs in the 1960s, a complex picture emerges, as Jeffrey Turner discusses in his Nashville case study. On the one hand, these campuses housed students who were among the most idealistic and daring foes of segregation, eager to abolish the Jim Crow system and all its indignities and inequities. And, in fact, as Jelani Favors and Cleveland Sellers point out in their chapters, an activist subculture was at times visible on top black campuses long before the 1960s—most notably at Fisk in the 1920s, in the wake of the Harlem Renaissance, at Howard amidst the rising NAACP legal battle against racial inequality in higher education during the 1930s, as well as other Depression-era HBCUs during the Old Left's Popular Front heyday. But the HBCUs were also centers of black assimilation and bourgeois aspiration, with a much higher percentage of first-generation college students than on predominantly white campuses (60% of black college freshmen in the 1960s came from families whose fathers had never completed high school vs. 25% for white college freshmen).[4] There was great pressure on black students not to rock the boat by challenging segregation. Such activism, after all, involved risking not only their physical safety and jail time but also their educational careers and their families' chances of social advancement. Activist fame could also lead to threats to family members or loss of jobs. Anne Moody, for example, in her classic civil rights memoir *Coming of Age in Mississippi,* wrote of her mother's alarm at a local white sheriff's warning that Anne was attending NAACP meetings at college. Anne recalled her mother threatening her that if "I didn't stop that shit she would come to Tougaloo and kill me herself."[5]

In fact, HBCU presidents often served as impediments to black student protest. Many had been selected by white trustees because they were gradualists opposed to mass protest, a tendency reinforced by the black colleges' dependence on white funding. In his memoir, *The Education of a Black Radical* (2009), D'Army Bailey expressed anger and anguish at the "Uncle Tomism" of Southern University president Felton Clark, who expelled Bailey and other students for participating in sit-ins against local Jim Crow businesses during the early 1960s. Bailey found that it "proved much easier to confront the 'external foe,'" Louisiana's segregationists, than "such antagonists" as Clark "in the black community who had long been empowered by the very oppressive segregationists we sought to reform." Bailey noted that "between 1960 and 1962 hundreds of student [protest] leaders were expelled from Negro land grant colleges in the South," a purge that has yet to find its historian.[6]

Subsequent surges in student activism were put down even more harshly at Southern University, with over 150 expulsions. Clark's successor, Leon Netterville, authorized a police invasion of the campus in 1972 in which tear gas was used to disperse the students occupying his office. Two unarmed student protesters were shot dead by a sheriff's deputy.[7] Southern was arguably the worst-case scenario, and it is true that some black college presidents openly identified with the civil rights movement. Had North Carolina A&T president Warmoth T. Gibbs not departed from his usual deference to A&T's white trustees by standing up for his students' political rights, the Greensboro sit-ins might have been crushed before they evolved into a historic mass movement.[8] But this was an unusual act of political courage, since state-supported black colleges were so vulnerable to white pressure. And even private black colleges—most of which were religiously affiliated—felt the heat, as Tougaloo president Adam Beittel learned when he paid with his job in 1964 for allowing his college to serve as a base for civil rights organizing in Mississippi.[9] At the end of the 1960s African American critics were still complaining about repression on "black college campuses [that] were run like feudal estates . . . with the President the feudal lord, the administrators—his vassals and the students his serfs."[10]

Given this repressive political atmosphere, documented in Joy Ann Williamson-Lott's chapter, it is all the more remarkable that HBCUs emerged as centers of the black freedom movement, whose young activists served as the spark plugs of the lunch counter sit-ins. Fisk University, one of these centers of HBCU student activists, is portrayed in Turner's chapter, which places Fisk in comparative context with its wealthier white neighbor, Vanderbilt University. Turner finds that initially, activists on both Nashville campuses struggled against similar social institutions and academic traditions that inclined students to avoid committing themselves to sustained political activism. But he also shows that student civil rights organizers at Fisk overcame such political lethargy, building an activist subculture earlier and mobilizing large numbers of their classmates against Jim Crow, while white student radicals at Vanderbilt who challenged segregation in the early 1960s remained an isolated, though dynamic, minority.

Black student activists in the South during the early 1960s out-organized not only their white counterparts on neighboring campuses but even the emerging New Left organizers of the more liberal North. Wesley Hogan's chapter attests that the Student Nonviolent Coordinating Committee, which evolved out of the sit-in movement of 1960, was organizing civil disobedience campaigns at a time when Students for a Democratic Society—the leading student radical organization in the North, Midwest, and far West—was still acting much like a debating society, more centered on talk and manifesto-writing than action.[11] The sit-in movement, in journalist Jack Newfield's words, sent

> shockwaves radiating from North Carolina . . . [that] quickly jolted Northern campuses out of a decade of silence and sloth. The television newsreels of fellow students being punched by hecklers and hosed by police pierced the split level dream of thousands of white Northern students. . . . In an estimated 130 cities and hamlets of the North, whites, mostly students, demonstrated in solidarity with their brothers [and sisters] in the South. The Uncommitted Generation was beginning to find a Commitment; the Silent Generation was beginning to find

its voice on a picket line; and the generation that wouldn't sign a petition was beginning to realize that a jail record could be a badge of honor. In those first few weeks, the sit-ins clearly liberated more white middle class students in the North than it did Southern Negroes.[12]

SDS president Carl Oglesby readily acknowledged the northern student movement's debt to SNCC: "At our best . . . [SDS is] SNCC translated to the North . . . on a . . . broader set of issues. Our best concern comes from SNCC."[13]

SNCC's reputation for training America's most daring and militant civil rights organizers, born in the sit-in movement, was reinforced by the way that its Nashville contingent refused to let the Freedom Ride campaign of 1961 go down to defeat after being disrupted by brutal racist attacks on the interstate buses that the riders sought to desegregate. SNCC activists put their lives on the line, enduring threats, arrest, and more violence to see that the Freedom Rides won the cessation of Jim Crow interstate bus travel.[14]

Equally daring was the SNCC effort to bring the vote to disenfranchised blacks in Mississippi, the South's most violently racist state, a crusade that, while not centered on civil disobedience, nonetheless caused a bloody backlash from that state's white supremacists. The bombings, beatings, and shootings that the black freedom movement endured in Mississippi led SNCC to accelerate its efforts to attract solidarity, donations, and volunteers from northern college campuses, culminating in Freedom Summer of 1964, when hundreds of mostly white student volunteers came south to assist in dangerous voter registration and freedom school work. Though designed to strengthen the challenge to white supremacy in the South, SNCC's outreach to northern campuses from 1962 through 1964 served as a catalyst that helped move SDS and the northern New Left from talk to action. SNCC modeled the most egalitarian of approaches to community organizing that would, as Hogan documents, inspire northern student radicals to enhance their political skills and willingness to challenge authority. This set the stage for the campus organizing that, through Berkeley's Free Speech Movement of fall 1964 (the first to bring to campus the mass civil disobedience that SNCC had used against racist white businesses) and then the antiwar movement (which began to surge with the mass teach-ins on the Vietnam War in spring 1965), helped make the 1960s an era of mass student protest nationally. Attesting to the leavening effect that Freedom Summer and SNCC had on campus activism and social protest nationally, SNCC founder John Lewis recalled, "The atmosphere of openness and breaking down barriers that we developed that summer extended far beyond issues of race. They extended into everything from sexuality to gender roles, from communal living to identification with working classes. And they live on today. . . . The Mississippi

Summer Project . . . led to the liberating of America, the opening up of our society. The peace movement, the women's movement, the gay movement—they all have roots that can be traced to Mississippi in the summer of '64."[15]

The lunch counter sit-ins and SNCC's militance in the early 1960s influenced not only the northern New Left but also mainstream civil rights organizations, including the NAACP and the SCLC. Historians credit the sit-in movement, the early SNCC, and the Freedom Rides with reigniting the civil rights movement, which had, in the face of massive resistance, been stalled since the mid-1950s after its initial early victories in the *Brown* decision, the Montgomery bus boycott, and the Little Rock school desegregation battle. Although Martin Luther King Jr., as the towering figure coming out of the Montgomery struggle, remained the freedom movement's most famous leader, this dynamic younger generation of activists, first emerging into the national news with the sit-ins, breathed new life into the movement. This is why Taylor Branch's Pulitzer Prize–winning history of King and the civil rights revolution called his chapter on the sit-ins "The Quickening" and identified the students as a "vanguard" responsible for "teaching" King "that oratory alone was not enough."[16] Historian Howard Zinn termed these mostly black young activists "the new abolitionists," the title of his 1964 book on SNCC, which he opened with the declaration that "for the first time in history a major social movement, shaking the nation to its bones, is being led by youngsters."[17]

If you add up SNCC's impact in passing the torch of student activism northward—inspiring SDS and the New Left—and SNCC's importance in reigniting the civil rights movement in the early 1960s and in becoming a central voice in the Black Power movement of the mid- and late 1960s, it is little wonder that SNCC became the best-known student activist organization in the South. Such SNCC leaders as John Lewis, Julian Bond, Diane Nash, and Bob Moses, as well as their successors in SNCC's Black Power era, Stokely Carmichael and H. Rap Brown, are the most famous leaders of any southern-based student group during or since that era. By comparison, the radical organization through which white southern students activists affiliated themselves with SNCC and the southern freedom struggle, the Southern Student Organizing Committee (SSOC), has been largely forgotten, as has its leaders. So have the leaders of student protests on predominantly white southern campuses, whose activism never led to the fame of such major northern figures of the New Left as Mario Savio or Mark Rudd.

Yet in a curious way, the form that SNCC's fame has taken has obscured consideration of its impact on southern campuses, especially the HBCUs. Since SNCC's activism in the early 1960s was directed primarily off campus (in pickets and sit-ins against Jim Crow lunch counters, stores, and transit companies and in voter registration work in poor black communities), historians of the southern freedom struggle have mostly studied SNCC in that off-campus context, as a civil rights organization, quite different from the way the northern New Left evolved and has been studied. The New Left's campus protests, most notably Berkeley's Free Speech Movement and the Columbia revolt, featured disruptive *campus* protests that put the spotlight on activism within the college gates. In contrast, civil rights and SNCC historians have, until quite recently, demonstrated very little interest in the "student" part of SNCC's name or identity.[18] They rarely followed the southern black student protesters back to their campuses, leaving relatively unexplored the questions Turner and Williamson-Lott, in their chapters, probe concerning how politically repressive, socially conservative HBCUs could become pivotal recruiting grounds for the black freedom movement.

Nor has New Left historiography been much more helpful. With the New Left often defined as white and middle-class, historians of that movement have tended to be interested in early SNCC's predominantly black organizers only insofar as they played their inspirational role of passing the torch of activism northward to the white student left.[19] It is not SNCC's black carriers of that torch but the SDS and the other radicalized white recipients of it who are the primary focus of New Left histories. Take, for example, Doug McAdam's classic *Freedom Summer* case study. Here you find a superb portrait of how and why a predominantly white, middle-class group of college students volunteered to risk their lives in the Mississippi freedom movement. McAdam employs sophisticated social science methods—qualitative and quantitative—to assess the ways that the Mississippi experience transformed these mostly white volunteers politically and personally. He even studied in great depth those who volunteered but didn't show up for Freedom Summer and compared them to those who had gone south.[20] But McAdam offers no such detailed analysis or compelling group portrait of SNCC's mostly black organizers, who by 1964 were veterans of the freedom movement in Mississippi and who mentored and led the white volunteers. Somehow the story of how the best and the brightest whites from Harvard, Berkeley, and other elite universities came south to join the freedom struggle in 1964 has been seen as a more dramatic story than that of the African American SNCC organizers in Mississippi, some of whom came out of HBCUs and played a far more important role in launching that struggle.

New Left historians have not even been able to offer a label for early SNCC. If SNCC's black leadership means that it was not New Left, then what was it? Not merely liberal, of course. Not Old Left, certainly. Not explicitly Black Power—at least not yet. How is it that SNCC pioneered New Left tactics, helped define the radically egalitarian New Left ethos, and inspired the New Left to activism, and yet is not itself considered New Left? If not New Left, early SNCC certainly represented a new kind of radicalism, which was at the very least New Left–*ish*.[21]

The failure of historians to resolve even this definitional problem has left the public almost clueless with regard to what made early SNCC so distinctive. This confusion was evident in a recent Black History Month issue of the *New Yorker* that offered a photo spread and online text on the civil rights movement, with historical and recent shots of key sixties movement leaders. Visually, the predominantly black southern student movement of the early 1960s was well represented, including the famous photo of the four North Carolina A&T students sitting-in at the Greensboro lunch counter in February 1960 juxtaposed with a shot of Joseph A. McNeil and Franklin E. McCain at the same lunch counter 50 years later. There were photos of SNCC leaders Bob Moses and James Forman and SNCC Freedom Riders Diane Nash and John Lewis. Forman and Lewis were shown marching with King. Lewis was described as the "then chairman of SNCC," who "at the age of 23 . . . helped organize the March on Washington" and who is today the "last surviving speaker from the march."[22] So SNCC comes off as the junior partner of Dr. King. The student wing of the civil rights movement is melded into the larger history of the heroic "black freedom struggle [that] defines the American experience . . . applying prolonged moral and political pressure to the promises of the Constitution and America's self-conception. Its culminating drama was Southern, nonviolent, and religious."[23]

But the distinctive radicalism of SNCC is barely alluded to in the *New Yorker* issue, represented briefly in the unexplained Diane Nash quotation on how "the history books and the media" erred in presenting the civil rights movement "as Martin Luther King's movement, when in fact it was a people's movement. If people understood that it was ordinary people who did everything that needed to be done in that movement instead of thinking, I wish we had a Martin Luther King now, they would ask 'What can I do?' Idolizing just one person undermines the struggle." Similarly, without attributing it to SNCC's militant ethos, the online *New Yorker* narrative noted that John Lewis's speech at the March on Washington, though not as eloquent as King's that day, was the most "ferocious."[24] Actually, King and other mainstream civil rights leaders pressured Lewis to tone down his speech, which was much more critical of the Kennedy administration's civil rights record than King dared to be in his classic "I Have a Dream" speech.

What this *New Yorker* issue neglected to explain, and what historians have failed even to label, was what Free Speech Movement leader Mario Savio (a Freedom Summer veteran) referred to as the early SNCC's "hyper-democratic" ethos, its stress on community organizing, its mistrust of hierarchy and celebrity leaders. SNCC's door-to-door organizing of Mississippi sharecroppers to vote after decades of exclusion from the political process was not telegenic enough to make the evening news—unlike those dramatic rallies King addressed. And since it never got on TV in the sixties, this grassroots democracy of SNCC activists, living in and with the people they were organizing, has not made it, as Bob Moses points out, into even the most famous documentary film about the civil rights movement, *Eyes on the Prize*. So arguably the most daring and radical organizers of the early 1960s South, SNCC's cadre of student and community workers, remain unlabeled by historians and at best dimly understood by the public, even though they empowered the poor and disenfranchised in ways that seem unparalleled in American history.[25]

SNCC did attract more media attention in the mid- and late 1960s because of the electrifying and (to white America) frightening Black Power oratory of its leader Stokely Carmichael (sometimes derided as "Stokely Starmichael" for seeming more interested in media attention than grassroots organizing). Even in its Black Power phase, however, the campus politics of the black student movement has been little studied or understood, and linking SNCC to the HBCUs in this era has proven problematic. With SNCC's focus shifting to northern ghettoes, which were a key base of the Black Power movement, the assumption has been that SNCC did little campus organizing. George Ware, SNCC's campus coordinator in the mid-1960s, questions this assumption, arguing that it is a myth that SNCC ignored the campuses in its Black Power phase and absurd to charge that all Carmichael did as SNCC chairman was give speeches and crave the media spotlight. Ware contends that after Carmichael's appearances he (Ware) would build SNCC chapters on those energized campuses, especially at HBCUs.[26]

But there was more to Black Power on the HBCUs than SNCC, as Jelani Favors's chapter shows with regard to North Carolina A&T. Favors depicts A&T as a center of the southern Black Power movement, giving birth to a new national group, the Student Organization for Black Unity, that would, in its campus Black Power organizing, pick up where SNCC left off. Favors raises important questions about the Black Power movement's impact on southern campuses—whether, where, and when the black student protesters of the 1960s won their struggle to render the HBCUs more politically free, less regimented socially, and open to such curricular innovations as Black Studies.

We do not know nearly enough about the ebb and flow of black student protest in the South during that time. It seems that after the big sit-in wave of the early 1960s, black student activism abated in the mid-1960s, only to come roaring back in 1968 after the King assassination and the Orangeburg massacre, and it surged again after the Jackson State massacre in 1970. The interval between the early and late 1960s surges in black student protest may be connected to exhaustion in those black churches and civil rights organizations that had previously organized African American community support for black student crusades against Jim Crow.

A decline in the energy level in these—to use sociologist Aldon Morris's term—off-campus "movement centers" may have contributed to a similar lull on campus. In his classic study of the freedom movement in Greensboro, historian William Chafe argued that after "the euphoria of victory" from the sit-ins "faded, black leaders began to realize the dimensions of the problems still remaining. It took time and organization to build a movement; only once in a generation, perhaps, could a people sustain the sacrifice and psychic turmoil of constant demonstrations. Mass protests could not be revived overnight."[27] But Chafe was speaking of generations in a city, not on campus, where there is a new student generation every four years. So his exhaustion explanation, viable as it may be in the off-campus context, seems problematic when applied to student politics.

The lull might connect to the strain in linking black campuses to the surging antiwar movement, which initially some black leaders disparaged as unpatriotic and a distraction from the civil rights struggle—a strain King himself experienced when his Riverside Church speech against the Vietnam War generated considerable criticism from blacks in 1967.[28] It seemed to have taken the outrage over the King assassination, Orangeburg, and Jackson to bring masses of black students out again in a new wave of protest in the movement's Black Power phase.

This question of the trajectory of student activism over the course of the 1960s is also in need of careful examination on the South's predominantly white campuses. It is too soon for definitive judgments, but tentative conclusions emerge from Gregg Michel's earlier study of SSOC, Jeffrey Turner's regional survey *Sitting In and Speaking Out,* and the essays in this volume as well as interviews and correspondence with southern student organizers.[29] What seems needed is a different framework for thinking about southern student activism than is used in histories of the northern New Left, especially with regard to the way the term *student movement* is employed. Yes, southern campus activists worked with local, regional, and national organizations of the civil rights and antiwar movements. They felt themselves part of those movements, part of the big-"M" movement of the sixties.[30] But not until the late 1960s—in much of the deep South, not until the strike wave in response to the Kent State shootings in 1970—did a progressive *mass student movement* arise on predominantly white southern campuses. So except in pockets of the urban, upper South and in parts of the black southern campus world, it makes little sense to use the term *movement* for the mid-1960s period as one would on campuses in the North, which had witnessed mass student protests led by New Left activists.

For much of the mid-1960s and even into the late 1960s, then, we may need to dispense with this northern frame, this equation of the student movement with mass campus insurgency. Instead we ought to research and think more about when, where, and how, to use Jack Newfield's term for the new radicals of the sixties, "a prophetic minority" sought to open the southern campus world to dissent. Progressive southern student activists challenged their classmates, raised in America's most conservative region, to question the South's racial and gender inequalities, the Cold War consensus, the repression of speech, and the paternalistic regimentation of campus social life. These dissidents championed a freer student culture that might in turn make the South more free and egalitarian.[31] The benchmark for judging southern student protest ought not to be whether campuses in Georgia or Mississippi could match Berkeley in the size and militancy of their demonstrations or the speed of their victories. Instead we should ask how well the southern students at Tougaloo, Fisk, and Southern, at UGA and Emory, and at the small rural colleges whose names are less familiar and less prestigious did in transforming their campuses from provincial Jim Crow institutions into more cosmopolitan colleges and universities.

This is not to say that leftist-led mass student protest never emerged on the South's predominantly white campuses, or that HBCU students in the late 1960s failed to mobilize as effectively as they had back in 1960. Turner's *Sitting In and Speaking Out* reveals that between 1968 and 1970 most major private and public universities in the South experienced at least one dramatic incident or confrontation growing out of student protests. In this time when southern campus activism was at its peak, the Vietnam War was the leading issue on the region's predominantly white campuses, and Black Power and minority access issues topped the concerns among African American students.[32] The surge of black student activism in the wake of the King assassination was in some ways akin to that of the sit-in surge of the early 1960s.

Part of our task in capturing the political dynamic of the southern New Left is figuring out what distinguished the centers of southern campus activism from the less active campuses. It may be that a higher degree of freedom and a critical intellectual and political sensibility fostered by a more cosmopolitan faculty and administration separated a campus such as Vanderbilt from colleges less conducive to student activism. As a former Vanderbilt SDS leader explained, on his campus the faculty and administration "tended to be more liberal" than the student body: "They readily allowed the creation of SDS. They never gave us a hard time. . . . In fact, the Dean of Men . . . publicly defended SDS on campus against the publisher of the *Nashville Banner* (a rabidly right-wing paper) whose publisher, James Stahlman, was . . . on the Vanderbilt board and wanted SDS disbanded (and its members expelled). The Administration absolutely refused, and even spoke about the need for political diversity on campus."[33] This differed dramatically from the situation on the many southern campuses—white and black—where political repression proved difficult to dislodge, perhaps a key to understanding the wildly divergent levels of student activism across the South.[34]

Turner's and Michel's books and many of the essays in this volume capture the excitement of this breakthrough of large-scale student protest in the South. Yet what is also striking is the movement's lack of consciousness about itself. Why wasn't there a stronger sense of the key late-1960s victories and battlegrounds in the South? In the southern narratives there is no sense that campus protests at regional hotbeds of activism, such as Duke, Vanderbilt, Fisk, Texas, Florida State, UNC, or Atlanta University, resonated in the South the way that events at Berkeley or Columbia did outside of it. What does it say that the best-known campus political events in the South during this era were the massacres of black students at Orangeburg and Jackson State?

The lack of a Berkeley- or Columbia-style narrative of a famed, left-led campus insurgency south of the Mason-Dixon line seems connected with chronology. Lacking the freedom and the mass support necessary for a Berkeley-style revolt in 1964, the southern campuses were slower to bring civil disobedience to campus. As SSOC organizer Sue Thrasher explained, "People knew they didn't have the numbers. On southern campuses [in the mid-1960s] people were well aware that they were a minority . . . speaking out. And so your tactics had to be a little bit more moderated. And so you had to think about safety and sustaining yourself over time."[35] Being so hesitant to take over an administration building meant that when such tactics came south, they no longer seemed path-breaking or radical. Indeed, by the time that disruptive tactics found their way on to leading southern campuses, in 1966 through 1968, they seemed so ordinary that just about nobody noticed when they first came to a southern campus. So while every schoolboy and -girl knows that the first mass sit-in off campus occurred in Greensboro in February 1960, to this day even historians of the 1960s don't seem to know (and have seldom discussed) when and where the first mass civil disobedience, the first disruptive sit-ins occurred *on a southern campus*.[36]

This leads us to the even more pressing questions about the student activism on the predominantly white campuses of the South: Did it matter? Did it have a major impact and prove politically or culturally transformative, either on campus or off? In most histories of the 1960s, these deep South universities play only a supporting role, stuck in the early 1960s (we never see them in the mid- or late 1960s), freeze-framed in a kind of collegiate version of Bull Connor: those racist students who rioted against the admission of James Meredith to the University of Mississippi in 1962. Or, in the case of the University of Alabama, the campus appears only as a prop for Governor George Wallace to make his self-serving Jim Crow stand at the school house door in 1963. But despite the segregationist bloviating of Wallace in Alabama and Ross Barnett in Mississippi, campuses at both Tuscaloosa and Oxford and across the South desegregated in the early 1960s.[37] What is not addressed in 1960s historiography is what became of this campus world *after* Jim Crow was kicked off campus. Several of the essays in this volume suggest that when we move to the mid- and late 1960s and the early 1970s, we see a southern campus world being transformed by the egalitarian social movements of the Vietnam era.

Striking examples of how even the most conservative deep South universities were shaken and changed by the student movement are provided in Gary Sprayberry's chapter on University of Alabama student radicalism from 1968 to 1970. He shows that in those years a vocal student movement emerged at Alabama and battled for free speech, peace, and racial and gender equity, leading to conflicts with the campus administration and heated clashes with a violence-prone police force. So by 1970 the University of Alabama no longer resembled the placid white campus of 1963 whose students had allowed Governor George Wallace to use it as a staging area for his segregationist speechifying.

Wallace found this out for himself when in April 1970 his attempt to speak at the Alabama campus earned him a rowdy Berkeley-style greeting, with hecklers, referring to Alabama's dismal standard of living, chanting "We're number 50, we're number 50" so vehemently that Wallace had to cut his speech short. Though Alabama was a campus that entered the 1960s without a single black student, by 1970 the university's African American students were organized politically, demanding greater black student admissions and expedited black faculty hiring as well as a Black Studies program.

An equally dramatic transformation was visible with regard to gender and sexuality on southern campuses. Kelly Morrow's chapter on sexual liberation activists at the University of North Carolina at Chapel Hill shows that in the early 1960s campus officials proved prudish and conservative on sexuality issues, doing nothing to provide birth control information to their students, punishing those who became pregnant, and refusing to use campus health services to deal with the needs of sexually active students. Morrow finds that in the late 1960s a coalition of radical physicians and feminist students—joined in the early 1970s by gay and lesbian activists—organized successfully to use the campus health service to deal in an open and egalitarian way with the full range of sexual issues that students faced. This form of activism spread across the South and the nation via sexuality handbooks that were collegiate precursors to the bestselling women's health and sexuality manual *Our Bodies, Ourselves* (1973).

The counterculture too made an impact on and near campuses in some southern college towns. Nicholas Meriwether documents this thoroughly in his micro-history of a head shop that thrived in Columbia, not far from the University of South Carolina. Influenced by the countercultural models from the San Francisco Bay area, the Columbia countercultural scene nonetheless had its own distinctive southern tone and products, and the same could be said for the underground newspapers that appeared in the 1960s South. The popularization of rock music and the spread of pot smoking among the young seeded a countercultural scene on and near southern campuses, offering an opening to political activists in challenging campus conservatism. Doug Rossinow's classic case study of University of Texas student activism—portraying the alliance between the New Left and Austin's counterculture (manifested in an underground newspaper and the start of "Gentle Thursday" countercultural happenings on campus)—suggests that such connections helped to yield the critical mass of dissidents needed to sustain a dynamic campus left. Nor has this "other South" disappeared, as evidenced by the continued presence of a lively rock scene near such campuses as the University of Georgia, which gave rise to such famed rock bands as REM and the B-52s and to this day supports an underground-style newspaper, *The Flagpole*. Clearly, the connections between the countercultural scene and political dissent in the South need further exploration.

Learning the history of its counterculture will not change the fact that Columbia, South Carolina, is not as famed for student dissent in the sixties as Columbia University in New York. This is because in 1968 that New York City campus experienced one of the most tumultuous student rebellions in American history, with five building takeovers, including one by militant black students, that lasted a week, culminating in some 700 arrests, a police riot that left more than 100 students injured, and a student strike that lasted until the end of the semester. There is simply no way that southern campus disruptions—including the takeover of the Russell House Student Center at the University of South Carolina in 1970—will ever get the attention of their northern counterparts.[38] The earliest, largest, and most famed New Left events, including the Port Huron Conference, the Berkeley Free Speech Movement, the launching of antiwar teach-ins at Michigan, Stop the Draft Week in Oakland, the Dow protests at Wisconsin, and the Columbia rebellion, occurred in the North. This is why after SNCC passed the torch of student activism to SDS in the early 1960s, the southern campuses and students disappear from most New Left histories, which are narrated with a northern accent rather than a southern drawl.[39]

Since the South will never replace the North in the mid- and late 1960s at the center of New Left and student movement histories, the question facing the new wave of sixties historians studying student protest south of the Mason-Dixon line is how the story of the southern sixties on campus fits into the national history of the decade's student movement. The temptation in early revisionism is inversion. So, yes, since Yankee-centered narratives of the New Left leave out the fact that as the Vietnam era dragged on, even campuses in the deep South saw militant demonstrations against the war, then the revisionist goal will be initially quite modest: getting such southern protesters into the national New Left and 1960s histories. No longer ought historians be unaware, for example, that after Kent State, antiwar protests on such southern campuses as the University of South Carolina culminated in student strikes, troops sent to campus, suspensions, expulsions, jailings, and a curfew imposed by the governor.[40] Such a revisionism would imply that north and south are just points on a map; that with the arrival of sixties-style student politics, southern distinctiveness melted away; that the once-hegemonic conservatism of southern campuses was as dead as Jim Crow. So whether you were in Columbia, South Carolina, or at Columbia University in New York, militant student protest had taken the campus world by storm. The revisionist conclusion, then, is that southern campuses came to resemble their northern counterparts, becoming part of the larger national student revolt. In other words, the payoff for all this new scholarship, reflected in the present volume, is bringing the South back into the union—only in this case it is a union of the sixties campus left and of the larger liberal academic culture of the American university.[41]

While this form of additive revisionism offers a useful corrective to all those histories that neglect or ignore late 1960s and early 1970s southern campuses, it is only a start for a new and more geographically inclusive history of the dissident sixties. Beyond revisionism, we need a deeper, more nuanced history, showing that in spite of some similarities, southern student activism often differed markedly from its northern counterpart. For example, though photos of the building takeover at the University of South Carolina or the burning of the University of Alabama's gym in May 1970 suggest that southern and northern students behaved identically in responding to the Cambodia invasion and the Kent State and Jackson State massacres, regional statistics tell a different story. Student protest was far less widespread in the South than in any other part of the United States that May. While 76 percent of colleges and universities in the Northeast reported protests having "significant impact" on campus operations and 68 percent of the Pacific states reported events of similar impact, only 41 percent of southeastern campuses had protests on such a scale. Only 3.4 percent of southeastern campuses reported student strikes that month, as compared with 29.5 percent of northeastern campuses.[42]

So when we move beyond small vanguards, which was what SNCC was in the early 1960s, and start thinking about the great mass of students, it seems evident that the regional dynamic of the student movement had reversed itself in the mid- and late 1960s. From 1960 through the summer of 1964, SNCC was the torchbearer for the student movement nationally, and in this sense the black South was leading the move nationally toward activism in that early period. Then, for much of the mid- and late 1960s and early 1970s, the North was leading the movement in innovative tactics and success in building coordinated waves of student protest, on campuses and off, from coast to coast. The reasons for this seem linked to the obstacles southern student organizers faced because their campuses were located in America's most conservative region. Here whites exhibited great anger over the challenges that the civil rights movement posed to the traditional white supremacist social order, that the antiwar movement posed to traditional definitions of patriotism, and that the feminist, gay rights, and related sexual liberation movements posed to Bible Belt orthodoxy. This southern political climate proved inhospitable to radical organizers, to mass civil disobedience, or even to progressive political demonstrations—on campuses where at least until 1968 students were far more likely to turn out for football or basketball games than for political protests.[43]

Again borrowing Newfield's terminology about the new student radicals of the 1960s constituting a "prophetic minority," we can best understand the distinctive dynamics of the southern student movement by acknowledging that the South's *prophetic minority*—envisioning an American free of racism, sexism, homophobia, and imperialism—faced the daunting task of organizing the region's *recalcitrant majority*: rightward-leaning white students. It is crucial, then, if we want to understand the southern campus left of the 1960s that we probe what it was up against with regard to the recalcitrant majority's conservative tendencies. Christopher Huff's chapter on conservative and reactionary student activism at the University of Georgia from 1965 to 1975 offers evidence upon which to start building that understanding.

Huff's essay grapples with the question that has long divided historians of the American right: How central was racism and an anti–civil rights movement backlash to the emergence of the New Right in the 1960s and beyond? Twenty-first-century conservatives prefer to think of their movement as being rooted in the lofty and philosophical anti-statism of William F. Buckley Jr. rather than in the crude racist backlash fanned by such segregationist leaders as George Wallace.[44] On campus, the Buckley brand of conservatism was represented by the Young Americans for Freedom, the organization he inspired and whose founding document, the Sharon Statement, was written on the lawn of his Connecticut estate. But Huff shows that some of the young right-wing militants at UGA grew so dissatisfied with the YAF's reluctance to get tinged with racism—YAF's refusal to embrace the neo-segregationist cause—that they burned their YAF charter and broke with the national conservative organization.

There is a distinctive and distinctively ugly history to the segregationist wing of the South's campus right. And it is a history that has yet to be synthesized into a coherent regional narrative. We get glimpses of it in the individual campus case studies of the most dramatic desegregation crises in the deep South. For example, E. Culpepper Clark's penetrating history of the Autherine Lucy case shows us the way political ambition and prejudice led white junior politicos at the University of Alabama to organize racist mobs so threatening to Lucy's safety that she had to flee the campus because her life was in danger.[45] This set in motion events that forced Lucy to end her bid to become the first African American student to matriculate at Alabama. Using the chronological frame of the "long sixties" or, as Taylor Branch dubbed it, "the King era"—an era of social change fueled by the surge in the black freedom movement, starting with the *Brown* decision and the Montgomery bus boycott in the mid-1950s—we might think of Alabama's racist white students who attacked Lucy in 1956 as the first New Right student militants of the 1960s.[46] And for those who define the New Left by its violence in the late 1960s, this Alabama activism suggests a right wing that was more than a decade ahead of its left-wing counterparts in its willingness to use violence, the difference of course being that the left sought to promote and the right to prevent democratic social change.

If we want to be more precise about chronology and stick literally to the 1960s, UGA would get bragging rights as the first campus in that decade to produce violent resistance to racial equality. In January 1961 UGA students, waving a "Nigger Go Home" banner, rioted outside Charlayne Hunter's dormitory, hoping to repeat the anti-Lucy mob's success by forcing the removal of Hunter, along with the other African American student, Hamilton Holmes, admitted to Georgia under a federal court order.[47] Trailing close behind these Georgia segregationists were the mobs of racist students at the University of Mississippi, who in 1962 contributed to the resistance to James Meredith's desegregation bid, a resistance that culminated in a bloody riot that left the Mississippi campus looking like a charred battlefield—in which federal marshals were wounded by gunfire and fatalities occurred, the first politically inspired killings on a college campus in 1960s America.[48]

It might seem simplistic, even unfair, to see these violent racist eruptions at Alabama, Georgia, and Mississippi as foundational events for the southern student right in quite the same way that the nonviolent, antiracist sit-ins that began at Greensboro in 1960 served as inspiring foundational events for the student left. After all, most southern campuses, in the wake of these failed deep South battles to retain Jim Crow, desegregated peacefully. But even while not willing to embrace violence, the 1960s generation was the last in the white South to have grown up as Jim Crow's children, and a hangover from that upbringing was a resentment of the forces of social change—whether the NAACP, the Warren Court, or the Justice

Department—responsible for forcing desegregation upon them and transforming the world they had known. Such attitudes would take the better part of the decade to erode.

The essays written by UGA students amidst the desegregation crisis of that campus suggest that in 1961 this erosion process had barely started. Most Georgia students, albeit disapproving of racist rioting, supported segregation and resented the civil rights movement and the courts for forcing the university to admit black students.[49] Similarly, more than three thousand students at the University of Mississippi signed a petition supporting Governor Ross Barnett's resistance to Meredith's desegregation crusade, praising the governor's "courageous defense of state's rights."[50] And even decades later, after serving as U.S. Senate Majority leader, Trent Lott, who was a Mississippi student in 1962, would in his memoir admit to feeling "anger in my heart over the way the federal government invaded Ole Miss" to impose integration.[51]

Though the black-led sit-ins against Jim Crow evolved into an impressive mass movement among HBCU students, which by 1961 had mobilized some seventy thousand participants, these were centered in cities mostly in the upper South and had less impact on white southern campuses, especially in the rural and deep South—other than to generate fear and criticism (except among a tiny group of radicals). The dominant collegiate culture and the students on most white southern campuses remained in the early 1960s, as historian Gregg Michel put it, "politically conservative, socially homogeneous, and culturally provincial."[52] Charles Eagles in *The Price of Defiance* (2009), his history of Ole Miss and the Meredith case, powerfully evokes this dominant white collegiate culture in 1962, whose tone was set by elitist fraternities and sororities. This was a culture centered on football games and beauty contests, assuming the effete role of a finishing school, promoting the social consciousness of a country club, taking racial segregation and white supremacy as givens, romanticizing the Old South, and proving largely indifferent to modern social science scholarship. "Ole Miss students," in the early 1960s, Eagles writes, "demonstrated a remarkable lack of interest in intellectual, aesthetic, and humanistic concerns," an assessment Dan Carter echoed in portraying the majority student culture at the University of South Carolina during this era in the foreword to this book.[53]

In contrast to the few white southern students who participated in the lunch counter sit-ins or joined SNCC, the segregationist demonstrations and rioting on the UGA, Alabama, and Mississippi campuses involved hundreds and at times thousands of white students.[54] These first mass protests on white southern campuses in the 1960s were on the right, not the left, and did not embrace the nonviolent civil rights movement—but vehemently, sometimes violently opposed it.

If we think of the sixties as defined by its movements to promote progressive social change, starting with the insurgency against Jim Crow, we see far more white southern college students starting the decade not on board with the sixties and the quest for a new future but clinging instead to the racial hierarchy and injustice inherited from the past.

Even when the violence ended, the desegregation process could prove both protracted and painful. At UGA, long after the riot, Holmes and Hunter, shunned by most white students, lived in a college town that remained segregated. The tension gave Hunter stomach problems and led Holmes to travel back to black Atlanta each weekend where he could feel safe and welcome.[55] It is only recently that Hunter could reflect on the humorous aspects of those tense times, revealing in a *New Yorker* interview that she was not above using Georgia's racism toward her own ends. Admitting to being a snob back then about UGA's physical education requirement, she evaded it by saying she would fulfill it with a bowling class— which she knew would not be feasible in the white bowling alley in Athens. She got it deferred again the next year by saying she wanted to enroll in a swimming class, which she knew would not fly since the white girls would refuse to go into the water with her. Her evasiveness was ultimately stymied when UGA came up with the novel idea of having her take archery. Racial discrimination in athletics also impacted her classmate Hamilton Holmes, a talented halfback who had co-captained his high school football team. UGA officials refused to allow him to break the color line in intercollegiate athletics, calling the prospect of his taking the field "risky. He could be killed. Deliberately."[56] Not until September 1967 did Nat Northington of the University of Kentucky become the first African American to play in a varsity SEC football game. As for the deep South, the UGA and Ole Miss football teams would not desegregate until 1971.[57]

This racial climate made it difficult for white student radicals to organize on many of the South's predominantly white campuses in the early 1960s. Bob Zellner, who took the job of organizing for SNCC on these campuses in 1961, found it tough going. The more he participated in SNCC civil rights actions, the easier it was for white campus officials to peg him as a dangerous agitator, whom most white students shunned.[58] YWCA organizers Mary King and Casey Hayden found that in this era, on campuses across the South, they "encountered hostile, indifferent, and scared students and faculty who had little interest in debating the merits of desegregation." For Zellner, white campus work proved so lonely and alienating that he directed more of his time to SNCC's black community organizing. "I felt quite estranged from the Southern students I was supposed to be talking to," Zellner reported.[59] Nor was this true only of radical organizers. On many southern white campuses in the early 1960s, students who dared to question the racial status quo were ostracized—and such peer pressure proved a major obstacle not only to organizing but even to discussing change.[60]

Nor was it just racist disdain for the civil rights struggle that posed barriers to building a student movement on historically white campuses. The lack of academic freedom and free speech posed serious obstacles. The case of James W. Silver, a professor at Ole Miss, was among the most poignant. His 1963 paper at the Southern Historical Association, "Mississippi: The Closed Society," yielded a backlash that revealed how closed to academic freedom his campus really was. Silver was harassed by state legislators (who called for his dismissal), investigated by private detectives, and charged by the regents in 1964 with "making provocative and inflammatory speeches calculated to increase racial tension and provoke racial violence." Since even a prominent professor could be hounded out of the South—Silver fled north to accept a professorship at Notre Dame—for expressing dissident ideas, students had good reason to be wary of engaging in radical activism.[61]

When the student movement nationally shifted its focus from race to Vietnam, as the war escalated in the mid-1960s, campus activists in the South again faced the toughest of organizing tasks, questioning the war in the most pro-military part of the country.[62] SSOC organizer Tom Gardner recalled that on many campuses it was initially difficult to obtain permission to give antiwar speeches and that at times political repression came from hawkish students, as at Appalachian State University, where a mob of several hundred students drove him from the campus, threatening to string him up.[63]

Considering all the obstacles student radicals faced on predominantly white campuses in the South during the 1960s, it is little wonder that historians of the New Left have for decades depicted the student movement as a mostly northern phenomenon. Books devoted to the southern student left have been few and relatively recent. At the top of this short list are Doug Rossinow's study of the New Left at the University of Texas, Gregg Michel's portrait of the Southern Student Organizing Committee, Jeffrey Turner's regional survey of the southern student movement, and Joy Ann Williamson's study of unrest at Mississippi's historically black colleges.[64] There is a logic to this pattern. Most historians who want to study student protest, like ambitious news reporters, go to the campuses where the action seemed to be, which of course, means such radical hotbeds as Berkeley, Columbia, Wisconsin, and Michigan.

But there is another, and arguably a better, way to think about this issue of regional focus. If we want to determine how major an impact the student movement of the 1960s had in changing America, the way to determine that is not to round up the usual suspects in the traditional northern centers of dissent but to see how well the movement penetrated an area like the South, which has historically been less amenable to left organizing. Much as you would tend not to assess a minister's oratorical abilities by judging only the reaction of the choir, one ought not judge a national student insurgency by probing only its northern epicenters. Although bringing out masses of students in Berkeley certainly made headlines, pushing southern student politics and culture even a little bit leftward seems in its own way equally significant. A student movement that could help transform southern campuses or society in political and cultural ways would obviously need to be looked at as more successful than a movement that could not penetrate the South.

Diverse as they are, the historians who contributed to the present volume share one thing: a rejection of that traditional notion that southern student activism in the mid-1960s was less important or interesting than its northern counterpart. Their essays attest that being a radical or liberal activist in the South was more difficult than it was in the North. In many ways it took more dedication, because at least until the late 1960s it often meant joining not a popular protest movement but a relatively small band of indigenous southern activists sailing against the wind in a historically conservative region—and often defying one's parents and classmates. These essays document that this sailing against the wind did pay off, resulting in the rise of a student left that had considerable transformative power on southern campuses.

The books by Turner, Michel, and Rossinow and the work of many of the historians represented in this volume—including Morrow, Meriwether, Sprayberry, Synnott, Whittington, and Huff—attest that the southern protesters of the middle and late 1960s and the 1970s (the end point of the long sixties) helped to transform the culture and politics of at least some of the historically white southern campuses. Through their persistence, southern student activists—black and white—managed to build on the work of the NAACP, further opening up formerly white campuses to racial diversity, first in the student body then in social life, in the curriculum (via Black Studies programs, and this was a major thrust on black campuses too), and finally in the faculty. Turner cites data suggesting that even at the University of Alabama the level of white student prejudice diminished dramatically, with the percentage of white students with no objections to sitting next to black students in class rising from 39.1 in 1963 to 88.3 in 1972.[65] Late-1960s southern student activists also championed academic freedom and free speech, bringing antiwar dissent, demonstrations, and civil disobedience to historically black and predominantly white campuses, pushing for an end to *in loco parentis* restrictions on student life—which tended to be sexist—and thereby helping to create space on southern campuses for freer lifestyles, the spreading of the counterculture, and ultimately gender studies programs.

That radical organizing was more challenging on predominantly white southern campuses as compared to the North might deter protest, but it could just as easily lead southern activists to be more pragmatic, patient, and moderate in their organizing strategies. This can be seen by comparing the University of North Carolina and UC Berkeley free speech battles. Although known as one of the South's most liberal campuses and a key center of regional activism, UNC in June 1963 faced a speaker ban imposed by the state legislature. The state barred from campus speakers who were Communists, advocates of the overthrow of the U.S. Constitution, and those who had refused to cooperate with anticommunist investigations. Despite student protests, speaker after speaker was denied access to UNC. Not until 1968 did students manage to get the ban lifted, an event that came not through mass protest but through a lawsuit. Contrast this with the Berkeley free speech battle, when a single semester of protest (fall 1964), including mass civil disobedience—a police car blockade, building takeovers, and a student strike— led the faculty academic senate to vote by a 7 to 1 margin to end the university's restrictions on political advocacy. The free speech victory in Berkeley took three months, after which the campus became a national center of antiwar dissent and mass actions against the Vietnam War. At Chapel Hill the victory took *five years*, and UNC in those years never approached Berkeley in its record of mass student protest.[66] But in both cases student dissent won out in the end, and while Berkeley was bigger national news, UNC, using more moderate tactics that seemed better suited to the South, secured the free speech it needed to return to its historic role as a center of southern dissent.

SSOC organizer Tom Gardner has a revealing term to describe the role of the student activists of the 1960s in transforming southern campuses. He calls southern activists "hegemites," likening himself and his fellow southern protesters to termites who nibbled away at the hegemonic racism, sexism, militarism, anti-radicalism, and intolerance of the region. And he points out that over time, termites can be "pretty damn effective."[67] Both he and Thrasher attest that over the course of the long sixties, southern campuses—though at different speeds depending on the degree of freedom and cosmopolitanism—changed profoundly. Gardner points out that while in the early 1960s it would have been difficult even to advocate racial integration at the University of South Carolina, by the early 1970s the student body had elected its first African American student government president. A University of Virginia student who only a few years earlier had tossed an egg in Gardner's face during an antiwar event was, after Kent State, telling Gardner how much he had learned about the war since he had come to college and, bedecked with an antiwar armband, joined Gardner in a campus protest against the war. And the progressive slate of candidates whose left politics would have marginalized them in the early 1960s was by 1969 sweeping the UVA student council elections.[68] Huff's chapter reports a similar moment of triumph in this era for radicals in UGA's student government elections.

The rise of women's liberation groups on southern campuses in the late 1960s and the early 1970s is another sign that student activism was fomenting change. Feminist manifestos and conferences began to appear on predominantly white southern campuses in 1968. There were notably strong women's groups at Duke University and the University of Florida as well as among students in Atlanta and New Orleans.[69] It is unclear, however, how deeply feminist organizing penetrated the HBCUs and more rural campuses—a question that needs to be pursued as the history of southern student organizing develops and gets more focused on gender.

It would be an oversimplification to attribute everything that changed on southern campuses to the New Left. The counterculture and the power of television, radio, and movies all played a role in wooing significant numbers of students from the conservative cultural norms of the region. "We're all watching television," as Gardner put it. "It's all getting groovy. So there is . . . desire not to be left out of this whole generational move, at least among a significant enough number of students" to change the mood and tone of the campuses.[70]

The ability of southern student activists to forge partnerships with churches and religiously based reformers seems to have been one of the keys to its success. The alliance between black student activists and the church-based freedom movement centers in African American communities has been emphasized by scholars of the movement, most notably Aldon Morris. But alliances between secular radicals and religious groups and leaders on campus also seem to have been important to student organizers from predominantly white campuses. On southern campuses, explains one New Left organizer, there was a "greater relationship with Christian groupings" than would typically be the case in the North: "The Vanderbilt SDS advisor was from the Divinity School. We mostly met in Christian student centers, whose directors were very supporting. None of us were even remotely religious—quite the opposite. But we respected these Christian allies and appreciated the support they gave. And it wasn't only Unitarians."[71]

Just listing the points of transformation in southern campus life raises questions about how to categorize the southern New Left of the late 1960s. Most of these achievements were more reformist than revolutionary. They were championed in a mostly nonviolent way by a southern New Left more able than its northern counterpart to work in coalitions with nonradicals. So we might think of the southern New Left as a left-liberal movement, truer to the reformist spirit of the early New Left—the New Left of the Port Huron era—than to the Marxifying and Weatherizing New Left of the late 1960s in the North. It seems that the southern

New Left, because it faced the more daunting task of melting what Bob Moses termed "the iceberg" that was southern racism and reaction, remained more sober and rooted in political reality than the increasingly ideological and dogmatic northern New Left.[72] Since the southern activists knew that they could not afford to engage in revolutionary posturing and sectarian squabbling, they appeared relatively free of these maladies of the northern New Left. This is not to deny that there were some black and white student radicals in the South drawn to Marxist-Leninism and that in the face of racist violence, armed self-defense and heated rhetoric about revolutionary violence held some appeal. But the most serious violence in the South came not from the student movement; it came from the movement's foes, and the shift toward a more ideological left came from the North, not the South.

It may be that the cultural conservatism of the South played a role in the way the region's white New Left expressed itself—that where the northern New Left was uninhibited and at times even coarse in its expressive style of politics, the white New Left in the South proved more reserved. While this may sound like a regional conceit, there does seem to have been a stronger sense of civility on the campus left in the South. As Tom Gardner observed, "The tone, the expectations, the necessities created a somewhat different reality" on southern campuses. "There were certain cultural norms that you had to pay attention to if you wanted people to go with you."[73] As one southern SDSer explained,

> Southerners are naturally more courteous, and Southern students tended to be more courteous in their organizing activities. They were certainly averse to dramatic activities that were intended to shock people into a new point of view. For example, a travelling organizer (I think he was Progressive Labor Party, or maybe its outgrowth, the May 2nd Movement—both of which proved to be heavily infiltrated with provocateurs) came to Vanderbilt and stated that he was going to pour gasoline on the informal campus pet (a beagle named George) and immolate the dog on the student commons to protest the use of napalm in Vietnam. It got the organizer almost universal hatred and defined the left as lunatics. Vanderbilt SDS denounced that tactic and said "Even we like George." To us, this person was acting out some infantile personal needs, not trying to build a movement.[74]

Generalizations about civility and moderation of expression, however, may be racially bound among southern activists. In the late 1960s black student activists, whether using epithets or militant rhetoric, at times expressed themselves in ways that shocked their white foes to a degree unmatched in the white southern New Left. It is quite possible that a double standard was being applied here, since white foes of the movement would likely be more shocked by black than by white militancy. But Chafe makes an important point in noting that by the late 1960s, "Blacks had simply come to the boiling point"; years of racial oppression had understandably yielded tough rhetoric as black student activists came to see that "civility within the context of oppression provides a veneer for more oppression. Only within a context of freedom can it be a vehicle for self-realization and fulfillment. . . . Where one group dominates another, the ground rules of discourse will always serve as an instrument of control."[75]

Being different from the North was at times helpful to southern student activists. There were, for example, advantages to the southern New Left's slowness to bring civil disobedience tactics to campus. Since they lacked the numbers to take over buildings in the South until after this had been done at Berkeley and Columbia, southern activists could learn from those northern campus battles—lessons that in some cases avoided pain and the price of what seemed excessive militancy. Gardner, for example, recalled that having taken over the ROTC building at UVA during the Kent State strike wave, he opted to end the takeover once the authorities read the injunction so as to avoid the injuries that occurred when police attacked protesters at the Columbia University sit-in. Having "seen the movie" and getting what happened in New York, he concluded that the Virginia movement did "not need busted heads," and so, having made their point, the protesters exited in an upbeat way, singing and marching minus the Columbia-style police violence and mass arrests.[76]

What is striking here is the white/black divide in the South. White campuses in the South were able to avoid Kent State–style tragedies. Yet, as we have seen, this was not the case with their southern black counterparts. Black student activists were murdered by law enforcement officials not only at Jackson State and South Carolina State College but also at Southern University and North Carolina A&T. And Sammy Younge Jr., a Tuskegee student activist leader, was fatally shot in 1966 in a dispute linked to his challenging the Jim Crow restroom restrictions in a gas station.[77] This black/white contrast underscores the need to be wary of easy generalizations about southern student protest, since when it came to race there was not one South but two. Though at times black and white protest seemed comparable, there were differences too—as with the issue of whether student protesters would face murderous violence—since in some respects the old color line lived on and white students enjoyed an immunity from police-inflicted bloodshed that was never available to their black counterparts.[78]

With so few studies completed yet on student activism at the HBCUs, it is impossible to draw definitive conclusions about its impact there. It does seem, however, that the black student activists of the 1960s had less immediate success in winning their demands for change on campus, such as free speech, a greater student voice in campus governance, and an end to presidential authoritarianism than in their anti–Jim Crow crusades off campus.[79] It is also striking that in the early 1960s, when black student activists were blazing new trails in the use of civil disobedience to battle segregation off campus, they did not use those sit-in tactics on campus. Thus it was white students in the North—starting at Berkeley in 1964—not black students in the South who first used mass sit-ins to blockade police and buildings on campus. It was not until later in the 1960s that black students would make extensive use of such disruptive tactics on campus. The mobilizations against Jim Crow in which HBCU students were active culminated in such historic victories as the Civil Rights Act and the Voting Rights Acts. But again, these enormous gains were centered off campus—enfranchising and empowering the black community—not reforming the HBCU campuses. On predominantly white campuses, by contrast, southern student activists seemed to have their greatest impact within the college gates, changing student life, expanding student rights, pushing formerly Jim Crow campuses at least a few inches closer toward genuine diversity.

Yet this contrast seems to have diminished during the Black Power era, when African American students used civil disobedience not only to demand but also to win Black Studies and other forms of political and cultural representation on HBCUs (as well as on white-majority campuses). James Edward Smethurst's *The Black Arts Movement: Literary Nationalism in the 1960s and 1970s* (2005) suggests that by the late 1960s HBCUs, most notably in Nashville and Atlanta, had become regional centers of the Black Arts Movement. And he credits HBCU Black Power activists with helping to create a constituency for this culturally nationalist upsurge. The role of African American faculty as well as students in promoting such cultural change on campus needs further exploration. So does the whole process by which cultural nationalism became incorporated into HBCUs, whose administrations, for all their vaunted political conservatism, somehow allowed for these changes at least in some of the urban HBCUs—hiring Black Arts writers, scholars, and artists.[80]

While distinctions between blacks and whites were central, they were not the only differences that accounted for variations in the southern political and cultural experience on campus. It mattered a good deal where a school was located. Urban and upper South campuses tended to display more cosmopolitanism and political tolerance then rural deep South campuses, which is why, as Turner's Nashville study shows, schools like Fisk and Vanderbilt could become centers of student activism. Although we need to better understand such regional centers of student activism in the South, we should avoid repeating the methodological mistake of New Left historians, whose focus on hotbeds of activism gave us a northern but not a southern New Left. We need a history of the southern sixties that gives us not one South, spotlighting only the centers of activism in the urban and upper South and at the big-name schools. We must look beyond the headlines and places where northern-style campus disruptions occurred, probing how dissent emerged at less hospitable places, including religious, rural, and authoritarian deep South colleges. Alex Macaulay's pioneering study of The Citadel is a model for such work, showing that even this famed South Carolina military academy, led by foes of the antiwar movement, a place where peace marches were simply not possible, could not keep that movement's influence from its campus—which he ingeniously documented by studying the appearance there of a dissident underground newspaper.[81]

If instead of trying to present the southern sixties on campus in northern terms we depict it in its own terms, we have much to learn from its distinctiveness. After all, the southern New Left displayed few of the excesses of its northern counterpart. It is a New Left minus the Weather Underground, less wedded to confrontational campus tactics and less prone to the left-liberal feuding that weakened both the Democratic Party and the student movement as a force beyond the campuses. By freeing us from focusing so intently and emotionally on those excesses of the northern New Left, the southern campus scene may lead to a more clear-sighted view of the movement's impact on higher education and American society. If instead of obliterating the North-South differences we study them closely, they may yield comparative histories that shed new light on the possibilities, limitations, and aftermath of the 1960s Left, North, and South.

Think again of the Berkeley and University of North Carolina free speech movements. Comparing them leads to a reconsideration of the way that historians have previously characterized the sixties' left-liberal-right political dynamic. Viewed alone, the Berkeley revolt seemed from a radical perspective to have a depressing political trajectory in that the feud between the left and liberalism, the Free Speech Movement and the UC administration, led to explosive political battles and mass civil disobedience that alienated the California electorate, weakened liberalism, and paved the way for the rise of Ronald Reagan and the New Right.[82] But the North Carolina case calls such conclusions into doubt. There the student protesters consciously avoided Berkeley-style civil disobedience tactics and maintained cordial relations with the liberal university administration. This more measured, gradualist resistance did win a (slow) victory for free speech in North Carolina (achieved in court) without Mario Savio–style oratory or polarizing protest tactics. Even so, the UNC free speech battle yielded a right-wing hero of anti-student backlash in the form of Jesse Helms, whose televised tirades had helped to inspire and sustain the speaker ban.[83] The parallels between Helms and

Reagan suggest that historians—myself included—may have engaged in oversimplification when we blamed the Berkeley student movement's confrontationalism for the backlash that carried Reagan and the right to power. The UNC case attests that right-wing foes of egalitarian change, appalled by any manifestation of student radicalism, were going to bait the student movement, no matter how moderate its tactics, playing to public fear of change with great skill and effectiveness.

Mentioning Helms and Reagan here (and Trent Lott, earlier) ought to underscore the importance of the right wing in the 1960s. So far the new scholarship on southern campus politics of the 1960s has (like this introduction) tilted a bit too much to the left. In our quest to rediscover the lost history of the southern student left, we ought not lose sight of the fact that the South exited the 1960s as it entered it, the most conservative region of the United States. We need more work like Huff's chapter on conservative student politics at UGA in the late 1960s, because a key legacy of the 1960s South, as Joseph Crespino's *In Search of Another Country: Mississippi and the Conservative Counterrevolution* documents, is its contribution to the Reagan ascendancy and the nation's rightward shift up though the George W. Bush era, a phenomenon many have referred to as the "southernization" of American politics.[84] Conservatives with links to the southern campus scene of the 1960s, from Trent Lott to Jesse Helms, played key roles in this turn to the right. We need to explore the role that the institutions of student life—from fraternities and sororities to student governments and right-wing political groups such as YAF—played in keeping millions of southern students recalcitrant about social change in the sixties and determined to prevent more progressive change ever since.

The question of legacies leads us back to the southern campus scene in our own time. If this is the campus world that the 1960s made, how are we to think of it? Campuses whose hard-won cosmopolitanism and at least smatterings of diversity relegated the provincialism of the old southern campuses to the dustbin of history? The presence of black faculty and students, Black, Women's, and Gay Studies programs on majority-white southern campuses and the rise of free speech and academic freedom throughout the region suggest that the campuses of the twenty-first-century South are closer to the future envisioned by its prophetic minority in the sixties than to its recalcitrant majority. So were the reactions of my students at UGA in the 1990s, who voiced astonishment when reading of the crude racism of their parents' generation after studying the UGA desegregation story. Yet when we pushed the comparison further, many noted the persistence of white fraternities and sororities, the underrepresentation of students of color on campus, the de facto segregation of student life (which left most with no friends outside of their racial group), and the segregated high schools from which many of them had come. This left some of them wondering how much really had changed.[85]

Looking beyond the college gates leads us to the question of what difference the progressive tendencies of southern colleges and universities have made in the region. Have they served as engines of progressive regional change? Liberal centers that make a difference politically? Or an academic subculture with little influence off campus, relatively progressive enclaves in a sea of red-state southern conservatism?

This amounts to a question of who won the civil war of the 1960s. And with America divided into red and blue states, this is not merely a southern question. In fact, it calls to mind Berkeley Free Speech Movement veteran Jack Weinberg's remark back in 1984, when a reporter contrasted the power of that movement's nemesis, Ronald Reagan (who at the time resided in the White House) with the sixties-generation student rebels (who seemed dispersed and powerless) and then asked "Who won?" Weinberg replied, "It's still too soon to tell."[86] In the wake of Barack Obama's election in 2008, which the student voter registration campaigns of the 1960s South and the Voting Rights Act made possible, Weinberg's words seem prescient. They remind us that so long as the ideas championed by the right and the left in the 1960s remain in play—with Washington being criticized for waging Vietnam-style wars abroad while refusing to wage anything resembling a War on Poverty at home—that decade's legacy will be contested, and our own work on the South in the 1960s will have contemporary resonance.

It is sobering, however, to see how little impact academic histories of the South, student protest, and race in the 1960s have had on popular memory. Cleveland Sellers makes this point powerfully in his closing chapter of this book, as he recounts how perplexed he was to learn that South Carolina students in the 1990s knew next to nothing about the Orangeburg massacre. Similarly, the students I teach and the high school teachers with whom I work in New York inevitably express shock after screening *Scarred Justice* because prior to seeing that documentary on the Orangeburg massacre, none had even heard of that tragedy. Nor had they heard of Sellers, though he was a prominent SNCC leader, was wounded at Orangeburg, was framed and jailed for inciting to riot—as part of the wave of repression provoked by the ghetto rebellions and white panic over Black Power in the late 1960s. Sellers's essay challenges us to enlarge the southern student movement's narrative arc so that it begins long before the 1960s—when black students in the New Deal era dared to serve as the first test cases for the NAACP's legal crusade against Jim Crow education, a crusade that culminated in the *Brown* decision—and to recognize that the movement's legacy is with us still.

Sellers's own trajectory from 1960s scapegoat to Black Studies pioneer and most recently South Carolina HBC president—whose son serves in the South Carolina legislature—is itself a testament to the change that the "unfinished revolution," as historian Jacqueline Dowd Hall terms it, brought to the South. The students' role in that revolution is a story that this volume sets out to tell. Our hope is that this history will spark more scholarship, teaching, and popular understanding of the organizing that Sellers and his generation of southern student activists—black and white—did to remake the South and the United States in the 1960s.

The organization of this book is roughly chronological. We open with a section on "Early Days: From Talk to Action" that explores how student dissent emerged from what had once been a sleepy campus political scene in the Jim Crow South. Wesley Hogan shows how the black-led Student Nonviolent Coordinating Committee (SNCC) in the early 1960s pioneered forms of direct action in protests against racism that became a model for student activists on a wide range of issues across the United States. Next, Joy Ann Williamson-Lott's study of political repression on black and white campuses in the Carolinas and Mississippi reminds us that the institutional weight of public colleges and universities—and the tradition of Jim Crow / Joe McCarthy antiradicalism—was in many cases arrayed against the political awakening that student protesters were seeking. Erica Whittington's chapter on the National Student Association's Human Relations Project then suggests that before black and white students could join hands in protest together, they first had to learn to communicate with one another and that a small but dynamic group of southern students was doing so even before the sit-in movement began in 1960. Marcia Synnott takes this human relations story to South Carolina, where she shows how students, mentored by older activists, built an interracial network that prodded even their moderate classmates to question Jim Crow, easing the transition toward a racially integrated campus world.

Part II, "Campus Activism Takes Shape," opens with Jeffrey Turner's comparative analysis of how student activism emerged on one black and one white urban campus, Fisk and Vanderbilt, in a city that was a hub of the upper South's civil rights movement. As the 1960s wore on, the Vietnam War came so to dominate political discourse that at least on predominantly white campuses it was often the primary focus of the student left. Gary Sprayberry's chapter on the student movement at the University of Alabama offers a window onto the turbulence the war could bring even to the deep South. But the left never had a monopoly on student activism in the conservative South, and Chris Huff's study of the University of Georgia's conservatives shows us how these activists battled over whether they were building a New Right or defending the Old South.

By the late 1960s, culture had become as much a cause for battle as politics on southern campuses. In Part III, "A Cultural Revolution and Its Discontents," Kelly Morrow's chapter shows how a coalition of feminist students, progressive physicians, and gay and lesbian activists worked to awaken campus authorities to the realities of the sexual revolution. The counterculture too challenged southern traditionalism, a process Nicholas Meriwether traces in his South Carolina case study. Although welcomed by many students, the cultural and political changes wrought by the 1960s frightened the governmental guardians of the status quo, including the FBI and the Jim Crow government's red squads, whose covert war against the New Left is documented by Gregg Michel in this section's closing essay.

Southern black student activism's shift from integration toward Black Power comes into focus in the book's closing section. Jelani Favors's chapter suggests that Greensboro, the early sixties launching pad of the interracial sit-in movement, emerged later in the decade as a fulcrum of the campus Black Power movement. This section ends with an essay by Cleveland Sellers, a SNCC veteran whose student activist years spanned the integrationist and Black Power phases of the freedom movement. Sellers ruminates about what America has chosen to remember and to forget about the freedom movement; he asks that Black Power, on campus and off, be studied anew, so that its cultural and political impact can be assessed fairly—free of the negative stereotypes panicky whites circulated in the 1960s.

NOTES

1. See Jeffrey A. Turner, *Sitting In and Speaking Out: Student Movements in the American South, 1960–1970* (Athens: Univ. of Georgia Press, 2010).

2. Dirck Halstead, "The Picture from Kent State," available at http://digitaljournalist .org/issue0005/filo.htm, accessed 13 June 2012; Scott L. Bills, ed., *Kent State / May 4: Echoes Through a Decade* (Kent, OH: Kent State Univ. Press, 1988), 1–61.

3. Jack Bass and Jack Nelson, *The Orangeburg Massacre* (Macon, GA: Mercer Univ. Press, 1984), 61–78. On the Orangeburg massacre, see also *Scarred Justice,* documentary film (California Newsreel, 2009); William H. Chafe, *Civilities and Civil Rights: Greensboro, North Carolina and the Black Struggle for Freedom* (New York: Oxford Univ. Press, 1980), 184–91; *The President's Commission on Campus Unrest* (Washington, D.C., 1970), 411–65; Tim Spofford, *Lynch Street: The May 1970 Killings at Jackson State College* (Kent, OH: Kent State Univ. Press, 1988); Mark S. Giles, "Race, Justice, and the Jackson State University [*sic*] Shootings," in *Historically Black Colleges and Universities: Triumphs, Troubles, and Taboos,* ed. Marybeth Gasman and Christopher L. Tudico (New York: Palgrave Macmillan, 2008), 107, 119; Tim Thomas, "The Student Movement at Southern University," *Freedomways* (First Quarter, 1973), 16; and Adam Fairclough, *Race and Democracy: The Civil Rights Struggle in Louisiana, 1915–1972* (Athens: Univ. of Georgia Press, 1995), 460. In addition to the student deaths listed in the text, another racially charged confrontation between law enforcement officers and students on a historically black campus ended in tragedy: At Jackson State College in 1967, the National Guard and local police fired into a crowd of black student protesters. But in this case it was a nonstudent who was killed. Benjamin Brown, a 22-year-old civil rights movement veteran and bystander at the demonstration, died of gunshot wounds when the officers fired on the crowd. See "Benjamin Brown," http://nuweb9 .neu.edu/civilrights/?page_id=776, accessed 13 Aug. 2012. The Kent State massacre sparked

more than a hundred campus protests per day between 5 May and 8 May 1970 and at least 350 student strikes. Before all the tumult ended, more than four million students (60% of the national student population) had been touched by the protests. By contrast, only 53 campuses erupted in mid-May in response to the Jackson State massacre, and most of these were historically black colleges. See Kirkpatrick Sale, *SDS* (New York: Vintage, 1974), 636–38.

4. *President's Commission on Campus Unrest,* 110. Andrew B. Lewis's study of SNCC leaders argues that their activism grew out of unrealized baby boomer aspirations for a comfortable middle-class life. But such aspirations were shared by most HBCU students both in and before the baby boom generation and far more often led to political apathy than risky radical activism. See Andrew B. Lewis, *The Shadows of Youth: The Remarkable Journey of the Civil Rights Generation* (New York: Hill and Wang, 2009), 38–62. On black student and faculty activism on the HBCUs prior to the 1960s, see Raymond Wolters, *The New Negro on Campus: The Black College Rebellions of the 1920s* (Princeton, NJ: Princeton Univ. Press, 1975); Richard Kluger, *Simple Justice: The History of Brown vs. The Board of Education and Black America's Struggle for Equality* (New York: Vintage, 1977), 126–31; and Robert Cohen, *When the Old Left Was Young: Student Radicals and America's First Mass Student Movement, 1929–1941* (New York: Oxford Univ. Press, 1993), 204–24, 245–46.

5. Anne Moody, *Coming of Age in Mississippi* (New York: Dell, 1978), 261.

6. D'Army Bailey with Roger Easson, *The Education of a Black Radical: A Southern Civil Rights Activist's Journey, 1959–1964* (Baton Rouge: LSU Press, 2009), 140; Fairclough, *Race and Democracy,* 265–71; Adam Fairclough, *A Class of Their Own: Black Teachers in the Segregated South* (Cambridge, MA: Harvard Univ. Press, 2006), 361–66.

7. Thomas, "Student Movement at Southern University," 16; Fairclough, *Race and Democracy,* 460.

8. Chafe, *Civilities and Civil Rights,* 95.

9. Joy Ann Williamson, "Black Colleges and Civil Rights: Organizing and Mobilizing in Jackson Mississippi," in *Higher Education and the Civil Rights Movement: White Supremacy, Black Southerners, and the Civil Rights Movement,* ed. Peter Wallenstein (Gainesville: Univ. Press of Florida, 2008), 130–31. See also Marybeth Gasman, "Perceptions of Black College Presidents: Sorting through Stereotypes and Reality to Gain a Complex Picture," *American Education Research Journal* (in press).

10. Thomas, "Student Movement at Southern University," 16.

11. See also Wesley C. Hogan, *Many Minds, One Heart: SNCC's Dream for a New America* (Chapel Hill: Univ. of North Carolina Press, 2007), 133; and Jennifer Frost, *An Interracial Movement of the Poor: Community Organizing and the New Left in the 1960s* (New York: NYU Press, 2001), 10–18.

12. Jack Newfield, *A Prophetic Minority* (New York: Signet Books, 1966), 40–41.

13. Ibid., 41.

14. Raymond Arsenault, *Freedom Riders 1961 and the Struggle for Racial Justice* (New York: Oxford Univ. Press, 2007), 179–208; Clayborne Carson, *In Struggle: SNCC and the Black Awakening of the 1960s* (Cambridge, MA: Harvard Univ. Press, 1995), 31–39; David Halberstam, *The Children* (New York: Fawcett, 1998), 248–325.

15. John Lewis and Michael D'Orso, *Walking with the Wind: A Memoir of the Movement* (New York: Simon and Schuster, 1998), 273. Even into the mid-1960s a new kind of community building thrived across racial lines among southern student activists, and this was an "important" attraction to white activists, who viewed interracial friendships, solidarity, and

romances as a welcome change from the racial repression and segregation they had grown up with in the Jim Crow South (Lee Frissell, e-mail to the author, 8 Mar. 2010).

16. Taylor Branch, *Parting the Waters: America in the King Years, 1954–1963* (New York: Simon and Schuster, 1988), 272–311; Taylor Branch, *At Canaan's Edge: America in the King Years, 1965–1968* (New York: Simon and Schuster, 2006), xii.

17. Howard Zinn, *SNCC: The New Abolitionists* (Cambridge, MA: South End Press, 1964, 1965, 2002), 1.

18. My interpretation of the way SNCC historiography has often been disconnected from the HBCUs has been shaped by the insightful discussion in Joy Ann Williamson, *Radicalizing the Ebony Tower: Black Colleges and the Black Freedom Struggle in Mississippi* (New York: Teachers College Press, 2008), 1–3. But for a recent SNCC study (2009) that offers some coverage of that connection, see Lewis, *Shadows of Youth,* 40, 46, 49–50, 55, 67, 68, 72, 83–84, 91, 191.

19. Newfield, *Prophetic Minority*; Todd Gitlin, *The Sixties: Years of Hope, Days of Rage* (New York: Bantam, 1993); Terry Anderson, *The Movement and the Sixties: Protest in America from Greensboro to Wounded Knee* (New York: Oxford Univ. Press, 1996).

20. Doug McAdam, *Freedom Summer* (New York: Oxford Univ. Press, 1988), 35–198.

21. Robert P. Moses interview in Ben Agger, *The Sixties at 40: Leaders and Activist Remember and Look Forward* (East Boulder, CO: Paradigm, 2009), 184–88; Robert P. Moses, interview with the author, 5 May 2011, New York City, available online at http://steinhardt .nyu.edu/historyintheclassroom/video. The best account of the Mississippi freedom movement is Charles Payne, *I've Got the Light of Freedom: The Organizing Tradition and the Mississippi Freedom Struggle* (Berkeley: Univ. of California Press, 2007). In this second edition Payne offers a valuable update to his brilliant bibliographical essay on the black freedom movement. But this work is centered off campus, as is the equally illuminating collection of cutting-edge civil rights scholarship, Emilye Crosby, ed., *Civil Rights History from the Ground Up* (Athens: Univ. of Georgia Press, 2011).

22. Platon, "A Civil Rights Portfolio," *New Yorker,* 15 and 22 Feb. 2010, 95–115.

23. Ibid., 96.

24. Ibid., 97; see http://archives.newyorker.com/?i=2010-02-15#folio=09, accessed Apr. 2010.

25. Moses interview with the author. Robert Cohen, *Freedom's Orator: Mario Savio and the Radical Legacy of the 1960s* (New York: Oxford Univ. Press, 2009), 64–66.

26. George Ware, telephone interview with the author, 15 July 2010, notes in author's possession.

27. Chafe, *Civilities and Civil Rights,* 156. Exhaustion may have contributed to the mid-1960s lull in student protest at the HBCUs in another way. SNCC organizers, veterans of the historic civil rights campaigns of the early 1960s, would have been uniquely qualified to build a mass black student movement in the mid-1960s. But by then much of this first generation of SNCC workers was burned out from years of dangerous anti–Jim Crow organizing in the deep South—suffering from a form of battle fatigue after enduring long periods of violence at the hands of white supremacists. See Cleveland Sellers, chapter 12 in this volume, for an eloquent discussion of this exhaustion and battle fatigue among SNCC veterans.

28. Charles Cobb to Tom Gardner, 25 Jan. 1967, copy in author's possession; David Garrow, *Bearing the Cross: Martin Luther King, Jr., and the Southern Christian Leadership Conference* (New York: Vintage, 1988), 543–56.

29. Turner, *Sitting In and Speaking Out*; Gregg L. Michel, *Struggle for a Better South: The*

Southern Student Organizing Committee, 1964–1969 (New York: Palgrave Macmillan, 2004); Sue Thrasher, telephone interview with the author, 9 Mar. 2010, transcript in author's possession; Tom Gardner, telephone interview with the author, 10 Mar. 2010, transcript in author's possession; Lee Frissell, e-mail to the author, 8 Mar. 2010, copy in author's possession.

30. The Movement was, as David Farber has put it, "a term widely used in the sixties era by progressive activists; it referred broadly to the linked struggles for a more egalitarian society . . . based on a more participatory democracy and an anti-imperialist world-view." Farber, e-mail to David Snyder, 15 July 2012.

31. Newfield, *Prophetic Minority*. A stunning example of how student dissidents in the South opened the campuses to critical views on race can be found in the civil rights photography of Jim Wallace, who in the early 1960s shot the local desegregation struggle in Chapel Hill for the UNC student newspaper (the *Daily Tar Heel*) at a time when there was a press blackout of the protests in most North Carolina newspapers. See Paul Dickson and Jim Wallace, *Courage in the Moment: The Civil Rights Struggle, 1961–1964* (Mineola, NY: Dover Publications, 2012).

32. Turner, *Sitting In and Speaking Out*, 183–262.

33. Frissell, e-mail to the author. Frissell's argument that faculty liberalism was an aid to the southern student left merits further exploration. For an example of early 1960s faculty liberalism on a historically black college that went well beyond the classroom, see Bernard Tapper, *Gomillion versus Lightfoot: Apartheid in Alabama* (New York: McGraw Hill, 1962), 31. What is needed is a history of southern faculty that assesses their impact on student politics, along the lines of Adam Fairclough's work on black school teachers in the Jim Crow South. HBCU faculty's relationship with the freedom movement and its student wing in the 1960s seems as complex and conflicted as that of the teachers Fairclough so brilliantly portrayed. See Fairclough, *Class of Their Own*, 355–90.

34. For a vivid account of political repression on a white southern campus, see Bob Zellner with Constance Curry, *The Wrong Side of Murder Creek: A White Southerner in the Freedom Movement* (Montgomery, AL: New South Books, 2008), 48–72. For an equally evocative discussion of repression at a historically black college in the early 1960s South, see Bailey, *Education of a Black Radical*, 46–53, 73–135.

35. Thrasher, telephone interview with the author.

36. Not even the most recent survey of southern student activism in the 1960s, Turner's *Sitting In and Speaking Out*, identifies where or when the first mass civil disobedience, sit-ins, and building takeovers occurred on a southern campus. But in our e-mail discussion, Turner agreed that "if the key word is 'mass' civil disobedience then UNC's disruptive campus sit-in in 1966 would be the first such on-campus demonstration in the South." He also points out, however, that "there were a few smaller episodes" on southern campuses earlier in the decade. In 1962, some students at Tulane connected with CORE were part of small interracial squads that came into the university's segregated cafeteria and demanded to be served, which led to the suspension of one of these student protesters. See Clarence L. Mohr and Joseph E. Gordon, *Tulane: The Emergence of a Modern University* (Baton Rouge: LSU Press, 2001), 223–27. Around the same time, students at Louisiana State University in New Orleans organized a boycott of their cafeteria for the same reason. Turner, *Sitting In and Speaking Out*, 65–66. Among HBCUs, Tuskegee students led by Gwen Patton and George Ware instigated some on-campus demonstrations in late 1965, including a "turn-over-your-plate" cafeteria demonstration. See Robert J. Norrell, *Reaping the Whirlwind: The Civil Rights Movement in Tuskegee* (Chapel Hill: Univ. of North Carolina Press, 1985),

170–78. Joy Ann Williamson concurs in this assessment but urges that we keep in mind that while mass sit-ins did not appear on HBCUs until later in the 1960s, some disruptive protest tactics appeared there earlier, most notably the boycott organized by Alcorn State students in Mississippi in 1957. That boycott "aimed at bringing business as usual to a grinding halt" and mobilized "almost the entire student body. . . . It didn't get much press outside Mississippi, though students were expelled, a president fired, and re-enrolling students had to sign a document never to protest again." Jeff Turner and Joy Williamson, e-mails to Robert Cohen, 18 Aug. 2011. Note, however, that compared to the campus building takeovers, which yielded mass arrests and police violence, of the mid- to late 1960s, even such boycotts seem moderate.

37. Michael S. Durham, *The Civil Rights Photography of Michael Moore* (New York: Stewart, Tabori, and Chang, 1991), 66–67; E. Culpepper Clark, *The Schoolhouse Door: Segregation's Last Stand at the University of Alabama* (Tuscaloosa: Univ. of Alabama Press, 2007), cover photo.

38. *The Gamecock,* 13 May 1970; *Student Activism Southern Style: Organizing and Protest in the Sixties and Seventies* (19–21 Mar. 2010), cover, 1, 3. See also Andrew Grose, "Voices of Southern Protest during the Vietnam Era: The University of South Carolina as a Case Study," *Peace and Change* (Apr. 2007): 153–67.

39. The major exception to the New Left narratives' erasure of the South comes when they mention the "Prairie Power" movement, that in the mid-1960s, as SDS leaders became more countercultural and geographically diverse, more of them came from midwestern and southern campuses. But this did not lead to studies of the southern campus milieu that produced such leaders. On Prairie Power, see Anderson, *Movement and the Sixties,* 148–49.

40. Melanie Knight, "The Free Speech Movement and the Antiwar Movement at the University of South Carolina," unpublished paper, abstract in author's possession.

41. Jeffrey Turner, "Conflict and Conscience: The Student Movement, The Sixties, and the South," unpublished manuscript, 754–59, copy in author's possession.

42. Richard E. Peterson and John A. Bilorusky, *May 1970: The Campus Aftermath of Cambodia and Kent State* (Berkeley, CA: Carnegie Commission on Higher Education, 1971), 60, 65.

43. Turner, "Conflict and Conscience," 313–39.

44. On the case for a conservatism that is not centered on race, see Lisa McGirr, *Suburban Warriors: The Origins of the New American Right* (Princeton, NJ: Princeton Univ. Press, 2001). The case for race and anti–civil rights movement backlash being central to the conservative revival is made powerfully in Dan Carter, *The Politics of Rage: George Wallace, the Origins of the New Conservatism, and the Transformation of American Politics* (New York: Simon and Schuster, 1995); and Joseph Crespino, *In Search of Another Country: Mississippi and the Conservative Counterrevolution* (Princeton, NJ: Princeton Univ. Press, 2007).

45. Clark, *Schoolhouse Door,* 53–90. For Martin Luther King's denunciation of the University of Alabama's racist student activists for their role in threatening Lucy, see "When Peace Becomes Obnoxious," sermon, 18 Mar. 1956, Dexter Avenue Baptist Church, in Clayborne Carson et al., ed., *The Papers of Martin Luther King, Jr.,* vol. 3 (Berkeley: Univ. of California Press, 1997), 207–8. For a penetrating look at the Georgian counterparts to these racist Alabama students, see Robert A. Pratt, "The Rhetoric of Hate: The Demosthenian Literary Society and Its Opposition to the Desegregation of the University of Georgia, 1950–1964," *Georgia Historical Quarterly* (Summer 2006): 236–59.

46. Branch's three-volume history of King and the Freedom Movement terms the era

from 1954 to 1968 as "the King years" in America. On the concept of a "long sixties" and with it a "long civil rights movement," see Jacqueline Dowd Hall, "The Long Civil Rights Movement and the Uses of the Past," *Journal of American History* (Mar. 2005): 1233–63; and Tom Hayden, *The Long Sixties: From 1960 to Barack Obama* (Boulder, CO: Paradigm, 2009), 1–92.

47. Robert A. Pratt, *We Shall Not Be Moved: The Desegregation of the University of Georgia* (Athens: Univ. of Georgia Press, 2005), 86–110; Robert Cohen, "'2-4-6-8 We Don't Want to Integrate,' White Student Attitudes towards the Desegregation of the University of Georgia, 1961," *Georgia Historical Quarterly* (Fall 1996): 616–45; Robert Cohen, "G-Men in Georgia: The FBI and the Segregationist Riot at the University of Georgia, 1961," *Georgia Historical Quarterly* (Fall 1999): 508–38.

48. Charles W. Eagles, *The Price of Defiance: James Meredith and the Integration of Ole Miss* (Chapel Hill: Univ. of North Carolina, 2009), 340–70.

49. Cohen, "'2-4-6-8 We Don't Want to Integrate,'" 624–45. On white southerners and their "fearful" attitudes toward the changes heralded by the civil rights movement, see Jason Sokol, *There Goes My Everything: White Southerners in the Age of Civil Rights* (New York: Knopf, 2006), 4–5.

50. Eagles, *Price of Defiance,* 332.

51. Trent Lott, *Herding Cats: A Life in Politics* (New York: Regan Books, 2005), 42.

52. Michel, *Struggle for a Better South,* 19.

53. Eagles, *Price of Defiance,* 10–24.

54. Calvin Trillin puts the crowd size at the UGA segregationist riot at "about a thousand." See Trillin, *An Education in Georgia: Charlayne Hunter, Hamilton Holmes, and the Integration of the University of Georgia* (New York: Viking, 1963), 52. The riotous crowd that attacked Autherine Lucy in Alabama was even larger. E. Culpepper Clark estimates that the crowd peaked at 3,000. See Clark, *Schoolhouse Door,* 73. The violent crowd at the Mississippi riot during the desegregation crisis peaked at somewhere between two thousand and four thousand. As Frank Lambert points out, this was a very large crowd when you consider that the University of Mississippi had only 4,500 students. This raises the question of how many rioters were students. Lambert cites estimates that at the outset of the night of protest, students constituted between 67% and 95% of the protesters but that as the violence escalated, the "percentage of students" involved in the disturbances "declined steadily." See Lambert, *The Battle of Ole Miss: Civil Rights v. States' Rights* (New York: Oxford Univ. Press, 2010), 118.

55. Trillin, *Education in Georgia,* 69, 83, 169; Pratt, *We Shall Not Be Moved,* 114–15.

56. Charlayne Hunter-Gault interview, http://archives.newyorker.com/?i=2010-02-15 #folio=09; Trillin, *Education in Georgia,* 4, 84; Charlayne Hunter-Gault, "Integrated Paths," *New York Times Magazine,* 31 Dec. 1995, 24.

57. Charles H. Martin, "Hold that (Color) Line!: Black Exclusion and Southeastern Conference Football," in *Higher Education and the Civil Rights Movement,* ed. Wallenstein, 166, 184–90.

58. Michel, *Struggle for a Better South,* 19.

59. Ibid., 236n24.

60. Tom Gardner interview.

61. David G. Sansing, *Making Haste Slowly: The Troubled History of Higher Education in Mississippi* (Jackson: Univ. of Mississippi Press, 1990), 198–202.

62. Turner, "Conflict and Conscience," 606–24; Tom Gardner interview.

63. Tom Gardner interview.

64. Doug Rossinow's *The Politics of Authenticity: Liberalism, Christianity, and the New Left in America* (New York: Columbia Univ. Press, 1998) was the first book-length study of the New Left on a southern campus. Next came William J. Billingsley's *Communists on Campus: Race, Politics, and the Public University in North Carolina* (Athens: Univ. of Georgia Press, 1999), which included several chapters on the New Left at Chapel Hill. Though not centered on campuses, Sara Evans's *Personal Politics: The Roots of Women's Liberation in the Civil Rights Movement and the New Left* (New York: Vintage, 1980) traces connections among the southern freedom movement, the student YWCAs, and women's liberation. Only in 2004 did a regionally focused study of the southern New Left appear: Michel's *Struggle for a Better South,* which looked at white leftist campus organizers across the South. Also useful are Joy Ann Williamson's important state study of student activism at HBCUs, *Radicalizing the Ebony Tower: Black Colleges and the Black Freedom Struggle in Mississippi* (New York: Teachers College Press, 2008); Harry G. Lefever's chronicle of Spelman College and the Civil Rights Movement, *Undaunted by the Fight: Spelman College and the Civil Rights Movement, 1957–1967* (Macon, GA: Mercer Univ. Press, 2005); and Charles U. Smith's edited collection *Student Unrest on Historically Black Campuses* (Silver Springs, MD: Beckham, 1995). Turner's *Sitting In and Speaking Out* offers the first regional survey of historically black and white southern student activism.

To date none of this published work has changed the national New Left narrative. While it is notable that Michel's SSOC study was included in John McMillian and Paul Buhle, eds., *The New Left Revisited* (Philadelphia: Temple Univ. Press, 2002), it remains to be seen whether student activism in the late 1960s South will be factored into national histories of the New Left and 1960s America. A look at the recent New Left historiography and histories of 1960s America is not very encouraging. Even the best of this work, Van Gosse's *Rethinking the New Left: An Interpretative History* (New York: Palgrave Macmillan, 2005), Maurice Isserman and Michael Kazin's *America Divided: The Civil War of the 1960s* (New York: Oxford Univ. Press, 2000), and David Farber's *The Age of Great Dreams: America in the 1960s* (New York: Hill and Wang, 1994) virtually ignore late 1960s southern campuses. Only Terry Anderson's *The Movement and the Sixties* (New York: Oxford Univ. Press, 1996) devotes a few pages to southern campus antiwar protests. Nor do the recent surveys of Black Power explore how this movement impacted black and white campuses in the South. See Peniel E. Josephs, *Waiting 'Til the Midnight Hour: A Narrative History of Black Power in America* (New York: Holt, 2007).

65. Turner, "Conflict and Conscience," 295.

66. William A. Link, *William Friday: Power, Purpose, and American Higher Education* (Chapel Hill: Univ. of North Carolina Press, 1995), 111–41; Billingsley, *Communists on Campus,* 218–19; Henry Mayer, "A View from the South: The Idea of a State University," in *The Free Speech Movement: Reflections on Berkeley in the 1960s,* ed. Robert Cohen and Reginald E. Zelnik (Berkeley: Univ. of California Press, 2002), 157–69.

67. Tom Gardner interview.

68. Ibid. Evidence of this liberalization process is found in Christopher A. Huff, chapter 7 in this volume. Georgia's conservative students could not muster enough campus support to win its campaign to force the school's band to return to its abandoned tradition of playing "Dixie" at football games.

69. Tom Gardner, *SSOC: A Brief History of the Southern Student Organizing Committee* (unpublished paper, University of Virginia, 1970), 19–20; Turner, *Sitting In and Speaking Out,* 271–77. It is surprising that more historians have not been studying the role of women

in southern student protest, since in addition to the book-length memoirs of such leading student organizers as Mary King and Anne Moody, female movement veterans have
compiled several rich anthologies of their memoirs. See Constance Curry et al., eds., *Deep
in Our Hearts: Nine White Women in the Freedom Movement* (Athens: Univ. of Georgia
Press, 2000); Faith S. Holsaert et al., eds., *Hands on the Freedom Plow: Personal Accounts
of Women in SNCC* (Urbana: Univ. of Illinois Press, 2010); Betty Collier-Tomas and V. P.
Franklin, eds., *Sisters in the Struggle: African American Women in the Civil Rights and Black
Power Movements* (New York: NYU Press, 2001); and Evans, *Personal Politics.*

70. Tom Gardner interview. In some southern states, such as Florida, the massive
growth of public higher educational institutions contributed to cultural liberalization.
Florida State University, which had once been a modest teachers college, expanded into
a research university in the 1960s, attracting cosmopolitan undergraduates, faculty, and
graduate students from both the South and other regions. Floyd Hammack, interview with
the author, New York City, 27 Sept. 2011.

71. Frissell, communication to the author. On the role of religion in the southern New
Left, see also Rossinow, *Politics of Authenticity,* 53–114; and Evans, *Personal Politics,* 27–37.
This alliance between church progressivism and student activism in the South began long
before the 1960s. See Cohen, *When the Old Left Was Young,* 211–15.

72. Tom Gardner and Sue Thrasher interviews.

73. Tom Gardner interview.

74. Frissell, communication to the author.

75. Chafe, *Civilities and Civil Rights,* 249.

76. Tom Gardner interview.

77. James Forman, *Sammy Younge, Jr: The First Black Student to Die in the Black Liberation Movement* (Washington, D.C., 1985).

78. There was at least one case, however, where police came close to shedding blood on
a predominantly white campus, Florida State University (FSU), on the evening of 4 March
1969. The FSU administration, after refusing to recognize the local SDS chapter—which
would have given SDS the right to meet on campus—called the police to evict the SDSers
who were defying the ban by meeting on campus. Led by an overzealous sheriff, 35 volunteer riot police, wielding loaded M-1 rifles, used fixed bayonets in arresting 58 student
activists—a display of force that outraged FSU faculty and students but did not result in
any shootings. On this "Night of the Bayonets," see Stephen Eugene Parr, "The Forgotten
Radicals: The New Left in the Deep South, Florida State University, 1960 to 1972," PhD diss.,
Florida State Univ., 2000), 1–2, 140–77; J. Stanley Marshall, *The Tumultuous Sixties: Campus
Unrest and Student Life at a Southern University* (Tallahassee, FL: Sentry Press, 2004), 3–181;
and David Lee McMullen, "Was Florida State Really the 'Berkeley of the South' in the 1960s
and 1970s?" *H-Net Reviews* (Sept. 2006).

79. Manning Marable, "The Quiet Deaths of Black Colleges," *Southern Exposure* (Mar.–
Apr. 1984), 31–39. But if black activists initially had limited success in transforming the HB-
CUs, they fared far better on historically white campuses. The cadre of African American
students who enlisted with the NAACP legal effort to end Jim Crow admissions in southern
college and universities helped win that epochal struggle. No historian has systematically
studied this generation of black students whose role first as litigants and then as the first
blacks at their colleges and universities made possible the toppling of Jim Crow on campus.
But there are excellent campus studies of their efforts in Wallenstein, ed., *Higher Education
and the Civil Rights Movement.* The late-1960s generation of Black Power activists on pre-

dominantly white campuses built on this success, pushing for greater curricular diversity, black admissions, and hiring. See Link, *William Friday,* 141–58.

80. James Edward Smethurst, *The Black Arts Movement: Literary Nationalism in the 1960s and 1970s* (Chapel Hill: Univ. of North Carolina Press, 2005), 326–42. On militant and effective HBCU Black Power protests in the urban South in the late 1960s and early 1970s, see Winston A. Grady-Willis, *Challenging U.S. Apartheid: Atlanta and Black Struggles for Human Rights, 1960–1977* (Durham, NC: Duke Univ. Press, 2006), 143–68.

81. Alex Macaulay, "'An Oasis of Order': The Citadel, the 1960s, and the Vietnam Anti-War Movement," in *Other Souths: Diversity and Difference in the U.S. South, Reconstruction to Present,* ed. Pippa Holloway (Athens: Univ. of Georgia Press, 2008), 328–40.

82. Cohen, *Freedom's Orator,* 216–23; W. J. Rorabaugh, "The FSM, Berkeley Politics, and Ronald Reagan," in *Free Speech Movement,* ed. Cohen and Zelnik, 511–18.

83. Billingsley, *Communists on Campus,* 16–19, 240–43; William A. Link, *Righteous Warrior: Jesse Helms and the Rise of Modern Conservatism* (New York: St. Martin's Press, 2008), 81–89.

84. Joseph Crespino, *In Search of Another Country: Mississippi and the Conservative Counterrevolution* (Princeton, NJ: Princeton Univ. Press, 2007), 1–17, 205–78; Dan Carter, *The Politics of Rage: George Wallace, the Origins of the New Conservatism, and the Transformation of American Politics* (New York: Simon and Schuster, 1995), 451–68; John Egerton, "The Southernization of American Politics," in *Where We Stand: Voices of Southern Dissent,* ed. Anthony Dunbar (Montgomery, AL: New South Books, 2004), 197–223.

85. UGA student essays in EFN 203, 1997–1998, copies in author's possession. On the enduring problems with racial discrimination and prejudice in southern fraternities, see Nadine Cohodas, *The Band Played Dixie: Race and Liberal Conscience at Ole Miss* (New York: Free Press, 1997), 232–53.

86. Jack Weinberg, speech at Free Speech Movement twentieth anniversary commemoration, Berkeley, California, 2 Oct. 1984, transcript in author's possession.

PART I

Early Days

From Talk to Action

CHAPTER ONE

Freedom Now!

SNCC Galvanizes the New Left

WESLEY HOGAN

Outside of the scholarly world, people have at best a hazy understanding that in the early 1960s, the Student Nonviolent Coordinating Committee, the Congress of Racial Equality, and Martin Luther King Jr. "passed the torch" of progressive activism to SDS and to the predominantly white and northern New Left. The story goes that the southern freedom movement fired off the opening salvos and then young campus activists north of the Mason-Dixon line finished the fight, ending a war and building gender, sexuality, and countercultural liberation movements. Three decades of important scholarship highlighting thick webs of personal and institutional connections moving from the South to the North (and the West)[1] has failed, however, to dislodge white America's paternalist notions about the role that northern white students played in the civil rights movement. This white paternalism was described most memorably by SNCC veteran and historian Julian Bond, when he barbed: "Rosa [Parks] sat down, Martin [Luther King] stood up, and the white kids came down and saved the day."[2] Yes, white students did come south to work in the movement, most famously in Freedom Summer: but they learned more than they taught, and what they learned, they carefully and passionately took back to their home communities. The civil rights movement, then, taught the whole New Left—sometimes directly, sometimes indirectly—how to organize for "freedom now." This story needs to be understood to comprehend 1960s America: the New Left owes a tremendous debt to SNCC and the black student movement. As my book *Many Minds, One Heart* attests, white kids didn't come down and save the day in Mississippi. Black kids and their adult allies in Mississippi's African American community saved the day on apathetic, politically dead campuses throughout the rest of the nation.

It is almost irresistible to look back on the decade as one marked by highly visible and often apocalyptic events set in motion by easily identifiable sectors of the population. Birmingham. The March on Washington. The Watts riots. The arrival of the miniskirt and the Beatles from Britain. Draft cards burned in Central Park. Women burning their bras at the Miss America competition. The Stonewall riots. Twenty thousand Chicano students walking out of the L.A. Central Unified School District en masse. What the country experienced was a protest movement generated by its youth. It was aimed at changing longstanding cultural habits.[3]

Those who remember newscasts from the civil rights era might have a series of images in mind as they think about these questions—white college students coming south to teach thousands of black youth during their summer breaks in freedom schools. But what if we've given credit to the wrong people? What if we still don't understand the nature and sources of the greater democratization of our own society in the 1960s and 1970s?

Bring to mind a new set of images. Forget for a moment the white Smith student teaching Jim Crow's children in a wooden church building in black Mississippi. Northern whites at elite schools learned from SNCC. Reverse the role of teacher/student, of hero/saved. Enter a well-heeled Episcopal church, marble floors and stained glass walls, across from Harvard's campus or the benches in front of the manicured lawns at the University of Michigan's Palmer Field. Observe students from Harvard, Smith, and Michigan listening, held rapt by Curtis Hayes (later Muhammad). Hayes, a teen from McComb, Mississippi, led the first sit-in at that violent town's Greyhound terminal. He was among the first Mississippi leaders of SNCC's daring and dangerous voter registration projects.

Hayes came to Harvard and Michigan in 1962 to share his knowledge about civil rights work. He was a black working-class kid from Mississippi teaching elite students. He "raised" their consciousness. Michigan sophomore Dickie Magidoff remembered Hayes as "a very young man, very shy, [who] had just unimaginable courage. He was only about twenty. It blew me away. He came up, and spoke at a couple of churches, and a few house meetings." Magidoff was thunderstruck by "how willing he was to risk his life. And it was clear he was risking his life. He was a very ordinary young man on some level." But "he was very clear about who he was, and what he had to do" in order to bring the country in line with its mission statement—freedom and opportunity for all.

It wasn't only Hayes's courage that was inspiring. Magidoff was learning from Hayes how a small group of committed students was making a significant difference in the country. They had found a way to act on their convictions and in so doing changed the national political calculus. This influence is visible in the SDS-SNCC relationship. Richard Rothstein wrote to Paul Potter that "the whole student movement," including SNCC, Students for a Democratic Society, and the rest of the New Left, "can all trace their spiritual and political ancestry to that day," 1 February 1960, when four young men sat down in Greensboro, North Carolina.

Adelaide Matteson and Susan Kent from Vassar wrote Charles McDew and Charles Jones, "We have been interested in the Freedom Rides since they began, but were not aware of their full value or nature until Tom Hayden spoke at Vassar on Wednesday, December 13. . . . We would like to participate in this movement or help in any way possible. We plan to arrive in Atlanta on January 18 with two or three other friends."[4]

About six months after nearly being beaten to death by white supremacist thugs in McComb, white southern college student Bob Zellner came to Ann Arbor. "We had a big argument about nonviolence," Magidoff remembered. He, Zellner, and another Michigan undergraduate, Bob Ross, sat in Ross and Magidoff's tiny two-room apartment one night. "We were not into [nonviolence] on principle. We didn't understand people being so passive," said Magidoff. Actually Zellner's activism was the opposite of passive, but it would be months before Magidoff began to understand that nonviolent direct action was the weapon breaking Jim Crow's chokehold on the nation's democratic aspirations. But from the outside, and without the experience, Zellner's weapon of nonviolence seemed like "passivity" to the Michigan boys. Zellner "had been beaten almost to death, had almost lost an eye six months earlier. And he was sitting here, in our kitchen-bedroom, saying that if they sicced a dog on him, and the dog was chewing on his balls, he would probably not fight the dog!"

Magidoff and Ross were incredulous. "You're just saying that!" they cried. "We were getting exasperated with it at one point, although we all got along very well," Magidoff remembered. "It was early groping with very difficult ideas. Zellner was such an absolutist about it."[5] It was, initially, a clash of cultures. It was also people thinking about change confronted with people bringing about change. This was a profound experiential difference. Southern visitors like Hayes and Zellner had actually found ways to live out their beliefs. They weren't just talking about "changing the world," they were doing it. And their methods were not just unacceptable, they were inexplicable. Predictably, Magidoff and Ross found the entire relationship a difficult challenge.

Some understood a bit faster than others. Martha Prescod Norman Noonan, an African American activist whose parents had been active in the Progressive Party, came to the University of Michigan looking to connect with blacks active in politics. Instead she found herself out of sync with a group of black sorority sisters "embarrassed to bring up" civil rights issues. Noonan heard Curtis Hayes and campus newspaper editor Tom Hayden speak and was so impressed that she helped form a group at Michigan called Friends of SNCC. For two years, she raised money, "sold records, arranged for speakers, [organized] cocktail parties." She also "got stories out to the newspapers and organized support demonstrations." After participating in the food and clothing drive for Greenwood, Mississippi, in the winter of 1962–63, she determined to go to the South herself, and that summer, she worked on the Greenwood voter registration project, followed by another year of community work in Selma.

Although Noonan did not see herself as part of the Students for a Democratic Society group in Ann Arbor, she was close to civil rights activist Casey Hayden, who at that time was Tom Hayden's wife. She attended some of the meetings in the Haydens' house in 1962. There were "a lot of ideas and feelings that were very similar at that point between SDS and SNCC people," she later recalled. "Not the level but the kind of commitment" was different. SNCC people asked: " 'Where is your body?' and 'How much are you willing to risk?' " At this point, Noonan found SDS "intellectually committed to change, but not willing to be active. . . . They might loan their car, but they were not the organizers."[6] Tom Hayden, who was an early founder of SDS, agreed. SNCC staff, he wrote back to SDS, "have decided not to protest but to transform as well, and that is revolution. They have decided that it is time right now—not in a minute, not after this one more committee meets, not after we have the legal defense and court costs promised—to give blood and body if necessary for social justice."[7] Peter Countryman at Yale started the Northern Student Movement after long conversations with SNCC leaders Charles McDew and Tim Jenkins. Jenkins was a SNCC member at Yale Law School. With the help of Tom Hayden's reports on McComb, Countryman pieced together the history of SNCC's first two years, as a guide for the NSM. Could this help northern students develop a blueprint for bringing the same quest for more humane social relations to their own localities?[8]

A similar dynamic was evident at the University of Texas. There was still one restaurant, the Piccadilly, that was not integrated by early SNCC people, and so students asked SDS, as its first project, to help them integrate it. Five or six people might not have been enough to run a picket line or to find enough nerve to protest. "But with thirty-five people we could do it," Texas student leader Robert Pardun remembered. "It felt like no individual person would be tremendously singled out." Seeing themselves together working toward a more democratic society gave them the strength to step out as individuals.

The Texas SDSers' education on the civil rights picket line taught them more about American society than any college class could. For six weeks, they set up picket lines outside the Piccadilly. A constant stream of counterprotesters drew police, and the police took pictures of everyone. One day a plainclothes police officer approached Pardun. "He said he had some really nice pictures of us," Pardun said, "and that if we would come down to the station, he would give us one." So they went down and met Lieutenant Burt Gerding. He gave them a picture from his stack and asked them to name other picketers. Rather than being intimidated, Pardun was "astonished. I thought that what we were doing was the country's work. That the country was built on freedom of speech, and freedom of assembly." The "Fourteenth Amendment gives people access to public accommodations" as well as the vote, he recalled. Although the laws had been passed in the previous century, others of previous generations had just not enforced them, and "now it was on my watch, and I was going to do it." Pardun "thought what I was doing was right, I was just kind of amazed that [Gerding] thought that he needed to be watching me."[9] So Pardun kept connecting SNCC activity to the campus through his SDS chapter.

Here, again, was the classic question small-d democratic organizers have been raising for generations in America. As Lawrence Goodwyn, the great historian of Populism, asked, How do we "move idea into action?" Ella Baker, mother and facilitator of an enormous variety of civil rights activities, brought together young students who had participated in the sit-ins in 1960 in order to discuss "what do we do next?" Noonan, Hayden, Countryman, and Pardun responded to "people doing something." That was SNCC.[10]

Whatever we call the phenomenon, the challenge remains the same. Realizing a problem, even identifying it, or, better yet, understanding its many manifestations: none of it alone will change anything. We can passionately discuss the problem, write position papers, or give eloquent speeches about it. We can even argue, in hindsight, that some understanding of a problem is a necessary prerequisite for resolving it. All true. Rarely if ever do any of these things change anything. Change only happens when people figure out what to do, how to translate idea into action.

Historically, it may well be the most difficult of all tasks—for individuals, for groups, for nations. The primary reason why cultures experience social movements so infrequently is as profound as it is basic: rarely do large groups of people figure out what to do. The primary problem is not that they don't share a "common awareness" or that they don't agree on a common understanding of what the problem is. And the difficulty most assuredly is not that people don't have a sufficient level of frustration or anger or alienation or even courage. The dilemma is that they haven't been able to generate a plan of action.

When people do figure out a plan of action—as in the American South in the early 1960s, in Prague in 1968, in Poland and East Germany in the 1980s, or in Egypt in 2011—we hear about it. We hear about it because the wheels of history begin to turn in new and unexpected ways. What yesterday appeared to be mostly unchallengeable and unchangeable suddenly collapses. It happened because people found a way to act.

Civil rights activists, and particularly in SNCC, found ways to act. They found ways to act that allowed them to destroy Jim Crow and the scourge of segregation, in the process becoming one of the most effective democratic movements of the twentieth century. They also found ways to act that deeply and systemically informed all subsequent movements of the 1960s. Blacks then taught whites how to act politically in a serious way. Indeed, we can show in hindsight that the extent to which movements such as the New Left, the antiwar movement, the women's movement, and others were successful was in crucial ways dependent upon their ability to have learned from civil rights activists.

The insight is not new to the organizers of any of these movements. But it is still a story that has not penetrated into the culture at large—even though it is a story essential to all those interested in moving ideas into action. And it is a story that, well studied and internalized, could teach us how popular politics can work. It could fundamentally expand our sense of possibility.

So what is it that civil rights activists in SNCC had learned, and how did it inform what later became known as the New Left? Let us revisit Julian Bond's satire of civil rights history—"Rosa sat down, Martin stood up, and the white kids came down and saved the day"—only now by retelling what happened with the benefit of the experiences and insights of the people who actually made the movement move.

SNCC is the founding generation of the 1960s student movement. SNCC organizers provided crucial assistance in generating the New Left. They did so in three specific ways. First, SNCC's civil rights activism in the South helped change both culture and climate on college campuses around the country between 1960 and 1964. Second, SNCC taught students on northern and western campuses how southern activism worked, and by virtue of asking for support, prompted college students in the North and West to start acting too. Such early activism nationwide included sympathy sit-ins, food and clothing drives, fundraisers, sending volunteers to the South, and providing brief "havens" for SNCC people who were close to burnout. Finally, SNCC created a new kind of inclusive and participatory, small-d democratic culture whose legacy shaped political actions on southern campuses but then spread well beyond the South into the wider culture of campuses in the North and West.

SNCC's pivotal role in first generating and then critically informing political activism in the wider culture was almost entirely unintentional. But by creating a powerful model—several models, actually—of moving ideas into action (immediately followed by letting actions refine ideas, and so on), SNCC began to serve as a magnet for northern youth interested in more than just talking about change. SNCC provided an experiential laboratory for those yearning to "do something" but unsure how to proceed.

Figure 1.1. SNCC activist Betty Poole of Tougaloo College was one of many movement veterans who spoke on northern campuses to recruit students into the freedom struggle. Here Poole describes for a student audience in 1963 how she and others in SNCC persisted in working to integrate Jackson, Mississippi, churches even after being jailed. © 1976 Matt Herron / Take Stock / The Image Works.

Students who later became major leaders of the New Left, including Peter Countryman from Yale, Tom Hayden from the University of Michigan, Paul Potter from Oberlin, and Betty Garman from Berkeley, had paid rapt attention to the activities of southern black youth ever since the sit-ins and Freedom Rides. Through institutions that brought together young people from both the North and the South—such as the National Student Association, the Methodist Student Movement, and the Congress of Racial Equality (CORE)—northern students met SNCC organizers. Without exception, the students not only learned but also were inspired, motivated, drawn in. Most were just plain awed by what the SNCC people had lived through.

And the word spread. Students who had learned from SNCC passed on their newly gained insights and often their newly informed passions. Such folk singers as Bob Dylan and Joan Baez appeared in Greenwood, Mississippi, at the height of the civil rights struggle in 1963. All of them—northerners such as Countryman, Hayden, and Dylan but also many more who had come in contact with SNCC—functioned in a way analogous to town criers: they passed on the ideas and experiences of the southern movement into the North and West.

Those who became highly visible (what we today might even call "overexposed") as student leaders by the end of the sixties jumped in and learned how to change things not because the Marines landed in Da Nang in 1965 but because they were both inspired and taught by what black teenagers were doing in the South in the earliest part of the decade. Tom Hayden and Al Haber of Students for a Democratic Society, Mario Savio of the Free Speech Movement, Bobby Seale and Huey Newton of the Black Panthers—all were educated, inspired, and/or fundamentally shaped in the crucible of the southern student movement. Meeting SNCC people, Hayden recalled, "was a key turning point, the moment my political identity began to take shape." He later wrote to his friend Mary King: "I hope for Mississippi and worry about Mississippi more than any project in the country, and could not do what I do [in Newark] without believing that it is directly important to the struggle down there."[11] Savio, his biographer Robert Cohen noted, never stood on the same experiential platform again after Freedom Summer: "Savio never would have stood up on the police car in Berkeley if he hadn't lived through the white terror in McComb earlier that summer. When you've faced down the Klan in Mississippi, you're not going to be fearful of a dean." Returning to Berkeley, he simply could not accept that the Berkeley administration knew more than he did about politics, local or national. And frankly, campus officials may not have realized that yet, but it was true; they didn't know as much as Savio. Black organizers in their teens and twenties in McComb had taught Savio a new way to practice politics, giving him a firm intellectual and practical grounding in small-d democratic organizing that first shocked and then overthrew administrators who thought they could curtail the free speech of student civil rights activists.

What Is Politics?

A University of Michigan freshman, Bob Ross, explained northern students' typical response to the civil rights movement. "I once thought politics was what you were for and against," he recalled of the heated campus debates on foreign and domestic policy. But then came the sit-ins. "Here were people *doing* something." To support these students, northern college campus groups sprang up, in particular Friends of SNCC and the Northern Student Movement. It is important to pause here and note: this was no simple division between "thinking" and "acting." Ella Baker, the longtime civil rights activist and SNCC advisor, modeled Gramscian "organic intellectual" thinking.[12] She forced people to think through consequences of their actions by asking questions and pushing the analysis. Largely thanks to Baker, there was within SNCC a heady intellectual culture rooted in analysis, action, and reflection grounded in mutual respect and curiosity rather than hard-edged grand philosophy and factional splits based on theoretical disagreements.

Elizabeth Hirshfeld, a Freedom Rider from Ithaca, was one of the first northerners to bring back direct word of the model of change she had experienced. She was also one of the first to translate that experience into extended activism in the North. To get out of Parchman Prison after six weeks, "we either had to accept the sentence, which was a six month sentence, or we could get out and challenge it. And CORE made us promise to raise our bond money if we wanted to get out. I agreed to do that. And actually that's how I learned fundraising." CORE and SNCC gave her the names of their contacts in Detroit, which turned out to be a group called Friends of the South, heavily laced with peace activists. This group organized her first speaking engagements.[13]

After a few attempts, Hirshfeld realized that her speeches were not as effective as they could be. She returned briefly to Ithaca and consulted someone from the speech department at Cornell, who "helped me put together my basic ten minute presentation. It was pretty effective, because it was full of detail that was just real interesting." She talked about what it was like to be in jail and testified to the wire brush beating SNCC legend Ruby Doris Smith had endured. She discussed "what the implications of it were for me and for my life" and why she had done it. She endeavored to explain why the work that SNCC did was so important and thus "why we needed for it to continue."[14] In short, she was clear, precise, specific. She addressed what later became known as both "personal and political."

So armed, she returned to Detroit and used this speech to organize a Friends of SNCC support group. The Friends of SNCC groups served as critical vehicles. They raised money for SNCC, built and maintained links between organizers in and outside the South, and provided a purpose around which northern students predisposed to civil rights could organize. SNCC always needed money, so Hirshfeld and others would periodically organize cocktail fundraisers, and "SNCC would send Sammy Davis Jr., and Harry Belafonte, and raise money for SNCC." Hirshfeld could fundraise, continue to develop her relationships with SNCC people in the South, and expand the network she had built up in Detroit.[15]

Hirshfeld also began to engage in direct action with high school students who were involved in her fundraising group. They picketed a Detroit bank that had all-white tellers and, after being arrested and released in one day, observed the Urban League negotiating with the bank. Black tellers were hired soon after. Hirshfeld's group went on to work on the issue of police brutality. She and Frank Joyce, a friend from Royal Oak, a suburb of Detroit, subsequently set up a city-wide tutorial program, the Detroit Education Project.[16] Hirshfeld's path to the South and back to the Midwest was far from unique. Thousands of students from New York to California took similar treks in the early 1960s.

Exposure to southern civil rights activism fundamentally shaped northern students. Many became less elitist and less theoretical. They were also catapulted out of their mostly uninformed assumptions about race. Above all, however, they learned basic lessons about organizing—about listening, recruiting, canvassing, collective decision-making, and putting ideas into action. By the end of 1964, Elizabeth Hirshfeld and some SNCC veterans who had gone north for school, as Tim Jenkins did, built a network of organizers outside of the South that spanned the country, clustered around Friends of SNCC groups, the Northern Student Movement, and Students for a Democratic Society. The northern travelers who came to the South now identified with legendary SNCC organizers Bob Moses and Charles Sherrod with an experiential precision they could not possibly have possessed prior to spending time on projects throughout the deep South. Those who came to visit did not learn as much as those who stayed on to help register voters for extended periods of time, but they learned enough to organize northern support. These links, made on the basis of personal connections and commitments, allowed the tremendous energy that SNCC was generating to flow northward and westward. The formation of this initial network was a leadership task that remained largely unrecognized at the time.[17] University of Texas student Sandra Cason (later Casey Hayden)—and Peter Countryman, Maria Varela, and others—simply shared information about how to organize and about events in the South that were not being covered in the media.[18] The democratic forms SNCC initiated in this period depended on the organization of many such groups—hundreds, and then thousands—that were independent of established power bases. It was grassroots activism that began to include thousands of people, increasing numbers of whom began to understand organizing as both a central and a fulltime job. Without them, there would have been no seemingly ubiquitous counterculture by the mid-1960s. And as we can now see, it was hardly "spontaneous."

Although the importance of organizing this informal network would not be clear for many years, it had two momentous consequences. First, it expanded the financial base and press contacts that enabled SNCC to continue its voter registration projects. Second, the resulting associations, initially created to support SNCC, would provide the personal connections whereby both the energy and skill base of those who were working within SNCC projects in the South could then push to the North and West.

Getting the Story Straight

So why don't we know this story already? Why, in 2012, do we need a new volume of histories sharing with us the role that southern students and southern campuses played in creating and expanding the New Left? At least two reasons stand out. The first describes a general cultural phenomenon: the response when deeply ingrained cultural beliefs are fundamentally threatened, when assumptions that previously governed one's life are shown to be false, yet one is determined to preserve the illusion. We may call this response "the battle cry of culturally embattled power" or, for simplicity's sake, "defensive condescension." The second, though related to the first, is a distinct version of cultural narrowness. It is actively bred in universities and colleges around the country and can be adequately termed "academic specialization": the widespread phenomenon of missing the forest for the trees.

The first point is so easily documented that it is almost painful. A review of the news coverage of both civil rights activism and the New Left in the 1960s, for instance, immediately reveals a stunning degree of condescension. Reporters, both shaping and mirroring the larger culture, were routinely not equipped, intellectually or experientially, to see, much less understand, what was in front of them. Civil rights and New Left activism, it seems, breached too many deeply ingrained assumptions. That politics was being made by non-elite young people was difficult enough to comprehend. That many of the activists were women was more difficult still. That it all started, and was critically informed by, young black southern activists was simply inconceivable to most white professionals—in both the media and the academy. Even among well-educated reporters the habits of white supremacy,

sexism, and cultural condescension were hard to break. And it was not just southern white journalists, such as Tom Waring or James Kilpatrick. Donald Jansen of
the *New York Times* gave white Mississippi Delta Council president B. F. Smith the
last word when describing civil rights workers' attempts to organize sharecroppers: the organizing would do "far more harm than good," the planter explained,
"And would be better spent in Harlem and other such areas where economic, racial, and crime problems appear to be much more serious than those of the area of
Delta of Mississippi."

Describing Nancy Mann, a Students for a Democratic Society organizer in
Newark, after a bad defeat for the community, journalist Douglas Davis quoted
her and wrote as follows: " 'If Harris loses we're going to have a fight here. Some of
the community people are carrying guns.' Her eyes are flashing. It is prom night all
over again."[19] This condescending dismissal of Mann's youth and "frivolous" gender
typify journalists' response to earnest attempts by this generation to chart a different path. Almost all journalists did not get the "first version of history" right. Ben
Reade provides another example of how distorted this first narrative could be. Of
Tom Hayden's work in Newark, Reade noted that his task was "to organize the poor"
—yes—and "to convince them that in their very powerlessness there lies the
roots of real power. It is a vastly more difficult job than organizing Negroes in the
South."[20] Such analysis showed just how little Reade understood how difficult it
was to organize people to go vote when it could cost them their lives.

A second reason we do not credit SNCC with a foundational role in the New
Left lies closer to home. The academy's pressures to specialize and institutional
pressures inhibiting interdisciplinary conversation and research have resulted in
four groups of academics whose research and scholarly networks intersect too infrequently: those who study the history of education, those who study the South,
those who chronicle the history of student movements, and those who research
the 1960s. These historiographies coexist, largely unaware of their large areas of
overlap, to the detriment of our greater understanding of the role that southern
students played in the New Left.

So let us revisit the question one more time: how and why can we be so sure
that the New Left—a movement most closely associated with campuses in the
Northeast, the Midwest, and the West Coast—traces its origins to SNCC and the
civil rights movement that flourished on southern, mostly black, campuses in
the early 1960s? After all, following World War II, many within U.S. society (and,
indeed, other societies around the world) perceived a common set of problems,
problems that at the time were often given grand abstract names such as oppression, bureaucracy, and alienation. With the benefit of hindsight, we can perhaps
improve on this general description by pointing out that many young people did

not feel heard but rather felt betrayed and cheated by what they saw as callous policies pursued by governments and corporations alike. Democracy, it seemed, was largely a charade, for the governed had no meaningful voice.[21] Even in the self-proclaimed beacon of the democratic world, the United States, whole segments of society were effectively disenfranchised, the economically disempowered young were sent off to war, and the outgoing president had warned against a "military-industrial complex" taking over the levers of power. What mattered, and thus was sanctioned in the United States, in short, was outcome, not democratic process.[22] People, it seemed, mattered little.

Jim Crow laws prohibited blacks from such basic citizenship rights as using a bus station, strolling in a city park, and most important, voting. As SNCC staff member and Mississippian Fannie Lou Hamer noted, "I could never treat nobody like we been treated. . . . I'm concerned about people running the government, but let it be people that we elect instead of pigs. I am sick of these hand-picked folk."[23]

Where, furthermore, was the role of people in a society increasingly dominated by transnational corporations? Where was the public scrutiny, input, or accountability in a culture in which corporate power directly benefited from the idea that people lacking formal education or economic resources were not qualified for self-government?[24] In the postwar United States, people in all regions of the country experienced alienation and powerlessness. "People were suffering," as presidential advisor Harry McPherson noted.[25]

Writing about their reasons for involvement in the New Left, many echoed Mitchell Goodman's observation that the movement itself was an impulse toward wholeness, "away from the atomized non-community of men helpless in the machinery of the centralized state."[26] As New Left activists Paul Potter, Greg Calvert, and Carol Neiman intimated, the increased emphasis on consumer spending and advertising in the postwar period weighed down this increased sense of alienation. The "guilt and self-hatred" promoted by the advertising industry to sell their products created, in words typical for the time, eloquent in style but short on specificity, an "army of object and objectified relationships promising us integrity and purpose but giving us instead the daily dose of humiliation, pain and emptiness."[27] Revolutionary politics, they felt, grew organically out of this "life-denying civilization."

As Potter stated, American society was not organized around meeting the needs of its citizens but rather around meeting the needs of its economy. "We turn off the TV; we are empty," he observed. "We finish with work; we are empty. We shut off the car; we are empty. We finish the Mr. Ice Cream Special; we are empty. . . . Why?"[28] Calvert and Neiman did not object to capitalism merely because some possessed more wealth than others—but rather because "capitalism is a power over our lives which forces us to do wasteful and meaningless things," when what they really wanted was "to do something radically different and marvelously new."[29]

With or without SNCC, modern societies like the United States had run up against fundamental conflicts and tensions. Young people were responding to lies, deceptions, and the hijacking of life's purposes by powerful elites from Mexico to France, Kenya to Czechoslovakia, Japan to the United States. In each society the conflicts played out differently, yet the legacy these movements left behind is dependent upon our ability to find and develop an accurate history: of their activities, their debates, their organizing traditions, their accomplishments and failures.

No doubt, many young students in the United States wanted to do "something radically different and marvelously new." Initially, however, they did not know how to translate that hope or vision into something tangible. They did not know how to act. That is, they did not know how to act outside of inherited cultural habits learned in the many hierarchical environments they occupied—schools, churches, families, and workplaces.

In the America of the 1960s, movement did not begin to happen until young people began to learn the lessons shared by Ella Baker and Fannie Lou Hamer with the SNCC students in the earliest years of the decade, the profound, simple, democratic lessons about learning and listening, about decision-making, and about finding one's own voice. Baker and Hamer may not have been our "founding fathers," but they certainly served as "midwiving mothers" for a more expansive version of American democracy. People came to SNCC's initial conference, even though they'd never heard of Dr. King's organization, SCLC. "We didn't know what this SCLC was about, but everybody we knew trusted Ella Baker and so they gave the okay to go."[30] When trying to reach consensus, the young people often went off on tangents and lost the central issue at hand. Baker used a technique she had developed through long years of organizing: she asked questions. "I was not too sure that I had the answer," she said later.[31] This style shaped early SNCC: from it they learned to focus on the most important issues under discussion but also allowed individuals to develop their own authentic responses. Above all, SNCC learned from Hamer and other southern black community leaders about how to find a way to act.

The steadfast, pure chutzpah of Hamer was a lesson to them. She was willing to risk her home, her job, her life. Were they? As students within SNCC began to internalize and then experiment with these lessons, they also started to share them with the rest of the nation. The New Left listened, and so long as its organizers emulated early SNCC's democratic ethos, the student movement thrived. It was only after Students for a Democratic Society turned away from that ethos in the late 1960s that the organization faltered, replacing egalitarian organizing with attempts to find any means necessary to bring an end to the Vietnam War and oppression in general. If there is to be a return to the organizing tradition that SNCC plugged into and developed in the early 1960s to topple Jim Crow, we will have to do a better job of listening to SNCC's history.

NOTES

1. See especially the important work of Patricia Hill Collins, Sara Evans, Bret Eynon, Jo Freeman, Doug McAdam, Robert Cohen, Jelani Favors, and Patrick Jones. See also Hasan Jeffries's *Bloody Lowndes: Civil Rights and Black Power in Alabama's Black Belt* (New York: NYU Press, 2009), which includes a fascinating account of the ways that Lowndes County, Alabama, descendants who migrated to Detroit kept the "movement pipeline" open to support and learn from their cousins who stayed in the South. For a wide range of ideological reasons, other writers have tried to downplay the impact of civil rights activists on northern democracy movements. For egregious examples, see James Miller, *"Democracy Is in the Streets": From Port Huron to the Siege of Chicago* (Cambridge, MA: Harvard Univ. Press, 1987); and Susan Brownmiller, *Against Our Will: Men, Women, and Rape* (New York: Ballantine, 1975).

2. The critical factor in determining who should come down, SNCC's Summer Project committee recommended, was a volunteer who "must be capable of understanding that the success of the Mississippi movement depends on the development of those who live and will remain in the state." Every summer volunteer who was interviewed had to answer the question, "Would you be willing to serve under a project director who was black?" Atlanta staff members worked on recruitment as well. James Forman later noted that "interviewers were instructed to pay very careful attention to that question, because that would determine perhaps more than anything else whether you should accept this person to work in the Summer Project." Forman also asked Ruby Doris Robinson "to go out and try to make every effort to recruit black people for the Summer Project. We made all sorts of efforts to do this so that people would not get the impression that there was an invasion of volunteers coming in who may not have been the same skin color as the majority of the people in Mississippi." Mississippi Summer Project Committee to Mississippi Summer Project Interviewers, 14 Apr. 1964, box 2, Robert Starobin Papers, State Historical Society.

3. Though the links between North and South seem natural, in the first few years of SNCC's existence, there were less than one hundred individuals who were deeply connected to people in both regions. Tim Jenkins, a black graduate of Howard and subsequent law student at Yale, was involved with early SNCC and the Northern Student Movement and served in the national office of the National Student Association. Maria Varela attended Emmanuel College in Boston, participated in early SNCC conferences, was present at the historic Port Huron conference of the Students for a Democratic Society (SDS), and by 1963 had moved into SNCC full time as an organizer and literacy educator. Peter Countryman, a white undergraduate at Yale, started the Northern Student Movement in the fall of 1961 as a vehicle to mobilize financial support and publicity for the activities of SNCC and CORE in the South. Other key bridgers included Bob Moses, Julian Bond, Stokely Carmichael (Kwame Ture), Ruby Doris Smith, Mendy Samstein, Dorothy Dawson Burlage, Martha Prescod, Julia Prettyman, and Jim Monsonis. Adults also linked students together through

their national networks, including Ella Baker, James Lawson, Connie Curry, Vincent and Rosemarie Harding, Anne Braden, Staughton Lynd, and Howard Zinn. For a more in-depth look at how these networks were created, maintained and expanded, see chapter four and appendix C of Wesley C. Hogan, *Many Minds, One Heart: SNCC's Dream for a New America* (Chapel Hill: Univ. of North Carolina Press, 2007).

4. Adelaide Matteson and Susan Kent to Chuck McDew and Charles Jones, 15 Dec. 1961, frame 747, reel 7, SNCC Papers; Rothstein, 19 Oct. 1964, box 19, Students for a Democratic Society Collection, State Historical Society of Wisconsin, Madison, Wisconsin; Dickie Magidoff, telephone interview with the author, 17 Nov. 1999.

5. Magidoff, telephone interview. Of course, given the assumptions prevailing within conventional political culture, it may have been inconceivable to Magidoff and Ross at that time that the reverse could be true: that they, not Zellner, were being "absolutist" in labeling Zellner's behavior as passive. Transparently, Zellner was in fact a veteran of front-line struggle against the southern caste system. There was nothing passive about it.

6. The Greater Boston and Michigan Friends of SNCC groups sent over 20 tons of food and clothing down to Greenwood in the winter and spring of 1963 and the winter of 1964, Charles McLaurin reported; see "Friends Send Food, Clothes," *The Student Voice*, 11 Feb. 1964, 2; "Food, Clothes Sent to Mississippi," *The Student Voice*, 18 Feb. 1964, 2; "Registration Up Since Food, Clothes Arrive," *The Student Voice*, 25 Feb. 1964; "News Roundup," *The Student Voice*, 2 Jun. 1964, 4; and Martha Prescod Norman, interview by Bret Eynon and Eileen Fishman, Apr. 1979, Bentley Library, Ann Arbor, Michigan. The other students involved in Ann Arbor's Friends of SNCC group were Helen Jacobson and Sue Wender; Jacobson worked for NSM, Wender for SNCC.

7. Tom Hayden, "Revolution in Mississippi," pamphlet first printed by SDS in Jan. 1962, 5; SDS Papers, State Historical Society of Wisconsin, Madison, Wisconsin, quoted in Miller, *"Democracy Is in the Streets,"* 60.

8. "The NSMCC: History, Structure, and Program," 5 Jan. 1962, frame 202, reel 1, Miriam Feingold Papers, State Historical Society of Wisconsin, Madison, Wisconsin.

9. Robert Pardun, interview with the author, 22 June 1998, Los Gatos, California.

10. For an in-depth look at precisely how SNCC transmitted its tactics, see Hogan, *Many Minds, One Heart,* chs. 4–5.

11. Tom Hayden, *Reunion: A Memoir* (New York: Random House, 1988), 126. Four years later, famous in his own right, he wrote to his friend Mary King: "I hope for Mississippi and worry about Mississippi more than any project in the country, and could not do what I do without believing that it is directly important to the struggle down there." Tom Hayden, Newark, New Jersey, to Mary King, 2 Oct. 1964, Mary King Papers, State Historical Society of Wisconsin, Madison, Wisconsin.

12. For more on Baker's intellectual influences, process, and impact on SNCC, see Barbara Ransby, *Ella Baker and the Black Freedom Movement* (Chapel Hill: Univ. of North Carolina Press, 2005); and Charles Payne, *I've Got the Light of Freedom* (Berkeley: Univ. of California Press, 1995).

13. Elizabeth Hirshfeld, interview with the author, 27 June 1998, Oakland, California. Interview and transcript in the author's possession.

14. Ibid.

15. Ibid.

16. Ibid.

17. Casey Hayden to the author, 21 Nov. 1999, e-mail in author's possession.

18. For example, in April 1963, she wrote to Sharon Jeffrey and Peter Countryman that they could do SNCC fundraising as an entrée into northern community organizing: "If you are trying to reach second level leadership, which I assume is your best bet (as it has been ours) in creating a constituency for yourselves, you will probably be working through civic clubs, churches, etc. That will probably mean you'll need lots of hand outs, pictures, etc." Casey Hayden to Peter Countryman and Sharon Jeffrey, 16 Apr. 1963, frame 661, reel 8, SNCC Papers.

19. Donald Jansen, "Negro Walkouts in Delta Spurred," *New York Times,* 7 Jun. 1965, 26; Douglas M. Davis, "Tom Hayden—The White Stokely," [New York] *World Journal Tribune,* 1 Jan. 1967, 4. See Robert Penn Warren's interview with Jackson State College students in 1964, available at http://whospeaks.library.vanderbilt.edu/search.php?record=33.

20. Ben Reade, "Prophet of the Powerless," *Renewal* (1965): 16–22, box 23, SDS Papers. This is quite a different perspective from that recently presented in *The Race Beat,* the Pulitzer Prize–winning book by Gene Roberts and Hank Klibanoff. Their focus is on how white reporters from the North were permanently changed by contact with the movement, but their conclusion is that without the media, the civil rights movement would have been like a "bird without wings." Roberts and Klibanoff, *The Race Beat: The Press, the Civil Rights Struggle, and the Awakening of a Nation* (New York: Knopf, 2006), 407.

21. For the most cogent and concrete statement, see Casey Hayden, "Raising the Question of Who Decides," *New Republic* 154 (22 Jan. 1966), 9. See also Kirkpatrick Sale, *SDS* (New York: Random House, 1973), 17–19; Bill Ayers, interview in Ron Chepesiuk, *Sixties Radicals, Then and Now: Candid Conversations with Those Who Shaped the Era* (Jefferson, NC: McFarland, 1995), 98; Greg Calvert and Carol Neiman, *A Disrupted History* (New York: Random House, 1971), 15–16; and Myles Horton with Judith Kohl and Herbert Kohl, *The Long Haul: An Autobiography* (New York: Doubleday, 1990), 169–71.

22. Noam Chomsky, "Prospects for Democracy," excerpts from a speech given at Massachusetts Institute of Technology, compact disc AK002CD, AK Press, 1994.

23. Fannie Lou Hamer, interviewed by Anne and Howard Romaine, 1966, transcript, Anne Romaine Papers, State Historical Society of Wisconsin, Madison, Wisconsin.

24. Casey Hayden, "Raising the Question of Who Decides," *New Republic* 154 (22 Jan. 1966), 9. See also Horton with Kohl and Kohl, *Long Haul,* 215–23.

25. Harry McPherson, *A Political Education* (Boston: Little, Brown, 1975), 301.

26. Mitchell Goodman, "Introduction," in *The Movement toward a New America: The Beginnings of a Long Revolution,* ed. Mitchell Goodman (Philadelphia: Pilgrim Press, 1970), viii.

27. Paul Potter, *A Name for Ourselves: Feelings about Authentic Identity, Love, Intuitive Politics, Us* (Boston: Little, Brown, 1971), 58–59; Greg Calvert and Carol Neiman, *A Disrupted History* (New York: Random House, 1971), 58–66.

28. Potter, *Name for Ourselves,* 58.

29. Calvert and Neiman, *Disrupted History,* 101.

30. Charles McDew, quoted in Cheryl Greenberg, ed., *Circle of Trust: Remembering SNCC* (New Brunswick, NJ: Rutgers Univ. Press, 1998), 34.

31. Joanne Grant, *Ella Baker: Freedom Bound* (New York: Wiley and Sons, 1998), 136.

CHAPTER TWO

Student Free Speech on Both Sides of the Color Line in Mississippi and the Carolinas

JOY ANN WILLIAMSON-LOTT

Southern colleges and universities became contested terrain as students involved themselves in the black freedom struggle. Trustees, presidents, and government officials argued that students entered into a contract when they enrolled and that their enrollment signified their willingness to follow institutional rules; defying regulations by participating in activism meant that students had forfeited their right to attend. Alternately, students argued that their citizenship status preempted any contractual obligations or *in loco parentis* mandates and provided them with constitutional protections. Students refusing to terminate activism forced administrators into battles regarding the difference between constitutionally protected speech and behavior and the right of an institution of higher education to control its property and constituents.

This chapter examines the curtailment of the First Amendment freedoms of speech, the press, and assembly at public institutions in the South. Though they constitute only a subset of institutions of higher education, examining public institutions is instructive. They were bound by constitutional mandates and court decisions in a way that private institutions were not. They were also at the center of the debate over the role of state-supported entities in the southern sociopolitical order. As far as white public officials were concerned, state-supported entities, including institutions of higher education, were there to fortify white supremacy. Violating the public interest necessarily triggered government intervention. On the other hand, students and their allies argued that tax dollars simply funded the institutions but that the academic community rightly controlled the institutions with regard to campus policy. And the extremity of state interference was most dramatic at public institutions. Legislators, governors, and other public officials vowed to break the back of the civil rights movement and promised that the state's colleges and universities would not enter the fray. Examining the battle for First

Amendment freedoms at public institutions provides a useful lens to assess the tensions between liberty and security during one of the most volatile times in our nation's history.

The Broader Historical Context: Civil Rights and Higher Education

Anticommunist and antifederal sentiment, a combination building since the 1930s, fueled white southern antipathy toward First Amendment freedoms in higher education. Many white southerners, resentful of federal intervention since Reconstruction, considered President Franklin Roosevelt's 1930s New Deal initiatives targeting the unemployed and working poor to be communist-inspired. They argued that the programs challenged the concepts of individualism, private ownership, limited government, and states' rights that provided the foundation of southern political and economic life. Equally important, the initiatives undermined white supremacy since New Deal programs "implicitly threatened the culture of dependency that had secured an abundant, cheap labor supply."[1] Subsequent federal policies substantiated white southern fears of a link connecting communism, the federal government, and shifting racial relationships. By the late 1940s, federal intervention enabled a black student to enroll in an all-white law school, outlawed the white primary, and mandated the desegregation of the military. Though translating these legal and congressional developments into reality took some time, southern whites considered these and other federal initiatives an un-American affront to their way of life.

The escalating black freedom struggle added fuel to the fire as southern blacks precipitated the federal interventions that forced changes in the southern racial landscape. The National Association for the Advancement of Colored People (NAACP) litigated against segregation and racial discrimination and organized boycotts and demonstrations. The push for national unity during World War II bolstered the attack on the racial caste system. Black participation in the war inspired the "Double V" campaign to achieve a victory against fascism abroad and against racial discrimination at home. The use of federal protections to achieve those rights infuriated conservative southern whites, who opposed them at every turn. Most southern white leaders believed that blacks should remain subservient and that the emerging civil rights movement was a communist plot. They considered resistance to racially liberal federal policies not simply self-serving but also patriotic.[2]

By the 1950s, the increased federal presence in higher education, and more importantly what that presence signaled in terms of racial equality, became a major

source of concern. The NAACP and the U.S. Supreme Court forced white southern institutions to alter their admissions policies and admit blacks. National philanthropic organizations such as the Rockefeller Foundation, the Ford Foundation,
and the Carnegie Corporation offered funding for development projects but required that institutions receiving the gifts not discriminate based on race. Federal
funding, whether through defense contracts, student tuition dollars from the GI
Bill and the National Defense Education Act, or research grants received by individual faculty had the same strings attached. National professional organizations
and accrediting bodies moved toward racial inclusion and against discrimination.
The marriage of race liberalism and federalism stoked southern white resentment
of federal involvement in higher education.

Public institutions of higher education therefore became important battlegrounds. Many southern public officials attempted to isolate students at both
black and white institutions from the black freedom struggle and curtail their
First Amendment rights when the exercise of those rights threatened white supremacy. Black students were of particular concern because they peopled the civil
rights movement and sometimes used their campuses as movement centers to organize and mobilize against the racial hierarchy. Public officials argued that white
students, as the region's future leaders, needed an education that taught them
to respect and perpetuate a racial hierarchy. Hence curtailing First Amendment
freedoms on white campuses would protect impressionable students from the
anti-American ideologies of communists and integrationists. As black and white
campus constituents demanded the right to teach and learn without state interference, one governor declared, "When academic freedom supersedes loyalty to one's
country, loyalty to one's state, and to our trust in God, it becomes an instrumentality of treason that profanes the faith of our nation."[3] That students deigned to
challenge the state's authority by participating in the civil rights movement proved
that campus administrators were not up to the task of maintaining control of the
campus. Theirs was a moral and patriotic obligation, and state officials refused to
be cowed by appeals to lofty ideals.

This chapter takes a case study approach and focuses on several notable examples of the battle for First Amendment rights in North Carolina, South Carolina, and Mississippi. Whether students fought against college or state officials,
they sought to make real their constitutional rights to assembly, press, and speech.
Students in other southern states fought for their First Amendment rights as well;
faculty, too, found their freedoms abridged by college or state officials; and examples of faculty and administrative support for students' rights exist. But a focus
on particular battles allows for a depth of treatment of the thorny issues involved.
The three cases cited are representative of trends across the South. Each enjoyed a

different reputation with regard to race liberalism, varied in the breadth of rights allowed, and employed different tactics to curtail those rights that threatened white supremacy.[4]

North Carolina was the most liberal of the three states. "The mood is at odds with much of the rest of the South," V. O. Key wrote in 1949. "It enjoys a reputation for progressive outlook and action in many phases of life, especially industrial development, education, and race relations." William Chafe described it similarly in his classic case study of Greensboro during the civil rights era. According to Chafe, a progressive mystique encouraged racial tolerance and moderation. Blacks lived a segregated reality and were disenfranchised, but key North Carolina politicians pursued a cosmopolitanism that required the rhetoric of racial tolerance and an enlightened citizenry. Evidence of the state's investment in education was that it funded ten white comprehensive institutions of higher education and five black institutions—more than any other southern state. That the University of North Carolina at Chapel Hill desegregated its undergraduate student body in 1956 and boasted the best reputation of all southern public institutions was a source of pride and bolstered the state's image as progressive in the South.[5]

South Carolina and Mississippi in the early twentieth century, on the other hand, did not pretend to be moderate oases. No doubt influenced by the fact that they had the largest proportions of black residents of all southern states, they "put the white-supremacy case most bitterly, most uncompromisingly, most vindictively." In place of a progressive mystique, political leaders in South Carolina and Mississippi drew on white fears of black domination to fuel racial conservatism. Until 1940, both states supported only one black college each, and they were the last two states to desegregate their undergraduate student bodies. The states' white flagship institutions functioned largely as social and cultural institutions rather than academic centers. Trustees and state officials cared about institutional reputation, but they concerned themselves with the opinions of state residents and regional peers rather than a national audience. The protracted battle against enforcement of federal rulings to desegregate their student bodies only strengthened their resolve and heightened the regional profile of their white institutions.[6]

However, by the civil rights era South Carolina and Mississippi were employing different tactics in their battle against black advancement. According to Marcia Synnott and R. Scott Baker, South Carolinians began to appeal to moderation in the 1950s and 1960s. South Carolina was different from Mississippi, Synnott states, "in that its leadership never abdicated its legal responsibility to the people—and to extremist elements." White supremacy was alive and well in South Carolina, but there a desire to avoid the violence and federal intervention that occurred in other states was also evident. According to Baker, "As demagogues in other states defied the courts, educational and political authorities in South Carolina sought legally defensible solutions to the problems posed by black demands for equality and access." With an eye toward the violence and disorder that occurred at the University of Alabama, the University of Georgia, and the University of Mississippi, South Carolina's governor, key state officials, and business leaders counseled the peaceful desegregation of Clemson University and the University of South Carolina in 1963. They portrayed desegregation as inevitable, argued that desegregating the state's public white institutions was the only way to avoid federal intervention, and promised to find legal ways to curtail black enrollment.[7]

And then there was Mississippi. Even "southerners . . . place[d] Mississippi in a class by itself." Racist rhetoric and extremism ruled the state. Officials oppressed black residents by spending less on the education of black children than any other state and prided themselves on having the fewest black registered voters. White politicians won elections by accusing each other of racial moderation and curried favor with the Ku Klux Klan, Citizens for the Preservation of the White Race, the white Citizens' Council, and a white electorate fearful of black domination. Governor Ross Barnett (1960–64) promised that "no school in our state will be integrated while I am your Governor" and appointed himself the registrar at the University of Mississippi to prevent James Meredith, a black man, from enrolling in 1962. Though Barnett failed to keep Ole Miss exclusively white, his actions sanctioned the violence, defiance of federal mandates, and white supremacist terrorism that accelerated along with the civil rights movement in the early 1960s. As late as 1967, racists attempted to sway white voters with a picture of a gubernatorial candidate addressing a racially mixed crowd with blacks standing in the front row and a caption that read, "Are these front row sitters going to determine the destiny of Mississippi? For the first time in our history we are faced with a large NEGRO MINORITY BLOC VOTE—William Winter's election will insure negro domination of Mississippi elections for generations to come. WHITE MISSISSIPPI AWAKE." The use of racist rhetoric in the late 1960s—after the passage of the Civil Rights Act and Voting Rights Act—was proof of Mississippi's lingering reputation as the last vestige of white supremacy.[8]

No matter the particular racial reputation or political tactics employed by the public officials in each of the states—progressivism in North Carolina, compromise in South Carolina, or massive resistance in Mississippi—black southerners put them to the test with escalating demands for the desegregation of public facilities including schools, voting rights, and equal protection under the law. Students at both black private and public institutions left campus to participate in sit-ins, demonstrations, and protests; advertised civil rights projects in the student newspaper; and recruited civil rights figures to speak on campus. To a much lesser degree, students at white institutions found ways to support the movement. All students faced the possibility of harsh punishment for their actions, but those at black or white public colleges attended institutions funded by the state and created in the spirit of maintaining the racial hierarchy. Public college presidents, hired by white boards of trustees and beholden to white legislatures, promised their superiors they would keep their campuses and students out of the movement. As Benner C. Turner, president of South Carolina State College, a black institution, stated, "It has always been the position of the College Administration that a college is an educational institution and cannot expect long to survive if it is allowed to become a political, social or economic battleground."[9]

Freedom to Assemble: Student Government Associations in Mississippi

Students at the University of Mississippi organized a student government in 1917. The organization advocated for student concerns but existed in a campus culture that emphasized social life and encouraged conformity. As one visiting journalist put it in 1962, "The range of political and social opinions is from Y to Z." Also, the student government was not as formidable or influential as the Greek system that controlled campus life. Political or racial moderates—who passed for radicals in Mississippi—gravitated to the campus newspaper, *The Mississippian,* not the student government. Responses to the violence surrounding Meredith's enrollment dramatized the difference between the two groups. While *Mississippian* editors condemned student participation in the segregationist riot, chastised Governor Barnett for escalating racial tensions, and encouraged friendliness toward Meredith, the student government condemned the violence that occurred but also protested "the forced admission of an unqualified student." It also voted to reprimand one editor for her liberal bias.[10]

Though lagging behind white colleges in the creation of student government associations (SGAs), most black colleges allowed students to form such organizations by the 1930s. Black students, then, found themselves in the paradoxical situation in which they could run for office and vote in campus elections but not local, state, or national ones. The incongruity of encouraging political participation on campus but not in American society was not lost on black students. Nor was the fact that black colleges practiced a paternalistic control over their students that was unmatched at white institutions. SGAs attracted these politically minded students who sought power as well as changes to the campus regulations and climate. Though student governments most often focused on grievances against the dress code, strict supervision of male-female contact, and lack of student representation on campus committees rather than black enfranchisement, their arguments mirrored the burgeoning black freedom struggle's demands for participatory democracy.[11] All of Mississippi's black public institutions prohibited the formation of civil rights–oriented groups, but administrators could not curtail political interests.

Students at Mississippi Vocational College initiated a boycott to demand the right to create an SGA in February 1957, marking the first large-scale disruptive event initiated at a black college in Mississippi during the middle twentieth century. Opened in 1950 as a way to stall the desegregation of the state's white institutions, Mississippi Vocational served a largely commuter student body. Still, students wanted to participate in campus decision-making. Their actions did not directly attack white supremacy, but they were influenced by the increasingly aggressive nature in which blacks advanced their grievances in the post-*Brown* era. Forty percent of the Mississippi Vocational student body staged a 36-hour walkout to demand their own student government to act as a liaison with the campus administration. A joint faculty-student committee existed, but students wanted more autonomy. Adding insult to injury, Mississippi's other black colleges (Alcorn A&M College and Jackson State College) had student-run organizations.

President James H. White and the all-white board of trustees promised to discuss the issue with students, and the walkout ended peacefully. However, President White stalled action on the issue for four years. Not until the 1961–62 academic year were students allowed to create a student government, and even then it was heavily censored.[12] Mississippi Vocational students never stated an intention to use the group for off-campus political aims. The civil rights movement had yet to gain a foothold in Mississippi at the time of the boycott, and students were more interested in campus advocacy issues. But their demand for a democratic voice on campus rattled the trustees and campus administrators and demonstrated that students would take drastic steps to achieve their ends. If students were willing to stage a boycott over a student government, the trustees worried, perhaps they would do the same for civil rights issues.

Events at Alcorn University and A&M College substantiated fears about student cooptation of registered student organizations for political aims. In early March 1957, Clennon King Jr., a minister and instructor of history, angered the Alcorn student community with a series of articles commissioned by the *State Times,* a white Mississippi newspaper known for its racism. In his articles, King associated the NAACP with communism, called Adam Clayton Powell a "dupe to Northern race trickery," and provided a thoroughly cleansed interpretation of American slavery. That pictures of Alcorn students appeared with King's articles did not help his cause. When the third installment of King's series appeared, the SGA organized a boycott and demanded King's firing. The all-white board of trustees responded by expelling the entire student body, firing the president for allowing the campus to get out of control, and renewing King's contract. Those students who wanted to re-enroll were forced to meet with the new president, John D. Boyd, and sign a statement vowing never to participate in campus protests again. Most students signed the statement and re-enrolled, but many were furious with Boyd and dubbed him a "white man's tool." Those who did not sign the statement or were identified as leaders in the walkout, including the SGA president, were refused readmission.[13]

Faculty at Alcorn, like at other black public colleges across the South, were in a precarious position. Some, like Clennon King, held racially conservative views. Others, however, supported the civil rights movement and student involvement in it. They refused to mark absent those students participating in sit-ins during the week, lent students their cars to attend demonstrations, raised money for bail when students were arrested, counseled restraint when administrators devised punishment for student activists, and used modern social science to undermine white supremacy in their classrooms. Such progressive faculty and students sometimes had tacit approval from administrators. Alcorn's president supported the students' critique of King even though it cost him his job.[14] Black public colleges could not become full-fledged movement centers like some of their black private college counterparts, but they posed enough of a threat that white officials kept tight control over them and appointed presidents who did the same.

Every year for the next several years, Alcorn students registered their discontent with Boyd's iron-fisted control of campus life. In 1959, the last straw was his interference with the election of Miss Alcorn and SGA officers. Boyd appointed a committee to oversee the elections and warned students, "You should be satisfied, as a committee, that such persons, as are nominated for positions, possess the right attitude toward law and order on the campus, as well as proper attitude toward responsibility of the administration in dealing with campus problems."[15] Students responded with another boycott and a list of demands that included an autonomous student government. Boyd closed the campus and expelled the student leaders.

In March 1960, a month after the first student sit-ins in Greensboro, North Carolina, and the same month as an attempted wade-in in Biloxi, Alcorn students again boycotted classes and issued a list of grievances. Smaller demonstrations occurred over the years until a two-week boycott rocked the campus in 1964. By this time, Mississippi had a full-blown black freedom movement, with demonstrations, boycotts, sit-ins, and litigation, and the state was preparing its violent resistance to Freedom Summer, sponsored by the Student Nonviolent Coordinating Committee (SNCC). Bolstered by escalating demands for participatory democracy off campus, hundreds of Alcorn students gathered on the football field, demanded to see the president, and insisted on "a student government free of administrative domination." Boyd repeated his past behavior and had all students rounded up and escorted off campus by the highway patrol.[16] It is not clear that the student government played a role in organizing demonstrations after the 1957 crisis, particularly since the administration had a stranglehold on the organization and students indicted it in their lists of grievances. But politically minded students very clearly played a role. Despite his best efforts, Boyd could not kill their aspirations to participate in a democratic environment.

To the horror of the Jackson State College administration, the board of trustees, and Mississippi public officials, Jackson State students appropriated the SGA for civil rights activities in a way that neither Mississippi Vocational students nor Alcorn students had. Their first organized act of defiance occurred when Jackson State students mobilized in support of the Tougaloo College (black and private) students arrested at a library sit-in in March 1961. About eight hundred black youth, including some not affiliated with Jackson State, congregated on campus near the library on the evening of the Tougaloo sit-in. According to James Meredith, a Jackson State student at the time, President Jacob L. Reddix attempted and failed to disperse the crowd. Reddix became so frustrated he began "snatching students at random and shoving them toward a [campus] policeman or dean with orders to expel them." Meredith remembered, "This incident introduced another factor into the demonstration, because it reminded the students of their many long-standing grievances against the administration."[17] The demonstrators finally dispersed when word came that city police were on the way, but protests continued the following day with a twofold focus: support for the Tougaloo students and grievances against the administration.

Governor Ross Barnett threatened to close the campus, and President Reddix threatened expulsion if students persisted. Students disregarded the threats, boycotted classes, and planned a march to the city jail. The SGA spearheaded the carefully orchestrated demonstration in which 50 students volunteered to march. According to Walter Williams, president of the Jackson State student body and member of the citywide chapter of the NAACP (the organization was banned from campus), "This was SGA sponsored. . . . We had passing NAACP support, but it was a student thing." Organizers asked all other students to attend a rally on campus to draw attention away from the marchers. While students at the rally sang songs and prayed, the marchers moved in a single-file line on each side of the street to avoid arrest for blocking traffic. Police swiftly and violently reacted to the demonstration with blockades, tear gas, billy clubs and—for the first time in Mississippi civil rights history—attack dogs. Reddix and the board of trustees

Figure 2.1. Police escort Tougaloo College students from the Jackson, Mississippi, public library following their attempt to integrate the facility in March 1961. Hundreds of Jackson State College students protested in support of the "Tougaloo Nine," eliciting threats from college administrators to shut down the campus. Courtesy of the Mississippi Department of Archives and History.

clamped down on students, enforced stiff rules and penalties regarding student conduct, and dissolved the SGA after accusing it of "embarrassing" the school. Reddix also expelled Walter Williams and created a puppet or quisling government in the student government's stead.[18]

It was fitting that Mississippi Valley, Alcorn, and Jackson State students demanded an autonomous student government, enlisting it as a change agent, and that their efforts would be thwarted. A student government, some black college officials and many whites worried, would represent a shift in the hierarchical structure of the university and give students a measure of authority and input. It was not that white officials and black public college administrators believed that citizenship training was irrelevant. In fact, Mississippi Valley, Alcorn, and Jackson State included the notion of education for proper citizenship in their mission statements. Such learning, however, was supposed to be confined to discussions in the history, government, or economics classroom. Students challenged this assumption when they translated republican theory into practice by demanding the right to form an advocacy organization and using it to challenge the administration and white supremacy.

SGAs at Mississippi's black colleges finally gained autonomy in the late 1960s. Due in part to constant student pressure, newly hired campus administrators and trustees recognized that black students should enjoy the same rights as white students. Also, the need to control the intimate details of student life lessened along with the waning of white supremacy. Rather than continuing to focus on off-campus issues, the SGAs focused on internal college reforms such as dorm regulations, visiting hours, and library regulations. In this way, the SGAs at black colleges began to function like those at white institutions. Students concerned with off-campus issues, including racial equality, joined the NAACP, SNCC, or other institution-specific groups previously banned from black campuses.

Freedom of the Press: The Student Newspaper in South Carolina

The ease with which students published inflammatory material in their campus newspapers varied in part on whether they attended a black or white institution. In general, students at black public colleges met the heaviest resistance. These campuses enrolled activist students who wanted to use the campus newspaper to advertise upcoming demonstrations or boycotts, but all content needed the approval of a faculty advisor who clearly understood that he or she was expected to monitor or censor material that linked the institution to the civil rights movement. Black college presidents refused to allow students to jeopardize the goodwill of state agents.

Faculty advisors to campus newspapers were in a precarious situation. Some advisors supported the civil rights movement and the concept of freedom of speech, although temperately. They allowed students to publish questionable material but attempted to mitigate its impact by altering harsh student language. Such tactics rarely worked at black public institutions. Florence Miller, an English professor at South Carolina State College—the only black public college in the state—was fired for such an infraction in 1956. Students at the college had joined an NAACP-sponsored selective buying campaign protesting segregation and discrimination in Orangeburg in 1955. By 1956, students expanded their efforts to include a boycott of the dining hall and of classes. Students used the campus newspaper, *The Collegian,* to discuss their actions. White trustees took sweeping action to regain control of the campus by expelling students, including the SGA president, and firing Miller. With regard to the student paper, the president refused to be drawn into such controversy in the future and explained to the student body, "While it is not forbidden that comments on controversial matters be printed in the college paper, final authority as to what shall be printed must rest in the President's office and not in the faculty adviser of the college paper."[19]

The status of the student press was very different—and student journalists freer—at the state's white flagship institution, the University of South Carolina. Students there used *The Gamecock* to register both liberal and conservative views on a host of topics, including the civil rights movement. They enjoyed their First Amendment rights in a way that did not exist at the state's black public college for at least two reasons. One, *individual* students at the University of South Carolina registered liberal opinions while students at South Carolina State College (and black private colleges in the state) transformed their campuses into movement centers where activists planned and initiated attacks on white supremacy. In other words, white students enjoyed more latitude in expressing themselves because the consequences of their liberal attitudes were not as urgent or widespread as those of the black students who peopled the movement. Two, state agents cared about the University of South Carolina's reputation. The white electorate, including powerful alumni, would not tolerate damage to the integrity of their alma mater and could punish officials for interfering in campus business at the election booth. Black South Carolinians could not exercise their electoral power since South Carolina prevented their participation in the democratic enterprise.

The differences between the black and white colleges in South Carolina was made clear as the civil rights movement gained momentum in the state. In 1955, the year before trustees expelled students and fired faculty at South Carolina State College for exercising their First Amendment rights in the campus newspaper, several University of South Carolina students wrote letters to the editor of *The Gamecock* after Chester Travelstead, the dean of the College of Education, was fired for publicly supporting desegregation. Their opinions on the wisdom of trustee action against Travelstead varied. Several students invoked faculty academic freedom to argue on Travelstead's behalf. One wrote, "It was not only [Travelstead's] right, but his responsibility as a leading educator to express his views in regard to such problems as long as he does not express these views as official University policy." Another lamented, "Not only was this rash and short-sighted act of the board of trustees a blow to academic freedom and freedom of discussion, it was a damaging blast at the very basis of the foundation of this or any other university—intellectual integrity." Others reminded readers that "we are in South Carolina" and said Travelstead should have "use[d] his damn head" and known better than to violate unwritten university policy.[20]

The appearance of both liberal and conservative opinions in the campus paper was a victory for freedom of speech, but it was not an unqualified victory. Certainly, state officials cared about the integrity of the institution and left the content of student publications to the discretion of college administrators. *The Gamecock* had enjoyed a long and proud history as an autonomous student newspaper. And, more importantly, the president and faculty supported First Amendment rights for students and academic freedom for faculty. In fact, the trustees fired Travelstead over the president's objections. Officials tolerated a few race-liberal students but refused to allow a faculty member to corrupt the minds of hundreds more. With the state embroiled in a desegregation campaign in the wake of the *Brown* decision, officials sacrificed dissident constituents when they considered them a threat to white supremacy. Faculty support for desegregation posed a danger; individual student opinions on the matter were only a nuisance.

Consequences for students changed, however, when they directly confronted the South Carolina power structure. The year following the Travelstead situation, R. L. Morton, a student and page in the South Carolina legislature, wrote an editorial for *The Gamecock* criticizing legislators for their obsession with segregation. He described them as closed-minded men "intent on circumventing movements which would abolish segregation of races in our state"; Morton declared their actions made him "ashamed to be called a 'Southerner.'" The university administration did not take action against him, but the legislature fired Morton from his position. Soon thereafter, *The Gamecock* published a petition signed by 85 students congratulating legislators on their decision.[21]

White trustees and public officials shared a common goal of halting the civil rights movement in the state and gladly sacrificed First Amendment freedoms when they conflicted with their interests; college administrators were in a different situation. The president of the University of South Carolina, though no raging liberal, believed in institutional autonomy from state interference. He sought to bring his university into the national educational mainstream by providing students and faculty with the protections widely supported in higher educational institutions across the nation. Because of the institution's status and prestige in the state, the president was able to protect students who voiced controversial sentiments in the college paper (though he could not protect a faculty member).

The president of South Carolina State College was in a different predicament. President Turner headed a black institution that lacked the respect or goodwill of state officials hostile to black advancement. Appointed in 1950, trustees selected him because he had been an able administrator at the college who worked well with the trustees and the state's elected leadership. More importantly, they chose him because he maintained conservative views on desegregation. Therefore, it is hard to imagine how the president could have acted differently. He was beholden to the legislature for appropriations and dared not offend them if he wished to keep the institution open. He was beholden to trustees for his job and dared not offend them if he wished to remain employed. He, like many of his counterparts in other southern states, most likely viewed his role as a pragmatic one that served the long-term survival of his institution. "It has always been the position of the College Administration that a college is an educational institution and cannot expect long to survive if it is allowed to become a political, social or economic battleground," he explained in his 1957 Annual Report. Allowing students to inflame white resentment, whether by publishing controversial material in the campus newspaper or participating in demonstrations, damaged the institution he swore to protect.[22]

Freedom of Speech: The Speaker Ban in North Carolina

As the civil rights movement made important gains, many southern officials used a combination of antiblack and anticommunist rhetoric to justify sweeping violations of First Amendment rights in the form of speaker bans. Northern legislatures and trustees enacted similar bans in the 1950s in response to lists of suspected communists compiled by HUAC. What differentiated southern officials from their northern counterparts was their use of race. Their anticommunism did not simply disguise racist motives; it was, in fact, sincere and strong. However, race was never far from their consciousness, and anticommunism and prosegregation frequently became proxies for each other. In the early 1960s as civil rights activists became more insistent and the movement grew, southern governors, legislators, and trustees merged their anticommunism with anti–civil rights activities. They considered it a moral and patriotic crusade and used all their resources toward that end.

As the civil rights movement escalated, the North Carolina legislature moved to create a blanket provision banning communists from the state's institutions of higher education. William Billingsley documents how the battle over the speaker ban unfolded at the University of North Carolina at Chapel Hill. Accusations of communist infiltration had dogged the university since the 1940s when the American Legion demanded that the university expel members of the Communist Party "or any other un-American group" from the campus. University administrators mollified the Legion by arguing that the university, like other northern and southern institutions during the Cold War, already maintained an anticommunist position. In 1963, however, conservative North Carolina legislators took matters into their own hands and enacted a broader speaker ban barring all public colleges from permitting on-campus speeches by Communist Party members, those who advocated "the overthrow of the Constitution of the United States or the State of North Carolina," and those who pleaded the Fifth Amendment when asked about their subversive activities or associations. The governor, a liberal moderate who lacked veto power, did not play a role in the speaker ban controversy and never issued a public statement about it.[23]

The speaker ban represented real fears of communist infiltration and threats to white supremacy. First, though McCarthyism ended in the mid-1950s, Americans still had reason to be on the alert for communist conspiracies. In the late 1950s and early 1960s, international developments including Russia's launch of Sputnik, the construction of the Berlin Wall, and the Cuban Missile Crisis dramatized threats to American power abroad and the geographical proximity of communists to American soil. Domestic events also heightened anxieties. The Supreme Court— to many a foreign entity that had alienated white southerners for years—issued decisions in 1962 and 1963 that rendered mandatory prayer and Bible reading in public schools unconstitutional. These rulings, many southerners believed, proved "the threat posed to a Christian nation by a godless doctrine" since they associated communism with atheism.[24]

By 25 June 1963, the date legislators enacted the speaker ban, civil rights activists across the South engaged in massive civil disobedience in the form of boycotts, demonstrations, rallies, and other direct action tactics. Activists in SNCC initiated voter registration drives and sit-ins that successfully forced establishments to desegregate. The Southern Christian Leadership Conference organized demonstrations and trained teachers for citizenship schools in which blacks learned to pass voter registration literacy tests. Freedom Riders traveled on buses to test compliance with federal antisegregation transportation laws. NAACP litigation desegregated institutions of higher education in all southern states. And several civil rights organizations finalized plans for the March on Washington for Jobs and Freedom to be held in August. In North Carolina, black activists and their white allies enacted similar initiatives, and immediately preceding the adoption of the speaker ban they confronted legislators at the hotel that served as their temporary residence, at the legislative building, and in the streets of Raleigh.[25] Federal protection for activists, in the form of Supreme Court decisions, presidential executive orders, and legislative mandates, proved to conservative white southerners that the federal government and civil rights activists were colluding with communists.

Even before legislators enacted the speaker ban, college trustees counseled presidents to prevent civil rights advocates—and others deemed subversive—from speaking on campus. In 1958, Martin Luther King Jr. and his staff planned a trip through North Carolina. Coming on the heels of King's high-profile involvement in the Montgomery bus boycott and his vocal support for the Little Rock Nine in Arkansas, many North Carolinians worried that King's appearance would spark violence. The belief that communists had infiltrated civil rights organizations and that King was himself a communist added to the concern. When attempting to find a location in the city of Greensboro, home to three white and two black institutions of higher education, King requested and was refused permission to use the auditorium at the black and public North Carolina A&T College. Instead, Willa Player, president of the black, private, and female Bennett College, invited King to speak there. Hundreds attended, including students from North Carolina A&T.[26] Two years later, four students from North Carolina A&T inaugurated the sit-in movement that swept the South.

The North Carolina speaker ban applied to all the state's campuses, but the primary target was the University of North Carolina at Chapel Hill. As the state's flagship white public institution, critics of the university argued that it belonged to the (white) citizenry and therefore should support the existing sociopolitical order. "At a time when the most fundamental of traditional social arrangements and values were coming under frontal assault," Billingsley explains, "this was a matter of paramount significance. . . . UNC was a too-liberal source of political authority that did not represent the traditional values of the region and state." The involvement of college youth, including those at the University of North Carolina, in disruption of the southern sociopolitical order made tight control of the campus imperative.[27]

Constituents inside and outside the university mobilized against the ban. President William Friday and Chancellor William Aycock, under duress from the legislature, enforced it. Like many of their counterparts, Friday and Aycock worried about legislative retribution in the form of lost appropriations and ill will. However, they did attempt to protect university integrity by placating angry legislators with anticommunist statements meant to prevent further legislative interference while quietly working to amend or repeal the ban. Faculty supported Friday's efforts, but many did not do so openly for fear of losing their jobs. The American Association of University Professors promised to advocate on behalf of the university and use the power of censure to persuade legislators to rescind the ban.[28]

Some of the ban's most outspoken critics, of course, were students. They sympathized with the delicate situation in which President Friday and Chancellor Aycock found themselves, but they argued that the campus administration owed its allegiance to the intellectual integrity of the institution and should work to ensure student rights. Soon after the bill's passage, the student body president wrote his counterparts at other North Carolina colleges and universities to enlist their help and coordinate their efforts in opposing the ban. In particular, he bristled at the "apparent lack of faith in the students of North Carolina and the proven quality of our faculties and administrators." Many students agreed that communism posed a threat, but they argued that students needed to "get first-hand information" on it in order to "carry out an effective war in defeating communism." They might be young, students argued, but they should be trusted and were fully capable of thinking for themselves.[29]

Students organized to support freedom of speech over the next few years as the legislature, trustees, and campus administration battled over control of campus policies. In 1966, the SGA unanimously adopted a resolution in support of proposed speaking engagements by Herbert Aptheker, a Communist Party member, and Frank Wilkinson, founder of the National Committee to Abolish HUAC. The newly formed Students for a Democratic Society (SDS) chapter sponsored rallies to draw attention to the issue. Individual members of both groups, with the assistance of sympathetic faculty, initiated a lawsuit against the university when the chancellor, under pressure from the trustees, denied approval of the Aptheker and Wilkinson speaking engagements. Finally, in 1968, a federal district court ruled in favor of the students. The court explained that it appreciated the legislature's concern regarding communism on campus, but it argued that the criteria by which speakers would be judged was far too vague. Still, the court did not throw open the doors of college campuses. The court explained, "University students should not be insulated from the ideas of extremists, but there is danger that the voices of reason, throughout the broad spectrum they cover, will remain unheard if the clamor of extremists is disproportionately amplified on university platforms. A more balanced program, unenslaved by sensationalism, but reaching it, too, would not be calculated to evoke legislative response." In short, the court warned students that there were boundaries around their right to hear controversial speech.[30]

Conclusion

The battle over the breadth of First Amendment protections looked in some respects remarkably similar at black and white public institutions. Control of funding and legislation enabled state officials to meddle in campus business and purge undesirable constituents when they saw fit. However, white institutions often mustered resources that could be used to their advantage and enlisted to resist government interference. Campus constituents exploited the fact that trustees and government officials cared about the reputation of white institutions. Mississippi officials did not interfere with the SGA at the University of Mississippi since it reflected conservative racial sentiment and South Carolina officials did not interfere with the student press at the University of South Carolina since the institution enjoyed a high profile in the region and the student newspaper had a large following off campus. Students at the University of North Carolina at Chapel Hill were able to garner enough national attention and support to force legislators to rescind the speaker ban.[31] On the other hand, trustees and government officials cared little about the vibrancy of black public institutions and even less about their reputations. The firing of the president and expulsion of the student body at Alcorn received little attention outside the black press. Many blacks, including activists and Alcorn alumni, were infuriated with the trustees, but they lacked the political power to intimidate the trustees into altering their decision. Their moral arguments about the evils of white supremacy and their constitutional arguments about First Amendment freedoms fell on deaf ears.

There also were differences among the three states. The breadth of students' rights and the backlash against student activists mirrored each state's political and racial reputation. Both North Carolina and Mississippi adopted speaker bans. In North Carolina, the state's progressive mystique led public officials to describe the ban as an anticommunist measure, not an anti-integrationist bill. The suspected association between civil rights leaders and the Communist Party USA meant that black activists could be targeted, and the black student protests immediately preceding the ban certainly influenced its passage. But the first two men prevented from speaking were, indeed, a communist and a critic of HUAC's red hunts.

In Mississippi, officials did not conceal the anti–civil rights movement aim of the ban. Updated in 1964, in the wake of Freedom Summer, which brought hundreds of white volunteers to the state to work in voter registration and Freedom Schools, the Mississippi ban specifically referenced an "invasion" of Mississippi by hostile "outside agitators" for the purpose of overthrowing local government and race rioting. Undeterred by the fact that North Carolina's speaker ban was headed to court in 1966, Mississippi officials, in the same year, revised their ban to strip campus committees and presidents of the right even to invite speakers to campus. They also prohibited speakers charged with a crime (which barred hundreds of civil rights activists or suspected communists who had been arrested or found in contempt of Congress), any person who advocated the overthrow of the United States (which included any activist not previously arrested), political or sectarian meetings sponsored by any outside organization on campus (which included organizations such as the NAACP, SNCC, SDS, and the Communist Party USA), and any speech on a political topic (which barred everyone else). Further dramatizing the difference between the two states was that the University of North Carolina thrived on its ability to attract students from across the nation while Mississippi officials sought to limit the number of out-of-state students to prevent the "possible creation of on-campus disturbances and to avoid trends toward ultraliberalism in our state by outside infiltration."[32]

Black colleges and their students' experiences varied across the three states as well. North Carolina officials queried the president of North Carolina A&T about the student sit-ins and registered disapproval but did not require the expulsion of the students. Student activists met a different fate in South Carolina and Mississippi. Whether expelled, required to sign statements vowing never to protest again, or denied organizational autonomy, white officials and black administrators heavily sanctioned black student leaders. Similarly, black students in all three states targeted off-campus concerns, but those in South Carolina and Mississippi also agitated for changes on their campuses. Still, South Carolina and Mississippi did differ, and the punishments meted out by white officials against student sit-in participants illustrate the difference between them. South Carolina officials did not abdicate their authority to extremists. Instead, they used legal methods to protect white supremacy and to intimidate activists. Local police did not allow violence against the sit-in participants, arrested them en masse, and singled out particularly vocal activists for hard labor at a prison work farm. In Mississippi, white police watched and even encouraged the savage beating of student and faculty participants in a 1963 sit-in at a Woolworth's lunch counter in Jackson. Only when the white mob began destroying store property did police step in, and then they arrested the sit-in participants for disturbing the peace.[33]

Even though black students at public institutions faced repression from a wide variety of sources, they persisted in their activism. Even in Mississippi, after trustees expelled the entire Alcorn student body and intimidated those who had wanted to re-enroll into signing affidavits in 1957, students, refusing to be cowed, initiated disruptive boycotts over the next several years. Youth, moral and political indignation, and a desire to be part of a larger movement for racial equality certainly fueled their dedication to activism despite certain sanction. So, too, did the climate of antiracism on black college campuses fortify student activists. Administrators at public black institutions sought to appease white officials invested in white supremacy, but they also worked to build strong institutions that provided a high-quality education. Faculty may not have openly supported the movement, but many did teach the radical concept of racial equality, whether in biology, philosophy, or civics courses. And students attended these institutions in the spirit of personal, familial, and racial uplift, not to remain second-class citizens. That student efforts turned to an attack on white supremacy may not have sat well with administrators or white officials, but the black college environment helped spur and sustain them. Along with their counterparts at private black institutions, those at public black institutions became an important vanguard in the black freedom struggle.

Evaluations of the success of student activism almost exclusively point to the desegregation of public facilities prompted by the sit-ins. Across the South, black students and their allies forced lunch counters, pools, beaches, waiting rooms, and other public spaces to admit blacks on an equal basis. A less celebrated consequence of student activism was the expansion of students' freedoms on their own campuses. Whether exerting constant pressure on college administrators or taking trustees to court, black and white students argued that they had not forfeited their rights at the ivory or ebony tower gates. Instead, they demanded the same freedom to assemble, publish, and speak as every other American citizen. The expansion of First Amendment rights on southern college campuses was a slow and uneven process, but student demands helped bring their institutions closer to the mainstream of higher education and make student rights a reality on southern campuses.

NOTES

1. Patricia Sullivan, *Days of Hope: Race and Democracy in the New Deal Era* (Chapel Hill: Univ. of North Carolina Press, 1996), 3; Bruce Schulman, *From Cotton Belt to Sunbelt: Federal Policy, Economic Development, and the Transformation of the South, 1938–1980* (New York: Oxford Univ. Press, 1991); Jacquelyn Dowd Hall, "The Long Civil Rights Movement and the Political Uses of the Past," *Journal of American History* 91, no. 4 (2005): 1233–63. The Communist Party USA helped organize black workers in the South, further inflaming fears of a communist-black agenda. See Robin D. G. Kelley, *Hammer and Hoe: Alabama Communists during the Great Depression* (Chapel Hill: Univ. of North Carolina Press, 1990).

2. Mary Dudziak, *Cold War and Civil Rights: Race and the Image of American Democracy* (Princeton, NJ: Princeton Univ. Press, 2000); Derrick Bell, *Silent Covenants: Brown v. Board of Education and the Unfulfilled Hopes for Racial Reform* (New York: Oxford Univ. Press, 2004); Gerald Horne, *Communist Front? The Civil Rights Congress, 1946–1956* (Rutherford, NJ: Fairleigh Dickinson Univ. Press, 1988); Kenneth O'Reilly, *"Racial Matters": The FBI's Secret File on Black America, 1960–1972* (New York: Free Press, 1989); Brenda Gayle Plummer, *Rising Wind: Black Americans and U.S. Foreign Affairs, 1935–1960* (Chapel Hill: Univ. of North Carolina Press, 1996); M. J. Heale, *McCarthy's Americans* (Athens: Univ. of Georgia Press, 1988); Jeff Woods, *Black Struggle Red Scare: Segregation and Anti-Communism in the South, 1948–1968* (Baton Rouge: LSU Press, 2004).

3. George Bell Timmerman, "Message to the Legislature," 15 Jan. 1958, cited in "Academic Freedom and Tenure: Allen University and Benedict College," *AAUP Bulletin* 46 (1960): 87–104, 95. Timmerman's statement was aimed at dissident faculty, but he and other public officials also attacked students.

4. The First Amendment and academic freedom are related but not synonymous. Courts draw a distinction between them: academic freedom is just that, a *freedom,* not a *right,* in that it provides protection against institutional sanction but does not command institutional subsidy for a constituent's individual interests or opinions. William Van Alstyne, "The Specific Theory of Academic Freedom and the General Issue of Civil Liberty," *Annals of the American Academy of Political and Social Science* 404 (Nov. 1972): 140–56. Even though some of the people discussed in the chapter used the phrases interchangeably, this chapter focuses on First Amendment rights, since the issue of academic freedom was often reserved for faculty and not students.

5. V. O. Key, *Southern Politics in State and Nation* (New York: Alfred A. Knopf, 1949), 205; William H. Chafe, *Civilities and Civil Rights: Greensboro, North Carolina, and the Black Struggle for Freedom* (New York: Oxford Univ. Press, 1980). Although the University of North Carolina campuses were desegregated in 1956, it happened only after a court order to do so. *Frasier v. Board of Trustees,* 134 F. Supp. 589 M.D. North Carolina, 1955.

6. Key, *Southern Politics,* 130. The Mississippi legislature opened Jackson State College in 1940 and Mississippi Valley State College in 1950. With regard to proportions of black residents, in 1949 South Carolina's black population stood at 42.9%, while Mississippi's stood at 49.2%.

7. Marcia Synnott, "Desegregation in South Carolina, 1950–1963: Sometime 'Between Now and Never,'" in *Looking South: Chapters in the Story of an American Region,* ed. Winfred B. Moore Jr. and Joseph F. Tripp (New York: Greenwood Press, 1989), 52; R. Scott Baker, *Paradoxes of Desegregation: African American Struggles for Educational Equity in Charleston, South Carolina, 1926–1972* (Columbia: Univ. of South Carolina Press, 2006), xvii. See also Philip G. Grose, *South Carolina at the Brink: Robert McNair and the Politics of Civil Rights* (Columbia: Univ. of South Carolina Press, 2006); Peter Lau, *Democracy Rising: South Carolina and the Fight for Black Equality since 1865* (Lexington: Univ. Press of Kentucky, 2006); Howard Quint, *Profile in Black and White: A Frank Portrait of South Carolina* (Washington, D.C.: Public Affairs Press, 1958); and Robert Coles, *Farewell to the South* (Boston: Little, Brown, 1972).

8. Key, *Southern Politics,* 229; Neil R. McMillen, *Dark Journey: Black Mississippians in the Age of Jim Crow* (Urbana: Univ. of Illinois Press, 1989); Ross Barnett, TV-radio address, 13 Sept. 1962, cited in Charles Eagles, *The Price of Defiance: James Meredith and the Integration of Ole Miss* (Chapel Hill: Univ. of North Carolina Press, 2009), 283; "Stop, Think, Consider: Awake White Mississippi," *Commercial Appeal,* 17 Aug. 1967, personal papers of William Forrest Winter, Jackson, Mississippi; Kenneth T. Andrews, *Freedom Is a Constant Struggle: The Mississippi Civil Rights Movement and Its Legacy* (Chicago: Univ. of Chicago Press, 2004). Winter lost the election but won in 1980. For an in-depth treatment of both public and private black colleges and their involvement in the Civil Rights Movement, see Joy Ann Williamson, *Radicalizing the Ebony Tower: Black Students and the Black Freedom Struggle in Mississippi* (New York: Teachers College Press, 2008).

9. Benner C. Turner, Annual Report, Jan. 1957, 80–81, cited in John F. Potts, *A History of South Carolina State College, 1896–1978* (Orangeburg: South Carolina State College, 1978), 92.

10. *New York Times,* 21 Oct. 1962 (first quotation), and *Jackson Daily News,* 16 Oct. 1962 (second quotation), cited in Eagles, *Price of Defiance,* 15, 377. See also David Sansing, *The University of Mississippi: A Sesquicentennial History* (Jackson: Univ. Press of Mississippi, 1999). Discussions of the editors of *The Mississippian* and the SGA reaction are included in Eagles, *Price of Defiance;* Frank Lambert, *The Battle of Ole Miss: Civil Rights v. States' Rights* (New York: Oxford Univ. Press, 2010); Nadine Cohodas, *The Band Played Dixie: Race and the Liberal Conscience at Ole Miss* (New York: Free Press, 1997); and Russell Barrett, *Integration at Ole Miss* (Chicago: Quadrangle Books, 1965). University of Mississippi faculty passed a resolution commending Sidna Brower, the reprimanded editor, for her articles, one of which earned her a Pulitzer Prize nomination.

11. Raymond Wolters, *The New Negro on Campus: Black College Rebellions in the 1920s* (Princeton, NJ: Princeton Univ. Press, 1975).

12. "Negro Students Stage Boycott," *Greenwood Commonwealth,* 22 Feb. 1957; "Negro Student Boycott Settled," *Greenwood Commonwealth,* 23 Feb. 1957; James H. White, *Up from a Cotton Patch: J. H. White and the Development of Mississippi Valley State College* (Itta Bena, MS: n.p., 1979).

13. Clennon King, "Negro Writer Hits America Race Myths," *State Times,* 3 Mar. 1957; "Adam Powell Called 'Dupe' to Northern Race Trickery," *State Times,* 4 Mar. 1957, 14; and "Real Uncle Toms May Come from North, Be College Bred," *State Times,* 6 Mar. 1957; Mis-

sissippi Board of Trustees of Institutions of Higher Learning Minutes, 9 Mar. 1957, Mississippi Department of Archives and History, Jackson, Mississippi; "Integration Feud Rocks Alcorn," *Chicago Defender*, 16 Mar. 1957, and "Ousted Miss. Students on Speech Tour," *Pittsburgh Courier*, n.d., Student Strikes and Protest Movements File, Alcorn State University Archives, Lorman, Mississippi; Medgar Evers, "Monthly Report: The Alcorn Situation," 25 Mar. 1957, in *The Autobiography of Medgar Evers: A Hero's Life and Legacy Revealed through His Writings, Letters, and Speeches*, ed. Myrlie Evers-Williams and Manning Marable (New York: Basic Books, 2005).

14. Jerry Proctor, "King Tries to Stop Student Walk-Outs," *State Times*, 8 Mar. 1957.

15. Trezzvant Anderson, "More Charges against Boyd Hurled at Alcorn," *Pittsburgh Courier*, 10 Sept. 1960, Student Strikes and Protest Movements File, Alcorn State University Archives; J. D. Boyd to J. A. Morris et al., 1 May 1959, enclosure in Corrine Craddock Carpenter to E. R. Jobe, 26 June 1960, box 4, Folder Corrine Carpenter, American Association of University Professors Papers, George Washington University, Washington, D.C. (hereafter AAUPP).

16. Student Body of Alcorn to President's Advisory Committee; Faculty of Alcorn A&M College to J. D. Boyd, 24 Mar. 1960, enclosure in Carpenter to Jobe; "Hundreds Sent Home," *The Free Press*, 9 May 1964; and "Alcorn Education Tragedy Gets Press Cover-Up," *The Free Press*, 9 May 1964, box 4, Folder Frank Purnell, AAUPP.

17. James Meredith, *Three Years in Mississippi* (Bloomington: Univ. of Indiana Press, 1966), 95. See also Anne Moody, *Coming of Age in Mississippi* (New York: Dell, 1968); Joyce Ladner, interview with the author, 13 July 2005; and Dorie Ladner Churnet, interview with the author, 5 Feb. 2006.

18. Meredith, *Three Years*, 93–98; Wallace Dabbs, "Jackson State College Students Stage Protest," *Clarion-Ledger*, 28 Mar. 1961; John A. Peoples, *To Survive and Thrive: The Quest for a True University* (Jackson, MS: Town Square Books, 1995), 58; "Report Classes Boycotted at Jackson State," *Jackson Daily News*, 7 Oct. 1961, Sovereignty Commission Record 10-105-0-4-1-1-1, Mississippi Department of Archives and History, Jackson, Mississippi (hereafter cited SCR and MDAH). Students worked closely with Medgar Evers, field secretary for the Mississippi NAACP and Jackson resident.

19. Benner C. Turner, "Report Related to the Recent Student Strike at South Carolina State College, April 9–12, 1956," 2, South Carolina State University Archives, Orangeburg, South Carolina; South Carolina State College Board of Trustee Minutes, 31 Oct. 1956, and 25 Apr. 1956; Fred Henderson Moore interview with William C. Hine, 21 July 1995, South Carolina State University Archives, Orangeburg, South Carolina.

20. Dew James, "Trustees' Action Considered Rash," and Jack Bass, "Travlestead Speech Found Intelligent," *The Gamecock*, 2 Dec. 1955; Billy Mellette, "Travelstead—We Are in South Carolina," *The Gamecock*, 9 Dec. 1955, University of South Carolina Caroliniana Library, Columbia, South Carolina. Separate treatments of the Travelstead affair are included in Alan Wieder, "The *Brown* Decision, Academic Freedom, and White Resistance: Dean Chester Travelstead and the University of South Carolina," *Equity and Excellence* 28, no. 3 (1995): 45–49; William C. Hine, "Civil Rights and Campus Wrongs: South Carolina State College Student Protest, 1955–1968," *South Carolina Historical Magazine* 97, no. 4 (Nov. 1996): 310–31.

21. Henry H. Lesesne, *A History of the University of South Carolina, 1940–2000* (Columbia: Univ. of South Carolina Press, 2001), 129; W. E. Solomon, "The Problem of Desegregation in South Carolina," *Journal of Negro Education* 25, no. 3 (Summer 1956): 315–23.

22. Benner C. Turner, Annual Report, 1957, cited in Potts, *History of South Carolina State College*, 92; and Grose, *South Carolina at the Brink*.

23. William Billingsley, *Communists on Campus: Race, Politics, and the Public University in Sixties North Carolina* (Athens: Univ. of Georgia Press, 1999), 10, 3.

24. Ibid., 7; *Engel v. Vitale*, 370 U.S. 421 (1962); *Abington Township School District v. Schempp*, 374 U.S. 203 (1963); Jonathan Zimmerman, *Whose America: Culture Wars in the Public Schools* (Cambridge, MA: Harvard Univ. Press, 2002).

25. Billingsley, *Communists on Campus*, ch. 4.

26. Chafe, *Civilities and Civil Rights*, 111–12.

27. Billingsley, *Communists on Campus*, 19.

28. Ibid.

29. John Dunne to William B. Aycock, 6 July 1963, Records of the Office of the Chancellor, William B. Aycock Series, University Archives, Wilson Library, University of North Carolina at Chapel Hill (hereafter cited UNC); Michael H. Lawler to the student body presidents of the constituent campuses of the Consolidated University, 21 Sept. 1963, Records of the Office of Chancellor, William B. Aycock Series, UNC; Transcript of the Britt Commission Hearings, 9 Sept. 1965, James G. Hanes, Speaker Ban Commission Papers, Southern Historical Collection, UNC.

30. *Dickson v. Sitterson*, 280 F. Supp. 486 (1968); "Resolution in Support of Free Speech from Student Government," 10 Feb. 1966, Records of the Office of Chancellor Paul Sharp, UNC.

31. Mississippi officials did interfere with the election of the editor of *The Mississippian*. Billy Barton, a senior, was accused of being a sit-in participant in Atlanta and a member of the NAACP. Neither was true, but he lost the editorship when rumors of his activism were leaked by the Mississippi Sovereignty Commission, a segregationist government entity. See "In the Colleges," *Southern School News*, Apr. 1961 and June 1962; W. J. Simmons to Albert Jones, 17 Aug. 1960, SCR 7-0-2-86-1-1-1 to 2-1-1, MDAH; and "Governor Refuses to Comment," *State Times*, ? Mar. 1961, SCR 7-0-3-85-1-1-1, MDAH.

32. Billingsley, *Communists on Campus*, 202–6; Mississippi State Board of Institutions of Higher Learning Minutes, 20 Aug. 1964, 5 (first and second quotations) and 20 May 1965, 7 (third quotation); Mississippi State Board of Institutions of Higher Learning, "Resolution," 17 Nov. 1966, cited in Donald Reagan Stacy, "Mississippi's Campus Speaker Ban: Constitutional Considerations and the Academic Freedom of Students," *Mississippi Law Journal* 38 (1966–1967): 488–507. The Mississippi board enacted the first speaker ban on 17 February 1955. A court ruled against the ban in 1969 after students from Mississippi State University took trustees to court. See *Stacy v. Williams* (1969) N.D. Miss. 306, F 2d Supp. 963; and Donald Cunnigen, "Standing at the Gates: The Civil Rights Movement and Liberal White Mississippi Students," *Journal of Mississippi History* 67, no. 1 (Spring 2000): 1–19.

33. Anne Moody, *Coming of Age in Mississippi* (New York: Dell, 1968); John R. Salter Jr., *Jackson, Mississippi: An American Chronicle of Struggle and Schism* (Hicksville, NY: Exposition Press, 1979). An obvious exception to South Carolina's reputation for compromise and restraint was the Orangeburg Massacre, when police shot into a group of South Carolina State students protesting segregation at a local bowling alley, killing three, in 1968. See Jack Bass and Jack Nelson, *The Orangeburg Massacre* (Macon, GA: Mercer Univ. Press, 1984).

CHAPTER THREE

Interracial Dialogue and the Southern Student Human Relations Project

ERICA L. WHITTINGTON

To mention southern student activism is to evoke the iconic image of four courageous students sitting stoically at a Woolworth's lunch counter in Greensboro, North Carolina, in February 1960. A wave of student-initiated demonstrations swept through the South in the months that followed. The press interpreted the student sit-ins that spring as the arrival of a new generation, no longer "silent" or "uncommitted" but dedicated to dismantling America's version of racial apartheid. Yet while direct action represented a history-altering break with past practice, the sit-ins were less a revolutionary rupture than a tactical evolution within a broader history of youth activism against racial inequality in the South. Among the antecedents to the sit-ins was the study and practice of human relations, an oft-overlooked means by which many southern students, both black and white, joined the freedom struggle.

This chapter considers the influence of the human relations tradition on the freedom movement by focusing on the National Student Association's Southern Student Human Relations Project, known informally as the Southern Project, which operated from 1958 to 1968. The Southern Project's primary initiative was an annual three- to four-week summer human relations seminar bringing white and black southern students together to study at a college campus outside of the South, where interracial gatherings were legal. Organizers typically selected fewer than 20 participants each year and matriculated approximately 150 participants during the seminar's active years, between 1958 and 1965.[1] The safe intellectual and emotional environment allowed participants to engage with the history and mechanics of southern segregation and to increase their understanding of their roles within it. Human relations seminars opened up new avenues for criticism of segregation and suggested new hope for an integrated society. A veteran of these seminars credited them with having taken the concept of integration out of the realm of the theoretical and demon-strated it at work in the real world. And all of us, black, and white, were shaken by the realization that, at base, despite all that we had been taught and led to believe, we wanted the same things and were not much different.[2]

Many participants formed their first cross-racial friendships at these gather-ings. Upon returning to their home campuses, many built local networks to sup-port civil rights activism throughout the South. Some Southern Project alumni later became leaders in the Freedom Movement, including Charles McDew, Casey Hayden, Joan Browning, D'Army Bailey, Bob Zellner, and Constance Curry, the Southern Project's director.

Human Relations in Perspective

Southern students often used the term *human relations* as code for race relations in the 1940s and 1950s when segregation was enforced by rule of law. By and large, however, scholars have not yet examined the concept's influence on the develop-ment of racial progressivism in the postwar South. This oversight is not entirely surprising. The enforcers of the racial caste system of the early postwar South were both powerful and dangerous, and the term's ambiguity made it easier to escape their notice. Once the Freedom Movement emerged into the open in the 1960s and "putting your body on the line" had become the true measure of devotion to the cause of equality, the human relations tradition was dismissed as "all talk." Yet in both concept and practice, human relations helped to provide an intellectual and moral foundation for the growing student opposition to racial oppression. Programs such as the Southern Project foreshadowed the development of a broad and inclusive freedom movement predicated on the universalism of human worth and dignity.

The concept of human relations first emerged in the 1930s and gained popular currency after World War II, as American educators and social psychologists ad-vanced the idea that community leaders, trained in the latest social scientific theo-ries, could become "change agents" for a more democratic society. Many saw it as a means to thwart the impulse toward authoritarianism by fostering tolerance and empathy for minority populations and teaching peaceful methods of conflict reso-lution. As both an academic field of inquiry and a thoroughly interpersonal en-deavor, human relations emphasized the potential of interpersonal contact to alter societal dynamics.[3] Combining theory with social action, the concept seemed a natural vehicle for challenging the southern color line.

Indeed, by the 1950s, both secular and religious progressive organizations had recognized human relations as a weapon against segregation. The American Council on Education, the National Conference of Christians and Jews, and the

Atlanta-based Southern Regional Council funded academic and community stud-ies of human relations. Notices advertising human relations meetings became in-creasingly common in 1950s campus newspapers, and it was a frequent topic of formal discussion at University Young Men's and Women's Christian Associations (YM/YWCA) as well as the National Student Association, a national confedera-tion of over 300 student governments. As both an ethos and a practical concept, human relations fit comfortably within the established rubrics of these progres-sive organizations. In the segregated South, the student YM/YWCA and the NSA created what historian Sara Evans has termed "free spaces": rare environments where blacks and whites could interact as equals.[4] Students from across the coun-try met at NSA conferences and regional meetings to discuss matters of interest to American students, including foreign and domestic policy. Drawing as well upon the emergent rhetoric of human rights, NSA forged campus ties with schools and students around the world, while also sharpening its critique of segregation in the South.

Creating the Southern Student Human Relations Seminar

In the fall of 1957, Ray Farabee, a law student at the University of Texas at Austin, became the president of the NSA, the nation's largest collegiate representative body. A veteran NSA member, the new president faced some pressing challenges that tested his considerable political skills, including negotiating the controversial issue of desegregation in higher education without alienating southern member universities.[5] The NSA's national and regional meetings had been desegregated since the organization's founding in 1947. Since that time, NSA had adopted a broad internationalist perspective that often conflicted with the nation's increas-ingly rigid Cold War approach to world politics. The organization expressed its ideals in language purposely reminiscent of the United Nations Charter and Franklin D. Roosevelt's "Four Freedoms." The NSA also organized a prestigious annual series of international summer seminars, convening small numbers of ex-ceptional American and international students for nine weeks of study, discussion, sports, shared housing, and cultural events. Their purpose was to build a social network of future world leaders whose personal relationships would in turn help to foster and sustain global cooperation and peace. Indeed, many alumni later became national and international leaders.[6] Farabee hoped that the cooperative model pioneered by the NSA's international seminars might be adapted to encour-age similar interaction between southern white and black students whose contact with each other remained severely circumscribed in their home communities.

    Southern youth, Farabee believed, were "more open minded" and "less bound by economic or other institutional factors" than were their parents.[7] In keeping

Figure 3.1. Ray Farabee, president of the National Student Association, presenting an award to Eleanor Roosevelt, 1957. Farabee, a Texan, was instrumental in developing the Southern Student Human Relations Seminars that brought together black and white students from southern campuses for discussions about racial integration. Courtesy Ray Farabee and the Wisconsin Historical Society.

with the prevailing assumptions of human relations, he felt confident that education and meaningful interaction across the color line would empower student leaders to challenge segregation.[8] To make his vision a reality, Farabee secured a two-year grant from the Marshall Field Foundation to host the Southern Student Human Relations Seminar. The SSHRS sought the participation of moderate and liberal-minded white and black southern student leaders for a three-week course of intensive study and discussion of human relations in their home region. The project's intentionally anodyne title contained no reference to race relations, reflecting Farabee's belief that it was more likely to attract mainstream "southern student leader types" if it did not "sound too radical."[9]

Yet charges of radicalism were nothing new for the NSA. Pitched affiliation battles took place routinely on southern campuses, as conservatives condemned the organization's comparatively liberal stances on race, federal education funding, and internationalism.[10] To some, a student organization such as the NSA had no business taking positions on such issues in the first place. In 1960, the University of North Carolina's student body president David Grigg criticized the

NSA's "very definite lack of emphasis on . . . 'purely campus problems.' "[11] Similarly, Lowell Lebermann Jr., who served as University of Texas at Austin (UT) Student Association president in 1962, ascribed NSA's "highly controversial" profile on the Austin campus in the late 1950s and early 1960s to its message that students could play an important role in national and international affairs. Grigg and Lebermann presided over recently desegregated public universities affiliated with the NSA, but the southern region had fewer member schools proportionally than the rest of the country.[12] It "was just an emerging idea at the time," Lebermann recalled, "that we could, as students, come together in a homogenous group and have influence."[13]

Notwithstanding its fairly liberal national leadership, the NSA had thus far transcended ideological division among its members by focusing primarily on issues of academic freedom and student representation. The majority of NSA member schools fell somewhere in the middle of the political spectrum, and left- and right-leaning students mixed easily at its annual conventions throughout the late 1940s and early 1950s. There were many like Grigg who, while sympathetic to the aims of the nascent freedom movement, worried that the NSA's intervention in the national debate over civil rights risked factionalizing the organization and prompting southern schools to disaffiliate en masse.[14]

Despite these fears, the inaugural SSHRS took place during the summer of 1958 at Ohio State University, beyond the reach of the southern color line. Farabee had scheduled the seminar to coincide with NSA's annual national convention, held that year at Ohio Wesleyan.[15] With help from an adult advisory committee of progressive southern clergyman, scholars, journalists, and educators, Farabee planned a three-week seminar targeting moderate southern students. He selected white and black participants more on the basis of their leadership potential than on their beliefs about human relations or segregation. Farabee "neither expected nor hoped" that every participant would "favor integration."[16] Seminar applicants differed in their understandings of human relations but expressed a universal interest in learning more about segregation and the history of race relations in the South.[17]

One applicant from Mississippi wrote that "change in the hearts of the south" was necessary in order "to form a more liberal and tolerant viewpoint concerning Negro Americans, as well as other persecuted and mistreated races of the world."[18] In placing the issue of racial justice into an international context, she echoed the sentiments of many SSHRS applicants. Others expressed personal shame about specific high-profile racial incidents in the South, such as the mob action to prevent Autherine Lucy from becoming the first African American to attend the University of Alabama in 1956.[19]

Fourteen southern students attended each of the first two seminars; they were chosen from a mix of schools that were integrated, segregated, and likely to integrate in the future.[20] The SSHRS curriculum addressed the history of southern race relations with a rigor and accuracy that likely would have scandalized many white southerners of the era. To prepare, the students read books and articles on the origins and evolution of racial oppression in the South, particularly in churches and schools.[21] Participants also maintained a reading load of between 100 and 180 pages of material per night during the seminar, including case studies of desegregation at colleges and universities and segregationist tracts distributed by the white supremacist Citizens' Council.[22] These hours of study imparted a new sense of intellectual confidence to seminar participants, who, as one organizer remarked, aimed to "realistically work with problems which their seniors are not acknowledging."[23]

Faculty advisor Warren Ashby, a professor of ethics and philosophy at the Woman's College in Greensboro, North Carolina, gave the opening address at both the 1958 and 1959 seminars. In his talks, Ashby connected southern racial dynamics to the new international pressures and responsibilities of the United States.[24] Other notable speakers at the 1958 and 1959 seminars included Ambassador to the United Nations Frank Graham, former first lady Eleanor Roosevelt, economist Vivienne Henderson, and author Harry Ashmore, along with Dorothy Tilly and Frederick Routh of the Southern Regional Council.[25] Participants grappled with sociology, physiology, and history; viewed relevant films; engaged in role-playing exercises; and wrote evaluation papers on themselves and their communities with respect to racial issues. Many also learned for the first time about earlier efforts to change southern attitudes on race, a proud tradition of progressive action of which they were now a part.

The SSHRS cultivated an atmosphere of demanding collaborative study, which in turn encouraged seminar participants to reexamine their own racial experiences and attitudes. They socialized together in integrated dormitories, cafeterias, student unions, and libraries. Seminar discussions often transformed into informal bull sessions running "late into the night," according to faculty advisor Ashby.[26] For many of the students, the experience shattered preconceived stereotypes.[27] Farabee himself was not immune to these leaping shifts of paradigm. During the 1958 seminar, he attempted to explain to Jan Porter, the black student body president of the University of Chicago, his lingering unease about the effects of interracial marriage on children. Porter replied that, for her children, "it would make no difference; they were going to be black one way or another." The truth of Porter's remark struck Farabee with tremendous emotional force, such that he could recall that moment, in all its clarity and power, 50 years later.[28]

The emotional experience of the SSHRS bore some resemblance to what later activists would call "consciousness raising."[29] The seminars allowed whites and blacks to speak to each other directly, and with unprecedented frankness, about the personal impacts of segregation. Most alumni wrote of gaining a better understanding of themselves, their peers, and how segregation affected whites and blacks differently. In his evaluation of the experience, a black student from Virginia reported feeling "less self-conscious in an inter-racial group" a few months after the 1958 seminar.[30] One white student from the same cohort wrote that, while he had considered himself an integrationist prior to the seminar, he now recognized having been "to a great degree on the southern defensive."[31]

"Defensive" was probably an apt description of many southern college students in the late 1950s, and indeed, personal revelation was quite common among seminar participants. Socially conditioned to accept segregation uncritically, both black and white participants often confronted deeply held feelings and beliefs of which they had not been previously aware. A white student from Little Rock, for example, acknowledged a change in his attitude toward segregation. "Living and working and sharing" with black students, he wrote, had convinced him that he had to be part of the "changes to come" in the South. He realized "that my own rights as an individual will not be fully secured" until all Americans enjoyed equal rights.[32] Others expressed regret that the seminar had not lasted longer. These reports confirmed precisely the kinds of insights that Farabee and the other organizers had envisioned prior to organizing the first SSHRS.

Seminar alumni also sent periodic updates on their activities, progress, and challenges to NSA headquarters. Anthony "Tony" Henry, a leader in both the University YMCA and NSA and one of the first African Americans to enroll as an undergraduate at the University of Texas, founded an interracial human relations student group after returning from the 1958 SSHRS.[33] With a large university and progressive faith community, Austin seemed particularly open to changing its racial status quo in the late 1950s.[34] At Henry's urging, several student groups organized a boycott of segregated campus restaurants.[35] After several low-key "sit-downs" at the popular Night Hawk diner, owner Harry Aiken agreed to desegregate his establishment and to urge other restaurants to do the same.[36] Other SSHRS alumni also reported persuading local businesses to desegregate, organizing weekly campus discussion groups, and convincing their school administrators to relax racially restrictive dormitory policies.[37] Nine months after the 1958 seminar, 9 out of the 14 attendees had sent back detailed accounts of similar efforts at their home campuses.[38] NSA distributed this information, along with a growing compendium of "Action Reports," to other students around the country who wished to attempt similar human relations and desegregation projects.[39]

The SSHRS evolved considerably in its first two years. In response to complaints about the overrepresentation of white males at the inaugural 1958 seminar, the 1959 version sought a more equal gender and racial balance. Seminar directors also added African American literature and speakers to the seminar. Farabee refined the seminar's purpose and objectives to reflect the lessons learned in 1958 and 1959, including jettisoning his early focus on racial moderates in preference for "educated southern youth with liberal racial ideas" and placing greater emphasis on "action" and "techniques" of "effective leadership."[40]

Farabee's selection of a successor demonstrated the seminar's shift toward a more activist-oriented approach. Capitalizing on the early success of the Southern Student Human Relations Seminars, the NSA secured funding from the Field Foundation in 1960 to expand the annual seminar into a year-round program with a fulltime director, known as the "Southern Project." NSA located its Southern Project headquarters in Atlanta, Georgia, and hired Constance Curry, a charismatic 23-year-old, as its first director. A native North Carolinian, Curry had been a prominent undergraduate student leader and NSA member at Agnes Scott College in Decatur, Georgia, and had organized interracial meetings in the South as chair of NSA's "Great Southern" region in 1953.[41] Curry's selection accelerated the Southern Project's transformation into a locus of student collaboration and organizing against segregation.

The Southern Project and the Sit-Ins

In February 1960, only a month after Curry began leading the Southern Project, the Woolworth's sit-in in Greensboro dramatically introduced the nation to student direct action. Though not the first of its kind, the sit-in demonstrations by four North Carolina A&T freshmen captured the attention of the national press as prior such actions had not and triggered an unprecedented groundswell of student-led civil disobedience across the South. Ella Baker, a skilled organizer and a firm believer in grassroots leadership, recognized the sit-ins as an organizing opportunity and convened an Easter weekend conference at Shaw University in April of 1960. Established civil rights groups, including SCLC and CORE, hoped to incorporate the students into auxiliary branches of their organizations. But Baker zealously defended the autonomy of the emerging student movement, encouraging the most dedicated among them, including Julian Bond, Lonnie King, and Marion Barry, to form their own organization. They did so, creating the Student Nonviolent Coordinating Committee. Though it began at the margins, SNCC quickly became the intellectual and emotional heart of the civil rights movement in the South, infusing it with the ideals of nonviolence and democratic equality.[42]

The link between SNCC and NSA's Southern Project was both immediate and strong. Curry looked to Baker as a mentor and as a conduit to other human relations workers in the region. The two women traveled together from Atlanta to the formative Raleigh student conference. When SNCC named Baker and Curry as official advisors, along with Harry Belafonte, Curry devoted a portion of the Southern Project's funds and resources to launching the new organization. According to Julian Bond, Curry was instrumental in connecting SNCC with NSA's extensive campus network, providing fertile ground for both fundraising and recruiting.[43]

Yet while the sit-ins transformed the political environment on many campuses, they also generated considerable confusion among racially liberal southern students. The SSHRS seminars of the late 1950s had emphasized resolving racial issues through noncoercive and legal means, as reflected in UT student Tony Henry's cautious approach to restaurant desegregation in Austin. Given its propensity to inflame, most human relations practitioners regarded direct action and protest as a last resort. The sit-ins were tactically at odds with this approach, leaving many progressive-minded students uncertain of how best to act in accordance with their beliefs. This was evident in the application for the Southern Project seminars from then on, which spiked sharply in the wake of the sit-ins. The seminars themselves also changed considerably from year to year in an attempt to keep pace with the swiftly changing patterns of southern student activism.

From 1960 to 1964, Connie Curry consulted with Will Campbell, a progressive white Baptist minister, on programming and selection of participants for the seminars. They chose students who seemed most willing to challenge segregation in their own communities. The purpose of the seminars remained largely unchanged: to provide "interpretive background" and "allow interracial, interpersonal experience" so that participants might view themselves as "citizens of the nation and the world" unbound by regional custom.[44]

Now that there was a more defined student movement to join, students sought not just social knowledge but practical instruction on how to combat segregation and racial prejudice. In her Southern Project application, Casey Hayden (née Sandra Cason) expressed a desire to learn about the "power structures" behind segregation and the "possibilities of action in existing channels, and . . . new channels, both on campus and off."[45] Hayden, along with other post–Greensboro Seminar participants such as Chuck McDew, Bob Zellner, and Joan Browning, was qualitatively different from applicants in the seminar's earlier years. As a student and YWCA leader at the University of Texas at Austin, she had already participated in direct actions to oppose segregation.

In contrast to the primarily introspective nature of earlier seminars, from 1960 to 1963 they included concrete objectives and tactics of civil rights activism.

After the 1960 seminar, consultant Will Campbell recommended that the Southern Project waste no time trying "to 'convert' the conservatives." A moderate
"leadership training" approach, Campbell warned, might just as easily "result in
developing some very fine leaders for the white resistors and their movements."[46]

Human Relations in Practice

Connie Curry's sympathies lay with Hayden and the other seminar participants
who were eager to apply human relations techniques to the problem of race. As
director of the Southern Project, Curry incorporated more specific programming
on methods of action into the 1960 seminar curriculum while retaining its original emphasis on study, fellowship, and personal reflection. Reverend James Lawson spoke to the 1960 participants on the philosophy behind nonviolent resistance
and led a role-playing exercise on civil disobedience. Valerie Brown, a white student from segregated Texas Christian University, wrote that the experience of being ridiculed, pushed, and called names while role-playing an African American
sit-in activist brought her face to face with the horrifying "realization of what it
means to be denied the right to be a person."[47]

As facilitators, Curry and Campbell challenged seminar participants to think in
broader terms about human relations in the South and to cultivate greater respect
for one another. Only in such an environment could they cease "wearing masks" of
politeness and honestly confront the harsh truths of racial injustice. Mutual recognition of the other person's common humanity, Campbell often told participants,
signaled the start of civilization and the symbolic first act of human relations. The
same impulse lay at the heart of student responses to racial discrimination. Justice
followed knowledge and understanding. There was not just "one way," Campbell argued, to oppose segregation. "Some," he said, "will march in picket lines and face the
jeers of neighbors and the jails of peers. Some will seek and find other ways."[48]

At its most powerful, the seminar offered participants a glimpse of what could
be. The spontaneous development of personal bonds among the students themselves played a key role in creating this remarkable dynamic. In the 1960 seminar,
a relationship sprang up between Valerie Brown and Chuck McDew, an African
American undergraduate and sit-in leader from South Carolina State College.
Most seminar participants had never been privy to an interracial romance. The
possibility and natural development of Brown and McDew's courtship revealed to
the seminar's participants how profoundly artificial the Jim Crow barriers separating black from white were.[49]

A few months after the 1960 seminar, McDew was arrested for sitting-in at a
lunch counter. He wrote Brown a letter from jail, describing for her the sights and

sounds of the experience. Outside, he wrote, he could hear the voices of four hundred supportive students singing "We Shall Overcome" and the national anthem. "Why can't we be a world of blind men," he asked. "Then we would all be free and equal. . . . Let me be me, Charles Frederick McDew, man, student, lover of life. I don't want to be that nigger with no personality, no body, just a dark blob. I want to be me with my color that I love, with my eyes, my body, my dreams and aspirations."[50] McDew's letter painted the aims of the struggle in vivid and deeply personal terms, but it also expressed a universal hope for individual acceptance and freedom. Brown published it in TCU's campus paper in the hopes that McDew's words might touch the consciences of white students who had no personal connection to the growing movement.

For other participants, the personal ties forged during the seminar made it difficult to return to their segregated home communities, where such friendships remained impossible. Bob Catlett, a white attendee from Virginia Polytechnic Institute (now Virginia Tech), invited Chuck McDew to his campus shortly after the 1960 seminar to speak on his protest experiences. McDew recalls having to hide in a church basement after being "almost lynched" during his visit by a group of hostile VPI students.[51] His harrowing experience was a stark reminder that while it was one thing to meet interracially outside the South, interacting as equals south of the Mason-Dixon Line still carried personal risk.

The 1960 national NSA convention in Minneapolis took place against a backdrop of rapid change on American college campuses. Knowing that the sit-ins would be a topic of fierce debate among the delegates, Connie Curry invited Casey Hayden, a participant in that year's seminar, to speak to the NSA Congress in defense of the tactic. The night before Hayden spoke, a panel discussion featuring African American veterans of the sit-in demonstrations flared into a contentious exchange over the wisdom and effectiveness of direct action. Hayden took the podium immediately following a white male southerner's fiery denunciation of the sit-ins as an abrogation of property rights. The organization seemed hopelessly split on how to respond to the historic developments.

Hayden's words turned the debate. The sit-ins, she argued, were a direct and loving expression of the ideals of the nascent civil rights movement.[52] In their passive resistance to injustice, the sit-ins modeled a moral society and represented the hope that "a just decision can become a reality in students walking and sitting and acting together."[53] To those who bridled at defying the law, Hayden replied that she did not view the law as "immutable, but rather as an agreed-upon pattern for relations between people. If the pattern is unjust . . . a person must at times choose to do the right rather than the legal."[54] She closed her address by recounting a famous exchange between Ralph Waldo Emerson and Henry David Thoreau. "When Thoreau was jailed for refusing to pay taxes to a government which supported slavery, Emerson went to visit him," Hayden said. "'Henry David,' said Emerson, 'what are you doing in there?' Thoreau looked at him and replied, 'Ralph Waldo, what are *you* doing out *there*?'" After pausing for effect, Hayden asked the audience, "What are *you* doing out there?"[55] The assembled students erupted in a standing ovation, and the NSA Congress voted overwhelmingly to endorse the sit-ins shortly after.

Hayden was not the only seminar participant to make an impact in the early 1960s. D'Army Bailey was already an active student leader at all-black Southern University in Louisiana when he participated in the Southern Project Seminar in 1961. As he later recalled, the seminar's intensive study of human relations, together with his first meaningful social interactions with white students, convinced him that racism was based on a fiction.[56] Amid discussions of racist and liberal viewpoints, scholarly racial analysis, and an "unusual sharing of emotions and motivations," Bailey "realized for the first time that there were whites who could honestly feel, relate to, and understand what it was like to be a Negro in America." For Bailey, the seminar experience was a kind of nirvana, where whites and blacks achieved a level of trust and unity he had never imagined possible: "We had a lot of fun because racial antagonism was being neutralized as we gradually let our guards down." Socializing informally outside of the formal programming was a revelatory experience. "We swam, played games, roasted hot dogs, and grilled hamburgers. At night we would sit around the campfire toasting marshmallows, singing 'Kum Bah Yah' to someone's accompanying guitar, listening to [the] banjo, or just watching the night sky, which seemed to have more stars than anywhere I had ever seen."[57]

There was an astonishing freedom, Bailey recalls, in truly being oneself, away from the eyes and expectations of administrators, politicians, and parents. "We were a small microcosm to be sure," he recalls, "but we were trying, usually with success, to deal with each other as human beings."[58] The seminar gave students the space to envision and even experience what they were fighting for. That such an experience could be obtained merely by leaving the South emboldened participants to resist the seemingly arbitrary restrictions placed on them in their home communities. Bailey would return to organize student protests at Southern University, for which he was later expelled.[59]

Similarly, Bob Zellner, a native white Mississippian, had also been involved in the movement prior to attending the seminar in 1961. He too remembers his experience at the Southern Project as "a watershed event." For Zellner, the seminar was a particularly vivid time of interracial fellowship, as it introduced him to powerful role models at a formative period in his life. He was particularly inspired by Will Campbell, whose actions and attitudes demonstrated, "in the same way that historian Vann Woodward taught . . . that one could be a good southerner and still oppose racial oppression and segregation."[60]

Human Relations and Civil Rights

In March of 1960, Lonnie King, Julian Bond, Herschelle Sullivan, Carolyn Long, Joseph Pierce, and other African American students from Atlanta published a full-page ad in the *Atlanta Journal-Constitution* titled "An Appeal for Civil Rights." Using the rhetoric of human relations, the article gave public expression to the goals of the emerging student movement, which far exceeded the mere ability to drink and eat in public restaurants. The ad outlined many of the specific injustices that African Americans were enduring in what was "supposedly one of the most progressive cities in the south" and declared "to the citizens of Atlanta and to the world" their intent to fight racial injustice with all nonviolent means necessary. "[We have] joined our hearts, minds, and bodies in the cause of gaining those rights which are inherently ours as members of the human race and as citizens of these United States," the ad's authors affirmed.[61] The students' platform cast the struggle in broad terms and demonstrated how the human relations tradition blurred the lines between human rights and civil rights.[62]

In keeping with this trend, the 1961 seminar sought a "broader context" through the inclusion of a Jewish student as well as an international student studying in the South, since, as Curry and the Advisory Board agreed, "human relations does not mean race relations only."[63] The Southern Project also spent more time planning and hosting trips to the South for international students, often at the request of the State Department. Accordingly, the 1961 seminar included a more thorough examination of the international implications of southern race relations.[64] Despite these changes, however, the seminar still emphasized self-reflection along with its new, more tactical focus. Southern Project leaders still asked students to consider their personal roles within, and relationships to, the existing system of segregation and how they could stay true to their beliefs. Improving human relations, Connie Curry wrote at the time, "is not always a question of 'doing' but actually of 'being.'"[65]

The relationship between human relations and civil rights remained fluid in the years following the Greensboro sit-ins. In 1961, the Southern Project began its own voter registration project coordinated by active SNCC member Dorothy Dawson. Yet Curry still tried to maintain a measure of distinction between the Southern Project's human relations work, such as the seminars, and its escalating civil rights activism. In practice, however, many adherents seemed uncertain of precisely where human relations ended and civil rights began. Some continued to view human relations as an academic tradition, while others saw it as an important mode of moral and political struggle.

For segregationists, however, the 1960 sit-ins removed all doubt about what human relations meant. Roy Harris, a Georgia attorney working in the racist Eugene Talmadge political machine and a regent of the University of Georgia, published a list of "race mixing" organizations and individuals that included the NSA Southern Human Relations Project and Connie Curry. Harris's intimidation efforts drew no distinction between "human relations" and "civil rights" organizations. A number of southern student organizations began quietly to distance themselves from the term, describing their work instead in terms of academic freedom, international affairs, and education.[66]

By the mid-1960s, even once-enthusiastic institutional supporters of the human relations approach were beginning to question its value. By the time the NSA asked for a renewal of its Field Foundation grant in November of 1965, much had changed since the first Southern Student Human Relations Seminar in 1958. Connie Curry had resigned as the Southern Project's director in early 1964, and Will Campbell and Ella Baker had also moved on. The 1964 and 1965 seminars incorporated material unrelated to race relations and in fact omitted human relations programming entirely, creating a very different experience than previous seminars.

Most importantly, the political environment in which the Southern Project operated had changed. Field Foundation executive director Leslie Dunbar weighed the Southern Project's grant proposal against four similar requests, one of which came from the Southern Student Organizing Committee, a newly formed white analogue to the increasingly militant and racially exclusive SNCC. In a letter to NSA president Philip Sherburne, Dunbar confessed his discomfort with extending the Southern Project's funding and wondered whether the "old human relations approach" had in fact become "outmoded."[67] Although the Southern Project's proposal was the strongest, Dunbar wrote, he saw "more realism in SSOC's methods and attitudes" and suggested that the two join forces in a final attempt to stimulate a white student movement in the South.[68] Dunbar's dismissal of human relations as obsolete and starry-eyed reflected a broadening acceptance among establishment white liberals that, as of late 1965, the dream of building a truly integrated civil rights movement in the South was over.

Realizing that the Field Foundation was preparing to drop the Southern Project's funding specifically because of its human relations framework, Sherburne concurred with Dunbar that "the day of inter-racial gatherings over tea and crumpets (or an RC and a Moon-Pie) is past, or that we should at least speed it on its way."[69] The NSA revised its grant proposal to omit the summer seminars entirely and to adopt SSOC's goal of organizing white students. "The pressing need,"

Sherburne wrote to Dunbar in March of 1966, was "to get these students to play their role in fully integrating the southern campus."[70]

The Field Foundation renewed the Southern Project's funding for two more years, with the caveat that the grant would be terminal. The NSA tapped Howard Romaine, who was active in SSOC, as the last director of the Southern Project. By Romaine's own admission, his tenure as the Southern Project's director was somewhat disappointing, and his 1968 report to the Field Foundation chronicling the Southern Project's final year struck a discouraged and almost apologetic tone. Given the political realities on most campuses, the Southern Project's goal of creating a white student movement in the South no longer made sense. "The activist, non-violent southern student civil rights movement has died (on black campuses)," Romaine wrote, "or has been transformed into a militant antiwar movement (on white campuses)."[71] Whereas the Southern Project's role through the early 1960s had been well defined, he continued, by 1967 "it had become almost impossible for a white person to work directly with the militant nationalist remnant of what was once SNCC and, simultaneously, it was no longer as clear how to involve whites now that their active participatory and supporting role in the movement was no longer desired by the blacks, and . . . their interest was often preoccupied with anti-war activities."[72] During the preceding year, Romaine had directed most of the Southern Project's resources toward Alabama, hoping to make a more measurable impact on a more modest scale. But the Southern Project's concentrated efforts there met with the same difficulties they had everywhere else in Dixie.[73] There simply was no longer a middle ground to move toward. Romaine's report reads as a kind of epitaph for the NSA Southern Student Project in Human Relations, which ceased to exist at the end of 1968.

Conclusion

Despite the civil rights movement's spiritual trappings and rhetoric, the American public tends to interpret the period as a moment of civic reform, its object the extension of full citizenship rights to a racialized and historically oppressed underclass. The very label—"civil rights movement"—specifically casts the struggle in the context of citizenship and legal equality. And indeed, viewing the movement in such terms makes it easy to understand the objectives of the students who endured taunts and physical abuse merely to sit at segregated lunch counters, who braved police dogs and fire hoses in orderly marches down the street, and who faced down a rain of bullets just to cross a bridge. They did these things, the story goes, as a strategic bid to reveal to the world the injustice of state-sanctioned segregation and ultimately to overturn it in American courts and legislatures.

Initially, the tradition of human relations appears to exist quite apart from this well-known version of civil rights history. Its approach contrasted sharply by holding to comparatively timid tactics of gradual and halting change and focusing more on the attitudes of individuals than on governing institutions. Human relations practitioners believed in the importance of education and interaction in formulating strategy and in respecting the rights and feelings of all stakeholders—even pro-segregationists. A moderate and deliberative approach to social change, they believed, would bring about more stable and enduring solutions to the problems of race prejudice and segregation than would direct action. Philosophically, civil disobedience rejected such gradualist assumptions as well as its "step-by-step" prescription for desegregation. The failure of human relations practitioners to keep pace with the movement after the sit-ins revealed the limitations of human relations and created a generational gap between older and younger activists. For those who rejected the idea of accommodating an unjust system, human relations quickly began to appear not merely passé but actually counterproductive.

Yet the history of the human relations approach to civil rights reminds us that, for many in the movement, there was more than just overturning the laws of segregation. A real psychological distance existed between passively disapproving of segregation, as many southerners did, and actively resisting it. The human relations tradition was vital in making the "next step" possible. Human relations played a key role in this emotional and intellectual evolution. It provided an entry point and philosophical framework for many in the freedom movement. Casey Hayden's experience illuminates the nexus between human relations and civil rights activism in the 1950s and the early 1960s. The work of human relations, Hayden recalled, was less about race than about "fostering healing and relationships that transcended race. This work undermined and defeated segregation on a personal level, just as bringing down the legal barriers would defeat it politically."[74] Ultimately, the aim of human relations was to instill a universal ethic of human respect and dignity within which there could be no place for racial prejudice.[75]

Connie Curry's characterization of human relations as a question of "being" as well as "doing" suggests one reason why human relations has been largely overlooked in the historiography of the civil rights movement. The public record is biased toward action, rather than personal reflection and interpersonal exchange. Events such as the NSA seminars created the types of personal conversions that led to civil rights activism, but revelations that take place on the personal level are harder to isolate. Yet they are crucial to our understanding of what sustained many activists who "put their bodies on the line" to fight against segregation. In addition to the well-known public record of speeches, organizing, arrests, and iconic imagery, there remains a vast and undiscovered record of conviction, belief, and faith. The evidence for human relations activities offers new insight into the emotional and intellectual roots of the civil rights movement.

The relationship between human relations and the freedom movement remains both problematic and understudied. Much of the existing history of the civil rights movement in the early 1960s focuses, as it should, on the sites at which brave men and women most directly confronted segregation, whether lunch counters, street corners, or county jails. The legacy of human relations is at best only intermittently visible in these iconic moments of confrontation. Yet accounting for that legacy is essential to understanding what brought many freedom workers to the front lines in the first place. The human relations seminars, particularly in the early years of the Southern Project, were far more than mere "tea parties" between blacks and whites. Before the Civil Rights Act of 1964, interracial assembly was not only dangerous; in the states of the old Confederacy, it was illegal. By participating in such activities, students defied the color line, confronted their own and each other's beliefs, and often transformed what they believed was possible.

Human relations programming and terminology are ubiquitous in the historical record, but "human relations" itself is often misinterpreted as an old-fashioned term for "race relations." Encompassing more than a means of struggle, human relations ideally modeled what students were striving for in their efforts against segregation. D'Army Bailey's memoir recounts the poignant and revelatory nature of the 1961 Southern Project seminar: "It does sound a bit far-fetched for a three-week seminar," Bailey later acknowledged, "but it happened. It happened because somewhere inside, each of us wanted it to. We wanted to be human beings, unlabeled and unclassified, and at least for a moment, *free*."[76]

There are many strands, many origins, to the long civil rights movement. The visible tension between different lineages of race consciousness and activism is worthy of reconsideration, as it helps to map the complex foundations of the freedom movement. In its focus on extralegal structures of power and in its ability to address the barriers that kept human beings apart, human relations generated a brief but pivotal historical moment of dialogue and awareness among twentieth-century southern students about the effects of segregation on themselves and others. The NSA's human relations seminars changed the minds and hearts of and lent courage to its young participants, many of whom went on to make important contributions to the struggle for equality. This orientation preceded notions of identity politics and perhaps ran counter to them. The concept of human relations became a framework for envisioning a world undivided by race, gender, and nationality. Direct action served the purpose of desegregating the South. But the story of the NSA Southern Student Human Relations Project offered a glimpse of a different South—one that was truly integrated.

NOTES

1. Fourteen students attended each of the first two seminars organized by Ray Farabee. Under Connie Curry's direction from 1960 to 1963, the seminars admitted between 16 and 20 students each summer. When Hayes Mizelle took over the directorship in 1964, he changed the curriculum and began to increase the number of participants. Thirty students participated in 1965, making it both the largest—and final—year of the SSHRS.

2. D'Army Bailey, *The Education of a Black Radical: A Southern Civil Rights Activist's Journey, 1959–1964* (Baton Rouge: LSU Press, 2009), 72.

3. The concept of human relations eventually gained popularity with business management trainers for the purpose of achieving greater organizational effectiveness, but in the 1940s and 1950s human relations concerns translated into a social activist orientation. See Laura Kim Lee, "Changing Selves, Changing Society: Human Relations Experts and the Invention of T Groups, Sensitivity Training, and Encounter in the United States, 1938–1980" (PhD diss., Univ. of California at Los Angeles, 2002).

4. Sara M. Evans and Harry C. Boyte, *Free Spaces: The Sources of Democratic Change in America* (Chicago: Univ. of Chicago Press, 1992).

5. A native Texan from Wichita Falls, Farabee's experience in youth organizations extended back to his high school years, when he had helped organize interracial regional "High-Y" YMCA conferences for high school–aged youth. At college, he quickly became a leader and active participant at the University of Texas YM/YWCA, which was integrated by national policy and had a long tradition of interracial gatherings and discussions on the issues of justice and peace.

6. Attendees included Kofi Annan and other youth who were presumed to be their nations' future leaders. We now know that the CIA covertly funded this seminar, and documents from the NSA archives in Wisconsin reveal that some American participants were instructed to record observations of the personal characteristics, mannerisms, and preferences of international student leaders for CIA files. *United States Student Association Records,* Wisconsin Historical Society, University of Wisconsin, Madison, Wisconsin. For more on the NSA-CIA connection, see Katherine Paget, "From Stockholm to Leiden: The CIA's Role in the Formation of the International Student Conference," *Intelligence and National Security* 18 (2003): 134–67; and Angus Johnston, "The United States National Student Association: Democracy, Activism, and the Idea of the Student, 1947–1978" (PhD diss., City Univ. of New York, New York, 2009).

7. Ray Farabee, interview with the author, 9 Sept. 2008, Austin, Texas, tape in author's possession.

8. Southern student leaders at national NSA congresses had called for a regional project of this type for several years. Ray Farabee, "Letter to Dear Friends," 13 Apr. 1959, folder "Curriculum and Program, 1959," box 7, *The Records of the United States National Students Association Southern Project,* King Center Archives, Atlanta, Georgia. (Hereafter cited as Southern Project Papers.)

9. Ray Farabee interview.

10. Indeed, some colleges dis- and re-affiliated with NSA from year to year according to the politics of student governments and the fluctuating intensity of opposition to the organization. Among the more prominent of the NSA's affiliation battlegrounds was the University of Texas at Austin. While UT students had played a pivotal role in founding NSA in 1947, the student body voted twice to disaffiliate between 1948 and 1953. UT re-affiliated in

1954, but in 1959 the UT Student Association again recoiled from the organization, placing it on campus probation for its "lack of flexibility" and "precocious delving into the national and international realms of government." *Daily Texan,* 25 Sept. 1959.

11. A conservative organization called the Southern University Student Government Association (SUSGA) formed in 1959 as a direct competitor to NSA; it admitted only white schools and purported to deal with campus-specific issues only. Though UNC did not affiliate with SUSGA, Grigg attended its second conference in 1960 to establish communication, as he felt that SUSGA was "the organization most representative of southern white student opinion . . . and is composed of schools with problems most similar to ours." He also hoped to persuade SUSGA members to attend NSA conferences, where he thought their viewpoints should be represented. "Statement by David L. Grigg," 11 May 1960, in the Student Government of the University of North Carolina at Chapel Hill Records no. 40169, University Archives, Wilson Library, University of North Carolina at Chapel Hill.

12. The state legislatures in Georgia and Mississippi forbade state schools from affiliating as members of NSA due to the organization's policies of support for desegregation and the sit-in movement. "Report of the Project's Activities, September–October, 1966," folder "Reports, 1966," box 3, Southern Project Papers.

13. David Scott Goldstein, "The Student Government Experience at the University of Texas at Austin, 1932–1933 to 1982–1983" (Honors thesis, Univ. of Texas at Austin, 1983), 316.

14. Subsequent events proved this fear to be somewhat unfounded. As historian Angus Johnston notes, "in fact southern white membership fell by only two schools—from 90 to 88—between 1959 and 1963," and attendance at NSA conferences increased more rapidly during these years than in any period since the NSA's founding in 1947. Johnston, "United States National Student Association," 310–11.

15. In 1958 and 1959 the core curriculum comprised the first two weeks, after which seminar participants attended the NSA National Convention while continuing to meet as a group. From 1959 to 1964, the seminar took place immediately preceding the national convention (always held on a midwestern college campus), and NSA encouraged Seminar participants to stay and attend the convention afterwards.

16. Ray Farabee, "Letter to Dear Friends," 13 Apr. 1959, folder "Curriculum and Program, 1959," box 7, Southern Project Papers.

17. Folder "1959 Seminar Participants," box 8, Southern Project Papers.

18. Folder "1959 Seminar Participants," box 8, Southern Project Papers.

19. Ray Farabee interview.

20. Warren Ashby, "Statement to Dean's Conference on SSHRS and Values," folder "11-Correspondence, Advisors, Speakers, Response Persons, 1958," box 6, Southern Project Papers.

21. The reading list included Harry Ashmore's *An Epitaph for Dixie* and *With All Deliberate Speed,* edited by Don Shoemaker, as well as White Citizens' Council and other segregationist tracts. Subsequent seminars would read C. Vann Woodward's *The Strange Career of Jim Crow,* Charles Grier Seller's *The Southerner as American,* and *Mississippi, the Closed Society,* by James Silver.

22. Ray Farabee, "Report: Southern Student Human Relations Seminar, August 3–29, 1958," folder "Background Information, Prospectus, Curriculum, 1958," box 6, Southern Project Papers.

23. Ibid.

24. Ashby was also chairman of the American Friends Service Commission College

Committee in the Southeastern Region. Ibid.; folder "Report to the Field Foundation, 1959," box 8, Southern Project Papers.

25. "Report: Southern Student Human Relations Seminar, August 3–29, 1958," folder "Report, 1958," box 6, and folder "Report to the Field Foundation, 1959," box 8, Southern Project Papers.

26. Warren Ashby, "Interim Report: August 15, 1959, Southern Students Human Relations Seminar," folder "Correspondence, Advisors, Speakers, Response Persons, 1958," box 6, Southern Project Papers.

27. One student evaluated the 1958 program positively overall but wrote that he thought students should have been notified beforehand that dorm space would be integrated.

28. Ray Farabee interview.

29. On the importance of consciousness raising and the women's movement in the 1960s and 1970s, see Sara Evans, *Personal Politics: The Roots of Women's Liberation in the Civil Rights Movement and the New Left* (New York: Vintage Books, 1979); Alice Echols, *Daring to Be Bad: Radical Feminism in America, 1967–1975* (Minneapolis: Univ. of Minnesota Press, 1989); and Ruth Rosen, *The World Split Open: How the Modern Women's Movement Changed America* (New York: Viking, 2000).

30. "The 1958 Southern Student Human Relations Seminar Final Evaluation, April 1959," folder "Evaluations, 1958," box 11, Southern Project Papers.

31. Bob Alexander, "Evaluation," folder "Evaluations I, 1959," box 7, Southern Project Papers.

32. "The 1958 Southern Student Human Relations Seminar Final Evaluation, April 1959," folder "Evaluations, 1958," box 11, Southern Project Papers.

33. "List of Participants, Southern Student Human Relations Seminar, August 3–29, 1958," folder "Background Information, Prospectus, Curriculum, 1958," box 6, Southern Project Papers.

34. Besides the University YM/YWCA, the Christian Faith and Life Community at UT was important in providing a space where students were encouraged to put their religious and philosophical understandings into practice, living in interracial dormitory space. See Doug Rossinow, *The Politics of Authenticity: Liberalism, Christianity, and the New Left in America* (New York: Columbia Univ. Press, 1998).

35. Casey Hayden, phone interview with the author, 10 Sept. 2008, tape in author's possession.

36. Campus-area restaurants in Austin desegregated with little controversy during the 1958–59 school year. Robert Hardgrave Jr., "Burden of the Past: Race at UT in the 1950s," 9 Apr. 1996, *Daily Texan,* "Integration and Segregation" vertical file, Center for American History, University of Texas at Austin.

37. These students attended Hampton Institute in Virginia, Dillard University in New Orleans, and Women's College in Greensboro, North Carolina. "The 1958 Southern Student Human Relations Seminar Final Evaluation, April 1959," folder "Evaluations, 1958," box 11, Southern Project Papers.

38. The alumni of the 1958 seminar were very active on their campuses: three served as student body presidents the following year, at least six more worked in their student governance associations, and one became a campus newspaper editor and co-chair of a human relations committee. "1958 Southern Student Human Relations Seminar Final Evaluation, April 1959," folder "Evaluations, 1958," box 6, Southern Project Papers.

39. "Student Participation in College Desegregation," folder "Action Reports, 1959," box 8, Southern Project Papers.

40. "Report of the USNSA Second Southern Student Human Relations Seminar," University of Illinois, 9 Aug.–3 Sept. 1959, folder "Report to the Field Foundation," box 8, Southern Project Papers.

41. As NSA chairperson of the Great Southern region, Curry organized a conference at the only location in Atlanta that would permit an integrated meeting—the Luckie Street YMCA. Curry remembered "the moment when the consequences of racial segregation first hit me personally was lunch hour at that Saturday meeting. . . . When noon came, the black delegates, some of whom were my friends form the national congresses, walked down the steps of the Y and headed toward Auburn Avenue to the black restaurants. The rest of us walked down the steps and headed in the other direction. I realized then that segregation took away *my* personal freedom as surely as if I were bound by invisible chains." Constance Curry, "Wild Geese to the Past," in *Deep in Our Hearts: Nine White Women in the Freedom Movement*, ed. Constance Curry et al. (Athens: Univ. of Georgia Press, 2000), 15.

42. See Wesley C. Hogan, *Many Minds, One Heart: SNCC's Dream for a New America* (Chapel Hill: Univ. of North Carolina Press, 2007).

43. Curry gave Julian Bond a key to the Southern Project office, where he was able to mimeograph SNCC newsletters and memos to other student organizations. According to Bond, Curry "was a bridge between the overwhelming number of black sit-in students and white students who were predisposed to join with us." Just as importantly, she "publicized the sit-in movement within the NSA network, interpreted it, and created an audience for us that might not have been there." Curry, "Wild Geese to the Past," 23–24.

44. "United States National Student Association Proposal for the Renewal of the Southern Student Human Relations Project," folder "Advisory Committee, Jan. 1962," box 1, Southern Project Papers.

45. Casey Hayden, "Reasons for My Interest in NSA Human Relations Seminar," 5 Apr. 1960, folder "1960 Third Seminar Applications—Accepted," box 9, Southern Project Papers.

46. Will D. Campbell, "Report on the Seminar," folder "Advisory Committee, January 1961," box 1, Southern Project Papers.

47. Brown wrote, "Imagine being burned on the back of the neck with a cigarette or having someone spit in your face and not even having a desire to strike back! And why—how are they able to attain this? In their training this becomes a part of them and they are able to look at you and say, 'These people are sick. I couldn't strike a sick man. I want to heal him.'" Valerie Brown, "Seminar Report," 14 Sept. 1960, folder "1960 Third Seminar Applications—Accepted," box 9, Southern Project Papers.

48. Will Campbell, "The Display of a Feather," *New South*, Jan. 1962, 7–8.

49. Casey Hayden was inspired to write a poem about this relationship just after the seminar, and both she and Connie Curry recall the impact of this union in their biographical essays in *Deep in Our Hearts*.

50. Curry et al., ed., *Deep in Our Hearts,* 20.

51. Charles McDew, conversation with the author, 20 Mar. 2010, Columbia, South Carolina, notes in author's possession.

52. Don Morrison, "White Coed Backs Sit-Ins, Gets Ovation," *Minneapolis Tribune*, undated copy from the personal files of Constance Curry, in author's possession.

53. Casey Hayden, "Onto Open Ground," in *Hands on the Freedom Plow: Personal Accounts By Women in SNCC*, ed. Faith S. Holsaert et al. (Urbana: Univ. of Illinois Press, 2010), 49–51.

54. Ibid.

55. Ibid.

56. D'Army Bailey, phone interview with the author, 30 Jan. 2009, tape in author's possession.

57. Bailey writes, "I realize that I say this at the risk of sounding ridiculous, that the experiences and feelings I describe may now seem incomprehensible. Perhaps it's like that line at the end of the old joke, 'you had to be there.'" Bailey, *Education of a Black Radical*, 67–72.

58. Ibid., 69.

59. Similarly, 1961 Seminar participant Walter Williams, an African American student at Jackson State College, became student body president but was kicked out of school when he spearheaded protests against Mississippi segregation laws.

60. Bob Zellner and Constance Curry, *The Wrong Side of Murder Creek: A White Southerner in the Freedom Movement* (Montgomery, AL: New South Books, 2008), 117–18.

61. "An Appeal for Human Rights," 9 Mar. 1960, folder 4, "Individual Protest Centers," box 1, Constance Curry Papers, Emory University Manuscript, Library, and Rare Book Collection, Atlanta, Georgia.

62. For more on human rights in twentieth-century American politics, see Elizabeth Borgwardt, *A New Deal for the World: America's Vision for Human Rights* (Cambridge, MA: Harvard Univ. Press, 2005).

63. Arthur Levin from the Anti-Defamation League was a regular seminar speaker on the relationship of racial and religious discrimination. "Minutes of the Southern Project Advisory Committee Meeting, January 31, 1961," folder "Advisory Committee—Jan. 1961," box 1, Southern Project Papers.

64. Among the additions to the 1961 seminar was a discussion session between Seminar participants and nine international student leaders from NSA's Foreign Student Leadership Project on "the meaning of Southern race relations in the world scene." "The Fourth Southern Student Human Relations Seminar August 1–18, 1961," folder "Advisory Committee—Jan. 1962," box 1, Southern Project Papers.

65. "United States National Student Association, The Third Southern Student Human Relations Seminar August 1–September 1, 1960, Report to the Marshall Field Foundation March, 1961," folder "Report to the Field Foundation, 1961," box 5, Southern Project Papers.

66. "Minutes, Southern Project Advisory Committee Meeting May 31, 1962," folder "Advisory Committee—May 1962," box 1, Southern Project Papers. See also Mary King, *Freedom Song: A Personal Story of the 1960s Civil Rights Movement* (New York: Morrow, 1987).

67. Leslie Dunbar, "Letter to Philip Sherburne," 24 Nov. 1965, folder "Field Foundation, November 1965," box 2, Southern Project Papers. As a longtime member of the Southern Regional Council (SRC), Dunbar was very familiar with the human relations tradition. From 1961 to 1965 he attempted to usher in "a great historic mind-changing" as the director of the SRC, especially through voter education projects.

68. Ibid.

69. Philip Sherburne, "Letter to Leslie Dunbar," 1 Dec. 1965, folder "Field Foundation, November 1965," box 2, Southern Project Papers.

70. Philip Sherburne, "Letter to Leslie Dunbar," 2 Mar. 1966, folder "Field Foundation, November 1965," box 2, Southern Project Papers.

71. Howard Romaine, "Director's Report, NSA Southern Project, 1967–1968," n.d., folder "Field Foundation, 1968–1969," box 2, Southern Project Papers.

72. Ibid.

73. Ibid. Romaine hired three staff members who were natives of Alabama and alumni

of Alabama universities. At a regional NSA meeting in Alabama, he brought on board Bob Zellner, a former NSA Project Seminar participant and a white Alabama native and organizer of poor whites, as well as Bernice Reagon, an African American freedom singer, both of whom were former SNCC workers. Zellner and Reagon led workshops on topics including white community organizing, student power, and black consciousness. These efforts were limited in their outreach, Romaine acknowledged, because the NSA conferences at which they took place attracted "student government types" more than "student activist types." Ibid.

74. Casey Hayden, "Fields of Blue," in *Deep in Our Hearts*, ed. Curry et al., 345.

75. Casey Hayden phone interview.

76. *Education of a Black Radical*, 70–71.

CHAPTER FOUR

Moderate White Activists and the Struggle for Racial Equality on South Carolina Campuses

MARCIA G. SYNNOTT

Despite a Jim Crow regime as oppressive as anywhere in the South, most histo-ries of the civil rights era in South Carolina stress the relative ease by which the state transitioned through the desegregation period. South Carolina had its share of Freedom Riders, sit-ins, and protest marches, particularly in Rock Hill, Or-angeburg, and Charleston. Nevertheless, the state largely escaped the crises that occurred in Georgia (Albany, Atlanta, and Athens), Alabama (Montgomery, Tus-caloosa, and Selma), and Mississippi (Oxford, Jackson, and Philadelphia). Radi-cal organizations such as the Student Nonviolent Coordinating Committee, the Congress of Racial Equality, and Students for a Democratic Society tended to find fewer recruits in South Carolina than in other southern states.

The conventional wisdom is that South Carolina escaped many of the episodes of racist violence that plagued other southern states because of the cool leadership of its moderates, such as Governors Ernest "Fritz" Hollings and Robert McNair. They avoided the extreme segregationist rhetoric of such demagogues as Ala-bama's governor, George Wallace. So South Carolina's political leaders rarely thrust the state into the national spotlight. Elements of this story may be true as far as they go, but such accounts miss the grassroots work accomplished by civic and student leaders, especially in the early 1960s. As Erica Whittington's essay in this volume demonstrates, the human relations movement was an effort to bridge the adult civil rights movement and student activists. The South Carolina Council on Human Relations was particularly effective and active in building such bridges. Its history attests that while the 1960s is often thought of as a decade whose pro-gressive movements were dominated by youth, mentoring from the older genera-tion contributed to building those movements and to shaping an antiracist ethos among the young. While these human relations groups did not generally provide for training activists per se, they promoted consciousness-raising that encouraged moderate white students to break with Jim Crow.

In part, the moderation of both the SCCHR and its South Carolina Student Council on Human Relations reflected the political realities of South Carolina, which took a middle-of-the-road approach to addressing racial problems. The SCCHR and its student council affiliate illustrate this prudence as well as the key role played by an older generation of advisors and mentors among student activists, especially in the status-conscious South. The SCCHR served as a conduit into lifelong activism for many students. Future leaders in academics and teaching, community service, law, the ministry, and politics received self-defining personal experiences through their participation in the SCCHR and the student council, demonstrating the enduring legacy of southern student activism.

The South Carolina Council on Human Relations and its Student Council on Human Relations sponsored integrated meetings and workshops where moderate and conservative college students could safely discuss racial issues in the last state in the deep South to desegregate its universities. The SCCHR, directed by Alice Norwood Spearman, and its student council, advised by Elizabeth ("Libby") Cowan Ledeen, paved the way for the peaceful desegregation of Clemson College and the University of South Carolina (USC) in 1963 and recruited black applicants to historically white colleges. Both councils collaborated in community development and antipoverty programs, educational tutorials, and voter registration. Moderate African American students influenced by the National Association for the Advancement of Colored People (NAACP) rather than by the Black Power movement also found friends in Spearman and Ledeen.

During its first five years, the student council expanded into a student movement in 23 of South Carolina's 31 colleges. Its Penn Center "stay-ins," described below, brought scores of students together each summer in the early to mid-1960s for discussions, sharing, and broadening of boundaries. The student council even managed to receive certification as one of 26 training agencies nationally—only four were in the South—for participating in the National Association of Intergroup Relations Officials–Eleanor Roosevelt Memorial Foundation Human Rights Internship Program.[1]

Spearman (1902–89) and Ledeen (1905–69) drew inspiration for their social activism from their liberal Baptist faith, their work with the student Young Women's Christian Association (YWCA), and their advanced degrees in religious education, earned, respectively, at Columbia Teachers' College and the Hartford Theological Seminary. Though Spearman was the granddaughter of one of South Carolina's largest slaveowners, her perspective on race was broadened by travel in

Europe and Asia, her work during the Depression administering Marion County's relief program, and her tenure as state supervisor for federal programs in adult and worker education. Positioned left of the New Deal consensus, she believed that President Franklin D. Roosevelt's relief programs did not go far enough in helping economically disadvantaged people.[2] She "wept" over many students' self-assumed white racial superiority: "They were," she recalled, "the most provincial, narrow-minded things I ever talked to in my life." Her persistent liberalism and cosmopolitanism shaped the South Carolina Council's programs, attracting small but dynamic groups of college students.[3] Spearman, observed Kenneth Dean, executive director of the sister Mississippi Council, was "the mother to a lot of young college people about race, politics, and progressive reform."[4]

Like Spearman, Libby Ledeen brought years of varied experiences to the SCCHR. A Baptist minister's daughter from Tennessee, she grew up in Greenwood, South Carolina, and Apex, North Carolina. Her work with the YWCA took her across the country. She directed religious education at the Congregational Church in West Hartford while her husband, Theodore John Ledeen, did special recreation work with migrant tobacco workers for the Connecticut Council of Churches. Moving to Columbia, South Carolina, Ledeen and her husband, a Congregational Christian Church minister, quickly involved themselves in mentoring students. She became executive director of the Community YWCA and directed Presbyterian student work for the Columbia area. Thus, Ledeen was well prepared for the multiple tasks of program director of the Student Council on Human Relations. She became Spearman's "junior partner" in the SCCHR office.[5]

In the 1960s the SCCHR became the first affiliate of the Southern Regional Council, a nonprofit organization that conducted research into racial discrimination and promoted voter education, to establish a student council. By June 1962, the student council had recruited some 280 students from 7 black and 13 white South Carolina colleges and universities. Under Ledeen's guidance, student council members held both one-day workshops and weekend conferences. Awakening to the civil rights movement, students discussed the role of students in the changing South with a special consideration of problems in higher education, economic growth and development, political life, citizenship, and religious life. Seeing an opportunity to break through "the conspiracy of silence," as Ledeen put it, they endeavored to persuade South Carolinians to embrace justice and racial equality. The student council succeeded in bringing moderate white students into the civil rights movement and in encouraging black students' demands for equal rights; it served as a model for other state student councils.[6] The student council's collegial tone was set by its first president, Charles Joyner, then a USC history PhD student who attributed his election to his talent with the guitar and knowledge of freedom songs.[7]

Spearman and Ledeen's vision for a statewide biracial student organization took on new urgency when African American students from Friendship Junior College held sit-ins in Rock Hill, South Carolina, on 12 February 1960, following the 1 February Greensboro, North Carolina, sit-in. Spearman quickly recognized that sit-ins were "the first effective demands by Negroes for social change; change in their status as consumers, citizens, and persons." They "dramatically pointed up again the urgent need for leadership recruitment and training, and for developing meaningful communication among Negroes and white people." After its 6 March open meeting became racially divided over the sit-ins, the SCCHR's executive board drafted, in closed session, a moderate statement for the press. The sit-ins were "an understandable protest by citizens of South Carolina against continued unequal treatment in the use of public facilities and services." Commending both the orderliness of the demonstrators and police restraint, the council offered "to initiate discussions and negotiations" leading to an acceptable solution that recognized all citizens were entitled to "the full rights and courtesies enjoyed by other citizens."[8]

That February, Thomas Gaither, head of the Claflin College chapter of the NAACP and a future field secretary of the Congress of Racial Equality, formed the Orangeburg Student Movement Association (SMA). Before their 1 March mass demonstration, the SMA trained about one thousand Claflin and South Carolina State College students according to the nonviolent principles of CORE and Martin Luther King Jr.'s Southern Christian Leadership Conference (SCLC). With only a few white student council members joining the sit-ins (since participation threatened them with police surveillance and possible dismissal from college), the sit-in movement in Columbia, the capital of South Carolina and location of USC, "was late, timid, and short-lived," observed Paul S. Lofton Jr., a student council member. With heavy participation by African American students, sit-ins in Orangeburg, Rock Hill, and Sumter were "considerably more turbulent and disruptive." On 15 March the Orangeburg SMA launched a demonstration coinciding with similar protests in Rock Hill and Columbia. Police hosed and gassed over a thousand students, filled Orangeburg jails, and caged another 350 demonstrators in a chicken stockade. There, in 45-degree weather, they sang "God Bless America" and "The Star-Spangled Banner." Among the two hundred students arrested for protesting at the Orangeburg courthouse were Gaither and South Carolina State College student Charles "Chuck" McDew, later to become the second chairman of the Student Nonviolent Coordinating Committee (SNCC).[9] In justifying these arrests, Governor Hollings said, "They think they can violate any law, especially if they have a Bible in their hands: our law enforcement officers have their Bibles, too."[10] Charged with "breach of the peace," the students appealed their sentences of $100 fine or 30 days in jail, citing their right to peaceful assembly. In 1963, the U.S. Supreme Court reversed the students' convictions and the ruling of the South Carolina Supreme Court.[11]

In Columbia, students at historically black Allen University and Benedict College, responding to sit-ins elsewhere, planned their own demonstration. To coordinate the black student campaign for integration, the South Carolina Student Movement was launched on 5 March.[12] Concerned that "outside, selfish, antagonist groups" were influencing students, Governor Hollings sent South Carolina Law Enforcement Division chief J. Preston "Pete" Strom to persuade the presidents of Allen and Benedict to call off a student prayer and song pilgrimage to the statehouse.[13] Despite such official harassment, the sit-in movement gathered steam; by the next school year, Spearman observed, the sit-ins were "in full swing."[14]

Official harassment continued. On 2 March 1961 police arrested and jailed 187 high school and college students marching from Zion Baptist Church to the State Capitol grounds, together with two NAACP adult leaders. Sentenced to a $100 ($50 for minors) fine or 30 days in jail for breach of peace, they, too, appealed their convictions to the U.S. Supreme Court.[15] The students had behaved in an orderly fashion, argued attorney Matthew J. Perry; those disrupting traffic were spectators, none of whom was arrested. NAACP Legal Defense Fund attorneys Jack Greenberg and Constance Baker Motley added their arguments, convincing the Supreme Court to reverse, in an 8 to 1 decision, the students' sentences. Their arrests, convictions, and punishments, wrote Justice Potter Stewart, "infringed the petitioners' constitutionally protected rights of free speech, free assembly, and freedom to petition for redress of their grievances." Once the demonstrations waned, Governor Hollings took satisfaction that "no one was hurt or seriously injured" during his administration.[16]

The sit-in movement caught on in other cities. Rock Hill's sit-ins gained national prominence on 6 February 1961 with SNCC's region-wide call for students to join the Friendship Junior College demonstrators. Four SNCC leaders arrived: Charles Jones from Charlotte, Charles Sherrod (Virginia Union University), Ruby Doris Smith (Spelman College), and Diane Nash (Fisk University). Arrested and convicted for demonstrating, Friendship Junior College students and the SNCC leaders were sentenced to 30 days in the York County Jail or the York County Prison Farm.[17] By serving out their sentences, they strengthened SNCC's "jail, no bail" policy. "Many SNCC staff and Ella J. Baker subsequently marked Rock Hill as the true beginning of the organization," said activist Mary King, "because of the way it blended SNCC people with a local movement." As a SNCC worker observed, "It was not until four outsiders joined with the Rock Hill students to fight a common enemy—segregation—that we realized until all are free, no one is free."[18]

Racial confrontation in Rock Hill again made headlines when, on 4 May 1961, the CORE-sponsored Freedom Riders arrived from Washington, D.C., en route to New Orleans for the 17 May anniversary of the 1954 *Brown v. Board of Education* desegregation decision. John Lewis, knocked down by white youths, declared that his rights were protected by the Supreme Court decision banning segregation in interstate travel, but he and others declined to press charges after the Rock Hill police broke up the fray.[19]

Against this escalating backdrop, the South Carolina Student Council convened its May conference on desegregation at the Penn Community Center on St. Helena Island. The Penn Center conferences provided the focal point for the work of the SCCHR and the student council for the next several years. Seventeen black students traveled from Allen University and Benedict, Claflin, and Morris colleges and from Atlanta's Morehouse, Morris Brown, and Spelman colleges to the coastal enclave. Eleven white students came from Clemson and Wofford colleges and USC. Spearman and Ledeen participated, as did Constance Curry of the Southern Student Human Relations Project and Southern Regional Council president James McBride Dabbs and his wife, Edith.[20] More than two hundred students and faculty participated. Student government and student religious leaders and campus newspapers editors proposed "a new student movement," which they called "the 'Stay-ins'—stay in South Carolina." By staying and working to improve race relations, white students believed that they, together with black students, could make South Carolina a more progressive state. White students actively encouraged black students, who began to learn "that the real tragedy of the South is not the Negro, for he will win, but the prejudiced southern white, who will need helping long after the so-called 'Negro problem' has been solved."[21] The student council's steering committee "democratically" planned two such conferences each academic year, giving members "leadership training."[22]

After attending the Penn Center and the workshops, reported Ledeen, student campus leaders and student council members became "instrumental in creating a social climate" for peaceful desegregation in South Carolina. Among encouraging signs were a Baptist Student Convention resolution "requesting that all Baptist colleges be opened to qualified students without regard to race" and a resolution at the state conference of Student Christian Associations, the first of its kind, calling for "the conference to study the whole matter of race relations in the light of our Christian Faith with the possibility of eventually becoming a desegregated conference."[23]

As massive resistance sentiment declined, Columbia's leaders began to work on racial problems, and here the SCCHR constructively participated. In 1961, Columbia Mayor Lester Bates met with Alice Spearman, Reverend Fred M. Reese Jr., a Methodist minister and chairman of the South Carolina Council, and planned "a quiet, orderly lunch counter desegregation" within the city. Bates courted local black elites while shrewdly allying himself with the city's white business community. Working behind the scenes, Bates met occasionally with moderate black leaders and various local "experts." From such conversations the dynamics of lunch counter desegregation in Columbia informally evolved. Under a trial plan in 1962, "all variety stores, drug stores and the like agreed to try-out providing desegregated service for a period of two weeks." With its staff members as observers or sitting at lunch counters, the South Carolina Council's quiet form of "direct action" helped the movement succeed, as did students, Columbia Council on Human Relations members, and other progressive whites.[24]

But the SCCHR paid a price. "Numerous anonymous phone calls" asked: "Is this the office of the NAACP?" A part-time black bookkeeper decided not to return after an aggressive white man barged into the office. Another white man identifying himself as a special representative of the U.S. Chamber of Commerce asked Spearman detailed questions about the council's history, leadership, and membership. She later learned that he investigated suspected Communists and reported them to the relevant authorities in Washington, D.C. A registered letter from the building's management told her to move the SCCHR office. Student council members also faced reprisals for their activism. Under political pressure, both M. Hayes Mizell and Charles Joyner found their $1,500 assistantships revoked, allegedly for academic weakness. But the real reason was that both had led the South Carolina Council's biracial Workshop for College Students. USC later renewed Joyner's assistantship, since he, unlike Mizell, had not actually participated in an earlier February 1961 sit-in at a Columbia Woolworth's.[25] Mizell would continue a distinguished public career on behalf of integration and educational reform. Joyner became a leading historian of slavery and southern life.

By January 1962, Governor Hollings recognized that "South Carolina's legal defenses will fall like a house of cards" when desegregation lawsuits reached the federal courts. Since "we are not going to secede," Hollings intoned, the press should begin to prepare "readers for the inevitable." Hollings met informally with business leaders and Clemson College administrators and also quietly communicated with J. Arthur Brown, president of the South Carolina State Conference of NAACP Branches, about finding a qualified black applicant to desegregate Clemson. Christopher Gantt, a rigger mechanic at the Charleston Navy Yard, agreed that his 20-year-old son, Harvey Bernard Gantt, then at Iowa State University, could apply to study architecture.[26]

Closely monitoring Gantt's lawsuit, the SCCHR provided its office for a conference with Gantt, his attorney Matthew Perry, and the Rev. I. DeQuincey Newman,

Figure 4.1. South Carolina Student Council on Human Relations members Charles Joyner and Hayes Mizell on the campus of the University of South Carolina, c. 1961. Like Mizell, student council members sometimes faced sanctions from their respective university administrators for their civil rights activism. Courtesy the South Caroliniana Library at the University of South Carolina.

field secretary of the South Carolina State NAACP. The Council's Education and the Schools Committee and its Student Council maintained lines of communication with faculty and students at Clemson and USC. As "the only continuous biracial channel," the student council invited Gantt to the Penn Conference Center in December. Discussing "the Student's Involvement in the Crisis of the South," they made, said Ledeen, "friendship and genuine acceptance a natural and normal part of The Clemson Story."[27] Hollings's farewell address in January 1963 called on the General Assembly to accept their responsibilities to maintain "law and order" and to "move on with dignity." Setting a new tone with his biracial inauguration day barbecue buffet, Governor Donald S. Russell then implemented a campus security plan to ensure Gantt's peaceful enrollment under federal district court order on 28 January.[28]

At their 1963 spring conference, student council members prepared for USC's desegregation. Working with campus chaplains, Ledeen planned "to bring student leaders and the Negro students seeking admission together for a conference."[29] When Columbia resident Henrie Dobbins Monteith's lawsuit came before the federal district court in June, USC acknowledged denying her admission because "she was a Negro." The judge ordered her admission. USC also admitted Robert G. Anderson Jr. of Greenville as a transfer student from Atlanta's Clark College and James L. Solomon, a Morris College instructor, as a graduate student in mathematics. They enrolled peacefully on 11 September.[30]

Yet USC's racial climate remained chilly, as documented by Ginnie Good, a sophomore from Kalamazoo College in Michigan, whom Spearman hired as an office intern in the spring of 1964. Good, a Marylander considered a "Yankee," discussed in her job report on "South Carolina—My Burden," learning "very quickly that another man's bondage directly affected my own freedom." She befriended Robert Anderson, who did not have family and friends in Columbia. This "very sensitive and alone young man" told her, "Ginnie, you're the only white girl that's ever treated me like I was a human being." But Anderson would not let her share the same couch in the Wesley Foundation lounge. For Good, "the tragedy that this nineteen year old college junior had never been recognized for his own worth is the tragedy of the South." Good was "continually amazed that Mrs. Spearman, the executive director, and Mrs. Ledeen, the program director, both white Southerners, could have turned out so open-minded and alive."[31]

Despite the integration of Clemson and USC under federal court orders, South Carolina's racial culture remained largely unchanged. What was needed was not only judicial desegregation but also an honest discussion of common problems and a commitment to seek mutually satisfactory solutions. So the SCCHR and the student council drew on their experience in encouraging biracial dialogue and in developing programs to help black South Carolinians. The student council offered new initiatives: tutoring younger students, registering voters, and assisting in community development and antipoverty programs. Educators lauded the tutorial program in Columbia for both "upgrading the students academically" and "in a very real way preparing them to live in an integrated society," since most of the students "have never before had contact with a white person who has accepted them as fellow human beings." The statewide student council collaborated with the Columbia Student Council on Human Relations, co-chaired by Mary Carlton O'Neal (USC, 1964) and by Benedict College student Mary Ann Eaddy.[32]

The Penn Center conferences remained crucial to the SCCHR's and student council's interactions with college students in the state. The 6–8 December 1963 conference drew 75 students from 15 South Carolina colleges. Addressing its theme, "The New Revolution: Challenge and Response," Vernon Jordan of the Southern Regional Council staff analyzed the civil rights revolution. Task force groups discussed "Feelings and Fears: An Honest Confrontation," "Ways of Work on the Local Campus," "The Role of the Church," "Student Responsibility in the Community," "Students and the Freedom Movement," and other such topics.[33] The student council's 10–12 April 1964 Penn Center conference on Africa drew the largest attendance ever, with 135 students coming from 15 South Carolina and 2 North Carolina colleges. Such a conference would promote international understanding and enhance America's image abroad, noted Hayes Mizell, a former graduate student member of the student council and in 1963 a foreign service reserve officer with the U.S. Information Agency. The USIA's Africa Division broadcast on African radio stations brief taped excerpts from the conference; it later distributed a more extensive story, with photographs, to African newspapers.[34]

The student council continued to extend its work throughout the state. Recognizing that education was vital to progress, the student council expanded its "Operation Search," the only program in South Carolina informing black high school students of college application steps. Members of its Recruiting Committee, chaired by Harvey Gantt, visited twelve communities to hold conferences with high school students. Because of its goal, "Beyond Tokenism," South Carolina received a higher percentage of Lehman Fund scholarships for blacks applying to desegregated colleges than any other state.[35]

To end the last vestiges of massive resistance to the *Brown* decision, student council members formed a Committee for a Compulsory School Attendance Law (CO-CO-SAL) seeking to reinstate the compulsory school attendance law—which had been repealed by the South Carolina General Assembly in 1955 when segregationists were of a mind to close public schools rather than integrate them. Chiefly functioning as an information-distributing committee to some five hundred selected citizens statewide, CO-CO-SAL "was handicapped by a lack of money, the fear of jeopardizing the tax-exempt status of the adult Council, by the lack of leadership and the unwillingness of the rank-and-file members to work," observed Mizell, who judged the student council's actual accomplishments as "modest," though it did foster "relationships that resulted in some students increasing their activism." In 1964, he moved to Atlanta to direct the National Student Association's Southern Student Human Relations Project.[36]

This period, 1964 through 1965, after the galvanizing moment of the sit-ins but before the broader radicalization of student groups such as SNCC and Students for a Democratic Society, was the high-water mark of the SCCHR and the student council. For Ledeen, it was an exciting, "more permissive" time than earlier, and it taxed her organizational ability, she confessed to Dan Carter, then a PhD student at the University of North Carolina at Chapel Hill. "We are working with many local communities," she wrote, "in assisting groups interested in the economic opportunity program, developing tutorials, implementing various facets of the civil rights law and doing a myriad things which need desperately to be done and which no other group is doing in [South Carolina]." She entreated Carter: "Please don't forget S.C. as you make your future plans."[37]

But new, more militant student groups were forming elsewhere. Some white South Carolinians hailed the formation of the Southern Student Organizing Committee in Nashville in April 1964. SSOC's manifesto, written largely by SDS leader Robb Burlage, proclaimed, "We, as young Southerners hereby pledge to take our stand together here to work for a new order, a new South, a place which embodies our ideals for all the world to emulate, not ridicule." By agreeing not to organize chapters in the South, SDS allowed SSOC to build up its own membership, which included about 5 percent blacks and other nonwhites. In November 1964, Libby Ledeen, together with USC and Winthrop College students, attended SSOC's first South-wide conference in Atlanta. The student council participated at SSOC's planning committee meeting in December and sent eight student leaders to the second SSOC conference in March 1965. Jerry Gainey, who in 1962 had presented to the state House of Representatives Education Committee a petition signed by 180 Clemson students opposing the segregationist private school tuition grant bill, was disappointed that the repressive political climate kept SSOC from generating white activism at Clemson. By 1967, however, "one of SSOC's most vibrant chapters" developed at the Baptist-affiliated Furman University in upstate Greenville. During its five years of activity, SSOC championed equal rights, university reform, and women's liberation, while opposing racism, segregation, poverty, and the Vietnam War.[38]

The positive experiences of student council members, together with their prevailing religious beliefs and strong commitment to racial justice, led them to serve others, often far beyond the borders of South Carolina, and this was one of the SCCHR's lasting legacies. Jerry Gainey served in the Peace Corps in Thailand, and another Clemson graduate, Hal Littleton, active in the campus YMCA, was elected student body president at Southeastern Seminary in Wake Forest. George Sadler entered Johnson C. Smith University, a historically black college in Charlotte, to prepare for the ministry. Mary Carlton O'Neal enrolled at Yale Divinity School. Wofford graduate Wiley B. Cooper entered Candler Theological School at Emory University. Henry Smith and J. P. Bethune (USC) finished a year of language study in Belgium before beginning a short term of service for the Methodist Board of Missions in the Congo. Paul Cash enrolled as the USC Law School's first black student, though he did not graduate. Ginnie Good went as an exchange student to Sierra Leone before returning to Kalamazoo College. Freddie Williams finished his first year of teaching in Darlington despite a serious automobile accident.

Noting their accomplishments, Ledeen exclaimed, "What an inspiration it has been to me to work with all you wonderful students."[39]

Ledeen and Spearman's reputation for mentorship was long remembered by student council members. One was Morris College student Freddie Williams. As an intern in the summer of 1962, Williams contacted federal and state agencies about their resources, conducted fieldwork and interviews, and attended community meetings.[40] Spearman put aside her own summer vacation plans to accompany Williams on field trips and encouraged him to work with USC Student Council member Dan Carter, whose critical perspective on segregation and massive resistance later contributed to his emergence as a leading southern historian who would go on to write the definitive biography of George Wallace. Carter and Williams met several times to discuss Williams's research project on local race relations.[41] Under Spearman's guidance, Williams drafted questions for his Florence city survey, for example: "In what ways have conditions changed in your community to affect Negroes; for better, or for the worse?"[42] Williams also cooperated with the newly formed Florence Committee on Negro Affairs in studying, with the help of youth groups, the entire Florence community. This committee obtained from the city council another baseball field for black youth and pointed out the unpaved streets, drainage problems, and poor housing in black neighborhoods. A voter registration drive added five hundred blacks and aimed to register another one thousand before the November election. "Only a few people are able to fight for freedom and equality," Williams observed, "because they are afraid of loss of position or job." Through his work at the South Carolina Council, Williams gained research and analytical skills and learned techniques of community organization. His report convinced Spearman: "No community will move until Negroes, fortified with the facts and a resolve to change things both for themselves and their children, confront the white people of their respective communities and offer cooperation toward building progressive communities, free of discrimination and offering full use of all public facilities to every citizen."[43]

Another student whose leadership talents were ignited under the tutelage of Spearman and Ledeen was Thomas Bradford Poston of Union, South Carolina (USC BA in psychology, 1965). Poston developed a range of skills by working on personnel, nominations, membership, finance, and public relations and by serving as a secretary for a Presidents' Council of local groups. He also served as state vice president of the student council.[44] He recruited 104 students and leaders from 15 South Carolina colleges for the October 1965 Penn Center conference, which focused on "Poverty in South Carolina." Among the speakers was the fearless Modjeska Simkins, assistant cashier of the black-owned Victory Savings Bank, director of publicity and public relations of the Richland County Citizens

Committee, and a vice president of the Southern Conference Educational Fund. While Poston agreed with Anti-Defamation League intern Melinda Friedman that "the conference lacked depth and long-range commitment on the part of the students," he emphasized that compared to previous conferences it had "much more substance." Acknowledging the difficulty of planning programs for students whose social awareness and biracial experiences ranged from minimal or none to the highly activist SDS members, Poston and the student council addressed, during four work-study weekends in February 1966, such urban and rural poverty issues in Charleston as the refusal to rent housing to blacks, restricted residential neighborhoods, and the urban ghettos.[45]

Another of Poston's responsibilities involved preparing for the Student Program for Economic and Educational Development for Underprivileged People (SPEED-UP), a collaborative project between the South Carolina Council and the student council, funded by a one-year Office of Economic Opportunity demonstration grant totaling $137,454. About 110 students from 23 South Carolina colleges worked on SPEED-UP teams in 28 neighborhood centers in 13 counties. More than two thousand children took classes with college student tutors in elementary English, mathematics, drama, art, sewing, and Negro History, and even more participated in afternoon recreational and cultural activities.[46]

Despite the exaggerated concern of Columbia College president R. Wright Spears that possibly "white students from Greenville might be living in Negro homes in Berkeley County—and vice versa," Poston, Ledeen, and Spearman were pleased with the results of SPEED-UP, which officially ended 1 September 1966 when the federal antipoverty program budget was cut. Poston felt his Eleanor Roosevelt Internship was "invaluable": "The dedication of the staff and the capability of the Executive Director have made more happen than is usually possible in a year."[47]

Ledeen and Spearman provided support during Poston's "draft crisis" in 1965. After the local draft board refused postponement until completion of his internship, Spearman wrote President Lyndon B. Johnson, emphasizing both Poston's maturity and contributions to the council's human relations work. For Spearman, *"Effective service on the home front may determine our destiny as a nation* even more crucially than our military EFFORTS ABROAD." Poston had, she wrote, "imagination, adaptability, creativity, sensitivity, and near-genius in working with all kinds of groups and individuals." Though taking issue with her reference to South Carolina as "provincial and backward," Colonel Donald H. Collins at the state's Headquarters of Selective Service acquiesced in the National Headquarters for Selective Service's request to postpone his induction.[48]

As an alternative to military service, Poston enlisted in the Peace Corps, for which he worked in Botswana. His "heart is often back in S.C.," he wrote Ledeen, wanting to know about the student council and SPEED-UP, what campuses had tutorial programs, and whether there were new staff members. He urged that Henrie Monteith, acting SPEED-UP director, involve international students. "Don't I wish," he wrote, "there were hundreds of S.C. college students rushing wildly about looking for all these things to do in the area of social change!"[49]

By the mid-1960s, many of South Carolina's white college students no longer felt threatened by the consequences of joining the student council, but they still perceived SNCC and SDS as radical. When in October 1963 Sam Shirah came to USC as white field organizer for SNCC, supported by the Southern Conference Educational Fund, he was arrested for trespassing, though the charges were later dropped.[50] Although some southern whites joined SNCC through the organizing efforts of Bob Zellner, an Alabama minister's son, that organization primarily attracted blacks and northern whites. In Georgia, SNCC was far more influential in pushing desegregation than in South Carolina.[51]

Columbia was "a place of excitement and challenge for students in the early 1960s," recalled Jean Toal, elected the first woman chief justice of the South Carolina Supreme Court in 1999. Compared to Mississippi, South Carolina was "a slightly easier" state to desegregate, but she acknowledged Orangeburg's real problems of racial and economic discrimination that led to blacks demonstrating against a segregated bowling alley on 8 February 1968. Shooting by state police killed two South Carolina State College students and a high school student and wounded 28 others. Among the wounded was Cleveland Sellers Jr., a native of Denmark, South Carolina, and a former SNCC program director who was sentenced to prison for allegedly causing the riot. Twenty-five years later, after passions had cooled, Sellers received a belated and well-deserved pardon from Governor Carroll Campbell. After serving as a faculty member and undergraduate director in USC's African-American Studies Program, Sellers was appointed president of Voorhees College in 2008. Governor Robert McNair ultimately accepted responsibility for the Orangeburg massacre.[52]

Before her retirement in September 1967, Alice Spearman's dedicated service as executive director was recognized by an honorary doctorate in humanities from Morris College (1964) and by appointment to the South Carolina Advisory Committee to the U.S. Civil Rights Commission (1965). But she felt "just burned out" by the increasing demands for staff interviews for planning, projecting, and coordinating programs. She was disappointed that "South Carolina did not develop a sophisticated, disciplined student sit-in movement in the early sixties, nor have students yet become an identifiable force for change," with the exceptions of Brad Poston and several others. Though the state did not produce "a civil rights movement comparable in any sense to the movements in Alabama or in Mississippi," the South Carolina Council under her directorship and its student council under Elizabeth Ledeen's guidance helped give "Negroes the confidence that they could win" and had broadened the intellectual and social horizons of white college students, awakening their moral responsibility to work for equal civil rights for all.[53]

NOTES

1. [Elizabeth C. Ledeen], "The Situation in the Colleges in South Carolina," c. fall of 1960, file "1961, Student Council, 1960–1969 & n.d.," box 10, South Carolina Council on Human Relations (SCCHR) Records, 1934–1976 (hereafter cited as SCCHRR), South Caroliniana Library, University of South Carolina, Columbia, South Carolina (hereafter cited as SCL). Prior to the formation of the South Carolina Student Council on Human Relations (hereafter cited as SCSCHR) in December 1960, a Student Intercollegiate Group in Columbia brought students together for discussions from USC; Columbia College, a Methodist-affiliated woman's college; the Lutheran Theological Seminary; Allen University, an African American Methodist Episcopal coeducational college; and Benedict College, an African American Baptist coeducational college.

2. Alice Buck Norwood, BA in history and literature from Converse College (1923), took courses at Union Theological Seminary and at the resident YWCA National Training School. She married Eugene H. Spearman, a dairy and tree farmer in Newberry, in 1935, and attorney Marion A. Wright, a former Southern Regional Council president, in 1970. See Marcia G. Synnott, "Crusaders and Clubwomen: Alice Norwood Spearman Wright and Her Women's Network," in *Throwing Off the Cloak of Privilege: White Southern Women Activists in the Civil Rights Era*, ed. Gail S. Murray, in the Southern Dissent Series, ed. Stanley Harrold and Randall M. Miller (Gainesville: Univ. Press of Florida, 2004; paperback, 2008), 49–76.

3. Alice Spearman Wright, interview with the author, 11 July 1983, Linville Falls, North Carolina, transcript, Oral History Program at SCL (hereafter cited as OHP, SCL).

4. Dr. Leslie Dunbar and Kenneth Dean, notes of conversation with author, 11 Nov. 1994, Atlanta, Georgia.

5. Elizabeth Cowan Ledeen's curriculum vitae, file no. 277, box 9 Staff, SCCHRR-SCL. She earned a B.S. in Home Economics from the Woman's College of the University of North Carolina in Greensboro. In 1968, with SCCHR's hiring of an associate director, she was shifted from directing student work and building up local councils to part-time director of information. Retiring in the spring, she died later in 1969. The Elizabeth C. Ledeen Scholarship at USC, awarded to an American or international minority student, honors her work with students.

6. Alice N. Spearman, quarterly report, Dec. 1959–Feb. 1960, box 9, no. 279; quarterly reports, Sept. 1960–Nov. 1960, and Dec. 1960–Feb. 1961, box 9, no. 280; [Ledeen], Situation in the Colleges in South Carolina; Purpose of the Student Program of the SCCHR; and Student Program of the SCCHR, 9 Jan. 1961, file "1961 Student Council, 1960–1969," box 10, SCCHRR-SCL.

7. Charles Joyner, " 'One People': Creating an Integrated Culture in a Segregated Society, 1526–1990," in *The Meaning of South Carolina History: Essays in Honor of George C. Rogers, Jr.*, ed. David R. Chesnutt and Clyde N. Wilson (Columbia: Univ. of South Carolina Press, 1991), 229–31, 214–44.

8. Martin Oppenheimer, *The Sit-In Movement of 1960* (Brooklyn, NY: Carlson Publishing, 1989), 146–52; minutes, executive board meeting of SCCHR, 6 Mar. 1960, file "Board of Directors, 1956–1961," box 8, no. 243; and Alice N. Spearman, quarterly report, June 1960–Aug. 1960, box 9, no. 280, SCCHRR-SCL; Paul Rilling, Anniston, Alabama, notes of telephone interview by author, 7 Sept. 1997; Rilling, interoffice memo to Harold Fleming and Paul Anthony, report on visit to South Carolina, 6 and 7 Mar., 10 Mar. 1960, series 4, reel 146, 0436–0438, Southern Regional Council Papers, 1944–1968 (hereafter cited as SRCP).

9. Paul S. Lofton, "Calm and Exemplary: Desegregation in Columbia, South Carolina," in *Southern Businessmen and Desegregation*, ed. Elizabeth Jacoway and David R. Colburn (Baton Rouge: LSU Press, 1982), 72, 75; Oppenheimer, *Sit-In Movement of 1960*, 169–71; William C. Hine, "Civil Rights and Campus Wrongs: South Carolina State College Students Protest, 1955–1968," *South Carolina Historical Magazine* 97 (Oct. 1996), 322–24; Harrison Salisbury, cover story, *New York Times*, 16 Mar. 1960; Thomas Gaither, "Orangeburg: Behind the Carolina Stockade," *Sit-Ins: The Students Report* (New York: CORE, 1960), 9–11; *Veterans of the Civil Rights Movement—Sit-Ins: The Students Report*, available at www.crmvet.org/docs/sitin/sitin-11.pdf; "Voices from the Civil Rights Movement in South Carolina: Charles F. McDew, Constance Curry, Matthew J. Perry, Harvey B. Gantt," in *Toward the Meeting of the Waters: Currents in the Civil Rights Movement of South Carolina during the Twentieth Century*, ed. Winfred B. Moore Jr. and Orville Vernon Burton (Columbia: Univ. of South Carolina Press, 2008), 337–58.

10. Ernest F. Hollings, quoted in Gaither, "Orangeburg," 10.

11. Oppenheimer, *Sit-In Movement of 1960*, 169–71; Hine, "Civil Rights and Campus Wrongs," 322–24; *Freedom and Justice: The Struggle for Civil Rights, Featuring the Photography of Cecil J. Williams* (1994), CQ Television Network, Inc., Cayce, South Carolina.

12. Oppenheimer, *Sit-In Movement of 1960*, 152–57; Spearman, quarterly reports, Mar. 1960–May 1960 and June 1960–Aug. 1960, box 9, no. 280, SCCHRR.

13. Lofton, "Calm and Exemplary," 75–76; Statement from Governor's Office, 10 Mar. 1960, file no. 15, and Press Release, 6 Apr. 1960, file no. 14, "Segregation," Papers of Governor Ernest F. Hollings, S.C. Department of Archives and History, Columbia; The Students to President J. A. Bacoats, News Release on sit-ins [1960?], file "Desegregation: Sit-Ins," box 35; "Students Disclaim Sit-Ins," [Columbia, S.C.] *State*, 18 Feb. 1961, clipping, file "Colleges and Universities: Allen University," box 40, SCCHRR, [Columbia, S.C.] *State*, 3 Mar. 1960, A-1, 9; 4 Mar. 1960, A-1, 9; 6 Mar. 1960, A-2; 11 Mar. 1960, A-1; 12 Mar. 1960, A-6; 15 Mar. 1960, A-1; 16 Mar. 1960, A-1, 5.

14. Wright, interview by the author, 10 July 1983, transcript, OHP, SCL; Spearman, quarterly report, Dec. 1960–Feb. 1961, box 9, no. 280.

15. Oppenheimer, *Sit-In Movement of 1960*, 155–57; *State*, 3 Mar. 1961, D-1.

16. *Edwards v. South Carolina*, 372 U.S. 229 (1963); Burke Marshall, *Federalism and Civil Rights* (New York and London, 1964), 9, 49–76; Senator Ernest F. Hollings, interview by the author, Columbia, South Carolina, 8 July 1980, transcript, South Carolina Political Collections, University of South Carolina Libraries, USC (hereafter cited as SCPC).

17. Alice N. Spearman to Paul Rilling, 9 Feb. 1961 and 20 Feb. 1961; and clipping, *Greenville News*, 12 Feb. 1961; and Margaret H. Gregg, letter to the editor, *Rock Hill Evening Herald*, 10 Feb. 1961, series four, reel 147, 0745, 0747, 0748, 0749–0750, SRCP; Spearman, quarterly report, Dec. 1960–Feb. 1961, box 9, no. 280.

18. Mary King, *Freedom Song: A Personal Story of the 1960s Civil Rights Movement* (New York: William Morrow, 1987), 316; Oppenheimer, *Sit-In Movement of 1960*, 149; John Hardy,

South Carolina Report, n.d., series 8, reel 22, 0823–0824, Student Nonviolent Coordinating Committee Papers (SNCC Papers), 1959–1972; Student Nonviolent Movement, News Release, "Jailed Sit-Ins Given Solitary," [c. Feb.–Mar. 1960], file "Desegregation: Sit-Ins," box 35, SCCHRR. See Barbara Ransby, *Ella Baker and the Black Freedom Movement: A Radical Democratic Vision* (Chapel Hill: Univ. of North Carolina Press, 2003). The Friendship Nine received the South Carolina NAACP's Civil Rights Advocacy Award at its annual Freedom Fund Celebration, 20 May 2011.

19. Taylor Branch, *Parting the Waters: America in the King Years, 1954–1963* (New York: Simon and Schuster, 1988), 415–16, 412–50, 451–91; David Halberstam, *The Children* (New York: Fawcett Books, 1999), 67–70, 246–57, 419.

20. Summary of Student Program: Eighteen-month Pilot Project, Dec. 1960–June 1962, file "Student Council 1962," box 10; Student Conference, Penn Center, Frogmore, South Carolina, 5–7 May 1961, file "Oct.–Dec. 1962," box 3; Spearman, quarterly report, Mar. 1961–May 1961, box 9, no. 280; Constance Curry to Libby Ledeen, 11 May 1961; [Ledeen] to Curry, 18 May 1961, thanking her "helpful leadership" and "arranging for the Atlanta students to participate," file "May–June 1961," box 2, SCCHRR; Alice N. Spearman to Paul Rilling, 28 Mar. 1961; Charles W. Joyner to Rilling, 17 Apr. 1961, 0700; Elizabeth C. Ledeen to Rilling, 2 May 1961, series 4, reel 146, 0697–0700, 0703, SRCP.

21. Evaluation of the Student Program, [1961/1962], file "Student Council 1961," box 10.

22. [Ledeen], report of program director, Dec. 1963–Feb. 1964, box 9, no. 281; report of Program Director, Mar. 1965–May 1965, box 9, no. 289.

23. Summary of Student Program: Eighteen-month Pilot Project; Elizabeth C. Ledeen to Dr. and Mrs. J. A. Bacoats, 5 Dec. 1961, file "Student Council 1961," box 10, Student Workshop, 3 Dec. 1961, series 4, reel 146, 1236–1237, SRCP.

24. Reverend Fred M. Reese Jr., interview by the author, Columbia, South Carolina, 13 Dec. 1994, transcript, OHP, SCL; Lofton, "Calm and Exemplary," 73–74, 77–78; *Columbia Record*, 10 Nov. 1955, B-1; *Anderson Independent,* 26 May 1954, 3; and "Weep No More Columbia," *Newsweek,* 3 May 1965. See Miles Richards, *A History of the Columbia Luncheon Club,* ed. Sarah McCrory (Columbia, S.C., 2005).

25. M. Hayes Mizell, Edna McConnell Clark Foundation, "The Impact of the Civil Rights Movement on a White Activist," Southern Historical Association, Fort Worth, Texas, 4 Nov. 1999, *MiddleWeb | Hayes Mizell Civil Rights Days,* available at www.middleweb.com/mw/resources/HMhistory.html.

26. Ernest F. Hollings, quoted in George McMillan, "Integration with Dignity: The Inside Story of How South Carolina Kept the Peace," *Saturday Evening Post,* 16 Mar. 1963, 17, 18, 20; Hollings interview; *Gantt v. Clemson Agricultural College of South Carolina,* 320 F. 2d 611 (1963); Maxie Myron Cox Jr., "1963—The Year of Decision: Desegregation in South Carolina" (PhD diss., Univ. of South Carolina, 1996), 14–143. Edmund L. Drago, *Initiative, Paternalism, and Race Relations: Charleston's Avery Normal Institute* (Athens and London: Univ. of Georgia Press, 1990), 276–77; Orville Vernon Burton, "Dining with Harvey Gantt: Myths and Realities of 'Integration with Dignity,'" in *Matthew J. Perry: The Man, His Times, and His Legacy,* ed. W. Lewis Burke and Belinda F. Gergel (Columbia: Univ. of South Carolina Press, 2004), 183–220.

27. Minutes, board of directors meeting, 12 Feb. 1962, box 9, no. 244; Spearman, quarterly report, Mar. 1962–May 1962, no. 280; Ledeen, program director, report of the SCSCHR, Penn Center, 7–9 Dec. 1962, in quarterly report, Dec. 1962–Feb. 1963, box 9, no. 281; "The Quotes of the Year," SCSCHR, file "October–December 1962," box 3.

28. Hollings interview; Hollings, quoted in McMillan, "Integration with Dignity," 20; M. Ron Cox Jr., "'Integration with [Relative] Dignity': The Desegregation of Clemson College and George McMillan's Article at Forty," in *Toward the Meeting of the Waters,* ed. Moore and Burton, 274–85. Judge Donald S. Russell, interview by the author and Herbert J. Hartsook, Spartanburg, South Carolina, 6 July 1992, transcript, SCPC; Leslie Skinner, "Sibling Institutions, Similar Experiences: The Coeducation and Integration Experiences of South Carolina's Clemson and Winthrop Universities" (PhD diss., Univ. of South Carolina, 2002); Harvey Bernard Gantt, interview by the author, Charlotte, North Carolina, 14 July 1980, transcript, OHP, SCL. After graduating with honors (1965), Gantt married Lucinda Brawley, the second African American to enroll at Clemson in September 1963. He earned a Master of City Planning degree from the Massachusetts Institute for Technology (1970), opened a successful biracial architectural firm in Charlotte, and was elected its mayor in 1983 and 1985.

29. S.C. Student Council Newsletter, 28 Jan. 1962 [1963], series 4, reel 146, 1239–40, SRCP; [Ledeen], report of program director, Mar.–May 1963, box 9, no. 290, SCCHRR.

30. Thomas F. Jones, vice president for research at the Massachusetts Institute for Technology, interview by the author, Cambridge, Massachusetts, 29 July 1980, transcript, OHP, SCL; Henry H. Lesesne, *A History of the University of South Carolina, 1940–2000* (Columbia: Univ. of South Carolina Press, 2001), 138–50. Monteith, a PhD in biochemistry and molecular biology from Atlanta University (1975), chaired the biology department at Morris Brown College in Atlanta and was program director for the W. K. Kellogg Foundation of Battle Creek, Michigan. She is currently director of community voices at the Morehouse School of Medicine. Professor Henrie Monteith Treadwell, interview by the author, Atlanta, Georgia, 14 Nov. 1980, transcript, OHP, SCL; Rebecca L. Miller, "Raised for Activism: Henrie Monteith and the Desegregation of the University of South Carolina," *South Carolina Historical Magazine* 109 (Apr. 2008), 121–47.

31. Spearman, quarterly report, Mar. 1964–May 1964, box 9, no. 281; Ginnie Good, job report, Career and Service Office, Spring Quarter, 1964; "South Carolina—My Burden," 3 July 1964, file "June–2 July 1964," box 3. Anderson served in Vietnam and worked in New York's social services, earning a social work degree from Hunter College. He died in 2009.

32. [Ledeen], reports of program director, Dec. 1963–Feb. 1964, box 9, no. 281; and Mar. 1965–May 1965, box 9, no. 289; Tutorials, SCSCHR, series 4, reel 146, 1722–23, SRCP.

33. [Ledeen], report of program director, Dec. 1963–Feb. 1964, box 9, no. 281.

34. [Ledeen], report of program director, Mar.–May 1964, box 9, no. 289; Ledeen to Hayes and Pat [Mizell], 29 Feb. 1964, file "February 1964," box 3. See *Finding Aid to the M. Hayes Mizell Papers, 1952–2005,* available at http://library.sc.edu/socar/mnscrpts/mizellmh.pdf.

35. Minutes, executive committee of the SCCHR, 25 Feb. 1964, box 8, no. 258; [Ledeen], reports of program director, Mar.–May 1964, June–Aug. 1964, Sept. 1965–Nov. 1965, and Dec. 1965–Feb. 1966, box 9, no. 289.

36. [Ledeen], report, Dec. 1964–Feb. 1965, box 9, no. 289; M. Hayes Mizell, "South Carolina: South Carolina Student Council on Human Relations," 15 Dec. 1965, M. Hayes Mizell Collection, file "News clippings-articles-authored works," box 5, SCL; Mizell, "The Impact of the Civil Rights Movement on a White Activist," *MiddleWeb Hayes Mizell Civil Rights Days,* available at www.middleweb.com/mw/resources/HMhistory.html. South Carolina's school attendance law was enacted in 1967.

37. Ledeen to Dan [Carter], 22 Oct. 1965, file "October 1965," box 3; USC History Professor Dan Carter, "Coming Home to Carolina," keynote address presented 27 Apr. 2002 at the 66th Annual Meeting of the University South Caroliniana Society.

38. Gregg L. Michel, *Struggle for a Better South: The Southern Student Organizing Committee, 1964–1969* (New York: Palgrave Macmillan, 2004), 37 (citing Jerry Gainey to Hayes Mizell, 16 Apr. 1964), 81–88, 119–29; Christina Greene, "'We'll Take Our Stand': Race, Class, and Gender in the Southern Student Organizing Committee, 1964–1969," in *Hidden Histories of Women in the New South*, ed. Virginia Bernhard, Betty Brandon, Elizabeth Fox-Genovese, Theda Perdue, and Elizabeth Hayes Turner (Columbia and London: Univ. of Missouri Press, 1994), 173, 174–82, 189; "The Quotes of the Year," file "October–December 1962," box 3; and [Ledeen], reports of program director, Sept.–Nov. 1964 and Mar.–May 1965, box 9, SCCHRR. Joseph Vaughn, the first black student to matriculate at Furman on 29 January 1965, was one of SSOC's founding members at this university. Courtney Tollison, "Moral Imperative and Financial Practicality: Desegregation of South Carolina's Denominationally-Affiliated Colleges and Universities" (PhD diss., Univ. of South Carolina, 2003).

39. Elizabeth C. Ledeen to Dear Friends, 3 June 1965, file "26 May–July 1965"; and Ledeen to Wiley [B. Cooper], 13 July 1964, file "5 July–August 1964," file 78, box 3; Spearman, quarterly report, Sept., Oct., Nov. 1963, no. 281, box 9, SCCHRR. In 1967, the first African Americans to graduate from USC's Law School since Reconstruction were Jasper M. Cureton and John Lake, transfers from South Carolina State University School of Law in 1965. Lesesne, *History of the University of South Carolina, 1940–2000*, 141–50.

40. Alice N. Spearman, executive director, Elizabeth C. Ledeen, program director, Gil Rowland, project director, Freddie Williams, student intern, Charlotte A. Hickman, director, membership—finance, quarterly report, June–Aug. 1962, box 9, no. 280.

41. Alice N. Spearman to Freddie Williams, 20 July 1962; and Williams to [Spearman], 23 July–2 Aug. 1962, file "July–September 1962"; Spearman, dictated 13 June 1962, to Williams, 14 June 1962, file "April–June 1962," box 3; Dan Carter, comment to Marcia Synnott, 21 Mar. 2010, "Conference on Student Activism, Southern Style: Organizing and Protest in the 1960s and '70s," USC, 19–21 Mar. 2010.

42. In South Carolina's Sixth Congressional District, Florence was the largest city in the Pee Dee area; 43% of its 84,000 people were nonwhite, and 30.7% of adults over 25 years of age were illiterate.

43. Spearman, quarterly reports, June–Aug. 1962 and Sept.–Nov. 1962, no. 281; Minutes, 12 Feb. 1962, file "board of directors 1962–63," no. 244, box 9; "Now Is the Time," SCCHR brochure, file "July–September 1962"; Williams's draft of Pilot Study in Florence and "History of Florence Negro Leadership from 1940–1962," based on his handwritten narrative of trips, 23 July and 2 Aug. 1962; Spearman to Mrs. Lemmie Ellerbe, president, Addie Pickens Club of Cheraw, 15 Oct. 1962, file "October–December 1962," box 3.

44. Spearman, quarterly reports, June–Aug. 1964 and Sept.–Nov. 1964, and quarterly financial report, box 9, no. 281; the SCCHR to Career Service Board of NAIRO, request for certification for participation in the NAIRO–Eleanor Roosevelt Memorial Foundation Human Rights Internship Program, file "December 1963," box 3; Spearman to Paul Anthony, 9 Feb. 1965, and Anthony to Spearman, 10 Feb. 1965, file "January–22 February 1965," box 3; Adlai Stevenson chaired the Eleanor Roosevelt Foundation; Ledeen, Plans of the SCSCHR for training an "Eleanor Roosevelt Intern," [ca. 1964–65], box 9, no. 290; Thomas Bradford Poston biographical sketch, Staff File, box 9, no. 277.

45. [Ledeen], report of program director, June–Aug. 1965, Sept.–Nov. 1965, Dec. 1965–Feb. 1966, box 9, no. 289; Brad Poston, reports of the administrative assistant, June–Aug. 1965, and Sept.–Nov. 1965, no. 288; Poston, Intern's first quarter report, 18 Nov. 1965, no. 290, box 9; Spearman, quarterly report, Sept.–Nov. 1965, box 9, no. 281; Spearman to National Committee Against Discrimination in Housing, 5 May 1966, file "Student Council," box 10.

46. Poston, report of the administrative assistant, Dec. 1965–Feb. 1966, box 9, no. 288; Jack Bass, "South Carolinian Doesn't Pussy-Foot about Life" and "Progress Continues in Human Relations," *Charlotte Observer,* 3 Jan. 1967, A-8; Spearman, quarterly reports, Mar.–May 1966, June–Aug. 1966, and Sept.–Nov. 1966, box 9, no. 281; Report I: SCCHR 1966–1967, box 8, no. 241; [Ledeen], report as program director, Mar.–May, 1966, and reports as extension director, June–Aug. 1966 and June–Aug. 1967, box 9, no. 289; Wright interview, 11 July 1983.

47. R. Wright Spears to Mrs. Theodore Ledeen, 28 Feb. 1966, box 24, "Program: Speed Up: general: January–March 1966"; [Ledeen], reports of program director, Dec. 1965–Feb. 1966 and Mar.–May 1966, no. 289; Spearman, quarterly report, Mar.–May 1966, box 9, no. 281; Bass, "South Carolinian Doesn't Pussy-Foot about Life"; Poston, quarterly report of the Eleanor Roosevelt Intern, Mar.–May 1966, box 9, no. 290; Edna Smith, report of student activities, June–Aug. 1967, file "Student Council 1967–69," box 10. Youth Educational Services (YES) in North Carolina temporarily operated both its own tutoring program and SPEED-UP; Governor Robert E. McNair vetoed South Carolina's participation.

48. Poston, Intern's first quarter report, 18 Nov. 1965; and Spearman, quarterly report, Sept. 1965–Nov. 1965; Spearman to Colonel Donald H. Collins, 15 Oct. 1965; Spearman to Gadsden Shand, 27 Oct. 1965; and Spearman to the President, 28 Oct. 1965, file "October 1965"; Colonel Collins to Alice N. [S]Pearman, 5 Nov. 1965, file "1–15 November 1965," box 3.

49. Excerpts from Poston's Letters to E.C.L. [Ledeen], 22 Sept. 1966, 16 Oct. 1966, and 23 Oct. 1966, box 4, no. 98.

50. For Sam Shirah's work and arrest, see Michel, *Struggle for a Better South,* 20–23; Sam Shirah, "Campus Visit Report (University of South Carolina)," SNCC Papers, series 4, reel 9, 332; and *The Gamecock,* 18 Oct. 1963.

51. Georgia Council on Human Relations, Nine Months Report—Oct. 1964–July 1965, series 4, reel 155, 0486–0501, SRCP.

52. Honorable Jean Toal, then associate justice, panelist in "Celebrating the Struggle: A Public Program, Dreams of Change: Remembering the Struggle for Civil Rights," USC, 21 Nov. 1996. Attorney General Daniel R. McLeod, interview by the author, Columbia, South Carolina, 15 May 1980, transcript, OHP, SCL; Jack Bass and Jack Nelson, *The Orangeburg Massacre,* 2d ed. (Macon, GA: Mercer Univ. Press, 1984); and Philip G. Grose, *South Carolina at the Brink: Robert McNair and the Politics of Civil Rights* (Columbia: Univ. of South Carolina Press, 2006), 239–40, 339n209.

53. Alice Spearman Wright, interview by Jacquelyn Hall, Linville Falls, North Carolina, 8 Aug. 1976, Southern Oral History Program, Manuscripts Department, Southern Historical Collection, Wilson Library, University of North Carolina at Chapel Hill, transcript, 87, 90–92; Wright interview, 11 July 1983; and Spearman, report of executive director, Sept. 1966–Nov. 1966, box 9, no. 281.

PART II

Campus Activism Takes Shape

CHAPTER FIVE

The Rise of Black and White Student Protest in Nashville

JEFFREY A. TURNER

The 1960s student movement in the South was built along the color line. The struggle to dismantle segregation provided the impetus for black and white southern students, who had not been significant political actors in the years before 1960, to mobilize. Beginning with the sit-in movement of 1960, the political spectrum widened on many southern campuses, opening up possibilities that had not existed for decades. This effect developed differently, however, on historically black and white campuses. Put another way, the sit-ins and other manifestations of the desegregation era created a paradoxical situation: a movement that sought the end of segregation had the effect, at least in the short term, of pointing out the continuing existence of a color line in southern student political mobilization. The difference, which revolved around the gap between how black and white students viewed nonviolent direct action, was more a matter of timing than trajectory. The tactics of the nonviolent direct action arsenal eventually were embraced by members of what by mid-decade might be called the southern New Left.[1] This dynamic—the interplay of racial, generational, and vocational identities of student activists and their tendency to build both bridges and walls—is at the center of the story of southern student activism in the 1960s.

The South in 1960 provided an unfriendly environment for student activism. On campuses throughout the region, the carefully planned "frivolity"[2] of Greek-letter societies often operated hand in glove with a political environment that stifled dissent. Nevertheless, a southern student movement developed around a number of movement centers that offered a mixture of characteristics that made activism possible.[3] Nashville was one of those centers. While the Nashville movement has received significant attention in print and in film, that attention usually has focused on the cadre of activists who generated the sit-in movement in their roles as activists.[4] But the focus on the heroes of the movement has obscured the role and impact of southern college campuses, black and white. How did the movement affect historically black colleges and universities, which produced many of the foot soldiers in the sit-in movement? What was the impact on predominantly white colleges and universities, many of which still officially excluded African Americans? It is the purpose of this essay to suggest some of the ways in which students engaged the movement and politicized campuses by focusing on two institutions, Fisk and Vanderbilt universities. Private institutions with high profiles in the South, these schools shared similarities in campus culture and academic reputation despite their residence on different sides of the color line. They thus provide revealing opportunities for comparison.

The Nashville Movement: An Overview

Nashville offers a useful prism through which to view the impact of the sit-ins on southern student political mobilization. The sit-in movement developed in many parts of the South, but the Nashville movement provided some of its most striking images and compelling leaders and much of its guiding philosophy. A city whose boosters dubbed it the "Athens of the South," Nashville was home to a range of colleges and universities of different institutional types. The two that provide the setting for this analysis, Fisk and Vanderbilt, were both leading private institutions in southern higher education. But other institutions—Meharry Medical College, Tennessee Agricultural and Industrial State University, and American Baptist Theological Seminary for blacks; Peabody Teachers College and Scarritt College for whites—also contributed activists who made Nashville an important locale for southern student protest. Collectively, they offer a good indication of the range of institutional types evident in southern higher education at the outset of the 1960s.

In 1960, the "Athens of the South" had a reputation for racial moderation, and the city's mayor, Ben West, nurtured this reputation. But Nashville remained a segregated city capable of directing violence at those who challenged segregation. "Nashville at that time was an odd mix of racial progressiveness on the one hand and conflict and intolerance on the other," SNCC leader John Lewis later observed. Though African Americans wielded some political clout, holding seats on the city council and positions in the police force, much of the city's public space—libraries, theaters, schools, hotels, and restaurants—remained segregated.[5] This mix of racial moderation and continuing segregation, in a city with a sizeable number of college students, played a significant role in the nonviolent direct action movement that developed in February 1960.

The organizing of sit-ins by college students in 1960 breathed new life into the civil rights movement and set in motion a process in which students became central actors in the dramas of the 1960s. Though the event that initiated the sit-in movement—a demonstration by four students from North Carolina Agricultural and Technical College at a Woolworth's in Greensboro, North Carolina—occurred on 1 February 1960, Fellowship of Reconciliation field secretary James M. Lawson Jr. had been leading nonviolent workshops in preparation for an assault on segregation in downtown Nashville for some months.[6]

Lawson, who moved to Nashville in 1958, provided the Nashville student activists who generated the sit-in movement with a galvanizing ideology that mixed the Gandhian philosophy and tactics of nonviolence with Christianity. At a practical level, this approach to social change used noncooperation to fight corrupt power under the assumption that political power depends on the cooperation of the subjects of that power.[7] But as Lawson taught his pupils in Nashville, nonviolent direct action was more than a tactic; it was a way of life. Bound together by their common experience, the students in Lawson's seminar became a sort of small counterculture.[8] According to Lawson, activists not only should resist the inclination to respond to violence with violence but also should love those employing violence. "It was not enough to resist the urge to strike back at an assailant," Lewis later recalled. " 'That urge can't *be* there,' he would tell us. 'You have to do more than just not hit back. . . . You have to *love* that person who's hitting you.' "

Christian love also bound together the members of the activist community. Members of Lawson's troupe believed that they were creating the ideal of the "Beloved Community," which in Lewis's later recollections was "nothing less than the Christian concept of the kingdom of God on earth." This community would not be structured like other communities; it would not be dominated by a strong leader. Instead, the Nashville student movement adopted a practice of rotating leadership, an approach that initially repelled some traditional campus politicos at Fisk.[9]

The Nashville student movement was avowedly interracial. Paul LaPrad, a white Fisk student who had recently transferred from a school in the Midwest and who had strong Quaker roots, became a regular participant in the Lawson-led seminars of the fall of 1959. When the Nashville movement hit the streets in early 1960, LaPrad, viewed by militant segregationists as a traitor to his race, became a prominent target for violent reprisals.[10] The ranks of the demonstrators in the spring of 1960 included several other white Fisk students: John Nye, Carolanne Anderson, and Barbara Biggar, all foreign exchange students.[11]

The Nashville movement's public phase began on 13 February, when 124 people, most of them black, made their way in the snow from a downtown church to sit in at several segregated lunch counters. Store owners responded by closing the lunch counters. This pattern continued off and on over the next two weeks.[12] Demonstrators encountered violent resistance on 27 February. Police overlooked the thuggish attacks on the student demonstrators while arresting 81 students for conducting the sit-in.[13] The sit-ins led to an Easter season boycott of downtown stores by African American shoppers. In April, the home of attorney Z. Alexander Looby, who had represented sit-in participants, was dynamited, prompting a student march to the courthouse downtown. Numbering in the thousands, the marchers, led by Fisk student Diane Nash, asked Mayor Ben West if he supported the desegregation of the lunch counters; he responded that he did. On 10 May, the city's counters were desegregated. Other forms of segregation, however, including movie theaters and restaurants, persisted over the next three years in Nashville and provided targets for continued nonviolent direct action demonstrations.[14]

The Sit-Ins and the Campus Political Culture: Fisk

The sit-ins provided the primary context for the political engagement of students at Fisk in the early 1960s. Fisk, in turn, provided the southern student movement with several of its most prominent leaders. Fisk had a history of fostering struggle against racial inequality. But Fisk's relationship with dissent was complicated. In the 1920s, Fisk students revolted against the restrictive policies of the university's president, Fayette McKenzie, which ultimately resulted in McKenzie's resignation. In the following years, the university raised its national profile, in the process developing into a cosmopolitan institution. The first black university to be placed on the approved list of the Association of American Universities, Fisk was the home of noted scholars and artists.[15] With a 1960–61 enrollment of 922 students—866 undergraduates and 56 graduate students—the school was large enough to foster a vibrant campus life.[16]

While Fisk continued to operate near the center of African American intellectual and cultural life, its dominant student culture often discouraged political activism. Fisk students could be expected to be better prepared educationally than members of their collegiate cohort at other historically black institutions in Nashville, but campus activists were in the minority. Rebels were, however, present. During the 1956–57 academic year, for example, some faculty and students, working with local affiliates of the Congress of Racial Equality and the National Association for the Advancement of Colored People, organized the Social Action Committee in an effort to challenge Jim Crow accommodations in Nashville.[17] Nevertheless, a more prominent concern of writers in the *Fisk University Forum*, the campus newspaper, during the late 1950s was the lack of political activity— a trend that was often connected to a perceived lack of intellectual energy on campus. "As long as the irresponsible, indolent, anti-intellectual attitude of this student body exists, the name of our college is going to become increasingly less meaningful," the editors of the *Forum* complained in early 1957.[18]

Such complaints of student apathy were common in the 1950s on black and white campuses. Commentators routinely complained about the disengagement of American youth. In November 1951, *Time* magazine made one of the earliest references to the "silent generation": "Youth today is waiting for the hand of fate to fall on its shoulders, meanwhile working fairly hard and saying almost nothing. The most startling fact about the younger generation is its silence."[19]

Criticisms of complacent 1950s college students were not restricted to white students. E. Franklin Frazier's scathing analysis of the black middle class, *Black Bourgeoisie,* argued that black colleges and universities created "money-makers," members of a class "without cultural roots in either the Negro world with which it refuses to identify, or the white world which refuses to permit the black bourgeoisie to share its life." Black students were listless, interested less in learning than in the social activities of the Greek societies. Black teachers, Frazier charged, held their positions merely to ensure their social status; they had little interest in literature or ideas, were conservative politically, and paid little attention to social questions. Frazier's career took him to several high-profile black colleges, including a stint at Fisk from 1929 to 1934. And though his criticisms were scathing, their existence suggests a more complex reality—one in which faculty such as Frazier helped at times to foster challenges to both Jim Crow and the complicity of black institutions.[20]

The application of this criticism to Fisk students appeared in the Fisk student newspaper before the advent of the sit-in movement, and it continued into the early 1960s. Such criticism suggests fissures in the student body—the presence of a subculture of students inclined to associate the life of the mind with political action and critical of others who, they felt, did not embody these characteristics. And, in fact, when Lawson began the nonviolence workshops, few Fisk students participated, and those who did generally resided outside the mainstream student culture. Marion Barry, for example, was a chemistry graduate student who came from a modest background and who had already experienced activism, having challenged a white segregationist member of the board of trustees of his undergraduate institution, LeMoyne College in Memphis. Barry found little in common with the students who gravitated to Greek societies and seemed to see political activity as beneath them. Another participant was Chicago-raised Diane Nash, a transfer student from Howard University who was surprised at the extent of Nashville's segregation. She later recounted asking fellow students if an organization existed that was fighting segregation. "And many, many people said they didn't know of one," Nash recalled. "And a few people asked me why I was trying to do that. Nothing was going to change and I was only going to get myself in trouble. And I had started thinking that Fisk students were apathetic." Eventually, Nash sounded out Paul LaPrad, a white transfer student, who directed her to Lawson's workshop.[21]

At the height of the sit-ins, however, Nash would find some of those skeptical students participating in the demonstrations. Indeed, for a period, in the spring of 1960, the sit-in movement became so large that it blurred the lines between campus subcultural groups as well as the lines between students and administration. The violence of 27 February seemed to give the Nashville movement momentum, galvanizing the black community's support for the students. Fisk president Stephen J. Wright announced his approval of the movement at chapel meeting the next day: "From all I have been able to learn they have broken no law by the means they have employed thus far, and they have not only conducted themselves peaceably, but with poise and dignity." The students, Wright stated, "have been exposed all their lives to the teachings of the great American scriptures of democracy, freedom and equality, and no literate person should be surprised that they reflect these teachings in their conduct."[22]

Activist students viewed Wright's support as significant. Faced with pressures from the community, from Fisk's board of trustees, and from worried parents, Wright had previously been cautious. Those forces were powerful, even if Wright, as the president of a private university, did not work under the same constraints encountered by public university presidents.[23] Nevertheless, Wright's public stand put him in the vanguard of college presidents who supported the sit-in movement, and it effectively opened the doors for widespread participation from Fisk students. On other occasions, Wright served as a force for moderation, encouraging students not to let their participation in the movement interfere with their attendance at classes. However, as the spring term continued, the sit-ins at times took on the feel of a sanctioned activity. Alongside the regular reports about mundane campus activities (a new photographic display in the library, "sons and daughters planning to go to the altar this summer"), the spring issues of the normally staid campus publications offered detailed summaries of the sit-ins.[24]

However, the apparently widespread unity of the Nashville student movement belied fissures that existed beneath the surface. One split existed along generational lines and surfaced later in the spring, as younger and older activists clashed over the movement's pace. Another breach existed along the campus subcultural lines that had previously seemed to dissolve. Lewis later described a November 1961 encounter on campus between demonstrators and a group of fraternity men "wearing dog collars around their throats and carrying their Greek paddles. They ran past us, barking like hounds, hollering and whooping and going through their fraternity ritual." Lewis recalled being stunned at the behavior, "to see these young black men swept up in this trivial silliness at the very moment that people their own age . . . were risking their lives . . . standing up for the future of all of us." Such incongruities existed on many campuses but were thrown in high relief in Nashville, where the committed core of the movement had undergone such intentional and intense schooling in nonviolence.[25]

As the Nashville movement's influence spread, activists such as Nash, James Bevel, and Bernard Lafayette found themselves drawn away from the city. Nash left college after her stint in jail in Rock Hill, South Carolina, gave her the feeling that a gap existed between the "real world" and a make-believe version that existed at Fisk and that this gap was complicit in the maintenance of segregation. If she stayed at Fisk, she could envision a future in which she would, as David Halberstam put it, "marry some black doctor, and live a black life parallel to the life of the wife of a white doctor." Indeed, Nash came to believe that real education about humanity and ethics occurred off the campus; college was more about credentialing.[26]

Lewis stayed in Nashville, transferred to Fisk, and attempted to keep the movement going. "I had become an oddity, a holdover of sorts," Lewis recalled. "Many of the professors at Fisk, as well as many of my fellow students, thought I was some sort of weird character, that I was not really in school but was just using Fisk as a base of operations, that I was some sort of transient activist, just passing through."[27] During this period, the Nashville movement expanded its targets from lunch counters to other kinds of public accommodations and began attracting a contingent of white students from Vanderbilt and Scarritt. But the workshops that had generated the Nashville student movement and made its participants the most conversant in the theory and practice of nonviolent direct action ended by the spring of 1961.[28] Lewis balanced his studies with continued direct-action attacks on segregated public establishments. In a March 1963 issue of the *Fisk University Forum* he reported on the status of four activists—one of them a Fisk student—arrested while attempting to desegregate the YMCA. Headlined "Sit-Inners Continue to Sit In," the article attempted to attract the notice of those students whose attention had lapsed.

That same month, another Fisk student, Ray Hanson, wrote an article expressing frustration with nonviolent direct action and speaking positively of self-defense advocate Robert F. Williams: "Can American Negroes be expected to sit tight and let the cigarettes burn out on their backs while other dark-skinned peoples the world over are daily shattering the myths of white supremacy?" Hanson asked, adding that progress did not always occur by "appealing for sympathy, turning the other cheek, waiting, waiting, waiting."[29] The term *Black Power* was still three years away from entering the national lexicon, and activists from Fisk and the Nashville community were still employing nonviolent direct action. But, in retrospect, Hanson's editorial can be seen as a preview of Black Power at Fisk.

Meanwhile, a couple of miles away at Vanderbilt University, a handful of students was just beginning to engage in nonviolent direct action.

Vanderbilt and the Sit-Ins

Vanderbilt is only two miles to the south of Fisk. During the first half of the twentieth century, the color line ensured that those two miles spanned a considerable social and political distance. Little contact occurred between the two schools, especially for undergraduates. Nevertheless, despite the significant gap in experience, some striking similarities between Fisk and Vanderbilt existed in the late 1950s and early 1960s. Both schools drew from a bourgeois clientele that gravitated to fraternities and sororities, and the dominance of these institutions helped to create a student political culture with a strong mixture of conservatism and apathy. Lee Frissell, a Vanderbilt student who was among the core of the campus left from 1963 to 1967, later recalled those similarities: "We were thrilled to find that the Fisk kids were very much like us . . . but, ironically, to us, far less political and generally more conservative, than we were. It probably had the same Greek percentage as VU. VU and Fisk are quite similar in many ways."[30] But while certain demographic realities helped to make a similar canvas on which the portrait of early 1960s student activism would be created, race and the politics of desegregation produced a very different painting at Vanderbilt.

In February 1960, Vanderbilt University was a culturally and politically conservative institution. Larger than Fisk, with a total enrollment of 4,121 (about half of them undergraduates in the College of Arts and Sciences),[31] its undergraduate programs were segregated, and though the numbers had dropped in previous years, most of its students were members of Greek societies, where the labels *southern* and *conservative* seemed practically synonymous. "Vanderbilt is a Southern university," observed undergraduate Roy Blount in a column in *The Hustler*, the student newspaper, in the early 1960s. "The majority of the people here come from people who have tried to make lazy Negro field hands work, have seen many Negroes and not many white men in knife fights, have given extra money to the yard man because he has spent all the rest on something he shouldn't and his children are hungry, and who remember fondly the old colored folks at home and are angered by Martin Luther King."[32]

Vanderbilt was, however, in transition. Though no African Americans had matriculated as undergraduates, its graduate programs had desegregated in 1954. One of the few black graduate students at Vanderbilt was James M. Lawson Jr., who was responsible for making Nashville the philosophical hub of the sit-in movement. Lawson's central role in the rise of the Nashville movement shook up Vanderbilt, challenging the university's student political culture, opening the door to a new form of political mobilization, and demanding student reassessment of the institution. But compared to Fisk, the process by which nonviolent direct action emerged as a viable means of political expression at Vanderbilt developed in slow motion.

Lawson brought the sit-in movement to Vanderbilt, though not in a way that quickly translated into student participation. Instead, Lawson's involvement in the Nashville movement prompted the university's administration to expel him in early March 1960 after local newspapers labeled him "the leading organizer" of the demonstrations.[33] The university's actions found support in the pages of its student newspaper, *The Hustler*. "Compared to other Southern schools," the paper's editors wrote, "Vanderbilt has bent over backwards in attempting to make its educational facilities available to qualified men and women, regardless of race. In view of this rather liberal (for the South) attitude, it is ironic that in the immediate future Vanderbilt will probably be vilified by critics in other sections of the United States for its handling of the case of James M. Lawson." To the editors, Lawson's actions resembled two other recent violations. In one episode, two students had been expelled for staging an impromptu "broadcast" through the carillon horns atop Kirkland Hall on campus. In another episode, a group of female students had been suspended for inciting a panty raid. "The 'sitdown' affair, in which Mr. Lawson has admitted a part, is of a far more serious nature," *The Hustler* concluded.[34]

In the following days, student and faculty groups on the campus took up the issue. The Vanderbilt student senate soon overwhelmingly approved a resolution endorsing Lawson's expulsion. But although conservatives controlled the student newspaper and student government, Lawson's supporters found other outlets. Divinity School students picketed Kirkland Hall in protest. Small American flags marked by a large black splotch and accompanied by a statement protesting the expulsion appeared throughout the campus. Lawson's expulsion sparked discussion on campus, and *The Hustler* agreed that students needed to engage the issue: "The Lawson case has proved at least one thing to us: that it is time for every Vanderbilt student to debate, with himself and with his fellows, the entire issue of segregation. As the South's future leaders, these students will likely be called upon to give an answer, and for the sake of everyone concerned, it had better be a good one."[35]

The Lawson case and the sit-in movement provided the backdrop for a renewal in the spring of 1960 of a longstanding campus debate over Vanderbilt's membership in the U.S. National Student Association. Founded in 1947, the NSA had no official connection to any national political group; student governments at member institutions simply voted to affiliate. But the organization did not avoid political issues. At the founding convention attendees passed a Student Bill of Rights that codified student academic rights and civil liberties and, significantly for the South, declared that those rights should not be limited on the basis of race, religion, or political views. In 1960, the group's national leaders endorsed and actively supported the sit-in movement, further alienating those who complained that the organization was too liberal, even radical, for Vanderbilt. According to one April *Hustler* editorial, the NSA's views "on the question of racial segregation are much too radical for most southerners—and most of the Vanderbilt student body is from the South." The editors continued, "Vanderbilt is not a hotbed of rabid segregationists by a long shot; neither, however, is it as liberal as most of the schools" in the NSA.[36] In early May, Vanderbilt students voted overwhelmingly to end the university's affiliation with the NSA in a nonbinding referendum.[37]

However, by September, the paper's new editors changed the publication's stance to favor continued NSA membership. The editors staked out a moderate position that decried the careless charges of communist influence sometimes levied against the NSA and acknowledged the inevitability of desegregation without actually endorsing the black freedom struggle. An editorial argued that the spring referendum had been voted down "mainly because of two loaded words—integration and communism—which its opponents brandished so frequently and slung so widely that hardly anyone bothered to look or think very deep into the real issue." The editors acknowledged the unpopularity of the NSA's support for integration but argued that membership in the group was crucial to Vanderbilt's continued relevance in the national debate on race relations.[38]

The Vanderbilt student senate continued the school's NSA membership during the 1960–61 academic year. Senate President Joe Roby and other conservative members pushed the body to adopt positions that would act as a conservative counterbalance within the NSA. In February 1961, a bill that would have criticized the NSA for attempting "to legislate the conscience of American college students" and condemned sit-ins as a "mass, organized violation of existing statutes" narrowly failed, in part because of the opposition of senate vice president Lamar Alexander. Although Alexander played a role in the bill's formulation, he opposed its passage because "it doesn't express as intelligently a position on our NSA's stand." Weeks later, the senate unified behind a bill opposing the sit-ins and their endorsement by the NSA. Wrangling over wording dominated much of the debate, such as whether the senate should call on the NSA to "cease" or "rescind" its actions, and in the end *The Hustler* suggested that the senators, though united in their support of the resolution, "were not of a united opinion as to what they were opposing." But Roby probably spoke for most when he took aim at the tactic of the sit-in, which he argued was "explosive" and represented an undesirable way to solve "an essentially legalistic question."[39]

In January 1962, senate debate turned from sit-ins to the desegregation of Vanderbilt after junior senator John Sergent proposed a bill establishing a student committee to investigate admitting qualified black applicants to all Vanderbilt schools. The discussion pitted opponents of desegregation against those who believed that integration was inevitable and that resistance would damage Vanderbilt's national reputation. Few opponents seemed willing to follow the lead of the anonymous student who argued, "Vanderbilt is one of the institutions of higher learning that still preserves the purity and superiority of the white race and I am definitely against integration." Instead, opponents more commonly argued about timing and process. Integration would proceed more smoothly in six years, they argued, when student attitudes would provide for a more welcoming environment and segregationist alumni would be less likely to withdraw financial support. Few proponents argued that segregation was immoral, instead taking the position that segregation was destined to end and that maintaining it would prevent Vanderbilt from being "a truly great university." In February, the student senate organized a campus-wide student referendum on integration. Students voted against the idea 862 to 661, with about 60 percent of the student body casting ballots.[40]

Over the ensuing months, however, *The Hustler* took a more assertive stand in favor of integration, led by editors Blount and Alexander. Blount's columns, peppered with sarcasm and colorful language, moved as close to an indictment of segregation as any writer in the paper had come: "'There ought to be a place,' students say, 'for people who believe in segregation.' There also ought to be a place for people who believe in going naked, but it ought not to be a university. We take our places around with us, and we have no right or power to impose them on other people or things. The Negro has been given his place, and he doesn't want it or deserve it." In the same April 1962 issue of the paper, Alexander warned that Vanderbilt was falling behind other southern universities by failing to end segregation.[41]

The decision to end undergraduate segregation came from Vanderbilt's board of trustees the following month. *The Hustler* celebrated the decision as a step forward but cautioned against "quick token integration" and warned that accepting Negro applicants over more qualified white applicants "just so that we can be integrated and our consciences can be salved and our critics silenced" would amount to reverse discrimination. The primary purpose of ending segregation was to realize the goal of a true university, and this ideal resided somewhere between the vision of a segregated "social club" on the one hand and a progressive "social crusader" on the other. The university should be "a community of scholars that welcomes other scholars. In this way Vanderbilt will do its job as a University, and in the process will help the Negro to gain his rights as a man."[42]

The Hustler's evolving embrace of desegregation suggested significant movement at a university that still had a self-consciously conservative student body. But
coming in 1962, more than two years after the advent of student sit-ins, what was
perhaps just as significant was the editorial's dismissive reference to the university
as a "social crusader." The stance suggested discomfort with, if not outright opposition to, nonviolent direct action.

Both responses to direct action soon became evident as a small group of
Vanderbilt students began sit-ins and picketing against segregated restaurants.
This wave of direct-action activities started in November 1962, when a national
conference of the Student Nonviolent Coordinating Committee meeting in Nashville led to demonstrations against two restaurants. In mid-December, physics
professor David Kotelchuck attracted local attention when a photograph of him
dodging a punch from a restaurant employee at a sit-in ran in the *Nashville Tennessean*. The university took no action against Kotelchuck, but the continuing
demonstrations and Kotelchuck's involvement unleashed debate on campus and
in *The Hustler*.

The Vanderbilt senate voted in December to denounce the demonstrations as
"injurious to the law-abiding citizens of the community." *The Hustler* responded
with an endorsement of the sit-ins that was less than full-throated: "Sit-ins aren't
good, but the discrimination they show up is worse, and that discrimination is
what must be either opposed, or rationally defended by responsible people." Three
years after the beginning of the sit-in movement, Vanderbilt students appeared
to be hovering on its periphery, offering commentary for or against but not con-
spicuously involved. Indeed, in January 1963, Blount described a sit-in that he and
several student senators had observed at the B & W Cafeteria, near the capitol
building in Nashville. Blount was uninspired by the demonstrators.[43]

Not until late spring 1963, when a new "campus liberal organization," PROD,
was formed, did any kind of movement toward student involvement in direct action become apparent. The organization initially sponsored lectures and discussion, but by the fall, PROD was poised to move from discussion to action.[44] The
organization, led by Ron Parker, a psychology graduate student, focused its attention on the Campus Grill, a segregated restaurant situated in the middle of
the Vanderbilt, Peabody, and Scarritt campuses. Some Vanderbilt divinity students had already begun to boycott the restaurant. In October, PROD announced
a picketing campaign, prompting the student senate to pass a resolution favor-
ing restaurant desegregation in Nashville but qualifying the resolution with a
statement that government had no right "to force a restaurant manager to alter
the management of his business in regard to whom he shall or shall not serve."
The Hustler, now edited by the more conservative Dick McCord, lampooned the

proposed picketing campaign as a "self-righteous and slightly ridiculous" move that "smacked . . . of children playing games," though the paper continued to endorse the goal of desegregation.[45]

PROD's life as a campus organization was shortened by a split between moderates and what one *Hustler* writer termed "vociferous radicals." But the Campus Grill campaign led to contacts among students from Vanderbilt, Scarritt, and Peabody. From Vanderbilt, graduate and divinity students were the most visible participants in the nonviolent crusade for desegregation.[46] They eventually joined colleagues from the neighboring colleges to form the Joint University Council on Human Relations. Members of the organization quickly developed a camaraderie based in part on a perceived set of common experiences as southern whites. They held meetings or parties almost nightly. More importantly, they initiated the first demonstrations that attracted participation from some Vanderbilt students.[47]

By April 1964, just as Vanderbilt was preparing to admit its first black undergraduate students, sit-ins at three Nashville restaurants not only attracted the participation of Vanderbilt students but also resulted in the arrests of four students. *The Hustler* continued to editorialize against the "misguided" demonstrations, and conservative students continued to flex their muscles in the student senate, but the political spectrum at Vanderbilt had widened to include direct action.[48] Moreover, activists from the city's white colleges had developed into a vanguard that would play a prominent role in the formation of the southern New Left, underlining Nashville's role as an important center for student activism.

Destroying the color line was the taproot of activism for this group of activists. Though the Southern Student Organizing Committee, which grew from this Nashville core, would eventually develop a broad agenda for social change, its origins lay in nonviolent direct action demonstrations aimed at ending segregation. Frissell, a Vanderbilt activist, later recalled the "great joy" that he felt in interacting with African Americans for the first time. As a sophomore, he participated in an Upward Bound tutoring program based at Fisk that helped prepare African American high school students for college. Social ties often mirrored the political agenda; close relationships that crossed the color line developed among black and white activists during the middle years of the decade.[49]

Nevertheless, despite the connections, what is perhaps more striking is the lack of significant contact and cooperation between Fisk and Vanderbilt activists as the decade progressed. The pages of the student newspapers at both campuses reveal little curiosity at either institution about the other. To a degree, this dearth of public interracialism is a reflection of the small activist communities at both schools in the years between the end of the sit-in movement and, at the end of the decade, the surge in activism inspired by Vietnam at Vanderbilt and Black Power at Fisk.

Figure 5.1. Demonstrations in 1963 at the Campus Grill, a segregated restaurant near Vanderbilt University, provided an opportunity for some Vanderbilt students to experience direct action protest for the first time—three years after the sit-in movement that was led by black students in the city. Courtesy Vanderbilt University Special Collections and University Archives.

At Vanderbilt, the students who considered themselves part of the movement were conscious of their position on the political and cultural periphery of student life. At mid-decade, Vanderbilt's activist community was still profoundly influenced by faculty and graduate students, especially in the Divinity School. Undergraduates who were willing to embrace the "liberal" label were decidedly in the minority. "We were rebels in virtually every way you could be a rebel," recalled

Frissell, who was among the founders of a campus chapter of Students for a Democratic Society in early 1965. "Most of all, we did not want to fit into Vanderbilt."[50]
Frissell and other radicals and liberals would spend the years between 1963 and
1967 carving out space on the left in an environment that was often hostile. Their
numbers would remain small. By 1967, as he prepared to graduate, Frissell would
express frustration to *Hustler* writer Tom Lawrence at the difficulty of organizing
a student movement on the left in such an unfriendly setting. "Most Vanderbilt
liberals want to leave Vanderbilt," Lawrence wrote in an article about an interview
with Frissell. "They are tired of running into The Brick Wall, which is Vanderbilt's
stolid, apathetic majority of students."[51] Given what was to come, this assessment
was perhaps overly pessimistic. While liberals and those on the left would not define the mainstream at Vanderbilt, the political spectrum would continue to widen
as Vietnam and "student power" joined race as motivating issues in the late 1960s.
Those issues would combine and help make possible a momentary broad mobilization at Vanderbilt that, in terms of participation, would resemble the widespread participation in the sit-in movement at Fisk in 1960.[52]

Meanwhile, two miles to the north, activists at Fisk would bemoan a lack of
politically and intellectually engaged students. For a brief period in 1960, the sit-
in movement had provided the context for a broad mobilization of Fisk students.
But by mid-decade, the cohort of activists was small. "Where are the radicals?"
asked Yolande "Nikki" Giovanni in the *Fisk University Forum* in 1967. "It's really a
sorry state of affairs when the Student Council President is the most militant cat
on campus."[53] But activism, animated by calls for Black Power and more student
power on campus, would grow at Fisk as well in the late 1960s.[54]

Conclusion

Only two miles apart, the campuses of Fisk and Vanderbilt occupied different
worlds in 1960. Nevertheless, despite their residence on opposite sides of the color
line, the students shared the common experience of inhabiting an academic environment with elements that strongly discouraged activism. Notwithstanding the
obvious differences, the political cultures of these campuses manifested some similarities. Both were dominated by a collegiate subculture centered on Greek-letter
societies whose political tendencies mixed conservatism and apathy and who were
inclined to resist involvement in the kind of provocative activism represented by
the sit-in movement. But the nature of that resistance was different on either side
of the color line. At Fisk, conservatism and apathy commingled with a history of
defiance, both of restrictions on campus and the racial discrimination that was, at
some level, a source of those restrictions. Despite the challenges that organizers

faced in their efforts to mobilize Fisk students, for a period in the spring of 1960 they were able to reach across the lines that divided student subcultures and mobilize significant numbers of Fisk students. While that kind of widespread participation was difficult to maintain, it lasted long enough to provide a model that student activists would attempt to recreate throughout the decade. By the end of that decade students at Fisk would turn a critical eye not only to discrimination in the Nashville community but also to perceived deficiencies on their own campus. By that time, the emphasis on interracialism that was at the core of James Lawson's workshops had been replaced by the separatism of Black Power.

The political climate at Vanderbilt in the late 1960s also would be much different, the political spectrum broader. But while race would continue to play a significant role at Vanderbilt throughout the decade—in large part driven by the growing presence of African American students on the campus—"student power" and Vietnam would mobilize larger numbers of Vanderbilt students. As they did elsewhere in the South on predominantly white campuses, the controversies created by the sit-ins ultimately created space to the left of an ordered ameliorative gradualism—a space for immediatists, not only on the issue of segregation but also on other issues. This development would provide the foundation for the southern New Left. But despite the vision of interracialism that would continue to animate many in the larger southern student movement—even after the rise of Black Power—a significant gap would continue to exist between black and white student activists.

NOTES

1. *New Left* most commonly refers to white activists, especially students, who mobilized around the Students for a Democratic Society vision of "participatory democracy" during the 1960s. In the South, the mobilization of white students at times resonated with this vision, though white southern activism during the decade drew even more on indigenous sources. I use the term *southern New Left* to refer to this phenomenon. Others employ a broader definition of the New Left. See, for example, Van Gosse, *Rethinking the New Left: An Interpretative History* (New York: Palgrave Macmillan, 2005), esp. ch. 1.

2. Willie Morris uses this expression in his description of the University of Texas in the 1950s in *North Toward Home* (Oxford, MS: Yoknapatawpha, 1967), 170–71.

3. These movement centers developed where strong manifestations of the sit-in movement appeared, and included, in addition to Nashville, Chapel Hill, Atlanta, Tallahassee, Gainesville, New Orleans, and Austin. For the early development of these movement centers, see Jeffrey A. Turner, *Sitting In and Speaking Out: Student Movements in the American South, 1960–1970* (Athens: Univ. of Georgia Press, 2010), 95–103.

4. The most detailed treatment of the Nashville sit-in movement is David Halberstam, *The Children* (New York: Random House, 1998). Halberstam, who covered the movement as a young reporter in Nashville, provides remarkable insight on the key personalities in the

movement, but the book relies almost exclusively on oral history interviews with those participants. John Lewis provides a revealing firsthand account in his autobiography, written with Michael D'Orso, *Walking with the Wind: A Memoir of the Movement* (New York: Simon and Schuster, 1998). Orlando Bagwell, director, "Ain't Scared of Your Jails (1960–1961)," *Eyes on the Prize*, 1986, focuses on the Nashville movement in the segment on the sit-ins. Paul K. Conkin, *Gone with the Ivy: A Biography of Vanderbilt University* (Knoxville: Univ. of Tennessee Press, 1985), 547–73, offers a detailed analysis of the expulsion of James Lawson from Vanderbilt as a result of his involvement in the sit-ins. No modern institutional history of Fisk exists, though Joe M. Richardson, *A History of Fisk University, 1865–1946* (Tuscaloosa: Univ. of Alabama Press, 1980) provides a useful overview of the institution's early years.

5. Halberstam, *The Children*, 105; Lewis with D'Orso, *Walking with the Wind*, 80 (quotation).

6. Halberstam, *The Children*, 11–17.

7. On the philosophy of nonviolent action and Gandhi's contribution to its development, see Gene Sharp, *Politics of Nonviolent Action* (Boston: Extending Horizons, 1973), 7–16, 82–87.

8. On the dynamic of Lawson's workshop, see Wesley C. Hogan, *Many Minds, One Heart: SNCC's Dream for a New America* (Chapel Hill: Univ. of North Carolina Press, 2007), 16–26.

9. Lewis with D'Orso, *Walking with the Wind*, 86, 93, 87.

10. Ibid., 91, 107.

11. Julia Moore, "From Jubilee Bell Tower," *Fisk News*, Spring 1960, 17; *Nashville Tennessean*, 2 Mar. 1960, 2. The spellings of some names vary depending on the source. The *Tennessean* cites "Carol Anderson" and "Barbara Bigger" as two of the exchange students.

12. *Nashville Tennessean*, 14 Feb. 1960, 10-a, 19 Feb. 1960, 4, 21 Feb. 1960, 2-a; Halberstam, *The Children*, 103.

13. *Nashville Tennessean*, 28 Feb. 1960, 1, 6.

14. On the bombing of the Looby house and the exchange with West, see Halberstam, *The Children*, 228–34; and "Ain't Scared of Your Jails (1960–61)."

15. Richardson, *History of Fisk University*, 135.

16. "College and School News," *The Crisis* 68, no. 8 (Oct. 1961), 517.

17. *Fisk University Forum*, 29 Jan. 1957, 1.

18. Ibid., 2.

19. "The Younger Generation," *Time*, 5 Nov. 1951, 46, 52.

20. E. Franklin Frazier, *Black Bourgeoisie* (Glencoe, IL: Free Press, 1957), 24, 78–85. On Frazier's academic career, which included periods at Tuskegee, Morehouse, Fisk, and Howard, see Anthony M. Platt, "The Rebellious Teaching Career of E. Franklin Frazier," *Journal of Blacks in Higher Education* 13 (Autumn 1996): 86–90. Langston Hughes launched a similar attack on black colleges in a 1934 article in *The Crisis*, focusing specifically on students at Fisk. Langston Hughes, "Cowards from the Colleges," *The Crisis* 41 (Aug. 1934), 226–28. On the complexities of black teachers and social change in the era of segregation, see Adam Fairclough, " 'Being in the Field of Education and Also Being a Negro . . . Seems . . . Tragic': Black Teachers in the Jim Crow South," *Journal of American History* 87, no. 1 (June 2000): 65–91, and, more generally, Fairclough, *Teaching Equality: Black Schools in the Age of Jim Crow* (Athens: Univ. of Georgia Press, 2001).

21. Halberstam, *The Children*, 2–24, 40–50, 60–63; Lewis with D'Orso, *Walking with the Wind*, 91–92; "Non-Violence and the Quest for Civil Rights," transcript of forum, John F.

Kennedy Library, 29 Mar. 2003, available at www.jfklibrary.org/Events-and-Awards/~/media/assets/Education%20and%20Public%20Programs/Forum%20Transcripts/Non-violence%20and%20the%20Quest%20for%20Civil%20Rights.pdf (quotation), accessed 1 Mar. 2010.

22. *Nashville Tennessean,* 29 Feb. 1960, 1, 2.

23. Presidents of black colleges often found themselves buffeted by opposing forces: conservative opponents of political activism and the activists themselves. In her study of Mississippi's black colleges during the Civil Rights Movement, Joy Ann Williamson argues that although private colleges were more insulated from interference by white segregationists than were their public counterparts, they still were subject to external factors that could limit activism. Williamson, *Radicalizing the Ebony Tower: Black Colleges and the Black Freedom Struggle in Mississippi* (New York: Teachers College Press, 2008), ch. 5. At Fisk, tensions between activists, often led by W. E. B. Du Bois, and the philanthropic organizations that provided so much of the funding for the university, surfaced time and again through the first half of the twentieth century. Wright's predecessor, Charles S. Johnson, a proponent of "slow and deliberate measures" in pursuit of black advancement, faced the opposition of Du Bois at the time of Johnson's appointment as president of Fisk in 1946, and he found himself navigating between conservative trustees and community leaders on the one hand and activists on the other throughout his presidency. See Patrick J. Gilpin and Marybeth Gasman, *Charles S. Johnson: Leadership beyond the Veil in the Age of Jim Crow* (New York: SUNY Press, 2003).

24. Lewis with D'Orso, *Walking with the Wind,* 109; *Fisk University Forum,* 24 Mar. 1960, 2 (quotation); *Fisk News,* Spring 1960, 16–18.

25. Lewis with D'Orso, *Walking with the Wind,* 185.

26. Halberstam, *The Children,* 268–69.

27. Lewis with D'Orso, *Walking with the Wind,* 185.

28. Hogan, *Many Minds, One Heart,* 53.

29. *Fisk University Forum,* 4 Mar. 1963, 2; 25 Mar. 1963, 2.

30. Lee Frissell, e-mail message to the author, 28 Apr. 2011.

31. *Bulletin of Vanderbilt University: General Catalog Issue* (1961–62), 600.

32. *The Hustler,* 12 Jan. 1962, 4.

33. Citing a section of university regulations dealing with student conduct at the scene of mob action or disturbance, Dean of the Divinity School Robert J. Nelson asked Lawson whether it was true that he had made statements urging Nashville students to continue their demonstrations regardless of the law. The regulation stated: "It shall be the duty of every student to discourage disorderly assemblage in large groups on or off the campus. . . . Students found at the scene of a riot or in an unruly mob shall be subject to immediate expulsion from the University whether or not they are active participants." Lawson responded with a two-page statement in which he declared that he endorsed not "defiant violation of the law" but civil disobedience "within the context of a law or a law enforcement agency which has in reality ceased to be the Law." University officials responded by asking Lawson to withdraw. When he did not comply, university officials expelled him. Ibid., 4 Mar. 1960, 1, 2.

34. Ibid., 4.

35. Ibid., 11 Mar. 1960, 1, 4.

36. Ibid., 29 Apr. 1960, 4.

37. Vanderbilt sent representatives to the National Student Congress, the NSA's annual

gathering, held at the University of Minnesota in the summer of 1960. The sit-in movement divided the congress and produced considerable tension, at one point pitting two white southerners—one from Vanderbilt, the other from the University of North Carolina—against each other. Vanderbilt student Joe Roby spoke for conservatives, arguing that the NSA's position on the sit-ins neglected the views of the majority of Vanderbilt's student body. In response, Curtis Gans, a former editor of the University of North Carolina's *Daily Tar Heel* who was serving as NSA vice president, outlined the reasoning behind NSA's support and declared that "the overwhelming sentiment of the nation" was behind the sit-in movement. Ibid., 23 Sept. 1960, 1, 6.

38. Ibid., 14 Oct. 1960, 4.

39. Ibid., 17 Feb. 1961, 1; 24 Feb. 1961, 1; 3 Mar. 1961, 1, 3. Alexander would go on to serve as governor of Tennessee, United States secretary of education, and a U.S. senator representing Tennessee.

40. Ibid., 9 Feb. 1962, 1, 10; 16 Feb. 1962, 1.

41. Ibid., 20 Apr. 1962, 4.

42. Ibid., 11 May 1962, 4.

43. Ibid., 30 Nov. 1962, 1; 4 Jan. 1963, 1, 2; 14 Dec. 1962, 1; 17 May 1963, 2; 11 Jan. 1963, 4, 10.

44. Ibid., 17 May 1963, 3; 18 Oct. 1963, 1. If PROD was an acronym, its full name was not identified in the pages of *The Hustler*. Lee Frissell, one of the founders, later recalled that the name was intended as a verb: "what we wanted to do to the South . . . prod it to act right." Frissell to the author, 2 May 2011.

45. *The Hustler*, 1 Nov. 1963, 1; 8 Nov. 1963, 4.

46. The predominance of graduate students in the early phase of mobilization at Vanderbilt and many other institutions in the South casts doubt on the idea that the sixties student movement should primarily be viewed as a generational revolt of youth against their elders.

47. J. Anthony Lukas, *Don't Shoot—We Are Your Children!* (New York: Random House, 1968), 153. These events in Nashville would lead directly to the formation of the Southern Student Organizing Committee, the leading organization of progressive white students in the 1960s South. On the group's Nashville origins, see Gregg L. Michel, *Struggle for a Better South: The Southern Student Organizing Committee, 1964–1969* (New York: Palgrave, 2005), 26–30.

48. *The Hustler*, 1 May 1964, 1, 4.

49. Frissell to the author, 29 Apr. 2011.

50. Ibid. On the founding of the Vanderbilt SDS chapter, see *The Hustler*, 28 Feb. 1967, 3.

51. *The Hustler*, 28 Feb. 1967, 3.

52. On Vanderbilt in the late 1960s, see Conkin, *Gone with the Ivy*, 612–46.

53. *Fisk University Forum*, 13 Jan. 1967, 4.

54. On Black Power as it was manifested at Fisk, see Turner, *Sitting In and Speaking Out*, 177–78.

CHAPTER SIX

Student Radicalism and the Antiwar Movement at the University of Alabama

GARY S. SPRAYBERRY

On 6 May 1970, two days after National Guardsmen gunned down four students at Kent State University, antiwar protests erupted on the campus of the University of Alabama. Hundreds of students fanned out across the university quad, chanting antiwar slogans, singing Bob Dylan's "Blowin' in the Wind" and the unofficial anthem of the civil rights movement, "We Shall Overcome." Large groups of demonstrators gathered beneath the balcony of the residence of President David Mathews, heckling the administrator for his staunch conservatism and his recent efforts to squelch free speech on campus. Afterwards, dozens of students marched into the middle of University Avenue and staged a sit-in protest, blocking traffic along the busy thoroughfare. Another group marched on the Student Union building, occupying it for more than twelve hours. As night wore on and as tempers flared, someone set fire to Dressler Hall, an old wooden gymnasium on the edge of campus. As the building burned to the ground, one hundred state police officers were ordered to the campus to disperse the student demonstrators and stabilize the situation. The following morning, President Mathews, at 34 the youngest president in school history, imposed a campus-wide curfew and urged students to remain calm in the trying days ahead.[1]

Few heeded his words. For several days after, the campus played host to countless demonstrations, as students and faculty alike added their voices and bodies to the expanding protest. A flame had been kindled. After the 6 May demonstrations, students presented Mathews with a list of demands, which included the removal of special rules governing female students and the lifting of speaker bans. On 13 May, after Mathews refused to concede to these demands, protests once again engulfed the university campus. Hundreds of students gathered at the Student Union building—the site of dozens of protests in the late 1960s and early 1970s—and refused to obey police orders to disperse. Shouting matches erupted between the demonstrators and pro-administration students. Just after eleven o'clock, police waded into the crowd of protestors, swinging nightsticks, grabbing fistfuls of hair, and knocking many to the ground. The student newspaper, the *Crimson White,* likened the officers to "vicious, hungry wolves in search of blood." Dozens of students were beaten and arrested. When the officers made the mistake of attacking a group of fraternity brothers who were merely observing the fracas, the entire campus united against the police and university administrators, forcing President Mathews to reconsider student grievances and demands.[2]

If the above events had transpired at Berkeley, at Ann Arbor, or at Columbia University, few would have taken note. Such actions on those northern and western campuses had become commonplace by 1970. But the notion that such demonstrations had occurred at the University of Alabama—arguably one of the most conservative schools in the nation—struck many as absurd. "It's like finding marijuana in your grandmother's jewelry box," quipped one professor. After all, this was the place where George Wallace had made his infamous "stand at the schoolhouse door" in 1963, and where, in February 1956, students had revolted when an African American woman named Autherine Lucy registered for classes. This was the school *Time* magazine had labeled "a bastion of idolized athletes and lionized coaches, pretty coeds, fervent fraternity men and racism." But, to the shock and dismay of many, antiwar activists did exist at the university. And their actions were not part of some spontaneous uprising, forged in the heat and chaos that followed the Kent State shootings. For years, a small radical youth movement had been coalescing on campus, resisting the administration's conservative rule, challenging the policies of a reactionary local government, exploring new forms of self-expression, and protesting against the Vietnam War.[3]

In the South, though, such actions came with their own peculiar set of circumstances and dangers. As one University of Alabama (UA) student said: "Living in the South and being a freak isn't like living just anywhere and being a freak. While we have our common bonds with freaks everywhere, there are things which are [completely unique] about being a Southern hippie." And he was right. These young radicals lived in a region where patriotism, political conservatism, social conformity, and respect for one's elders were deeply rooted. According to a 1967 Gallup poll, southerners supported the Vietnam War in greater numbers than other Americans. They accounted for almost one-third of the soldiers who fought in the conflict and 28 percent of the men killed in action. A sense of duty and honor pervaded the South. To some, fighting for the country proved the best way to assert your manhood and affirm your patriotism. The students who were growing out their hair, burning draft notices, smoking grass, or shouting down school administrators at antiwar rallies were not only risking public censure and bodily harm; they were inviting shame and dishonor to their families.[4]

Besides giving us a better understanding of the characteristics and social pa-
rameters of the countercultural South, the study of student radicalism at the University of Alabama yields further lessons for scholars of the New Left. First, we
realize the limits of social activism at southern universities and colleges in the
1960s and the overall ineffectiveness of certain left-wing organizations. For years,
a relatively small group of radical students at UA had been challenging the administrations of Frank Rose and David Mathews, demanding fewer restrictions on
free speech and more power for student government. Realizing that such students
lacked influence across campus, the presidents could effectively ignore them. In
fact, until the shootings at Kent State, the student movement at UA seemed more
like a patchwork of special interest groups than a cohesive front against authority—too weak and too diffuse to effect meaningful change. But in May 1970, when
Tuscaloosa police officers savagely attacked fraternity and sorority members, thus
uniting liberal and conservative students against the administration and local officials, President Mathews began to concede to student demands.

The upheaval at UA demonstrates, too, that local and regional issues were just
as important as the Vietnam War in galvanizing the student movement. Vietnam
was, of course, the common thread that united New Left activists across the nation, from campus to campus. But at UA, a repressive local police force, the lack
of free speech on campus, discrimination against African American students, and
antiquated *in loco parentis* rules proved just as persuasive as the war in stirring
discontent and inspiring action. The tactics of UA activists closely resembled the
strategies of the nonviolent civil rights movement and rarely displayed the kind
of revolutionary fervor associated with radicals in the North and West. In retrospect, the demands of Alabama students seem modest: the repeal of mandatory
food contracts, the lifting of speaker bans, more student representation on university committees, and monthly meetings with the president. And their methods
for achieving these demands—sit-ins, petitions, candlelight vigils—could never
match the violent rhetoric or action of groups such as the Black Panthers or the
Weather Underground. In fact, the only real violence on the Alabama campus
throughout the May 1970 demonstrations emanated from the Tuscaloosa police
and the surreptitious activities of an FBI informant.

Evidence that this historically conservative campus was undergoing a cultural
and political metamorphosis had become quite visible by the late 1960s. Nowhere
was this more evident than in the Twelfth Avenue district near the campus—a
place the local newspaper, the *Tuscaloosa News,* had dubbed a "micro–Haight
Ashbury" after the famed hippie enclave in San Francisco. The apartments and
duplexes that lined Twelfth Avenue had seen better days, but they were cheap and
the students settled there in droves. "The housing in that area is as bad as any

housing in this city," said Tuscaloosa Police Commissioner James Chancy. "You talk about slums. Some of these apartments are really slums." All along Twelfth Avenue, the fraternity and sorority symbols displayed in previous years had been replaced by peace signs and exhortations to "drop out." "For several years the freek [*sic*] community has been growing here in Tuskaloosa [*sic*]," read an editorial in *High Gauge,* a local underground newspaper. "The hair has been growing into mountainous piles—apartment windows explode with color before the naked eye—lovely sweet smelling smoke scents the air—we dance to joyous music against Sunday afternoon blue sky." Wild, free-flowing parties would draw in dozens of revelers on the weekends, consuming several blocks along Twelfth Avenue. Students would gather around kegs of beer to talk about sex, the war, music, and politics, speaking of such things with a candor that doubtless would have shocked their parents. Many had grown weary of their parents' middle-class lifestyle and the conformity and hypocrisy of modern life and were seeking alternative ways to live. They were developing a culture that would parallel their growing political radicalism.[5]

It took a while for such changes to reach the deep South, but by the late 1960s they certainly had. At times, this behavior invited scrutiny from local authorities who, in the minds of students, tended to lump drug users, antiwar activists, and campus radicals into a single group. Quite often, the police would crash parties along Twelfth Avenue, raid suspected drug dens, and drop what one student termed the "ax of cultural repression." On 4 October 1968, the Tuscaloosa Sheriff's Office raided the Haight Hut, a head shop located near campus, and arrested two students, Bud Silvis and John Mullis, for possessing and selling LSD. Nine others, all university students, were apprehended and charged with vagrancy. Days after the raid, a co-owner of the Haight Hut, Robert C. Ford, told the *Crimson White* that police had not uncovered any drugs on the premises. The deputies seized water pipes, incense, and beads, taking "between $125 and $150 worth of merchandise," he said, "but found no drugs." Another one of the arrested students lamented, "I never realized we live in such a police state. It's one thing to have theoretical rights, but it's another thing to get those rights." On 18 October, despite testimony from three investigators that no drugs had been uncovered at the Haight Hut, a Grand Jury indicted Silvis and Mullis for the possession and sale of dangerous narcotics. Silvis never stood trial. Hours after his indictment, he shot himself in the head and died en route to the emergency room. "Bud G. Silvis died because there was no alternative," one student wrote to the *Crimson White.* "Bud Silvis, honor student, chemistry lab instructor, former Lt. Colonel in AFROTC died in order to be free. . . . No drugs were found at the Haight Hut because there were none. But that did not deter the Police because the Police were not necessarily interested in drugs alone. The Police were interested in Bud Silvis, because, to them, Bud Silvis was a symbol of everything that they fear and hate."[6]

On campus, students waged similar battles with school administrators, who seemed hopelessly lodged in the past. They fought to lift free speech restrictions and to extend more power to student government. One of the earliest clashes came in the fall of 1968, when the Democratic Student Organization asked permission from the Student Life Committee to invite Black Panther Eldridge Cleaver, SDS founder Tom Hayden, Yippie Jerry Rubin, and Communist historian Herbert Aptheker to the UA campus to speak. On 12 October, President Frank Rose wrote to Jack Drake, the DSO chairman, denying the organization's request. The president did not specifically address why these particular individuals had been barred from speaking. Instead, he focused on the right of the institution "to control its own destiny" and "have its own influence on the quality or shape of its educational product." He wrote, "It is my understanding that the [DSO] is stating that a chartered student organization has the constitutional right to have any speaker that it so desires; and that the educational institution . . . has no authority or right to make any judgements about who may or may not use its facilities. . . . The University cannot claim for itself . . . absolute rights in this matter. Thus, to the question of whether a student organization has an absolute right to hear any speaker of its own choice, the institution must reply that it does not." Drake wrote back to President Rose, wanting to know why he had not "considered our speakers individually nor assigned any specific reasons for objecting to any particular speaker." He never received a satisfactory reply. The DSO told the *Crimson White* that the "right of chartered campus organizations to bring speakers to campus goes to the heart of a free institution. . . . Unfortunately, the University's decision to ban these speakers is part of a consistent policy toward 'leftist' speakers." A few days later, Drake and the DSO filed a civil suit against President Rose and the University of Alabama, seeking to enjoin the plaintiffs from banning the four speakers from campus.[7]

In the midst of its speaker ban controversy, the DSO planned to hold "a rally against the Vietnamese War" on 21 October on the steps of the Student Union building. According to Mike Stambaugh, former president of the DSO, President Rose immediately nixed the idea for the demonstration, informing the students that "they would be allowed to assemble on the Union steps for 10 minutes after which they would be required to move on to be silenced in the confines of Foster Auditorium." School officials said that they offered the use of the auditorium after receiving word from a Birmingham television station that four hundred students from various colleges had made plans to attend the peace rally. They were worried about the crowd size and their ability to provide adequate security to the students.

Rather than comply, the DSO voted to move the rally off campus to the Canterbury Episcopal Student Center. Stambaugh resigned in disgust, believing that the organization had acquiesced to pressure from the administration. He had presumably wanted to force a confrontation.[8]

The 21 October rally proved a tense affair. Fifty members of DSO gathered at the Student Union building at noon and marched in silence to the Canterbury Student Center. The demonstrators put tape across their mouths to protest "the lack of free speech at [the] University." Dozens of other students heckled and jeered at them as they marched past. Investigators under the command of Floyd Mann, state director of public safety, had been invited to the campus to observe the rally. Several city policemen were also on hand as the marchers filtered into the Student Center. According to some reports, Colonel Beverly Leigh, the UA police chief, pointed out "students to 'state investigators' as they took pictures and wrote down names of those coming out of the DSO meeting." Tuscaloosa police arrested a reporter for the *Southern Courier* for "disorderly conduct" after he snapped a photograph of a state investigator. The police confiscated the Polaroid image and tore it up. Jim Baines, a congressional candidate from Alabama's seventh district, asked the officers, "On what charges are you taking that man in?" The police took Baines in custody as well, charging him with "vagrancy."[9]

Tension and fear began to build on the UA campus. "Recent events including vagrancy arrests, the speakers case, and the student suicide have all tended to bring about a situation of several warring camps," Professor Richard Singer, faculty advisor for the DSO, told the *Crimson White*. "Many students are angry, upset and scared of police action. And they are worried about police retaliation." Following the arrests at the Canterbury Student Center, 15 students wrote a letter to President Rose inquiring about Colonel Leigh's involvement at the DSO rally. They wanted to know why Leigh had identified certain students to state investigators, and they expressed concern over reports that the Colonel kept a brown notebook containing the names of campus subversives. "It seems as if Col. Leigh was there for reasons other than protecting University students," the letter read. Larry McGehee, executive assistant to President Rose, denied the existence of the brown notebook and tried to downplay Leigh's actions at the rally. "[Leigh] did point out to city police several reporters who were present and he did identify, at their explicit request, two students," he wrote. "He took no initiative in offering such identification. In fact, in the case of the two students, the city police already knew who the students were, but wanted to be sure of their facts. . . . We are satisfied that the actions of University personnel at the time, while capable of speculation and misinterpretation, were genuinely geared to the protection of University students and to the insuring of orderly assembly."[10]

The students would not allow the matter to dissipate. On 30 October the DSO staged another rally on the steps of the Student Union building to protest police harassment. A hundred students and a handful of faculty members participated. In obvious reference to the 21 October rally, several protestors jokingly snapped photographs of the dozens of spectators and campus police officers on hand. Tommy Thompson, the new DSO president, urged the crowd "to come and join us." Many did. Others were more reluctant, telling the *Crimson White* that they were afraid of police retaliation. The following day, Jim Zeigler and Jason Braswell, members of the Student Government Association, appeared before the Tuscaloosa City Commission to ask "why we have been subjected to continued police harassment." "The feeling of concern on campus is not just among left-wingers," Zeigler said. "Even the supporters of Gov. Wallace are concerned with the action of city police in recent weeks." Police Commissioner George Ryan defended the actions of the officers at the Canterbury Student Center. "Anytime the University administration calls us out there, we go to do a job, not to baby-sit and coddle students," he told Zeigler. "These weren't just students being arrested. . . . Son, did you know those are outside agitators?"[11]

The war of words between the students and city government continued into the spring semester of 1969. On 13 April the police showed up at an apartment building along Twelfth Avenue—the "micro–Haight Ashbury district"—to investigate violations of a city ordinance, which forbade drinking in public. When they arrived, people were in the streets dancing and drinking beer. A policeman seized a cup from one of the students, poured it out, and then handed it back to him. The student threw the cup at the officer. Four revelers were jailed. The *Crimson White* accused the police of harassment and of conducting a "witch-hunt." The arrested students later reported that they had been treated "roughly" by the police. In a report published in the *Tuscaloosa News,* the arresting officer dismissed such charges as frivolous. He wrote, "Some students act like they can behave in any manner in our city and violate the rights of our taxpaying citizen majority, and still not be interfered with by [police]." A few days later, at a city commission meeting, Jim Zeigler got into a shouting match with Police Chief W. M. Marable, warning that if the harassment continued, the students would be more "inclined to listen to radical leaders." When the police chief tried to interject, Ziegler told him to "learn some manners" and quit interrupting. Marable exploded: "Just shut up! That's enough out of you!"[12]

After the meeting, Commissioner George Ryan asked Marable to investigate the 13 April incident and report back to the city commission. Marable said that he could find "no evidence of misconduct or illegal acts on the part of the officers." By his estimate, they had shown "leniency" to the students by not hauling more of them into jail. Marable concluded: "Policemen are human, they are 'of the people, by the people and for the people,' but they are not the criminal, the Anti-American demonstrator, or the draft dodgers, nor the destructive and militant dissenters who hate all things American. Our function is to protect decent citizens from those who violate our laws—and that we intend to keep doing."[13]

UA officials worried about the growing unrest among students. "Several department heads, particularly in the sciences, have reported to me conversations with graduate students who have knowledge of various . . . radical student groups on campus," wrote Douglas Jones, dean of the College of Arts and Sciences. "There are approximately five different groups on campus now with little or no uniform purpose in mind. . . . One brick through one glass door would destroy a $75,000 piece of research equipment in chemistry; the same would hold true for the computer center." He lamented the fact that there were no guidelines in place to deal with student demonstrations or the possible takeover of a campus building by radicals. "It seems to me that if one of our science buildings is forcibly entered, stringent measures should be employed to get them out of the building as quickly as possible," he said. "To inform the faculty after a confrontation begins will be useless. They need to know ahead of time what the official stand of the University will be if trouble develops." Days later, Ervin R. Van Artsdalen, chair of the Chemistry Department, reported to Dean Jones that someone had broken into one of the instructional laboratories and "carefully booby-trapped three doors with bottles of concentrated hydrochloric acid, so arranged that when anyone would unlock and open the door from the outside, the acid would be spilled upon the door and probably also upon the person of the man involved." Van Artsdalen dismissed the action as a "vicious practical joke rather than general campus uprising." But he urged the administration to enhance security in all of the science buildings.[14]

Tensions between student radicals and the administration reached a boiling point in March 1970, when the Student Government Association announced plans to bring activist Abbie Hoffman to campus for the Emphasis '70 program, an annual political forum held at the university. The SGA hoped the program would include a debate between Hoffman and former governor George Wallace, who was in the middle of a tight gubernatorial primary campaign with the incumbent governor, Albert Brewer. Wallace refused to participate, saying that he would not "debate someone who wasn't a gentleman." President David Mathews killed the idea as soon as he heard about it, telling reporters that due to Hoffman's recent conviction in the "Chicago Seven" trial, there was "considerable legal uncertainly about" allowing him to speak. A day after the announcement, dozens of students planted themselves outside Mathews's office and refused to budge until the president changed his mind. Mathews, though, held his ground.

Hearing that Hoffman's appearance had been cancelled, Wallace decided to show up for the Emphasis '70 event on 16 March. As soon as he took the podium, he was greeted by a throng of noisy hecklers, who wore black arm bands and hoisted signs that read: "Weirdos for Wallace." The former governor told them: "I've taken on the pros and you look like a bunch of amateurs." But when chants of "We're number 50, we're number 50"—a not-so-subtle reminder of Alabama's socioeconomic ranking among other states—began to drown out the PA system, Wallace cut it short. In the days following Wallace's speech, angry students sent editorials to the *Crimson White,* demanding to know why Abbie Hoffman had not been allowed to speak. They camped out in front of the president's mansion, heckled administration-approved speakers, and organized free speech rallies throughout the month of April.[15]

Off campus, students faced even more scrutiny from local police. On 1 May 1970 a sheriff's deputy visited a residence along Riverview Drive in Tuscaloosa to serve a subpoena to a potential witness in a civil suit. As soon as he stepped onto the front porch, the deputy claimed that he could smell marijuana. Leaning forward to knock on the door, he noticed two messages etched into the woodwork. The first one read: "You can't enter unless invited." The second one, scrawled into the doorframe itself, stated plainly: "Bill went to the moon." Ignoring the first message, the officer entered the house and, according to a *Tuscaloosa News* reporter, found himself transported "into a different world." Scattered all about the house were large plastic bags packed with "bulk marijuana," along with measuring scales, seeds, pipes, rolling papers, and other paraphernalia. The deputy discovered improvised hothouses along the wall of the living room, where dozens of young cannabis plants emerged from fresh, warm soil. Upstairs in the "cutting room," where "psychedelic posters" adorned the walls and beer cans littered the floor, the officer stumbled upon several more bags of marijuana. He also found a notebook filled with "unusual scribbling," which "seemed to have been done by someone 'high' on drugs." In one passage, someone had written, "We see Fred walking across the campus . . . life is such a damn bore."[16]

Next door in the garage, which had been converted into makeshift living quarters, the deputy found strange neon lights and colorful beads hanging from the ceiling. A couple of ratty-looking mattresses were flung haphazardly upon the floor, surrounded by islands of trash and dirty laundry. Realizing that he had indeed crossed into a "different world," the deputy immediately radioed for help. Within minutes, an army of detectives, uniformed officers, reporters, and city attorneys had descended upon what Commissioner Chancy called one of the largest "marijuana factories" ever found in Tuscaloosa County.

Figure 6.1. Segregationist icon George Wallace is forced to cut short a 1970 address at the University of Alabama as progressive students heckle him over the state's dismal record on social services and poverty. Courtesy The W. S. Hoole Special Collections Library, the University of Alabama.

Coming only a few months after Mayor C. Snow Hinton had vowed that "all the resources of the City of Tuscaloosa are going to be concentrated on stopping [the] punks who are selling drugs," the discovery of the house on Riverview Drive served as a tremendous boon to local authorities. A week later, as antiwar demonstrations raged on the UA campus, police apprehended the two students who shared the residence and booked them on a variety of drug charges. In the coming weeks and months, the two detainees were joined by several of their classmates, as the city redoubled its efforts to impede the flow of illegal drugs. Moreover, the arrests served notice to all the "hippies" and "long hairs" that the governing powers of Tuscaloosa had their eyes upon them and were, according to one local attorney, determined to "destroy a movement which irreverently challenges their myths, their country, their idols, and, in fact, their whole life-style."

Captain Robert Sawyer, who belonged to the Tuscaloosa Police Department's "drug education section," agreed. He told the *Tuscaloosa News* that most of the drug users at UA hailed from the school's "thought and theory" departments. "They don't like the present establishment," he said. "[They] don't like authority, and they think they are being held down." Sawyer concluded that most users were "generally students who feel they should never have to work and that America should become some kind of welfare-utopia state."[17]

The same day that officials discovered the "marijuana factory" on Riverview Drive, rumors began surfacing that Abbie Hoffman's co-defendant in the "Chicago Seven" trial, Jerry Rubin, was somewhere on campus and would make an appearance at the upcoming "Festival of Life," a rock concert sponsored by the student-led Experimental College. School officials assured the public that the rumors were false. Students, after all, had not asked if Rubin could speak on campus, so there was little chance he would be making an appearance. But Rubin did show up at the 3 May concert, strolling onto the stage to wild applause. He hoisted what he called the Yippie flag, a solid black background with a marijuana leaf embroidered in the middle. He told the crowd they should smoke dope and enjoy life. To emphasize his point, Rubin allegedly lit a marijuana cigarette and smoked it onstage. He encouraged the students to challenge the authority of the University and local officials, telling them that the administration does not run the school, students do. He said: "I am everything George Wallace says I am." The school promised sanctions against the student organizers for not going through the proper channels to bring Rubin to campus. The "Festival of Life" concert had been approved by the administration, but no "outside speakers had been registered" by the Experimental College. A former student said: "The people on this campus have been censored by Mathews and the power structure too long. If you want the power to do something, you just do it. When people get together and decide to do something, it all works out." Others saw it differently.

One parent wrote to Mathews: "I was sorry to hear that Jerry was sneaked . . . on campus but my son thought he was repulsive and mentally deranged."[18]

The conflict between students and administrators reached its crescendo after the U.S. invasion of Cambodia and the deaths at Kent State. On the night of 6 May, two days after the shootings at Kent, the newly formed Tuscaloosa Women's Liberation Movement organized a candlelight vigil on the Quad to honor the dead. Students had asked President Mathews to declare a moratorium on classes, but he refused (although he did grant permission for the flag to be flown at half-mast on campus). The vigil began as planned, with more than one thousand students descending on the Quad to remember the victims of Kent State. Hundreds of candles flickered in the darkness, as participants read poems and sang "Blowin' in the Wind." Afterwards, they walked over to the ROTC building and placed candles along the sidewalk and front entrance. Inside, several members of the ROTC braced themselves for an onslaught, convinced that the protestors had intentions of ransacking the building.

Some of the demonstrators were not satisfied with the candlelight vigil and wanted to do more. Someone yelled out, "Let's go to Mathews!" Hundreds of students raced across University Boulevard and heckled Mathews beneath his balcony window, demanding he come out and talk to them. The president was not home at the time. The group remained on the president's lawn for an hour, ignoring the pleas of faculty members to leave. One of the students, Stoney Johnson, urged everyone to "stay all night long," or at least until Mathews made an appearance. "We're going to get the man here if we have to go get him ourselves," he shouted. Around ten o'clock, at Johnson's behest, a large group of students walked into the middle of University Boulevard and held a sit-in protest, blocking traffic for several minutes. Afterwards, several of them marched down and seized the Student Union building, holding it throughout the night, liberating hundreds of dollars' worth of sodas and junk food. Sometime after midnight, Dressler Hall, an old wooden gymnasium, was set ablaze. Fearing further destruction, Governor Albert Brewer sent in one hundred state troopers to restore order.[19]

The following day, when the troopers arrived on campus, they immediately made their presence known, donning riot gear and driving loitering students from the Quad. For several days they remained on campus, menacing the protestors, intimidating students and faculty alike. They were everywhere. "They were pugnacious, obnoxious . . . very self-righteous," remembered one student. "[They] knew that they had God, George Wallace and Albert Brewer on their side. And they weren't taking anything off anybody. That was kind of scary. They seemed to be a little bit out of control." With the troopers' help, Mathews declared a curfew and ordered a ban on all assemblies. The troopers enforced the rules with impunity.

"The campus is a police state," said one student. "The protests and all were over last night until the police waded in. Now things are real uneasy." A group of students hung a sheet from the balcony of the Union Building, which bore a single message in large brown letters: "1984 is here."[20]

Several protests were organized over the next couple of days but were quickly dispersed by authorities. On 8 May, for instance, students planned to hold a "teach-in" on the Quad to discuss the Kent State shootings and other issues gripping the campus. Around three o'clock, as dozens began to arrive for the event, 50 helmeted state troopers lined up "military style with their riot sticks and tear gas equipment." Colonel Leigh told SGA president Jim Zeigler that he could not guarantee the safety of students. "If you go ahead on out there, I am not going to say that nothing is going to happen," he said. "I am not bluffing." After a tense few minutes, the students elected to vacate the Quad.[21]

Despite the restrictions on public gatherings, the students found ways to get their message across to the administration and the community. Back on the night of 6 May, the students who had seized control of the Student Union building drew up a list of demands to present to President Mathews. This included an end to speaker bans, "the immediate granting of all Black student demands," "amnesty for everyone involved in the protests," removal of outside police forces, "student control of student funds," monthly meetings with the president, and the lifting of special restrictions for female students.[22]

Two of the issues—the restrictions on female students and the concerns of African Americans at the university—had been simmering for many months. Groups such as the Association for Women Students and the Tuscaloosa Women's Liberation Movement had been demanding changes to the *in loco parentis* rules since 1968. They wanted to extend curfew hours for female students, allow more unmarried women to live off campus, and permit male students to visit female dorms. Despite opposition from concerned parents, the UA administration began implementing some changes in the fall of 1968. For instance, female students aged 21 and over could now live off campus if they so desired. In the spring of 1969, the university began allowing female students to visit male dormitories during designated weekend hours. In December, the administration extended the curfew for other female students from 11:00 p.m. to midnight. In early 1970, the University finally removed the curfew for women with at least 60 credit hours. Despite the advancements, the students who took over the Union building on 6 May demanded more. They wanted the administration to abolish all curfews "regardless of age or class standing," allow men to visit female dormitories, establish "off-campus living rights regardless of age," and create a "fact-finding committee to investigate possible pay and promotion differences for women faculty members."[23]

The protestors were also sensitive and responsive to the demands and problems of African American students. Following the integration of the university in 1963, the black student population had grown slowly but steadily. In May 1971, a full year after the antiwar demonstrations, there were still only 340 African Americans out of a total of 13,000 students at UA. Many of them still felt socially and culturally isolated from the rest of the campus. Back in 1968, several black students organized a chapter of the Afro-American Association and presented a list of demands to President Frank Rose. They asked for more courses in African American history, a black officer on the campus police force, "housing without discrimination," and the hiring of more black professors. By the end of the 1968–69 academic year, the AAA could point to many signs of progress at the university, including the addition of black history courses, a float in the UA homecoming parade, more African Americans appointed to student-led committees, and the hiring of a black campus police officer. But more work remained. The aftermath of the Kent State shootings created the opportunity for black and white activists to unite against university officials. The demonstrators who seized the Union building on the night of 6 May accused the administration of being "unsympathetic toward the black student's experience on the campus." They wanted President Mathews to act immediately and decisively to implement black demands, including the creation of a Black Studies department, the establishment of an Afro-American Center, the hiring of African American professors, the "recruitment of black athletes," and the "desegregation of fraternities and sororities."[24]

While a majority of faculty members remained silent about the protests or continued to throw support to the administration, there were a few who openly sided with student activists and their cause. Back in April, dozens of professors from a variety of disciplines had attached their names to a "Petition for Peace" in the *Crimson White*. They called on members of the university community to "express their dissatisfaction with current U.S. Policy in South East Asia" by supporting the upcoming "Peace Fast of April 13–15." On 6 May, hours before the Tuscaloosa Women's Liberation Movement's candlelight vigil on the Quad, Iredell Jenkins, chair of the Philosophy Department, spoke to a group of students on the steps of the Union building. He urged them to remain nonviolent when protesting the senseless deaths at Kent State. "Violence and public disturbance would defeat any purpose we have here," he said. "The most frightening thing in this country now is the divisiveness—this country is breaking apart." Jenkins concluded his address with an appeal to the government to send "every plane the U.S. owns" to Vietnam "to bring back right now every boy there." Other professors joined the students in demanding a two-day moratorium on classes to honor the Kent State shooting victims. Dr. Joseph Bettis, chair of the Religion Department, said that each student should "act according to his conscience and take whatever actions he thinks necessary to cause suspension." Following the 6 May demonstrations and the burning of Dressler Hall, Jenkins, Bettis, and other professors helped organize the Student-Faculty Coalition and urged the administration to consider the list of student demands.[25]

President Mathews, however, had other intentions. After pledging to keep the university open and work "to find reasonable solutions to real problems," he rejected all of the demands of student activists. In a 12 May statement to the "University Community," the president explained,

> The cause of genuine reform here has been seriously threatened by association with the disruptions we have seen in the last several days. I am, therefore, calling on every member of the University community to make it perfectly clear that disruptions and threats of disruptions will meet with unequivocal condemnation. Some real problems that we have been working on this year have now been drawn into focus at this time of campus unrest. We should all be greatly concerned not to respond to these problems in such a way to give any appearance of making disruptive tactics work or improperly to associate these problems with radicalism. *For that reason, I would hope that everyone would understand the necessity of deliberately refraining from any announcements of future changes in this particular setting.*

Mathews pointed to the recent reforms that had been implemented in regard to the rights and privileges of female students. "We have made more changes recently than ever in our history," he said. As for the demands of African American students, Mathews highlighted the very recent hiring of five black faculty members and a handful of administrators. He also alluded to the creation of the Afro-American Grievance Committee, which had been meeting regularly over the previous year to find solutions to the myriad problems facing black students. The president concluded, "Whether we progress or not will depend entirely on whether . . . we can demonstrate to ourselves and others that we can differ and decide, like people of reason, without resorting to even the suggestion of disruption or mass pressure. This University is very important to a great many people. I hope that you will join me in trying to keep it open."[26]

Following the president's statement, letters and telegrams streamed in from across the state, commending Mathews for his hard-line stance. "We certainly do not agree with the demands made by the students—neither by the women students nor the blacks," wrote one resident. "Campus disorders have caused me to 'about face' completely concerning the 18 yr. old's right to vote. I certainly don't want these college youth choosing my public officials if their judgment is no better than indicated." Another writer objected to the involvement of faculty members in the demonstrations. "Please do not allow a few Liberal long Hair Proffesors [*sic*] to stay at the University and lead a bunch of Bums to destroy it," he wrote. "I hope you weed all of this trash out—you have the people behind you. Do not let these Bums make our Great University another Berkley [*sic*] or Yale." Other respondents were more succinct: "Stand firm. Force if necessary. We support you."[27]

On campus, however, the president's remarks were met with mounting disgust. One student wrote, "[If] Dr. Mathews had bothered to come out of the Crystal Palace and [talk] with students and/or faculty more frequently so that they would know what he was doing and so that he would know what their problems were, we *probably* would not have all this mess on our hands!" On the night of 13 May hundreds of students converged on the Quad again, protesting the president's refusal to consider their demands. This time, they were met by pro-administration demonstrators, who carried signs reading, "Fight pollution / Send hippies to Cuba" and "A Good Hippie is a Dead Hippie." The two groups stood toe to toe, shouting at one another. When the arguing seemed destined to erupt into violence, state troopers informed the two groups that they had ten minutes to clear out or face arrest. Before the allotted time had expired, the troopers and local police moved in, swinging nightsticks, pulling hair, and shoving people into police cars. The *Crimson White* concluded: "It was as if Adolph Hitler had returned from the grave to put every student in [a grave] of their own."[28]

Several students who were not involved in the demonstrations were beaten by police and tossed into jail—actions that led many self-styled conservative students to criticize Mathews's management of the crisis. "These incidents of beating and unlawful arrest made me sick and filled me with fear," one student wrote to Mathews. "I can't grasp your reasons for such a course of action—what do you hope to prove and to whom? We are students; we are your people, why betray us. I've always felt that I was middle-of-the-road on most issues, but I feel that its now time for me to take my stand, a stand of decency. The incidents of last night have caused me, and many of my peers, to resent you and the police." One student, Richard Winstead, a former all-state basketball star and member of the Delta Kappa Epsilon fraternity, arrived at the "Deke House" with his date just as the police were pursuing students from the Quad. Members of the fraternity stood on the lawn of the frat house, watching the drama unfold. Several police officers formed a wedge and headed down University Boulevard toward the Deke House. Without provocation, they marched headlong into the onlookers, beating anyone who stood in their way. One of the officers hit Winstead's date in the back of the head. Winstead yelled out: "Leave her alone. Don't touch her!" Five or six officers tackled Winstead, threw him into some bushes, and savagely beat him with nightsticks.[29]

Tuscaloosa police arrested another student, Charles Schwartz, outside an Orange Julius near the campus, charging him with "failure to obey an officer." According to his father, he had been at someone's house all night with his girlfriend and had not participated in the demonstration. After taking Schwartz to the police station, the officers reportedly sprayed him with kerosene or insect repellant and ordered him to strip naked. The officers told "him his long hair and beard contained bugs." "While this was going on the police officers were laughing," Schwartz's father wrote to President Mathews. "He did not know what charge he was arrested on until the next day after he was out on bond." The elder Schwartz, a veteran of World War II, Korea, and Vietnam, questioned why he had risked his own life to defend a country that could violate the rights of its citizens in such a callous way. "When my son is arrested on a public street for no other reason than he had a beard, and is subjected to the indignities performed by the Tuscaloosa police department, then I have to ask myself why did I fight against the Nazis and against the communists," he wrote. "[W]hen this sort of action is condoned by you and the governor of the state one begins to wonder if maybe these young radicals are not right after all."[30]

Even newspaper reporters were not immune to the violence. Just before the police ordered the students to disperse, journalist Wayne Greenhaw walked over to an open-air corridor near the Student Union building to use a pay telephone to call in a story before his 11:00 p.m. deadline. Seconds later, a frantic student ran past with a police officer in close pursuit. Before the officer passed, he made sure to stop and take a swing at Greenhaw with his nightstick. Greenhaw somehow dodged the blow and then ran away as fast as he could. He managed to blend in with a large group of students, who were desperately trying to get away from police. More than 50 students were arrested during the protests, and dozens were pummeled with billy clubs. According to most accounts, only one phrase could aptly capture what had happened: police riot.[31]

The brutal attacks on the evening of 13 May were a turning point for the movement at UA. Before this traumatic conflict, the protests had been confined to a relatively small group of radicals. The beatings of Richard Winstead and other fraternity brothers, however, united liberal and conservative students against the police and school administrators. "That was the solidarity on this campus," one professor remembers. "The freaks and the frats both joined against this nonsense." One fraternity member said: "You know, we never believed the black students about police brutality. We thought the freaks deserved whatever they got. Now it's close to home." Wayne Greenhaw reported that sorority women, who would not have dared participate in such protests in the past, were now leaning from their windows and yelling to passing police cars, "Pig! Pig!" Sorority and fraternity members alike displayed signs in front of their respective houses calling for an end to the Vietnam War. The mood on the campus was surreal. Student David Lowe, a self-described "hippie long hair," rode his motorcycle past the Deke House a few days after the violence of 13 May. He stopped at the traffic light in front of the house and noticed several fraternity brothers out on the lawn. He raised his fist in the "revolutionary salute." The Dekes turned and raised their fists in solidarity.[32]

For the next few days, demonstrations continued unabated, with the student body and president both refusing to give in. The Student-Faculty Coalition called for a campus-wide strike, but it failed to materialize. President Mathews paid a visit to the Deke House and apologized for the previous violence but vowed to enforce the assembly ban. On the night of 15 May another building, a small warehouse, burned to the ground, as students clashed openly with state troopers and local police. On the night of 18 May, three days after police shot and killed two students at Jackson State College in Mississippi, dozens of students held another candlelight vigil on the Quad. Sixty "riot-trained state police" confronted the students as they placed candles along the steps of Denny Chimes, a bell tower that had been a campus icon for decades. After someone began throwing objects at the troopers from the balcony of the Student Union building, Major John Cloud of the Alabama State Troopers declared the gathering "an unlawful assembly." More than 40 students were subsequently arrested. With the campus seemingly ready to explode again, SGA president Jim Zeigler submitted a plan to President Mathews to make final exams optional, which would result in students leaving early. Eight thousand students signed a supporting petition. Days later, Mathews approved the SGA plan and the campus cleared of students overnight. By virtue of the semester's end, peace had been restored; the "movement had left with the summer vacation."[33]

Throughout the summer of 1970, many of the students arrested during the demonstrations were put on trial. As the cases wended their way through the legal system, more information came to light concerning the May protests. The ACLU lawyers who defended many of the activists discovered that students had not actually been responsible for much of the violence and unrest on campus. Part, if not all, of the blame could be placed at the feet of the police and state troopers, who had employed heavy-handed tactics to subdue the crowds. Attorneys Jack Drake, Ralph Knowles, and George Dean, representing nearly one hundred of those arrested in May, also uncovered evidence that students had nothing to do with the burning of Dressler Hall. Their investigations revealed that Charles Grimm, an informant for both the FBI and Tuscaloosa police, had actually set the fires. He was arrested with the demonstrators but mysteriously left town before his court date and was therefore never prosecuted. According to the three attorneys, Grimm had been recruited by the FBI to infiltrate the local movement, identify its leaders, "encourage conflict and division within the University community," and provoke the students into committing acts of violence. He also did undercover drug work for the Tuscaloosa police, helping the department make "thirteen arrests for drug abuse." The attorneys also linked Grimm to several additional acts of arson and violence around the campus. For instance, on 18 May it was allegedly Grimm who "threw a bicycle pedal, a softball, and a brick" at officers from the balcony of the Student Union building, prompting Major Cloud to declare the candlelight vigil "an unlawful assembly." Four nights earlier, Grimm reportedly tossed six Molotov cocktails into the street in front of the Denny Court Apartment complex. When police arrived, they arrested several students, giving one of them a severe beating in the process. If such accounts were indeed true, the FBI and local police were the instigators of much of the unrest that had gripped the UA campus in May. To this day, Grimm has not been held accountable for his actions.[34]

In September 1970, as students arrived on campus for the start of the fall semester, many sought to rekindle the movement. Concerts and teach-ins were planned. An underground newspaper, *High Gauge,* went into circulation. The pressure began to build again. This time, however, school administrators were more receptive to student demands. During the summer, the newly appointed University Council Committee on Campus Unrest, composed of students, faculty members, and administrators, had conducted a study of the May demonstrations. They made several recommendations that would strengthen the relationship between the University and city government, "establish a marshaling system to handle large public demonstrations," and open lines of communication between students and the administration. For instance, student representatives were appointed to the University Council for the first time in school history. A booklet, "Student Rights and Responsibilities," was distributed at the beginning of the fall semester in an effort to inform students about their rights as members of the university community. The administration also hired Floyd Mann, the Alabama public safety director, to replace Colonel Beverly Leigh and restructure the campus security forces, making them more "service-oriented" and student-friendly. The administration even planned to organize a number of "discussion groups," consisting of students, members of city government, police officers, school administrators, and local businessmen in the hopes of improving relations between "town and gown."

By most accounts, the demonstrations had shifted the political terrain on campus. More reforms would be implemented in the coming months and years, as the administration loosened its grip on the student body and began to show some consideration for its opinions and aspirations. By the mid-1970s, most of the remaining restrictions for female students had been eliminated, giving women the freedom to come and go as they pleased. In 1975, a women's studies program was introduced at the university—the first of its kind in the southeast. School officials also granted students greater leeway in choosing outside speakers, thus lifting the ban on free speech. In February 1974, for example, the Afro-American Association invited famed activist Angela Davis to campus, sparking outrage across the state. "I can't believe that you will allow Angela Davis, a self confessed Communist, to speak at the University of Alabama," one resident wrote to President Mathews. "I trust you will use your authority to see that this enemy of our way of life is not allowed to speak in this state (tax payers) university." But Mathews defended the AAA's right to bring Davis to campus. "It is true that a group of students invited the speaker in question to make a public address, but the University would have no authority to intervene," he explained. "Public speech is regulated by the Constitution, and if an individual is allowed [by the] law to speak in the country in all public places, no particular agency can prohibit such a speech in its location." Jefferson J. Coleman, director of alumni affairs, concurred. "I can understand why many people are repulsed by Angela Davis," he wrote. "On the other hand, there must [be] a place in this world where one can freely say what they believe and think, and I believe a University is a most appropriate place for that. We believe that a great majority of the faculty and staff of the University of Alabama, as well as a great majority of the citizens of the State of Alabama have great faith in our youth. . . . [We] do not believe that a person such as Angela Davis will corrupt them."[35]

Progress was made along the racial front as well. More Black Studies courses were added to the curriculum, and the university began funding special events, like Black History Week. In 1971, after the AAA sued the legendary coach Paul "Bear" Bryant for discriminating against black athletes (the suit was eventually tossed out), two African American players, Wilbur Jackson and John Mitchell, joined the UA varsity football squad. In 1976, Cleo Thomas became the first African American student to be elected president of the Student Government Association. These were, by all accounts, significant strides and reflected a willingness on the part of the university community to correct past injustices. Yet countless inequities remained. By the fall of 1975, there were still only 13 fulltime black faculty members at UA, representing about 2 percent of the total faculty. A Black Studies program had not yet been implemented, the Afro-American Cultural Center had failed to emerge, and fraternities and sororities were still segregated (and would remain so until the early twenty-first century).[36]

Many students bristled under the slow pace of advancement. "The University of Alabama, as many other predominantly White institutions, has taken this cornerstone-right from the foundation of American democracy and replaced it with its own cornerstone of Institutional [Racism]," the AAA charged in a 1975 report. "It has become imbedded in the every day workings of this University constantly depriving the Black students of their inherent rights and [privileges] under the constitution of this land and the Laws of God." The AAA would continue to apply pressure to the administration throughout the 1970s, organizing periodic boycotts and marches "to arouse the social consciousness of this nation and marshall the eyes of the people to monitor the course of the movement." Problems would persist, but the spirit of activism unleashed in 1970 insured that school officials would no longer be able to ignore the concerns of students. As *Time* magazine observed: "When dissent can transform an Alabama . . . it can happen anywhere."[37]

NOTES

1. *Tuscaloosa News,* 7 May 1970; *Crimson White,* 7 May 1970.

2. *Crimson White,* 14 May 1970; *Tuscaloosa News,* 8–14 May 1970.

3. *New York Times,* 24 May 1970; *Time,* 1 June 1970. For additional information on the Autherine Lucy affair and George Wallace's "stand in the schoolhouse door," see E. Culpepper Clark, *The Schoolhouse Door: Segregation's Last Stand at the University of Alabama* (New York: Oxford Univ. Press, 1995).

4. *High Gauge,* 13 Aug. 1970; John Ernst and Yvonne Baldwin, "The Not So Silent Minority: Louisville's Antiwar Movement, 1966–1975," *Journal of Southern History* 73, no. 1 (Feb. 2007): 106.

5. *Tuscaloosa News,* 4 Mar. 1970; *High Gauge,* 13 Aug. 1970.

6. *Crimson White,* 8, 10, 22, and 29 Oct. 1968.

7. Jack Drake to the Student Life Committee, 27 Sept. 1968; Frank Rose to Jack Drake, 12 Oct. 1968; Jack Drake to Frank Rose, 13 Oct. 1968, folder "Democratic Student Organization, 1968," box 03, President David Mathews Papers, Stanley Hoole Special Collections Library, University of Alabama, Tuscaloosa, Alabama; *Crimson White,* 15 Oct. 1968; *Jack Drake v. Frank Rose,* 68–653 (Northern District of Alabama, 1968).

8. *Crimson White,* 29 Oct. 1968; Dean John L. Blackburn to Michael Stambaugh, 19 Oct. 1968, and Larry T. McGehee to Harry A. Edgar, 6 Nov. 1968, folder "Democratic Student Organization, 1968," box 03, President David Mathews Papers.

9. *Crimson White,* 24 Oct. 1968; Jim Zeigler et al. to Frank Rose, n.d., folder "Democratic Student Organization," box 03, President David Mathews Papers.

10. *Crimson White,* 29 Oct. 1968; Jim Zeigler et al. to Frank Rose, n.d., and Larry McGehee to Harry A. Edgar, 6 Nov. 1968, folder "Democratic Student Organization, 1968," box 03, President David Mathews Papers.

11. *Crimson White,* 5 Nov. 1968.

12. *Tuscaloosa News,* 27 and 29 Apr. 1969; *Crimson White,* 21 Apr. 1969; Minutes of the Tuscaloosa City Commission, 17 and 29 Apr. 1969, City Clerk's Office, Tuscaloosa, Alabama.

13. *Tuscaloosa News,* 30 Apr. 1969.

14. Douglas E. Jones to David Mathews, Raymond McLain, Willard Gray, Larry McGehee, and John Blackburn, 16 May 1969, and Ervin R. Van Artsdalen to Douglas E. Jones, 20 May 1969, folder "XV 23," box 20, President David Mathews Papers.

15. *Tuscaloosa News,* 4–7, 9, 15, and 17 Mar. 1970; *Crimson White,* 17, 19, and 23 Mar. 1970.

16. *Tuscaloosa News*, 2 May 1970.

17. *Tuscaloosa News*, 2 and 8 May, 1 June, and 13 July 1970; Minutes of the Tuscaloosa City Commission, City Clerk's Office, Tuscaloosa, Alabama; 18 Sept. 1969; *High Gauge*, 13 Aug. 1970.

18. *Crimson White*, 4 May 1970; *Tuscaloosa News*, 4 May 1970; Mrs. Don Darnell to David Mathews, 7 May 1970, folder "XV 27," box 20, President David Mathews Papers.

19. *The University Report*, 7 May 1970; *Tuscaloosa News*, 7 May 1970; *Crimson White*, 7 May 1970.

20. Radio program on the 1970 student uprising on WUAL, University of Alabama, May 1990; Donald A. Brown, "A Walk Down University Avenue," in *Birmingham* (monthly publication of the Birmingham Chamber of Commerce), May 1970.

21. *Tuscaloosa News*, 9 May 1970.

22. *Tuscaloosa News*, 10 May 1970.

23. Joab Thomas to University of Alabama Students, n.d., and "Demands of Student-Faculty Coalition," n.d., folder "XV 37," box 20, President David Mathews Papers; Jeffrey A. Turner, *Sitting In and Speaking Out: Student Movements in the American South, 1960–1970* (Athens: Univ. of Georgia Press, 2010), 273.

24. "Demands of Student-Faculty Coalition," n.d., folder "XV 37," box 20, President David Mathews Papers; Turner, *Sitting In and Speaking Out*, 220–21.

25. *Tuscaloosa News*, 10 May 1970; Pat Bradburn to David Mathews, 12 May 1970, folder "XV 27," box 20, President David Mathews Papers; *The University Report*, 12 May 1970; *Crimson White*, 9 Apr. and 7 May 1970.

26. *Tuscaloosa News*, 13 May 1970; "Statement to the University Community by the President of the University of Alabama," 12 May 1970, folder "XVI 2," box 20, President David Mathews Papers; Joab Thomas to University of Alabama Students, n.d., folder "XV 37," box 20, President David Mathews Papers; Turner, *Sitting In and Speaking Out*, 221. According to Joab Thomas, the Dean for Student Development, there were three black administrators on campus at the beginning of the 1969–70 school year. Five African Americans were quickly added to the faculty: Lena Pruitt (College of Business and Commerce), Hycel Taylor (Department of Religion), Archie Wade (College of Education), E. O. Jones (Department of Biology), and Walter Wrenn (Social Work Department). They were slated to join the rest of the faculty at the beginning of the 1970–71 school year.

27. Mrs. Joseph G. Stewart to David Mathews, 13 May 1970, folder "XV 27," box 20, President David Mathews Papers; R. C. Perdue to Mathews, 15 May 1970, folder "XV 29," box 20, President Mathews Papers; Dr. and Mrs. G. I. Weatherly Jr. to Mathews, 13 May 1970, folder "XV 35," box 20, Mathews Papers.

28. David P. Currie to David Mathews, 13 May 1970, folder "XV 28," box 20, President David Mathews Papers; *Tuscaloosa News*, 14 May 1970; *Crimson White*, 14 May 1970.

29. David Patterson to David Mathews, 14 May 1970, folder "XV 28," box 20, President David Mathews Papers; "Statement by Richard Winstead" and "Public Statement by Mary Cynthia Potts," n.d., folder "XV 41," box 20, President David Mathews Papers.

30. Charles M. Schwartz to David Mathews, 17 May 1970, folder "XV 41," box 20, President David Mathews Papers; *Tuscaloosa News*, 20 May 1970.

31. Radio program on the 1970 student uprising on WUAL, May 1990; *Time*, 1 June 1970.

32. Ibid.

33. *Tuscaloosa News*, 15–21 May 1970; radio program on the 1970 student uprising on WUAL, May 1990.

34. *High Gauge,* 24 Sept., 5 Oct. 1970.

35. Available at www.as.ua.edu/womensstudies/site/about.html, accessed 2 Aug. 2011; William T. Johnson to David Mathews, 28 Jan. 1974, Mathews to William T. Johnson, 4 Feb. 1974, and Jefferson J. Coleman to Dudley S. Powell Jr., 25 Feb. 1974, folder "XVII, Student Organizations: Afro-American Association, 1972–1974," box 20, President David Mathews Papers; *Time,* 1 June 1970.

36. Tommy Wells to SGA Senators, Apr. 29, 1971, folder "XVII, 8, Student Organizations—Afro American Association, January–April 1971," box 22, David Mathews Papers; "Integration of College Athletics," *Encyclopedia of Alabama,* available at www.encyclopedia ofalabama.org/face/ArticlePrintable.jsp?id=h–1668, accessed 1 Aug. 2011; *Crimson White,* 10 Feb. 1976; Joab Thomas to Sylvester Wilson, 20 Oct. 1975, folder "XVII 12," box 22, David Mathews Papers.

37. "War on Institutional Racism—Charges," 6 Oct. 1975, folder "XVII," 12, box 22, David Mathews Papers; *Time,* 1 June 1970.

CHAPTER SEVEN

Conservative Student Activism at the University of Georgia

CHRISTOPHER A. HUFF

In October 1970, several members of the Young Americans for Freedom chapter at the University of Georgia voted to withdraw from the national organization and form the Campus Conservative Club. To emphasize both the finality of the decision and the growing discontent with YAF's national leadership, the students burned the group's charter. Founded in 1960, YAF became the largest student organization for right-leaning students during the 1960s. By the end of the decade, however, factional infighting divided the group and created a crisis of leadership within the organization. According to Steve Barnes, president of the YAF chapter at UGA at the time, the decision to separate from the national organization resulted from this crisis. UGA conservatives expressed particular concern over the amount of power national leaders exercised over its chapters. For Barnes, the issue of local control proved paramount, and he argued for more autonomy of action at the grassroots level; the kind of action Barnes and his supporters decided to pursue would become clear over the next several years. First as the Campus Conservative Club and later as the Union of American People, UGA's conservative student activists dedicated much of their time to fighting gains made by African Americans and homosexuals on campus. The existence of a YAF chapter at UGA during the 1960s signaled the desire to connect with a growing conservative movement. By the early 1970s, however, UGA student activists had largely abandoned the developing ideas of the New Right. Instead, they held tight to the rhetoric of race and region.[1]

A substantial body of scholarship on post–World War II American conservatism has emerged over the past several decades. These works explore how conservatives across the country developed a movement that coalesced in the 1950s over a shared belief in anticommunism but became increasingly concerned with the nation's moral values by the 1970s. While these scholars have displayed great persistence in uncovering the story of postwar conservatism, they have also largely overlooked the story of conservative students on the nation's college and university campuses.[2] To be sure, most discuss the development of YAF and its role in the failed 1964 presidential campaign of Arizona senator Barry Goldwater, but they also push the group to the wings after president Lyndon Johnson's landslide victory in that election.[3] Historians of the 1960s era and the New Left have also viewed the role of right-leaning students in much the same way as scholars of conservatism, relegating them to the background following their failure in the 1964 election.[4]

While students have been largely overlooked in the rise of the New Right, the importance of race continues to be debated among scholars of modern conservatism. Dan Carter's work on George Wallace, for example, argues for the centrality of race in the rise of the right as the former Alabama governor and presidential candidate replaced "the age-old southern cry of 'Nigger, nigger'" with the "political equivalents of apple pie and motherhood: the rights of private property, community control, neighborhood schools, union seniority." More recent works contest Carter's argument, instead making race one part of a more complex set of social and political factors tied to the postwar process of suburbanization. Matthew Lassiter argues that "the overreliance on race-reductionist narratives ... downplays the centrality of class ideology in the outlook of suburban voters." Lisa McGirr states that in order to protect their "affluent white havens" in the suburbs, conservatives in Orange County, California, attacked civil rights legislation with constitutional arguments based on the ideas of states' rights and the overextension of federal power. Although fueled by "deep-seated racial biases," McGirr's conservatives chafed at the overtly racist rhetoric employed by many southern politicians. These studies and others have helped create a more nuanced understanding of the rise of the New Right but have not ended the discussion regarding the importance of race in the development of modern conservatism.[5]

An examination of conservative student activism at the University of Georgia furthers the discussion of these topics. It provides a window onto the largely overlooked activities of the campus right during the late 1960s and early 1970s, a transformative period for the national conservative movement. It also reveals the tight grip that racism still held on some southern conservatives. In the first years of the 1970s, proponents of a virulent strain of racism emerged as the dominant voice of conservatism on the Athens campus. Yet these campus conservatives did not go unchallenged or remain isolated from the changes happening within conservative circles. Events at UGA showed how southern conservatives struggled with the process of merging into a larger movement, often picking and choosing which issues and strategies worked best in their local environment.

Young Americans for Freedom at UGA, 1965–70

In November 1965, the UGA student senate approved a campus chapter of Young Americans for Freedom. A first attempt in August had failed due to a lack of interest in the group, but by late fall the group had grown enough to resubmit its petition for approval.[6] The inability of UGA's activists to generate interest initially reflected the differences between southern conservatives and those associated with YAF outside the region. Loyal to the Democratic Party and the "Solid South" since the end of Reconstruction, southern conservatives started throwing their support behind the Republican Party after the passage of the Civil Rights Act of 1964. As a result, conservative Republican Barry Goldwater won every deep South state in that year's presidential election, although it would take longer for the region to develop a truly functional two-party system.[7]

YAF's desire to avoid taking a public position on the civil rights movement impeded the organization's ability to win over southerners. YAF opposed the Civil Rights Act, to be sure, but its reasoning echoed that of Goldwater, who argued that the law violated the constitutional balance between state and federal power. By the mid-1960s, however, as it was becoming clearer that "states' rights" was becoming a euphemism for continuing Jim Crow by other means, the YAF would refrain from taking a stand in the ongoing southern political and cultural battles that defined the civil rights era in the region.[8] Hence the YAF tended to remove itself from the field precisely at the time that southern conservatism was reorganizing itself along racial lines. These differences over race and party loyalty meant that prior to 1965, YAF maintained only a nominal presence in the South.

At the University of Georgia, two factors contributed to a change in attitude toward the organization. First, YAF existed as the only vehicle for conservative students who wished to become politically active, even if this meant supporting an organization with a problematic agenda. Sam Dickson, a UGA undergraduate and one of YAF's first members at UGA, often disagreed with the organization, despite having been a member since high school and serving as the university chapter's president in 1967. Dickson felt "disillusioned" with the group as early as 1964, since it did not share his views on "racial difference and an isolationist foreign policy." He stayed with the group but clashed with national leadership in 1965 over the passage of the Hart-Celler Act, which abolished immigration restrictions put in place by the National Origins Act of 1924. Dickson opposed making immigration for nonwhites easier, but the YAF national office told him to reconsider a campaign against the act since "the issue had undertones of racism."[9] Nevertheless, the lack of other campus-based conservative groups kept students such as Dickson connected to YAF through the end of the decade. Second, the escalation of the Vietnam War and the growth of the New Left prompted both northern and southern conservatives to reconstruct organizational and political counterweights. As the war began to overshadow civil rights and a left-based student movement developed, YAF began confronting the New Left over its growing radicalization and confrontational tactics.[10]

At UGA, the YAF chapter focused its attention on the campus New Left starting in the 1966–67 academic year. By spring 1967 a small chapter of Students for a Democratic Society had formed at UGA and began protesting against a wide variety of issues, including racism in Athens, the Vietnam War, and the continuing enforcement by the school administration of *in loco parentis* rules. Concern among campus conservatives grew after a three-day sit-in organized by members of the school's SDS chapter over the issue of coed rights in April 1968. Targeting a student newspaper article indicating that several YAF members at UGA supported the demonstration, the group issued a statement clarifying its position. The organization expressed its dislike of some coed rules but emphasized strongly its opposition to "so-called techniques of non-violence" and applauded school officials for not giving in to mob rule. The group continued its attack against the New Left by distributing a flyer entitled "WHY WE PROTEST!" In this document, the YAF chapter at UGA aimed to expose "the unsavory background and composition of groups like Students for a Democratic Society and the Southern Student Organizing Committee [SSOC]" by exploring possible connections between these groups and communist organizations. According to the flyer, "the majority of college students in Georgia . . . oppose the radical views of this fringe group," and "will not be fooled by efforts to enlist their support."[11]

During 1969 and 1970, YAF attempted to combat the New Left through programs and organizations that built coalitions between conservative and moderate students who supported law and order on campus.[12] While returning from YAF's Southern Regional Conference in March 1969, Antony Weaver and two other YAF members at UGA decided to start a campus-wide petition drive to let students voice their displeasure with the New Left–generated violence. Weaver used the Majority Coalition Campus Action Kit, a creation of the national YAF which, according to an advertisement in the group's magazine *The New Guard*, "provides the necessary information for organizing to combat the New Left Radicals on the college campus."[13] Using the kit to form the PRO-UGA Committee, Weaver and other YAF members at UGA spent several weeks collecting signatures. They presented the petition, which contained over 3,300 names, to university president Fred C. Davison on 22 April. The petition stated that "we are here for an education, not a revolution" and encouraged the administration to "expel and/or to take prompt legal action against any person(s) or groups of people taking part in any disruptive acts on our campus." The success of the petition led Davison to tell an alumnus that "although there is a small SDS organization here . . . there is a much larger chapter of the Young Americans for Freedom."[14]

YAF members at UGA formed two more groups during the following academic year. In the fall of 1969, several YAF members at UGA formed the Student Majority Opposed to Simplistic Solutions. The group's chairman, Jimmy Jordan, created the organization as a means of opposing the Moratorium to End the War in Vietnam, a demonstration that involved millions of Americans in October of that year. Hoping to counter the potential success of a second Moratorium event planned for November, Jordan founded SMOSS. He believed that the majority of students on campus supported the war, and he urged them to wear blue arm bands on the day of the antiwar demonstration as a way of showing their support for President Nixon's policies.[15] The last organization backed by the YAF chapter at UGA, the Student Committee for a Responsible SGA, circulated another petition in May 1970. This time, the conservative activists condemned the decision of the Student Government Association to hold a referendum on U.S. policy in Vietnam and the killings at Kent State.[16] In the petition, Dickson, Steve Barnes, and Martin O'Toole blasted the wording of the referendum, arguing that it was "shoddy" and lacked "conservative" policy choices regarding Vietnam. This petition drive proved less successful than previous ones, garnering a little over one thousand signatures, half of which came from an "eleventh hour drive" the day before the committee submitted it to the student senate.[17]

The Campus Conservative Club, 1970–73

The actions of the YAF chapter at UGA from its founding in 1965 up to 1970 demonstrated a close tactical alignment between campus conservatives and the national organization. The group, however, contained several members who questioned the larger goals of the national organization. The success of YAF during the 1960s rested on a fusion of traditional conservatives and libertarians in the organization. Following the 1969 national convention, this balance collapsed. The national office, composed of "trads," purged libertarians across the nation from positions of leadership. Victims of the purge leveled charges of authoritarianism against the group's leaders, which were not altogether unfounded since the national office had begun dictating policy to local chapters in an attempt to maintain control over the organization. The more rigid control exhibited by the YAF national office encouraged several factions within the organization to leave, including those that existed on the right wing of the conservative movement, which had been largely neutralized during the ten years of YAF's existence.[18] At UGA, several YAF members seized this opportunity to adopt an agenda that more closely reflected their beliefs and created the Campus Conservative Club in October 1970.

At UGA, the debate within YAF between moderate conservatives and right-wingers had been brewing for some time. Dickson recalls that by 1970 the YAF chapter at UGA had grown "schizophrenic" due to the growing animosity between these two factions. Jordan, a moderate, battled with Dickson, O'Toole, and others over the direction the group should take, a conflict that contributed to the burning of the YAF/UGA charter and the formation of the CCC.[19] Jordan hoped to keep campus conservatives in ideological alignment with the national movement. Dickson and his allies, however, exploited the schism in the YAF national office to push campus conservatives further to the right.

Within days of its founding, the CCC released the first issue of its "Right On!" newsletter, a mimeographed broadsheet containing articles on a variety of right-wing causes. In Issue no. 1, dedicated to a discussion of the United Nations, the CCC explored how membership in the organization threatened U.S. sovereignty. In the second issue, the CCC argued that "super-rich international capitalists [i.e., Jews]" funded the Bolshevik Revolution in 1917. It also reported that the Demosthenian Literary Society would host an upcoming lecture by John McLaren of Emory University, who would explain how the "depression of 1929 was artificially induced" and "brought untold profits to the banks," another thinly veiled anti-Semitic reference.[20]

Issue no. 3 of "Right On!" touched off a heated exchange over racism that generated harsh criticism of the CCC from both the right and left on campus. In that issue, the group commented on the week-long campus visit of famed sociologist Gunnar Myrdal, author of *An American Dilemma: The Negro Problem and Modern Democracy*, which played an important role in the U.S. Supreme Court's decision to declare de jure segregation unconstitutional in the 1954 *Brown v. Board of Education* case. "Right On!" attacked Myrdal over a statement quoted in an Atlanta newspaper in which he said that the "inferiority dogma" whites had used to justify segregation had been destroyed by scientific research. The CCC countered this statement with its own argument that the only dogma that existed in academia was the "dogma of equality" and listed several academics who refuted the claim of equality between the races.[21] In its next two issues, the CCC continued professing its belief in racial inequality, pushing its arguments further by stating that "this fallacious theory [racial equality] is the foundation of liberalism and radicalism and the source of all the disastrous social policies emanating from Washington D.C."[22] The group also issued a challenge to its opponents, offering to debate the issue of equality in the pages of the *Red and Black,* the campus newspaper. The paper's editors accepted, and the two sides squared off in the 11 February 1971 issue, each presenting "scientific" evidence to support its position.

The CCC's advocacy of white supremacy in "Right On!" and the *Red and Black* generated a strong backlash against the group. Moderate conservatives, many of whom had belonged to the YAF chapter at UGA before the chapter splintered the previous October, attacked the racist views of the CCC. In a letter to the paper, former UGA YAF chairmen Jimmy Jordan and William Moredock claimed that "the views expressed in 'Right On!' can hardly be called those of a responsible conservative. They are tainted with racism and all other symptoms generally associated with super-right-wing paranoia." They went on to label the authors of "Right On!" as "right-wing radicals who have co-opted the respectable title of conservatism in order to mask their somewhat less respectable goals." Richard Meno, a member of a new but short-lived YAF chapter at UGA, said that the CCC should instead be called the "Youth for Reaction and Racism," since the group's racial attitudes were "totally contradictory to American conservative thought" and that it had "misrepresented the views of the young conservative movement."[23] While this debate did reflect the changing racial views of some students, it did not develop from an increase in the number of African American students on campus, who consistently made up less than 4 percent of the student body during the first half of the decade.[24]

Both liberal and conservative critics of the CCC argued that the group shared the beliefs of the John Birch Society (JBS), a claim that CCC member Tom Mahler denied.[25] This denial would not seem unusual for most conservatives by 1971. While the JBS played an important role in helping develop a grassroots conservative movement during the late 1950s and early 1960s, by the early 1970s the organization had dwindled in size as many of its members abandoned the group. It also lost the support of prominent conservative activists. As McGirr notes, by the early 1960s conservative leaders who had relied on the popular and stridently anticommunist JBS to build a conservative groundswell had distanced themselves from the group, hoping to "forge a new image of respectability by redefining the movement's boundaries, with the society well outside them." This effort succeeded; as the group became marginalized it created new alliances with fringe groups on the far right.[26] Mahler's denial of an ideological affiliation between the CCC and the JBS could possibly be taken to indicate that the group had distanced itself from the increasingly extreme views of the JBS. A closer examination of "Right On!," however, reveals that the CCC was more concerned to distance itself from the Birchers' bad reputation than their hard-right ideas. Close scrutiny of "Right On!" articles makes it clear that during its existence the CCC closely identified with the racist ideology of JBS competitor, the Liberty Lobby.

Founded in 1958 by Willis Carto, the Liberty Lobby followed a neofascist set of beliefs. According to Sara Diamond, Carto "would frame the problems of Soviet 'expansionism' and anti-colonial national liberation movements as racial . . . in their origins" as well as promote a "conspiratorial analysis of world events."[27] The group's fondness for conspiracy theories should have made the Liberty Lobby and the JBS close allies, but the two groups disagreed on the issue of race. While the JBS favored policies that tacitly threw support behind white supremacy, ideas of racial inferiority and anti-Semitism were not part of the official JBS platform. The Liberty Lobby, however, grounded its ideology in biological racism and anti-Semitism. For Carto, these issues fell under the heading of "populism." Carto used the term both as a wedge between the right wing and the moderate conservative movement and to develop an ideological umbrella under which he could fit a set of beliefs centered on "nationalism, conspiracism, biological racism, and 'free enterprise' anti-communism."[28]

During the late 1960s and early 1970s, the Liberty Lobby focused on three "populist" core issues—championing the cause of Rhodesia, tax reform, and opposition to mandatory school busing.[29] The CCC expounded repeatedly on these same issues in its newsletter. In addition to the statements listed above regarding international financiers and arguments for biological racism, "Right On!" discussed the Nixon administration's support for economic sanctions against Rhodesia and its opposition to school busing, claiming that this latest effort in the "experiment of integration" would lead to the "physical endangering of white children." The CCC displayed its support for the Liberty Lobby most directly in an article entitled "Administration Repression Against the Right" in which it decried attacks by the Internal Revenue Service against the group, described by the CCC as "America's largest conservative organization." In an interview for a campus publication, O'Toole deployed the Liberty Lobby's vocabulary, stating that he did not "classify himself as a conservative in the strict sense" but instead "feels he is a populist."[30]

In addition to their support for Liberty Lobby causes, the CCC continued the battle begun by the YAF chapter at UGA against the campus New Left but added its own assaults against a more general "left wing bigotry" that existed at the university. The group attacked the campus left on several fronts, including its campaign to end ROTC programs; the relationship between student government and the campus chapter of the Young Socialist Alliance; and the Committee on Gay Education, an activist group for gays and lesbians on campus.[31] The CCC also fought with the administration. In May 1971, the university announced a change to its policy regarding the placement of literature by political organizations in student mailboxes. Up to this time the CCC had been distributing "Right On!" through the campus mail system, but the new policy required all campus political groups to place literature on tables next to dormitory mailboxes. According to the CCC, Richard Armstrong, head of the Housing Office, changed the policy after he had received complaints from New Left "radicals" regarding the distribution of "Right On!," an accusation Armstrong denied. Unable to get the policy reversed, the CCC promised to "complain *loudly* to our friends in the Legislature, the Board of Regents, and the Executive branch of the state government." This proved no idle threat. Campus conservatives had received support and encouragement from state leaders during the 1961 desegregation crisis and would rely on similar connections to push their agenda forward over the next several years.[32]

In January 1972, the CCC confronted the Housing Office over the distribution through dormitory mailboxes of a pamphlet entitled "I Am a Person." Part of the "Growth Program," an attempt by the university to create a more tolerant attitude on campus toward race, gender, and sexuality, the CCC considered the pamphlet political in nature, making its distribution a violation of the policy passed the previous year. The group wrote an article about the program in "Right On!" and mailed approximately one hundred copies of the newsletter and the pamphlet to state legislators and the university system's Board of Regents. In the article, the CCC complained that the administration had sided with the "hip degenerates against normal people" by "advocating a permissive attitude toward homosexuality and other hip cultural vices." The tactic did convince administrators to halt the program, explaining that "the type of programs we initiated are still somewhat controversial."[33]

In early 1972, the CCC took offense at a less controversial decision by UGA marching band director Roger Dancz to stop playing the song "Dixie" during football games and to change the name of the Dixie Redcoat Band to simply the Redcoat Band. Citing his reasons for the changes, Dancz mentioned an incident during a football game between UGA and Clemson University in which an African American member of the Georgia marching band was harassed by white Clemson fans "to 'Play Dixie, nigger;' [and who] then began slapping him on the back, ramming his mouth into the mouthpiece and cutting his lip." Dancz's decision may also have been influenced by the desegregation of the varsity football team. In 1971, five players made the freshmen squad, three of whom would take the field in Sanford Stadium for the 1972 season. Most of the campus seemed to have no problems with Dancz's decision. Several years later, former dean of students O. Suthern Sims reflected on the change, stating that "the campus was just more liberal then, just accepted not playing it. It was fashionable to be more active about the war and racism in general; it wasn't noticed that much." O'Toole, president of the CCC, decidedly did notice and attempted to generate outrage on campus and among alumni over the decision not to play "Dixie" but failed to raise any real concern. But as the CCC evolved into a campus political party, the playing of "Dixie" became a cornerstone in a developing right-wing ideology held by campus conservatives that increasingly focused on issues of southern identity.[34]

The Union of American People, 1973–75

By the fall of 1973, the Campus Conservative Club had transformed itself into the Union of American People party. The decision of the CCC to reconstitute itself as a political party reflected the changing nature of campus politics at UGA. During the 1960s, New Leftists in Athens had little use for student government. Members of the campus's Greek system had long maintained a tight grip on leadership positions and attempted to exclude controversial issues, such as the Vietnam War or racial politics, from discussion. Activists in SDS and other groups tried working with campus leaders on several occasions to create meaningful changes at UGA, but even the most progressive student government officers disapproved of the radical politics and confrontational tactics of the New Left. As a result, these attempts failed to meet with any kind of success. By the first years of the 1970s, however, changes in campus culture brought New Left activists directly into student government. The liberalization of American society did not bypass UGA, as an increasing number of students embraced progressive politics. In addition, the Greek system lost control of student government as membership in fraternities and sororities dwindled. Seeing an opportunity, New Left students reconsidered their attitudes toward student government and came to the conclusion that it might now be possible to effect meaningful change through the traditional corridors of campus power. Consequently, an increasing number of New Left activists won election to various offices in the first years of the new decade.

The movement of New Leftists into student government marked the final stage in a prolonged period of activism at UGA. Beginning with the formation of an SDS chapter in 1967, the next six years witnessed the development of a diverse community made up of liberals, radicals, feminists, and pacifists, among others. In addition to the 1968 sit-in, a massive demonstration at UGA against the Kent State killings led to a two-day closure of all schools in the University System of Georgia. By the early 1970s the campus possessed a particularly active chapter of Vietnam Veterans Against the War and several other antiwar groups. The early years of the decade also saw campus feminists founding W.O.M.E.N. (Women's Oppression Must End Now) and homosexual activists organizing the Committee for Gay Education. Members of these groups won election to various offices in the early 1970s. As part of Coalition, a prominent leftist student political party of the day, they eventually gained control of student government in the spring 1973 elections.[35]

Figure 7.1. University of Georgia marching band director Roger Dancz lynched in effigy by conservative students protesting Dancz's decision to remove "Dixie" from the Redcoat Band's repertoire. Courtesy Hargrett Rare Book and Manuscript Library, University of Georgia Libraries.

In response to these changes, the CCC reconstituted into a political party as part of its ongoing effort to confront liberals and leftists on campus. The Union of American People developed a unique slate of policies based on white southern identity and conservative ideals regarding gender and sexuality. To spread its message, the UAP began publishing "The People's Observer," a short newsletter that explored the group's positions on campus matters and occasionally touched on other right-wing issues, particularly those dealing with race. Billing itself as "the only moderate to conservative political party on campus," the UAP revealed its platform for the 1974 SGA elections in the newsletter's first edition. In addition to positions on tuition, grades, and campus parking, the UAP platform contained two race-based planks. First, it aimed to get a university rule repealed that required dormitory residents to live with an assigned roommate for at least two weeks before requesting a move. Billed as a "freedom of choice" issue, race actually fueled the UAP's opposition to this policy, since the group expressed concern that a white student would be forced to live with a black student for at least 14 days. The group's last platform plank, however, eventually generated a great deal of trouble for the university over the next several years. Proclaiming that "the suppression of our regional traditions and history help to create a rootless individual," the UAP promised to get the playing of "Dixie" reinstituted at sporting events and that the marching band would regain its former name as the Dixie Redcoat Marching Band.[36]

The UAP did not consider this a problem unique to UGA but indicative of a "general tendency in recent years to run down and demean the culture and heritage of majority students." As evidence of this trend, the UAP cited cases in which African Americans led the fight to suppress the use of the Confederate flag at southern university sporting events, condemned the portrayal of "southern rednecks" in popular films such as *In the Heat of the Night,* and cursed the widespread dissemination of writings by "anti-Southern turncoats" Erskine Caldwell and Willie Morris.[37]

The UAP did not restrict its ire to the suppression of southern cultural traditions. It also focused a sustained attack on campus homosexuals. By the early 1970s UGA possessed a dedicated community of gay activists. In addition to forming the Committee on Gay Education, several gay men had been elected to student government, and openly gay men and lesbians served on the faculty. Conservative students had made their opposition to homosexuality clear as early as 1969. On several occasions during the late 1960s and early 1970s the Demosthenian Society passed resolutions condemning homosexuality, arguing that it should be "recognized as an emotional disease" and that the group should go on record "condemning the . . . Committee on Gay Education." The UAP lambasted the university for allowing monies collected through student fees to pay for programs that benefited homosexuals, including the creation of a Gay Crisis Line, which "only encouraged homosexuals to think of themselves as normal," and various social functions, such as dances at which female impersonators performed. Through its newsletter, the UAP discussed the extent to which homosexuality had established itself as an acceptable presence on campus. In 1974 alone "The People's Observer" noted that an associate professor of English had openly declared herself a lesbian; a new group for gay professors, the Gay Academics Union, had been founded; and the leader of a gay student group had spoken to UGA classes about homosexuality. The UAP held back little in discussing its opposition to homosexuals on campus, labeling the leaders of the Committee on Gay Education "chairthings" instead of chairmen or chairwomen and claiming that, through its support of gays and lesbians, the university "had [sunk] into the muck and mire of permissiveness and perversion."[38]

While the UAP's strong position on race and region placed its members at odds with a national conservative movement that attempted to create a more complex and subtle vocabulary in regard to race during in the 1970s, the group's focus on homosexuality also put it firmly in the middle of a changing conservative critique of American life. By the 1970s "the center of grassroots activity moved away from the anticommunism . . . of the early 1960s and towards new single-issue campaigns. As a result, various forms of 'domestic corruption' became the new targets of attack." For conservatives, these new targets represented the worst elements in an increasingly permissive society created by the youth culture of the 1960s and a series of liberal Supreme Court decisions.[39] Of specific concern were abortion, feminism, and gay liberation. As with other conservative groups around the country, the UAP adopted positions on these issues, but its refusal to abandon its direct assault on African American gains ensured that its critique of American culture would be seen through a specifically southern lens. To the UAP, this made sense, since southern culture stood as the ultimate benchmark for what American society should look like. The group claimed repeatedly that it defended the "dispossessed majority" who represent the "Christian European element which gave our nation the distinctive stamp of its character."[40]

The UAP's support for southern culture, along with opposition to homosexuals and the creation of a Black Cultural Center on campus, existed as the primary planks in its platform for the 1974 SGA elections. In the weeks leading up to the 17 April election, the UAP published several issues of "The People's Observer" that explored its positions and how the party stood apart from candidates from the other two major parties, the leftist Coalition and the moderate Onward. The group expressed its support for biological racism as it argued against the continuing process of school desegregation occurring across the South. The UAP also dedicated almost an entire issue to explaining why "DIXIE MUST LIVE!!" Despite its right-wing position on race and opposition to homosexuality, the UAP polled better than expected in the election. Its slate of candidates for student government's executive positions (president, executive vice president, and administrative vice president) gained nearly 20 percent of the vote, forcing a runoff election between Coalition and Onward. UAP presidential candidate John McEachern noted that the party was "quite pleased with the election results," while John Roddy, executive vice president candidate, stated that "it's only the beginning for us."[41]

Opinions differed on why the UAP had done so well. In its postelection analysis, the group proclaimed victory and argued that the results provided "dramatic proof that those who have built their party upon the queers, black militants, chronic malcontents, etc. have completely misjudged the sentiments of the student body." The UAP also vowed not to support either party in the runoff election, stating that the group existed as more than a political party. "While others . . . may compromise and make deals, we proclaim the truth of our creed," the UAP argued. Its leaders further promised to continue representing "the dispossessed majority," which was under attack "from rapacious minorities bent on plundering our heritage."[42] But others, including former dean of men William Tate, believed that the UAP's position on the playing of "Dixie" specifically led to the SGA election result. According to Tate, even UAP founder Martin O'Toole expressed surprise at how much attention the "Dixie" issued generated.[43] The UAP would focus on the "Dixie" issue over the next 18 months.

During the fall of 1974, the UAP kept "Dixie" a primary concern in its newsletter. By November, enough interest regarding the issue had been generated on campus that SGA president J. Rivers Walsh, a moderate conservative, called for a student referendum. Walsh's decision revealed the contested nature of student politics at UGA. The student senate, the body responsible for approving referendum items, refused to include the "Dixie" question as part of a larger referendum election. As a result, Walsh presented the issue in a separate referendum held on 14 November.[44] On that day, the UAP organized a rally attended by three hundred people to show support for the playing of "Dixie." Standing on a podium decorated with many Confederate flags, UAP member Mike Johnson stated that "this is the chance . . . for the majority student on this campus to stand up and be proud of his cultural heritage," while O'Toole lamented that "we have few symbols of our past left to us, consequently a symbol like 'Dixie' is very important to us." In a turnout that involved 21 percent of the student body and exceeded the previous spring's SGA elections, voters approved the return of "Dixie" to the marching band's repertoire by a three-to-one margin. Band director Roger Dancz, however, issued a statement the same day explaining his reasons why he had stopped playing the song three years earlier and asserted that the band would not abide by the referendum results.[45]

Dancz's refusal to play "Dixie" drew attention from a variety of off-campus sources. Over the next several months, local and regional newspapers published op-ed pieces critical of Dancz's position. Nationally syndicated radio commentator Paul Harvey offered a story of the issue the day after the referendum, quoting Dancz as saying that "under no circumstances" would the song be played.[46] The university administration supported Dancz, a move that, along with results of the referendum, led the UAP to launch a major campaign against the band director and in favor of "Dixie." "The People's Observer" printed numerous articles calling for Dancz's dismissal, and starting in the spring, the UAP enlisted the help of supportive alumni in its cause.

During the April 1975 G-Day game, the annual football scrimmage that brought thousands of alumni and university supporters to campus, the UAP distributed copies of "The Georgia Observer." Essentially a re-named "People's Observer," the newsletter discussed the "Dixie" debate. Hoping to generate outrage among alumni regarding the state of affairs in Athens, the flyer also explored how the administration and faculty had failed as teachers and had abandoned the "entire idea of moral leadership." To support its argument, the UAP revealed several examples of homosexuals serving in leadership positions and discussed the activities of "black militants" on campus. To make its message as clear as possible, the UAP included a picture of a female impersonator performing at a school function.[47]

The publicity had the effect that the UAP intended. G-Day game attendees took copies of the "Georgia Observer" back home, and soon university administrators began receiving letters from upset alumni. James Bankston, a member of the Class of 1959, wrote President Davison that he was "shocked to learn the level the student body [had] reached in electing a homosexual as president of the student body" and noted that he would find it difficult to continue his support of the school or let his child attend. William Stewart expressed his concern over the "Dixie" issue and also noted that "if only *one* item that appeared in that publication is true, then we are in a heap of trouble."[48] Indeed a heap of trouble did occur, but at the instigation of the UAP, not those it criticized.

The UAP's campaign to remove Dancz and return "Dixie" to the marching band repertoire reached its zenith during the 1975 football season. Local and regional newspapers had been running opinion pieces about the "Dixie" issue in the weeks leading up to the game between UGA and the University of Richmond on 1 November, most of them critical of the decision to stop playing the song. The day before the game, the UAP and its supporters raised a banner across Lumpkin Street near campus reading "PLAY DIXIE! FIRE DANCZ!"—the same slogan the UAP had repeatedly printed in "The People's Observer" over the previous year. Public awareness of the controversy led to a raucous halftime ceremony. While the Redcoat Band played on the field, fans in the stands sang "Dixie" at full volume. A plane flew over the stadium trailing a banner with the "Fire Dancz, Play

Dixie" slogan. Campus police also confiscated a large Confederate flag that a fan attempted to hoist aloft.[49]

The controversy simmered over the next several weeks. While Dancz received support for his decision from various groups, including the administration, the Campus Ministry Association, the Georgia Music Educators Association, and the Redcoat Band itself, local press and alumni continued to voice displeasure at the band director's decision. On 9 November, O'Toole appeared on an Atlanta radio show to discuss the controversy; he received overwhelming support from listeners who called in. For the final home game of the season against Auburn University on 15 November, the UAP printed up a new edition of "The Georgia Observer" that included a facsimile of the school's Annual Fund pledge card. The "Fire Dancz, Play Dixie" slogan had been emblazoned over the card, which the UAP encouraged alumni to send back to the university instead of a donation to the fund.

The "Dixie" controversy slowly diminished after the end of the football season, as the university received only 71 UAP pledge cards and almost three dozen angry letters over the next several months. By this time O'Toole had graduated; despite promising to do so, he failed to revive the issue during the 1976 football season.[50] By April 1976 the UAP had also effectively stopped operating as a student political party and did not run candidates in the SGA spring elections. In fact, the low voter turnout and the election of an independent candidate for SGA president suggests that the student body had grown tired of the intense partisanship that had defined UGA student politics during the first half of the 1970s.[51]

In the fall of 1974, a campus magazine profiled the UAP in the wake of its strong showing in the SGA elections the previous spring. Although the author entitled the article "The New Conservatism," UAP leader John Roddy rejected attempts to label him a conservative, preferring to be known as a populist and employing the language used by several national right-wing groups. Roddy dismissed Young Americans for Freedom as "just a clique of elitists" who "looked down their noses at the workers, the common people." Such were the dispossessed white majority who, according to Roddy, were poised to take back the nation. Citing the anti-busing riots in Boston that year, he believed that white Americans were experiencing not just the "rebirth of a race" but also a spiritual awakening that began in the South but would soon spread to the rest of the nation.[52]

Despite this optimistic outlook, the story of far-right activism at UGA reveals the liberalization of campus life and politics rather than a return to the conservatism that defined the school prior to 1965. While only a small leftist core at UGA joined SDS or other radical groups on campus during the 1960s, a majority of students did embrace the opening up of American society that occurred during that tumultuous decade. By the middle of the 1970s, the administration had abandoned attempts to guide the moral education of students, allowing for an increased amount of personal freedom and expression. Recreational drug use increased, especially marijuana use. Students even participated in "streaking," a trend sweeping the nation that involved sprinting nude through public places. In addition, gay men and women openly served on the faculty, while homosexual students championed gay liberation causes. Finally, African American enrollment at UGA continued to increase, albeit slowly. But the story of right-wing conservatism at UGA also demonstrates the intransigent sense of regional pride felt by many students. While rejecting the overt racism and anti-Semitism of the CCC and the UAP, they did support the "Dixie" campaign and its use of symbols and rituals from the South's troubled past.

The story of right-wing activism at UGA also complicates the narrative of conservatism's resurgence in the 1960s and 1970s. While moderate conservatives on campus attempted initially to bring UGA into the national movement through membership in YAF, by 1970 campus right-wing activists had largely rejected this relationship, opting instead for an agenda based on regional identity and white privilege. While conservative activists at UGA initially organized around national issues such as the Vietnam War, by the mid-1970s they were focusing attention on causes specific to the South and, ultimately, to the UGA campus. It is true that UGA's right-wing activists embraced the national movement's criticism of American cultural life, particularly its opposition to homosexuality. But the founding of the Campus Conservative Club, the creation of the Union of American People, and the refusal to accept the mainstream conservative movement's more subtle approach to racial issues demonstrate clearly the importance of local conditions to the development of political activism.

Although quite different from the existing story of conservative student activism, which focuses on YAF, it remains to be seen if what occurred at UGA is unique. Grassroots studies of the New Right have revealed a complex political movement in the nation's cities and suburbs from the 1950s to the 1970s. The story of conservatism at UGA suggests that the same result may occur when the focus shifts from town to gown.

NOTES

1. Ray Tilley, "YAF Burns National Charter," *Red and Black*, 15 Oct. 1970, 1.

2. For more on the rise of modern American conservatism, see Mary C. Brennan, *Turning Right in the Sixties: The Conservative Capture of the GOP* (Chapel Hill: Univ. of North Carolina Press, 1995); Dan T. Carter, *The Politics of Rage: George Wallace, the Origins of the New Conservatism, and the Transformation of American Politics* (Baton Rouge: LSU Press, 1995); Joseph Crespino, *In Search of Another Country: Mississippi and the Conservative Counterrevolution* (Princeton, NJ: Princeton Univ. Press, 2007); Kevin M. Kruse, *White*

Flight: Atlanta and the Making of Modern Conservatism (Princeton, NJ: Princeton Univ. Press, 2005); Matthew D. Lassiter, *The Silent Majority: Suburban Politics in the Sunbelt South* (Princeton, NJ: Princeton Univ. Press, 2006); Lisa McGirr, *Suburban Warriors: The Origins of the New American Right* (Princeton, NJ: Princeton Univ. Press, 2001); and Jonathan M. Schoenwald, *A Time for Choosing: The Rise of Modern American Conservatism* (New York: Oxford Univ. Press, 2001).

3. YAF has been the subject of two book-length treatments, but only Gregory Schneider's *Cadres for Conservatism: Young Americans for Freedom and the Rise of the Contemporary Right* (New York: NYU Press, 1999) traces the history of the organization beyond the 1964 presidential election. See also John A. Andrew III, *The Other Side of the Sixties: Young Americans for Freedom and the Rise of Conservative Politics* (New Brunswick, NJ: Rutgers Univ. Press, 1997). Rebecca Klatch has produced a wonderful study that compares activism by members of YAF and SDS. See Klatch, *A Generation Divided: The New Left, the New Right, and the 1960s* (Berkeley: Univ. of California Press, 1999).

4. The earliest works about the decade largely ignored activism on the right, instead crafting a narrative built around the importance of left-based national groups, particularly Students for a Democratic Society (SDS). See David Farber, *The Age of Great Dreams: America in the 1960s* (New York: Hill and Wang, 1994); Todd Gitlin, *The Sixties: Years of Hope Days of Rage* (New York: Bantam, 1987); and James Miller, *"Democracy Is in the Streets": From Port Huron to the Siege of Chicago* (Cambridge, MA: Harvard Univ. Press, 1987). Many recent works have moved beyond SDS to expand our understanding of the complex nature of activism in the sixties, including writing YAF and conservatism more fully into the history of the era. But, again, the story of conservative student activism generally ends with the 1964 election and does not explore grassroots campus activism. See Michael W. Flamm and David Steigerwald, *Debating the 1960s: Liberal, Conservative, and Radical Perspectives* (Lanham, MD: Rowman and Littlefield, 2008); Maurice Isserman and Michael Kazin, *America Divided: The Civil Wars of the 1960s*, 3d ed. (New York: Oxford Univ. Press, 2008); and Mark Hamilton Lytle, *America's Uncivil Wars: The Sixties Era from Elvis to the Fall of Richard Nixon* (New York: Oxford Univ. Press, 2006).

5. Carter, *Politics of Rage*, 11; Lassiter, *Silent Majority*, 6; McGirr, *Suburban Warriors*, 182.

6. Jack Brookner, "Cox Initiates New Policy on Charters," *Red and Black*, 6 Aug. 1965, 5; Ron Taylor, "Improvement in Advisement Sought in Senate Resolution," *Red and Black*, 18 Nov. 1965, 1.

7. The "Solid South" is a term used to describe the control that the Democratic Party held over electoral politics in the south from roughly the end of Reconstruction to the middle of the 1960s. See Dewey W. Grantham, *The Life and Death of the Solid South: A Political History* (Lexington: Univ. Press of Kentucky, 1988). For the purposes of this essay I define the South as the eleven former Confederate states and the deep South as South Carolina, Georgia, Alabama, Mississippi and Louisiana. For an overview of Republicans in the South during the 1960s, see Numan V. Bartley, *The New South, 1945–1980* (Baton Rouge: LSU Press, 1995), 384–95.

8. Schneider, *Cadres for Conservatism*, 58–60.

9. Sam Dickson, interview with the author, Atlanta, Georgia, 29 Jan. 2011. Several members of UGA YAF and other conservative campus groups were approached to be interviewed for this essay, but all except Dickson declined to discuss their participation in student activism at UGA.

10. Schneider, *Cadres for Conservatism*, 58, 110–12. No study of YAF in the South yet exists, so conclusions regarding the organization's development are preliminary at best.

11. "A Statement of Policy Concerning Student Demonstrations," *The Reasoner,* special edition, undated, box 5, Louise McBee Papers, Hargrett Library, University of Georgia, Athens, Georgia; "WHY WE PROTEST!" box 56, Fred C. Davison Papers, Hargrett Library, University of Georgia, Athens, Georgia.

12. Schneider, *Cadres for Conservatism*, 120–21.

13. Antony Weaver and James Baldwin, "University of Georgia YAF Forms Majority Coalition," *The New Guard,* Summer 1969, 25.

14. Fred C. Davison to W. E. Towson, 2 June 1969, box 56, Davison Papers, Box 56, Hargrett Library.

15. Robinette Kennedy, "SMOSS Group Organizes to Support Nixon Policies," *Red and Black,* 11 Nov. 1969, 1.

16. Protests erupted on college campuses across the country following the announcement by President Nixon that the United States had invaded Cambodia on 30 April. At Kent State University in Ohio National Guardsmen fired into the crowd, killing four students and injuring nine others.

17. Ray Tilley, "Committee Culminates Drive, Presents Petition to Senate," *Red and Black,* 21 May 1970, 1.

18. For more on the battle between libertarians and traditional conservatives in YAF, see Schneider, *Cadres for Conservatism*, 127–41.

19. Sam Dickson interview.

20. "Right On!" 1, no. 1 (16 Oct. 1970), 1; 1, no. 2 (30 Oct. 1970), 1–2. One of the first student organizations at the university, the Demosthenian Literary Society (DLS) existed for much of its history as a debating society but by the 1960s developed a reputation as a haven for right-wing conservative students. For more on the DLS's racial politics, see Robert A. Pratt, "The Rhetoric of Hate: The Demosthenian Literary Society and its Opposition to the Desegregation of the University of Georgia, 1950–1964," *Georgia Historical Quarterly* 90, no. 2 (Summer 2006): 236–59.

21. "Speakers at the University of Georgia, September 25, 1970–February 24, 1972," box 53, Davison Papers; "Right On!" 1, no. 3 (15 Nov. 1970), 1–2.

22. "Right On!" 2, no. 1 (12 Jan. 1971), 1; 2, no. 1 (3 Feb. 1971), 1.

23. *Red and Black,* 9 Feb. 1971, 4; 26 Jan. 1971, 4.

24. In 1971, Assistant Director of Admissions Anthony White estimated that five hundred black students attended UGA ten years after desegregation occurred. A 1973 study showed that 536 African Americans attended UGA out of a student body of 20,318. Terry Fetner, "Black Enrollment Climb Anticipated," *Red and Black,* 11 Nov. 1971, 1; Mitchell Shields, "Report Shows Enrollment Shift," *Red and Black,* 9 Nov. 1973, 1.

25. Don White, "Right On!—Childish Rantings," *Red and Black,* 24 Nov. 1970, 4; 26 Jan. 1971, 4; "CCC Prints 'Right On!'" *Red and Black,* 28 Jan. 1971, 2.

26. McGirr, *Suburban Warriors,* 218–25. A controversy developed over the influence of the JBS on YAF during its first years of existence. See Andrew, *Other Side of the Sixties,* 102–4; and Schneider, *Cadres for Conservatism,* 48–52.

27. Sara Diamond, *Roads to Dominion: Right-Wing Movements and Political Power in the United States* (New York: Guilford Press, 1995), 85–86. For more on the history of the right wing of the modern American conservative movement, see Chip Berlet and

Matthew N. Lyons, *Right-Wing Populism in America: Too Close for Comfort* (New York: Guilford Press, 2000); Euan Hague, Heidi Beirich, and Edward H. Sebesta, eds., *Neo-Confederacy: A Critical Introduction* (Austin: Univ. of Texas Press, 2008); Jean Hardisty, *Mobilizing Resentment: Conservative Resurgence from the John Birch Society to the Promise Keepers* (Boston: Beacon Press, 1999); and George Michael, *Willis Carto and the American Far Right* (Gainesville: Univ. Press of Florida, 2008).

28. Berlet and Lyons, *Right-Wing Populism in America,* 181; Diamond, *Roads to Dominion,* 86; Schneider, *Cadres for Conservatism,* 51; Diamond, *Roads to Dominion,* 149–50.

29. Diamond, *Roads to Dominion,* 154.

30. "Right On!" 1, no. 1 (15 Nov. 1970), 1; 2, nos. 1 (12 Jan. 1971), 2; 3, no. 1 (1 May 1971), 1, 2; *Impressions* 6, no. 2 (Winter 1972), 8.

31. "Right On!" 1, no. 2 (30 Oct. 1970), 2; 5, no. 1 (Winter 1972), 1.

32. "Right On!" 3, no. 1 (1 May 1971), 1–2, emphasis in original; Jon Hamm, "Dorm Program Halted under Fire," *Red and Black,* 4 Feb. 1972, 5; Robert Cohen, "G-Men in Georgia: The FBI and the Segregationist Riot at the University of Georgia, 1961," *Georgia Historical Quarterly* 83, no. 4 (Fall 1999): 521–22; Robert A. Pratt, *We Shall Not Be Moved: The Desegregation of the University of Georgia* (Athens: Univ. of Georgia Press, 2002), 107–8.

33. "Right On!" 5, no. 1 (Winter 1972): 1–2; Hamm, "Dorm Program Halted," 1.

34. William Tate, "Personal Observations," box 39, William Tate Papers, Hargrett Library. The integration of college football in the deep South met with almost no resistance from conservative whites. Michael Orland suggests that the desire of southern football fans to maintain a competitive edge at the national level forced the quiet acceptance of the change. See Michael Orland, *Bowled Over: Big-Time College Football from the Sixties to the BCS Era* (Chapel Hill: Univ. of North Carolina Press, 2009), 57–88.

35. Christopher A. Huff, "Radicals between the Hedges: New Left Activism at the University of Georgia, 1963–1975," MA thesis, Univ. of Georgia, 2005.

36. "The People's Observer," 1, no. 1 (Feb. 1974), 1, 2.

37. "The People's Observer," no. 6 (15 Apr. 1974).

38. Minutes of the Demosthenian Literary Society, 19 Nov. 1969, 111; 24 Feb. 1972, 348, Hargrett Library; "The People's Observer," no. 2 (Mar. 1974), 1; no. 4 (12 Apr. 1974), 1; no. 8 (13 May 1974), 1.

39. McGirr, *Suburban Warriors,* 217, 226.

40. "The People's Observer," no. 11 (Summer 1974).

41. "The People's Observer," no. 3 (3 Apr. 1974); no. 5 (15 Apr. 1974); "Both Parties Predict Victory," *Red and Black,* 18 Apr. 1974, 1. Roddy's statement proved untrue. In the 1975 SGA elections the UAP won approximately 10% of the vote and had disbanded by the time of the 1976 election.

42. "UAP: Election Statement of the Union of American People," "The People's Observer," no. 6 supplement (3 May 1974).

43. Tate, "Personal Observations," box 39, William Tate Papers, Hargrett Library.

44. Memorandum from J. Rivers Walsh to Jay Blackburn and Senate Elections Committee, n.d., box 53, Davison Papers.

45. Buddy Waller, "UAP Culminates Campaign Plans," *Red and Black,* 14 Nov. 1974, 6; Nancy Black and Thomas R. Franklin, "Students Approve 'Dixie' by 3–1 Vote," *Red and Black,* 15 Nov. 1974, 1.

46. William Tate, "Personal Observations," box 39, Tate Papers.

47. "Georgia Observer," no. 1 (Apr. 1975), box 53, Davison Papers.

48. James K. Bankston to Fred Davison, 29 Apr. 1975; William H. Stewart to Fred Davison, 30 Apr. 1975, box 53, Davison Papers.

49. William Tate, "Personal Observations," box 39, Tate Papers.

50. Ibid.

51. "Morgan and Snelling Win," *Red and Black,* 15 Apr. 1976, 1.

52. Tom Steadman, "The New Conservatism 1974," *Impressions* 9, no. 1 (Fall 1974): 31.

PART III

A Cultural Revolution and
Its Discontents

CHAPTER EIGHT

Sexual Liberation at the University of North Carolina

KELLY MORROW

During October 1970, students in Morrison Dormitory at the University of North Carolina at Chapel Hill sponsored "Sexual Revolution Month."[1] Throughout the month, hundreds of male and female students trekked across campus, crowding Morrison's lobby to view displays of detailed anatomical models, horrifying illegal abortion tools, and samples of contraceptive devices. They also found a small library that included a new handbook created for UNC students listing local places where they could obtain contraceptives and safe abortions at a time when these products and services were illegal in many areas of the United States. Students watched films and participated in discussions about birth control, abortion, homosexuality, venereal disease, and childbirth, and many came to hear "the most controversial speaker on campus," physician Takey Crist, who had "a long reputation at UNC for being blunt with the facts of sex."[2]

The events at Morrison Dormitory were part of a wave of campus activism that helped to shape the meaning and direction of the sexual revolution in the early 1970s. At UNC alone, over 50 sexual liberation activists, as I will refer to them, created practical services and educational programs that touched the lives of thousands of student supporters.[3] Similar efforts were occurring during the same period with varying degrees of success on campuses across the South and the nation. Inspired by the civil rights, antiwar, and student power movements, student and faculty sexual liberation activists banded together in a cross-generational effort to contest a sexual culture grounded in hypocrisy, shame, and silence. Through their efforts, they promoted a new model of sexuality based on the values of openness, knowledge, and gender equality.[4] In doing so, they helped to transform the sexual landscape of the campus and embody a version of feminism that included men as well as women.

Tracing the actions and ideas of sexual liberation activists draws attention to an underexplored strand of the sexual revolution. Although the sexual revolution is commonly portrayed in popular and political culture as a time when unmarried intercourse rates skyrocketed, this view is misleading and fails to account for the dramatic changes in sexual discourse at the core of the revolution.[5] Historian Beth Bailey argues that the sexual revolution was largely an attempt to combat the hypocrisy of a public ideal that expected young people, especially women, to remain chaste until marriage, with the reality that many young, unmarried college students were having sex.[6] Sexual liberation activists believed that this disjuncture between ideals and behavior caused secrecy and shame and made it extremely difficult for young people to protect themselves from the negative emotional and physical consequences of sex. For these activists, liberation could be achieved not only by exposing this hypocrisy through greater openness about sexual desires but also by democratizing knowledge about sexuality to ensure young people's sexual health and happiness.

In order to achieve these aims, sexual liberation activists promoted equality inside and outside of the bedroom, and their ideas represent an important aspect of second-wave feminism. Scholarship is now emerging that takes us beyond the conventional narrative of second-wave feminism that had focused on urban, middle-class women in formal women's rights organizations as well as the divisions between radical and liberal feminists. Historians such as Anne Valk argue that we need to look at the "cross-currents of second-wave feminism" that include both self-identified feminists and those who did not identify as feminists but who worked to end gender inequality and oppression.[7] Sexual liberation activism shows us that men were an important component of this group. Male and female activists worked together for equality and reproductive justice and attempted to change the gender consciousness of men as well as women in order to promote sexual relationships based on mutual honesty, trust, desire, and pleasure.

To reveal broader themes about the evolution of the sexual revolution on college campuses and how these changes influenced gender ideology and women's experiences, this chapter focuses on UNC. Although we may imagine that southern states, such as North Carolina, remained wrapped in a cloak of Bible Belt morality, sexual liberation activism simultaneously found its way down south and radiated from it. This type of activism did not germinate only on the coasts or come from the ideas and beliefs of a few radicals; it had multiple origins on liberal college campuses from northern California to North Carolina. UNC developed its own activism while in conversation with universities and organizations around the country.[8] By the early 1970s, however, its leaders rose to national prominence, and its innovative programs became models for many universities, colleges, and even high schools throughout America, thus making it an ideal case study to examine this type of activism.

A Changing Campus Scene

The 1960s witnessed dramatic changes in the gender dynamics and policies at the University of North Carolina. The school had admitted a limited number of junior and senior female students since 1897. The few first-year female students allowed to enter the university in the early 1960s had to be permanent residents of Chapel Hill and major in "feminine" subjects such as fine arts, medical technology, pharmacy, physical therapy, nursing, or dental hygiene. Although UNC did not admit women on an equal basis to men until 1972, by the fall of 1964 the university was accepting female first-years regardless of residency or major, which brought the number of female undergraduates into the twentieth percentile range for the first time.[9]

UNC's deans of undergraduate affairs feared the possible sexual effects that more women on campus would have on the student body, especially when coupled with what they perceived as the chaos of student activism that began with the civil rights movement and now involved free speech and antiwar protests. Administrators felt that it was their duty to protect students against the negative consequences of sex but limited their vision to upholding and reinforcing the sexual double standard. Their goal was to promote abstinence and to control female students' sexual behavior by limiting their autonomy and opportunities for sexual expression. To prevent the anticipated escalation of sexual activity caused by the new admissions policies, UNC's administrators reinforced old *in loco parentis* rules and erected new ones for women. The dean of women believed, "Women must be the standard bearers. . . . [E]very society must have a function for women, which is somewhat different from that for men; and education should reveal this concept."[10] Women under 25 were required to live in university housing, were locked in their dorms after designated hours, and had to sign out and receive permission to leave campus. Male students were largely exempt from these rules.

Beginning in 1967, these rules began to give way, and penalties became more lenient as the Association of Women Students demanded full equality. The passage of Title IX in 1972, which barred gender discrimination in education programs that received federal funding, ensured that female and male students faced the same rules. Nevertheless, the dean of women adamantly resisted the dismantling of women's rules throughout the late 1960s and early 1970s because, like much of the American public, she feared that their repeal intensified what she saw as a rising trend of university women increasingly engaging in sexual intercourse compared to the recent past.[11] College students in the late 1960s were undoubtedly more open than their parents' generation about their sexual activity, yet most contemporary studies found that there had been little change in the rate of unmarried women having intercourse when compared with Alfred Kinsey's data about the previous generation.[12] Despite the statistics, however, the deans, the media, and the public used anecdotal evidence to claim that a change in behavior had occurred.[13]

Oral contraceptives often took center stage in this anecdotal evidence. "The Pill," first put on the American market in 1960, became the emblem of the sexual revolution. By 1969, 8.5 million American women took oral contraceptives, making it the most popular birth control method in the nation.[14] Yet among female students at UNC, only a small minority took the Pill, according to a 1968 study. Sixty percent of those surveyed either had not used contraceptives at all or had depended on unreliable methods, such as withdrawal, rhythm, or douching the first time they had intercourse, and 40 percent of the students used nothing or unreliable contraceptives each time they had sex.[15] Despite the deans' and general public's panic, it seemed that the Pill—or any other reliable contraceptive device— had little effect on unmarried college students' sexual behavior.

Many college women did not use birth control devices, because their schools restricted access to them. In 1967, a survey showed that 96 percent of American college and university student health services refused to prescribe contraceptives to unmarried students; by 1970, 72 percent of these still retained their policies.[16] UNC's Student Health Services fell into this category. Administrators believed that denying birth control devices to female students was an extension of their *in loco parentis* policies to prevent students from having intercourse. Physicians at the Student Health Services also shamed students for requesting contraceptives. These doctors repeatedly reinforced the double standard by responding to female students' requests by stating that they were not "going to help in promoting promiscuous behavior in young people," that their female patients' behavior was not "lady like," or that "sex, like wine, should not be guzzled."[17] In addition to delivering such sermons, some doctors sent letters to students' parents telling them of their daughters' requests. Many pharmacists and private physicians in the community also responded to young women with lectures and refusals.

If a student became pregnant, she faced few options. Official policy in the late 1960s mandated that she should "present herself as soon as possible to the Student Health Service," where she would receive aid in dealing with the "problem in an ethical and confidential manner." This usually meant notifying her parents and suspending her from school until she gave birth.[18] If a woman decided to solve the problem on her own with an illegal abortion, she could face "disciplinary action ... not because of the pregnancy *per se* but because of the illegal fashion in which the student attempted to resolve the problem."[19] North Carolina had liberalized its abortion laws in 1967, making "therapeutic abortions" legal in cases in which the pregnancy resulted from rape or incest, impaired the life of the woman, or posed the risk of a giving birth to a child with "grave physical or mental defect."[20] To obtain a therapeutic abortion, three doctors had to approve the procedure, and until mid-1971, women under 21 had to have a parent or guardian's permission.[21] Obstetrician-gynecologists at UNC's Memorial Hospital tended to interpret the law liberally, authorizing the procedure on the grounds that a continued pregnancy would impair the woman's health by causing depression or attempted suicide.[22] Nonetheless, most UNC students did not have accurate information about the law, lacked a parent's approval, or did not know which doctors they could trust to assist them. Unlike the OB/GYNs at Memorial Hospital, most physicians at Student Health Services refused to help pregnant students who wanted to terminate their pregnancies. As one student recalled, a doctor told her there was nothing he could do for her and then "went into a long story about the children on his desk and he had always wondered how they [the children] would feel if [his wife] had gotten an abortion."[23] Therefore, if students chose to abort, they frequently did so under illegal, unsafe, or emotionally fraught circumstances.

A Physician's Crusade

Takey Crist, a young physician at UNC, watched the number of women on campus increase, the controversy over women's rules erupt, and Student Health Services' policies evolve throughout the late 1960s and early 1970s. What he observed eventually pushed him to become a sexual liberation activist leader and one of the most powerful advocates for gender and sexual equality on campus. Crist grew up in rural, eastern North Carolina, where his Greek Cypriot parents ran a hotel and restaurant. Unlike many American households, the Crist family discussed sex openly. As he remembers, "It's always been part of the natural process of being a human being in my family. . . . It was never a stigma to talk about it." This openness, however, was at odds with the social mores of his community. "When I was in high school, if a young woman got pregnant . . . she disappeared. . . . We didn't talk about it."[24] These patterns of silence about sexuality continued when Crist attended UNC as an undergraduate on a football scholarship and then as medical student in the early 1960s.

Two experiences during his training as an OB/GYN propelled Crist to devote much of his life to helping women secure reproductive freedom. During a medical internship in Charleston, South Carolina, in 1965, he was horrified at what he saw on the OB/GYN ward of the hospital: "On the weekends, we would always see women who had gone somewhere for an illegal abortion. The wards on the OB/GYN service on Monday, you could smell the infection and the disease and it just left an impression on you." When Crist returned to UNC for his residency, the 29-year-old, now-married physician had another experience that connected the horrors he was seeing in Charleston to the policies of the university. In 1966, a female student with a red catheter lodged in her uterus from a 50-dollar illegal abortion arrived at Memorial Hospital. Crist remembered with vivid detail, "She lost her uterus. She lost her ovaries. She had an abscess. She was put in ICU and of course, at that time, if you became pregnant, you got kicked out of school for unwoman-like conduct. Remember, the male, he wasn't involved."[25] Crist was outraged over the personal and physical losses that pregnant women had to endure, while the men who impregnated them lost nothing.[26] He was convinced that the university administration and Student Health Services were largely to blame for students' sexual ignorance and medical problems. He complained in the *North Carolina Medical Journal,* "It is as though pregnancy were being forced on a girl for stating that she was sexually active [to a Student Health Service physician] when in truth she was acting responsibly to herself, her boyfriend, and society."[27] Appalled by such practices, Crist began a crusade to assist students with their sexual problems and, in doing so, helped to initiate a wave of campus activism.

In the late 1960s, Crist, along with a few of his colleagues in UNC's OB/GYN Department, began vocally opposing the university's policies on pregnancy and abortion.[28] In combating the situation at the Student Health Service, these OB/GYNs made it known that students could come to them for contraceptives, legal abortions, and nonjudgmental discussions about their sexual feelings. In the 1970s, they set up a clinic where students could obtain birth control devices and abortion advice without patronizing morality lectures or demands for marriage licenses.[29] When female students did not have money or the resources to overcome restrictions for legal abortions, Crist later explained, "We would draw 30 cc's of blood, inject it in the woman's vagina, and say, 'Look, one of the residents is on call tonight. You go over to the hospital, the infirmary, and tell them you're having a miscarriage.'"[30] Through legal and extralegal means, doctors in the OB/GYN Department were able to help some women, but it was clear to them that a more organized system was needed to reach all the students at UNC, not just those lucky enough to hear about their efforts through the grapevine.

Throughout 1970, Crist visited dormitories and sororities on campus in order to assess students' reproductive knowledge and provide them with basic sexual information.[31] To gauge their understanding, he administered an informal questionnaire to six hundred female students. Of those who were sexually active, over 25 percent could not answer a single question about ovulation, anatomy, contraception, and basic sexual function. None of the women answered all of the questions correctly, and only 59 percent successfully answered half. These findings confirmed what he had witnessed in the clinic: UNC students lacked basic knowledge about sex as well as access to the products and services they needed to protect themselves. Crist's belief that "contraception and sex education [went] hand in hand" and that "one cannot give out contraception without . . . talking about human sexuality" led him to implement a new plan to reach all UNC students.[32]

In the summer of 1970, Crist recruited Tom Blush, Richard Mier, and Donald Rollins, three medical students from around the country who wanted to work with him. As Rollins explained, "I don't want to become a doctor just to push pills. . . . I want to be in there helping with the real problems of society."[33] The medical students agreed with Crist that one of the most pressing "real problems" was the lack of sex education for college students. Calling themselves the "Sex Men," the medical students, under Crist's supervision, created a handbook tailored to UNC students, *Elephants and Butterflies . . . and Contraceptives.*[34] In 1968, students at McGill University created the first sexuality handbook tailored for a campus community, and similar ones were beginning to appear on campuses throughout the United States.[35] In 1969, a women's liberation group in Boston began to compile a similar booklet more exclusively for women, which eventually was published commercially as *Our Bodies, Ourselves* in 1973.[36] Although that would be the most famous handbook, it began as one of many local projects that included *Elephants and Butterflies.*

When presenting the handbook for the first time, the medical students explained, "The sexual revolution we have heard so much about may be only a minor insurrection as far as the contraceptive habits of college students are concerned."[37] It was time for a new direction based on knowledge, responsibility, and equality. The handbook's title (besides evoking imagery of female and male anatomy) was based on an E. E. Cummings story about an elephant and butterfly who fall in love, protect each other, and discover the world together. By reprinting the story on the opening page, the authors represented sexual relationships as a partnership based on caring and trust. The first section addressed female and male anatomy and sexual function because they believed, "Effective contraceptive practices are reliant upon a healthy appreciation and solid understanding of male and female physiology."[38] The handbook even had a passage explaining the female orgasm, a central rallying point for second-wave feminists who had been drawing links between sexual pleasure and women's emancipation.[39] The male authors also invoked feminist language and ideology by asserting that women's "traditional role as passive, submissive weaklings who have no active interest in sex is changing with our new generation of maturing students." The second section of the booklet focused on contraceptives, explaining each method's effectiveness, side effects, and how to overcome psychological barriers by emphasizing the link between birth control

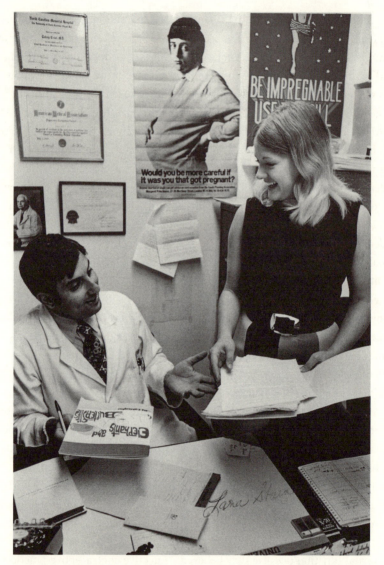

Figure 8.1. Sexual liberation activist Dr. Takey Crist and student activist Lana Starnes with a copy of *Elephants and Butterflies . . . and Contraceptives,* the popular handbook on sexuality they designed for the students of University of North Carolina at Chapel Hill. Courtesy Sallie Bingham Center for Women's History and Culture, Duke University.

and openness: "Honest, frank, and loving communication is the key to contraceptive effectiveness as well as sexual happiness in general."[40] The booklet then went on to discuss venereal diseases and to list places in Chapel Hill that would provide contraceptives, pregnancy tests, and safe abortions.[41]

Students Enlist in the Cause

After completing the handbook in August, the three medical students returned to their respective schools, leaving Crist in charge of publicity and distribution. He wanted to ensure that every student had a copy and hoped that its release would provoke a new dialogue on campus. Crist also anticipated a battle with the administration, so he began to build a coalition of undergraduates. UNC students, like many on campuses across the United States, had been involved in numerous progressive and even radical forms of protest in the 1960s. They had held sit-ins to integrate local businesses, demonstrated against a campus speaker ban of Communist Party members, rallied against the Vietnam War, and went on strike with African American food workers.[42] Students also had turned their attention to their own surroundings and charged that the impersonal, mechanical "multiversity" was a main source of alienation from one another and their academic work. Calling for "student power" as a way to obtain a more meaningful, relevant education, they fought to increase their participation in the school's governing bodies and their control over the curriculum.[43] As one UNC student explained, "Students have stopped listening and they are beginning to talk themselves. They are now working their way into the system."[44] Sexuality soon became a central aspect of student power demands, in no small part due to the release of *Elephants and Butterflies*.

In attempting to tap into student activism, Crist turned first to the leaders of student government. Tommy Bello, the student body president active in organizing Vietnam War protests, fully supported the handbook. He wanted to use the momentum of *Elephants and Butterflies* to form a committee that could compose a formal petition giving voice to the "grievances from students that have been to the infirmary and have been given morality lectures and not treated as patients, but in an unprofessional manner."[45] Mary Vallier, president of the Association of Women Students, was also enthusiastic about the handbook. The association's fight against *in loco parentis* had taken over almost its entire agenda during the previous two years, and its new president wanted to expand beyond "rules and rules alone."[46] To coincide with the release of the handbook, she planned a series of sex education symposia and discussion groups in each dormitory and sorority similar to the women's liberation movement's consciousness-raising efforts.[47]

Another emerging campus activist, sophomore Robert Wilson, had been independently planning a "Sexual Revolution Month" for his dormitory and asked Crist to "be the number one speaker." The physician agreed, and they decided that these events could also serve as a platform for promoting the handbook and the ideology embedded within it.[48]

These three young white students formed the initial support network for Crist.[49] They believed that *Elephants and Butterflies* could create a new awareness of the need for sex education, but first they had to secure funding for its publication. The last thing administrators wanted was more student demands, let alone demands centered on sex. They refused to allocate funds for the printing and distribution because they believed that it would outrage taxpayers, alumni, and the press, including Jesse Helms, North Carolina's rising media and New Right political star.[50] Crist lamented the struggle with the administration in a letter he wrote to Tom Blush, a fellow sexual liberation activist: "Putting it very mildly this book has caused an uproar on this campus."[51] Crist sent off letter after letter defending *Elephants and Butterflies*. He was not above emotional persuasion, arguing at one point, "I am not sure I have adequately justified in my mind the price the university wants to place on the young 21 year old female who might die from an illegal abortion or from unwanted pregnancy."[52] Finally, ECOS, Inc., a student-run nonprofit group, agreed to print and distribute the handbook.[53] On 18 September 1970, ten thousand copies hit the stands at the student store, and within five days, all were gone; there were about eighteen thousand undergraduate and graduate students at the time.[54] Congratulatory letters and requests for copies poured into Crist's office. Within six months, *Elephants and Butterflies* went into its third printing and found its way to universities across the country, all custom-made to list local contraceptive and abortion providers.[55]

The release of *Elephants and Butterflies* succeeded in bringing together students and faculty activists who were committed to sexual liberation. While male physicians had played a leading role in earlier activities, the success of *Elephants and Butterflies* opened the door for many undergraduates and women to take on leadership roles. Sophomore Lana Starnes chronicled the events surrounding the handbook in the student newspaper, the *Daily Tar Heel*. Recognizing its appearance as a moment when radical change was possible, she wrote in a November 1970 editorial, "The questions are now out in the open and are being discussed freely. . . . It's time we came out of the dark ages and talked about our problems truthfully and openly." Starnes warned that she often witnessed "very intelligent women who were almost totally ignorant of their bodies."[56] Starnes and the doctor became friends and allies as she chronicled Crist's visits to dorms, symposia, and lecture halls across the state. She experienced a life-changing moment when she accompanied Crist to a lecture at a college in Raleigh, North Carolina. A few women approached her to ask her some questions. Starnes remembered, "That was the turning point! I found that because of my talks with Takey and writing about *Elephants and Butterflies* I had learned enough that I could answer questions myself."[57] Crist also realized the depth and breadth of her knowledge and pitched an idea to her: together they could write a question-and-answer sex column in the *Daily Tar Heel*.

Ignoring criticism from the administration, Crist and Starnes published their first column, also titled "Elephants and Butterflies," in December 1970. The weekly column ran for the next three years, using a question-and-answer format in which students wrote to the student-doctor team about their sexual problems and curiosities. Inquiries ranged from the history of tampons and the probability of catching venereal disease in a swimming pool to why women fake orgasms and how to compare abortion prices in different states.[58] Unlike the handbook, the column began to address gay and lesbian issues by confronting stereotypes and arguing against the notion of sexual deviance.[59] Virtually nothing was taboo; sexual liberation activists were opening up all aspects of sexuality to public discussion on campus.

In the column's second year, Starnes largely took over writing it, while Crist primarily double-checked it for medical accuracy. Starnes's equal responsibility in the column and accumulation of knowledge reveal the ways in which sexual liberation activism overlapped with the women's health movement. She eventually identified as a feminist who believed that women's sexual ignorance directly related to their oppression and hoped that her column would aid in their struggle for sexual and gender liberation. By cooperating with Crist in writing the column, she became a lay practitioner and educator and one of thousands of feminists around the country reclaiming medical knowledge of sexuality and the body for ordinary people.[60]

Starnes, Wilson, Vallier, Bello, and Crist embarked on independent yet intertwined activities throughout the fall of 1970, but by semester's end, these sexual liberation activists felt that it was time to unite their efforts. Starnes and Crist formed the Committee for Human Sexuality in order to place all their activities under an umbrella organization. Starnes, Wilson, Crist, and a graduate student from the Department of Maternal and Child Health served as committee chairpersons. The board of directors included faculty from the Department of Maternal and Child Health, the Carolina Population Center, the Department of Health Education, and the School of Social Work. A few doctors from Student Health Services and administrators who realized that change would occur with or without them even joined the board.[61] This would be a collaborative project where male and female students, physicians, faculty, and administrators could organize and discuss sexual issues on equal footing.

The committee's first goal was to create a sex education course for undergraduates. Since at least the 1920s, some universities had offered courses with sexuality as a theme, but most had titles such as "Hygiene" or "Marriage and Family Living," which assumed and encouraged that students' sexual relations would take place within the institution of marriage. Well into the 1960s, most of these courses attempted to promote conventional gender roles and the sexual double standard.[62] As Crist observed, "The marriage or family courses offered do little more than explain parental roles and how to budget a family income."[63] The Committee for Human Sexuality wanted its class to be different. This meant, however, that it would be more controversial. Fearing political repercussions, the university refused to fund the course, and the committee had trouble finding a department willing to associate itself with the undertaking.

After months of searching for a home for the class, the Public Health Department agreed to offer the course for credit hours, even though it offered no other undergraduate courses.[64] This decision, however, came with several conditions: the course coordinators could "*not* advertise . . . in the *Daily Tar Heel* or any other newspaper. Students [would have] to find out about it through word of mouth."[65] The Department Chair also warned that "the course should be a sober and scientific reflection on the issues of sexuality . . . and not to look as if we are the initiators of the sexual revolution which has occurred quite without the benefit of our sponsorship."[66] Crist assured him that the "students would not be given any 'how' information," and the emphasis would be on "*responsible* sex."[67]

On 1 February 1971, two hundred students filled a lecture hall for the inaugural for-credit course, Topics in Human Sexuality. Crist began the first lecture by telling the students that the purpose of the course "is to challenge students with concepts and issues of human sexuality and to provide students with the opportunity to creatively integrate these concepts and issues into their total perspective of self and society." He continued, "We anticipate that a basic result of making this challenge and providing this opportunity will be that students will have an increased capacity to make better informed value choices."[68] The organizers of the course intended to change how students viewed sexuality, experienced sex, and interacted with each other. Every Monday night, students listened to lectures by Crist or a guest speaker about abortion, birth control, venereal disease, sex and the law, sexuality and religion, the population problem, or "the college student and sex."[69] Students then dispersed into small discussion groups, usually led by students, where they talked about sexual experiences and worked on collaborative projects.[70]

Student letters praising the course poured into the offices of administrators and department chairs. Janelle Urnay summed up many students' feelings: "This course is more relevant to my every day problems and needs than any other course I have taken this semester." She explained that the most important aspect of the course for her was "that it has broadened my perspective concerning homosexuality, abortion, masturbation, and how to cope with my own needs." The course not only taught the students about their own bodies but also encouraged them to examine their ideas about how others expressed their sexuality. Although the course focused on heterosexual sex, the organizers made a conscious attempt to integrate lesbian and gay issues into its content, which not only benefited students in that community but also encouraged straight students to be more tolerant. A heterosexual man reported on the gay male subculture at Chapel Hill for his final project in the class. In the paper, he admitted that he had been quite apprehensive: "[My] Eastern North Carolina upbringing had never brought me in contact with homosexuals. Sure, I'd read all the accounts about them in *Time* and had even seen a couple but had never been in an environment dominated by gay people." He left a gay bar "with a different attitude towards homosexuality. . . . I realized that homosexuals were a rejected minority of human beings with most of the same ambitions, faults, and feelings as the rest of society."[71]

By the next fall, Topics in Human Sexuality had an enrollment of about 250 and a waiting list of over 400. Nevertheless, despite its popularity, the course ran into financial difficulties. During the first semester, Crist taught for free, and sexual liberation activists raised $700 from private donors and departments to cover guest lectures and course materials. The next fall, they received only $200 from the School of Nursing. Although Crist had acquiesced to the administration's requests the previous semester to keep the course out of the press, he went public with the issue of funding and potential threat of cancellation. He had built a rapport with many students and knew that they would support him. Crist blasted the administration and all the departments on campus in the *Daily Tar Heel*: "Somebody better come up with the money to run this course. We're talking about peanuts. . . . We are turning away from 400 to 500 students each semester. . . . Why?"[72] The course had the support of a large number of students whose anger about the funding issues reached a boiling point over the following few days. Various departments attempted to assuage the tension. The chairman of the Health Department argued that he had no knowledge of funding issues, and the director of Student Health Services offered funds, probably to keep Crist from further damaging its reputation. Eight days after Crist's media tirades, various departments finally came up with the necessary funding.[73]

Building on the course's success, Wilson, a founding student member of the Human Sexuality Committee, came up with an idea for a peer counseling service.

He believed that UNC still lacked "campus resources to aid students in integrating sexual expression into the context of interpersonal relationships" and an "adequate formal loci" for students to obtain "necessary information."[74] Moreover, the inherent hierarchy of the classroom or doctor's office dissuaded many students from seeking help. A peer counseling service would be a site where power and knowledge would flow horizontally, to and from peers, rather than vertically down from medical and faculty "experts" to students. Wilson secured space and funds from the student government to set up the counseling service and then found help from an unexpected source: Student Health Services.[75] Student Health Services had been revising its policies about sexuality and reproduction—no doubt in response to sexual liberation activists' demands—and did not want to risk further estrangement from students.[76] It even created a new position, coordinator of human sexuality, filled by Dr. Caroline Dixon.[77]

In early October 1971, Wilson began advertising in the *Daily Tar Heel* for volunteers for a counseling team. Thirty-seven undergraduate students, graduate students, and community members responded. Wilson and Dixon ran three three-hour training sessions in which students learned about physiology, anatomy, contraception, pregnancy, and abortion. They also participated in role-playing exercises, because Wilson wanted to ascertain whether volunteers had the "openness and sensitivity" to become counselors and to root out any "Kama Sutra extremist," who he believed "could prematurely and unjustly influence decisions" of students who used the service.[78] Wilson did not want counselors to push their views on students or for the service to be associated primarily with sexual technique instruction. Rather, like the other endeavors of sexual liberation activists, the counseling service sought to promote frankness, responsibility, scientific knowledge, and rational choices.

The Human Sexuality Information and Counseling Service opened on 18 October 1971, offering in-person counseling as well as a telephone hotline for students who wished to remain anonymous. In the first year of its existence, it handled 1,091 cases.[79] This overwhelming response suggests that students still had many unanswered questions about sexuality and that sexual liberation activists were fulfilling a pressing need on campus. Students inquired about a variety of sexual matters. Common questions included how to tell whether one was pregnant, whether oral sex could cause conception, how to prevent painful intercourse for women, where to obtain birth control devices and abortions, what caused male impotence and premature ejaculation, and how women could best achieve orgasm.[80]

The counseling service attempted to change how the counselors and the students they helped understood their sexual relationships and gender identities. Many counselors participated because they saw the service's goals as central to second-wave feminism. Former counselor Margaret Scales recalled, "I was not sexually active. I was not a lesbian. I was not in need of an abortion and all that. But, I was very interested in women's health and as a feminist. . . . I was very interested in . . . the information sharing part of it."[81] Like members of the women's health movement, the student counselors believed that they could liberate themselves by gaining knowledge about their bodies and passing it on to others. The service also dovetailed with the women's health movement in its abortion counseling. Counselors who chose to specialize in abortion received special training from psychiatrists and gynecologists, who taught them how to talk to women about their choices and to explain procedures.[82] Because of the restrictions on and high prices of therapeutic abortions in North Carolina, counselors often referred women to New York clinics, where abortion had been legalized in 1970—without a residency requirement. The counselors visited the clinics before recommending them to "see that they really are legitimate, see how clean they were, and talk to the people."[83] These counselors became extremely educated about abortion and, as a result, were able to empower themselves and the women they helped.

The counseling service represents how women and men worked together for a feminist cause. Although men filled most leadership positions, as they did in most New Left mixed-sex groups, women quickly rose in the ranks at the counseling service and in other sexual liberation activities. Moreover, the counselors worked together to try to change the gender consciousness of men on campus by fighting against the double standard, which had placed reproductive concerns solely in the hands of women. For example, counseling service posters in dorms and classrooms featured a cartoon of a young man giving the "OK" sign and asked, "Hey Charlie . . . did you score last night?" The poster went on to pose a series of questions to the male student: "Was she on the Pill? Does she have an IUD? Did you remember your condom?" The final statement of the poster read, "Hey Charlie, birth control is your responsibility too!!"[84] Sexual liberation activists believed that women had as much right to a fulfilling and pleasurable sex life as men, but this was impossible unless men shared in the burdens of preventing unwanted sexual consequences.

In 1972, the counseling service expanded its focus to include lesbian, gay, and bisexual (LGB) issues. This was in large part due to outside pressure from the LGB community, which was beginning to organize into a mass movement in the South as well as the rest of the country.[85] Former counselor Sara Spencer remembers that when the service began, counselors "had not gotten any training in gay counseling. So the gay people themselves, both men and women, came along and said, 'If you're going to have a sexuality counseling service on campus, this has got to be a component of it.'"[86] LGB counselors performed regular duties in addition to being "resources to the other counselors" and speaking to various groups on campus about gay issues. The service helped to create a network of LGB activists while increasing their visibility on campus. As a direct result of engaging in these activities, counselor Daniel Leonard cofounded the first gay liberation organization at UNC in 1974.[87]

The participation of LGB counselors in the service also changed the consciousness of straight counselors and led to gay-straight alliances. Straight counselors had advocated acceptance of homosexual sexual acts and identities, but many had little personal experience with the LGB community until those students joined the service. Wilson recruited gay members but felt some trepidation. When entering a meeting of gay men, Wilson thought himself "so liberal that I'm vulnerable to the idea of being gay, and I'm going to go in and be tapped with a magic wand and suddenly have interest in men." He remembered, "It was like about six seconds [before] I was totally fine, and that was behind me and then we went on to our business."[88] Margaret Scales gave a fellow female bisexual counselor a ride home one night. She recalls, "All of a sudden I got this sweat—I thought she was going to reach over and grab my crotch, and at that point, I realized that I was so unsophisticated. . . . So that was a great wake-up call for me."[89] Just as the service could alter the gender consciousness of men, it also affected how heterosexual students thought about and interacted with the LGB community. As Wilson reported, "Even if our Counselors were the *only* people who the Service helped . . . our existence is justified."[90]

Conclusion

By 1973, sexual liberation activists had created an astonishing number of services and institutions at the University of North Carolina. Students now had a medical clinic offering contraceptives and advice, a handbook and course devoted to helping them understand their bodies and sexual lives, and a newspaper column and a peer counseling service to answer questions about sexuality. In 1973, an article in the student paper even complained about "all the sex information that has been crammed down your throat since you got to Carolina."[91] Sexual liberation activism seemed to lose some of its intensity in the following years as information saturated the student body, programs became institutionalized, student leaders graduated, and Takey Crist left the university to open a private practice. Yet we should not underestimate what these activists achieved in such a short time.

Sexual liberation activists succeeded in shifting the university's relationship to students and students' relationships with each other and their own bodies along feminist lines. They challenged the double standard by creating a new public dialogue about sexuality and offering male and female students a new gender ideology grounded in the ideals of mutual responsibility, honesty, and respect. Their actions and ideas thus reveal that second-wave feminism had multiple origins and trajectories. Like many activists in the era, these activists did not associate with a single movement, such as civil rights, women's liberation, student power, or gay liberation but rather saw themselves as part of them all and part of a larger struggle for human liberation and social justice. They represent a web of alliances in which adults fought for the rights of students; men advocated reproductive justice; and straight students helped to carve out an affirming and accepting atmosphere for lesbian, gay, and bisexual students.

Sexual liberation activism complicates popular understandings of the sexual revolution. The historic upheaval in sexual manners and mores is often remembered by the American public as a sexual free-for-all. Conservative pundits and politicians especially have pushed a definition of the sexual revolution as "the creation of a new social order based on moral relativism, hedonism and individual gratification."[92] They explicitly connect the sexual revolution to college students in order to discredit many of the New Left movements in which these young people were involved and to wage their contemporary battles to curb women's reproductive rights, limit sex education, and restrict gay rights. The students and faculty in this study did not define the sexual revolution as sleeping with as many partners as possible or participating in wild orgies. When they talked of "revolution," they talked of the dissemination of sexual knowledge, gender equality, and the acceptance of diverse sexual identities.

NOTES

1. Robert Wilson to Takey Crist, Aug. 1970, folder "Coed and Politics," box 6, Accession 2004, Takey Crist Papers, Rare Book, Manuscript, and Special Collections Library, Duke University, Durham, North Carolina (hereafter cited as TCP).

2. Jerry Klein, "'Sex Month' Entertains," *Daily Tar Heel,* 10 Oct. 1970, 1.

3. These activists did not use a single name to describe themselves and their activities. Some considered themselves sex educators at the forefront of the sexual revolution; others saw themselves as part of a movement to legalize birth control and abortion; many identified primarily as feminists. Although they came from different orientations, I use the identifier "sexual liberation activist" because in addition to working together, they shared common goals, tactics, and philosophies.

4. Sexual liberation activism is very much a part of Van Gosse's idea of a "movement of movements" and what Jacquelyn Dowd Hall describes as the "long civil rights movement." Van Gosse, "A Movement of Movements: The Definition and Periodization of the New Left," in *A Companion to Post-1945 America,* ed. Jean-Christophe Agnew and Roy Rosenweig (Malden, MA: Blackwell, 2002), 278; Jacquelyn Dowd Hall, "The Long Civil Rights Movement and the Political Uses of the Past," *Journal of American History* 91, no. 5 (Mar. 2005): 1233–63.

5. Conservatives in particular are invested in this portrayal of the sexual revolution. See Leon Kass, "The End of Courtship," *Public Interest* 126 (2002): 39–63; and Mary Eberstadt, "Is Food the New Sex?" *Policy Review* 153 (2009): 25–40. Alan Petigny makes a similar argument about behavior change: Alan Petigny, "Resisting the Complacency Narrative: Sixties Social Unrest and Its Relation to the 1950s," *Reviews in American History* 34, no. 2 (2006): 241.

6. Beth L. Bailey, "Sexual Revolution(s)," in *The Sixties: From Memory to History,* ed. David Farber (Chapel Hill: Univ. of North Carolina Press, 1994), 235–62; Beth L. Bailey, *Sex in the Heartland* (Cambridge, MA: Harvard Univ. Press, 1999). See also David Allyn, *Make Love, Not War: The Sexual Revolution, an Unfettered History* (Boston: Little, Brown, 2000).

7. Anne M. Valk, *Radical Sisters: Second-Wave Feminism and Black Liberation in Washington, D.C.* (Urbana: Univ. of Illinois Press, 2008), 2. See also Anne Enke, *Finding the Movement: Sexuality, Contested Space, and Feminist Activism* (Durham, NC: Duke Univ. Press, 2007); and Katarina Keane, "Second-Wave Feminism in the American South, 1965–1980" (PhD diss., Univ. of Maryland, 2009).

8. Exact numbers of sexual liberation activists are difficult to pinpoint because people moved in and out of groups and activities and often did not participate in all activities on a given campus. Moreover, while UNC had many different sexual liberation activities, it represents one end of the spectrum. Hundreds of other campuses may have had only one or two activities and 10 to 20 activists devoting a significant amount of time to them.

9. Joan Page, "UNC Doors Open Wide to Freshmen Coeds," *Chapel Hill Weekly,* 1 Nov. 1964; Gene Marlowe, "UNC-CH Lifts Restrictions on Women" *News and Observer,* 25 June 1972, 7. See also Pamela Dean, *Women on the Hill: A History of Women at the University of North Carolina* (Chapel Hill: Division of Student Affairs, Univ. of North Carolina at Chapel Hill, 1987).

10. "Dean Carmichael Stays 'Consistent' as Coeds Change," *News and Observer,* 23 Mar. 1973; Carmichael to Dean of Student Affairs at the University of North Carolina, 10 June 1969, folder 1:29, box 2, Katherine Kennedy Carmichael Series, Records of the Office of the Dean of Women, University Archives and Record Service, Wilson Library, University of North Carolina at Chapel Hill (hereafter cited as RDW).

11. For example, see "Campus '65: The College Generation Looks at Itself and the World around It," *Newsweek,* 22 Mar. 1965.

12. Alfred C. Kinsey et al., *Sexual Behavior in the Human Female* (Philadelphia and London: W. B. Saunders, 1953), 286–88; Harold I. Leif, "The Essence of the Revolution in Honesty," *Marriage Council News* (Nov. 1971), 5; Seymore L. Halleck, "Sex and Mental Health on the Campus," *Journal of the American Medical Association* 200, no. 8 (1967): 684.

13. Alan Petigny, "Illegitimacy, Postwar Psychology, and the Reperiodization of the Sexual Revolution," *Journal of Social History* 38, no. 1 (2004): 63–79.

14. See Elizabeth Siegel Watkins, *On the Pill: A Social History of Oral Contraceptives, 1950–1970* (Baltimore: Johns Hopkins Univ. Press, 1998).

15. Karl E. Bauman, "Selected Aspects of the Contraceptive Practices of Unmarried University Students," *American Journal of Obstetrics and Gynecology* 108, no. 2 (1970): 203–9.

16. L. Barbato, "Statistical Report of U.S. Survey on 'The Pill,'" paper presented at the American College Health Association 45th Annual Meeting, Washington, D.C., 1967, folder 12, box 4, Sexual Freedom League Records, Bancroft Library, University of California, Berkeley, California.

17. Barry Parker, "UNC Students Getting Truthful Sex Education," *News and Observer,* 9 Mar. 1972; Johanna Schoen, *Choice and Coercion: Birth Control, Sterilization, and Abortion*

in Public Health and Welfare (Chapel Hill: Univ. of North Carolina Press, 2005), 168; Crist, Record Sheet, 13 July 1970, folder "Interviews Coeds," box 13, TCP.

18. James A. Taylor to C. O. Cathey, 10 Mar. 1967, series 1, folder 12, box 1, Records of the Office of the Vice Chancellor for Student Affairs, University Archives and Record Service, Wilson Library, University of North Carolina at Chapel Hill (hereafter cited as RVC).

19. Cathey to Carmichael, Cansler, Hedgpeth, and Taylor, 8 Sept. 1967, series 1, folder 12, box 1, RVC.

20. Jaroslav F. Hulka, *Therapeutic Abortion: A Chapel Hill Symposium* (Chapel Hill, NC: Carolina Population Center and Department of Obstetrics and Gynecology, 1967), folder "Abortion, 1969–1991," box 7, Jaroslav Hulka Papers, Rare Book, Manuscript, and Special Collections Library, Duke University, Durham, North Carolina.

21. For more on abortion, see Leslie J. Reagan, *When Abortion Was a Crime: Women, Medicine, and Law in the United States, 1867–1973* (Berkeley: Univ. of California Press, 1997); Schoen, *Choice and Coercion*; and David G. Warren to Charles H. Hendricks, 21 July 1971, folder "Contraception and the Law," box 13, TCP.

22. Takey Crist, interview with the author, Jacksonville, North Carolina, 30 Nov. 2007; see all letters in folder "Abortions, Psychiatric Letter," box 3, TCP.

23. Crist, Record Sheet, 5 Feb. 1970, folder "Interviews Coeds," box 13, TCP; Crist interview.

24. Crist interview.

25. Ibid.

26. Crist, "Sex Education," n.d. [1970], folder "Grant," box 10, TCP; Andrew H. Malcolm, "College Ferment '71," *Today's Health* 49, no. 4 (1971), 27–33.

27. Takey Crist, "Something Is Happening on Our College Campuses," *North Carolina Medical Journal* 33, no. 1 (1972): 42–44.

28. Crist and the other doctors in his department were part of a long and complicated history of OB/GYNs supporting the struggle for reproductive justice. Physicians were among the leading proponents of criminalizing birth control and abortion in the name of the "professionalization of medicine" in the late nineteenth century. Throughout the twentieth century, however, a few played key roles in supporting women's quest for reproductive autonomy, risking their careers and jail time by providing birth control products and services to women who wanted them. Moreover, many OB/GYN were at the forefront of the legal and political battle for legalization. Crist and sexual liberation activists were aware of this history to various degrees. Nevertheless, the archival and oral history evidence suggests that they did not dwell on this long history. Most sexual liberation activists at UNC characterized their work as truly innovative and revolutionary but failed to ground it in a larger historical narrative about the birth control and abortion movement. For more on doctors' involvement in the struggle for reproductive justice, see Linda Gordon, *The Moral Property of Women: A History of Birth Control Politics in America* (Urbana and Chicago: Univ. of Illinois Press, 2002); Reagan, *When Abortion Was a Crime*; and Schoen, *Choice and Coercion*.

29. Hulka to Crist, 12 May 1970, folder "Health Ed. Clinic Coeds UNC," box 11, TCP.

30. Crist interview.

31. Crist, "Development of Health Education Clinic and Educational Materials for High Risk Sexually Active Women," n.d. [1970], folder "Health Ed. Clinic Coeds UNC," box 11, TCP.

32. Crist to Hendricks, 20 Dec. 1970, folder "Health Ed. Clinic Coeds UNC," box 11, TCP.

33. Malcolm, "College Ferment '71."

34. Richard Mier, Donald Rollins, and Thomas Blush, *Elephants and Butterflies . . . and Contraceptives,* 1st ed. (Chapel Hill, NC: ECOS, 1970), box 6, TCP.

35. Donna Cherniak and Allan Feingold, eds., *Birth Control Handbook* (Montreal: Donna Cherniak, Allan Feingold, and the Students' Society of McGill Univ., 1968); Malcolm, "College Ferment '71."

36. Kathy Davis, *The Making of Our Bodies, Ourselves: How Feminism Travels across Borders* (Durham, NC: Duke Univ. Press, 2008).

37. Richard Mier, Donald Rollins, and Tom Blush, "Elephants and Butterflies: A Report for the Carolina Population Center's Summer Research Program," 17 Aug. 1970, folder "E&B: Final Report," box 7, TCP.

38. Mier et al., *Elephants and Butterflies,* 4.

39. See Jane F. Gerhard, *Desiring Revolution: Second-Wave Feminism and the Rewriting of American Sexual Thought, 1920 to 1982* (New York: Columbia Univ. Press, 2001).

40. Mier et al., *Elephants and Butterflies,* 6.

41. Ibid., 17–18.

42. For an excellent overview of UNC student protests movements, see University of North Carolina Manuscripts Department, "I Raised My Hand to Volunteer: Student Protest in 1960s Chapel Hill," available at www.lib.unc.edu/mss/exhibits/protests/, accessed 6 Sept. 2011.

43. David Farber, *The Age of Great Dreams: America in the 1960s* (New York: Hill and Wang, 1994), 158–59, 193–97.

44. Rick Gray, "Changes Came on Campus," *Daily Tar Heel,* 11 Jan. 1971.

45. Crist, interview with Tommy Bello, Aug. 1970, folder "Coed and Politics," box 6, TCP.

46. Mary Vallier to New Students, [Aug. 1970], folder "Policies," box 2, RDW; Renée N. Lansley, "College Women or College Girls? Gender, Sexuality, and In Loco Parentis on Campus" (PhD diss., Ohio State Univ., 2004).

47. Jessica Hanchar, "Sex Education Symposium Slated by Women Students," *Daily Tar Heel,* 23 Sept. 1970, 1.

48. Robert Wilson to Crist, Aug. 1970; Crist to Wilson, 25 Aug. 1970, folder "Coed and Politics," box 6, TCP.

49. It is important to note that sexual liberation movement leaders were overwhelmingly white. A few possible explanations are because the percentage of African American students at UNC was so small—only 1.5% by 1968—while black student activists tended to focus on civil rights movement issues, including transforming the university through achieving better pay for black workers and fighting for African American studies. Moreover, African American students' relationship to the sexual revolution was different from that of white middle-class students given the entrenched racial stereotypes of oversexualized black men and women and the different historical relationship African Americans had to contraceptives, abortion, and sterilization that often involved force and manipulation. Schoen, *Choice and Coercion*; Susan Cahn, *Sexual Reckonings: Southern Girls in a Troubling Age* (Cambridge, MA: Harvard Univ. Press, 2007); Rickie Solinger, *Wake Up Little Susie: Single Pregnancy and Race before Roe v. Wade* (New York: Routledge, 1992); J. Derek Williams, "'It Wasn't Slavery Anymore': Foodworkers' Strike at Chapel Hill, Spring 1969," MA thesis, Univ. of North Carolina at Chapel Hill, 1979).

50. Ethel Nash to Moye [Freymann], 14 Sept. 1970; memorandum by Crist, 15 Sept. 1970; Dr. J. Hulka and Robert Blake to Dr. Moye Freymann, 11 Sept. 1970, folder "Coed and Politics," box 6, TCP.

51. Crist to Tom Blush, 24 Sept. 1970, box 7, TCP.

52. Crist to Dr. Arden C. Miller, 11 Sept. 1970, box 7, TCP.

53. ECOS is not an acronym. It is the full name of the student group, and the students chose to capitalize all of the letters in it.

54. Robert Smythe to Mark Smythe, 20 Mar. 1971, folder "E&B Correspondence," box 7, TCP.

55. Folder "E&B Correspondence," box 7, TCP. Copies of *Elephants and Butterflies* were distributed to college and universities throughout North Carolina and in the Southeast, including to UNC at Wilmington, the University of Kentucky, the University of Tennessee, Florida Technical College, and Sandhill Community College in South Carolina. UNC Student Stores, Elephants and Butterflies Accounting Memo, n.d. [1973], folder "E&B: Accounting from UNC Stores, Sales," box 9, TCP. See also folder "E&B Correspondence," box 7, TCP.

56. Lana Starnes, "Sex Education Needed Badly," *Daily Tar Heel*, 4 Nov. 1970, editorial page.

57. Margaret Bobo, "Lana Starnes: The Women Who Helped Bring 'Elephants and Butterflies' to UNC," *Daily Tar Heel*, 9 Feb. 1973, 1, 5.

58. Lana Starnes and Takey Crist, "Elephants and Butterflies," *Daily Tar Heel*, 7 Feb. 1972, 21 Jan. 1972, and 4 May 1972.

59. Starnes and Crist, "Elephants and Butterflies," *Daily Tar Heel*, 27 Mar. 1972 and 15 Oct. 1973.

60. Sandra Morgen, *Into Our Own Hands: The Women's Health Movement in the United States, 1969–1990* (New Brunswick, NJ: Rutgers Univ. Press, 2002).

61. "Board of Directors, Human Sexuality Committee," n.d. [1971], folder "Committee for Human Sexuality, 1971," box 12, TCP. The Carolina Population Center was founded in 1966 and helped to fund and support many sexual liberation activities on campus. The population movement in North Carolina had roots in the state's eugenics policies that dated back to the 1920s. Arguing that certain eugenic theories could be put to use to elevate the white race, eliminate poverty, save taxpayers' money, and improve maternal and child health, health and state officials used a patchwork of voluntary and coercive welfare policies to try to control poor women and African American women's sexuality. As eugenic arguments about improving the race began to lose cultural and political capital in the 1960s, population control rhetoric replaced it as a central justification for controlling poor women's reproductive capabilities. It was in this context that the Carolina Population Center was founded in 1966 with about three million dollars in private and public funds. Although most of its programs were aimed at poor women, Takey Crist and others in the OB/GYN Department managed to secure some funds for sexual liberation activities to help college students. See "UNC Project Given Grant of $800,000," *News and Observer*, 27 Oct. 1965; Wade Jones, "UNC Receives Birth Control Research Grant," *News and Observer*, 14 Jan. 1969; Crist interview; Donald T. Critchlow, *Intended Consequences: Birth Control, Abortion, and the Federal Government in Modern America* (New York: Oxford Univ. Press, 1999); and Schoen, *Choice and Coercion*.

62. See Janice M. Irvine, *Talk about Sex: The Battles over Sex Education in the United States* (Berkeley: Univ. of California Press, 2002); and Jeffrey Moran, *Teaching Sex: The Shaping of Adolescence in the 20th Century* (Cambridge, MA: Harvard Univ. Press, 2000).

63. Crist, "Something Is Happening."

64. Robert Reid Wilson, interview with the author, Chapel Hill, North Carolina, 27 Sept. 2005.

65. Crist to Dr. Steuart, 23 Nov. 1970, folder "HEED 33," box 10, TCP, emphasis in original.

66. Guy Steuart to Crist, 11 Jan. 1971, folder "HEED 33," box 10, TCP.

67. Crist to Steuart, 15 Jan. 1971; Art Jones to Guy Steuart, 25 Nov. 1970, folder "HEED 33," box 10, TCP, emphasis in original.

68. Crist, HEED 33 Introduction, n.d. [Fall 1972], folder "HEED 33 Introduction," box 11, TCP; Minutes MHCH 140 and HEED 33, "Human Sexuality Working Notes 1: The Structures and Purpose of the Human Sexuality Course," 21 July 1972, folder "Human Sexuality—Committee for Human Sexuality, 1972," box 12, TCP.

69. Crist, "Outlines for Lectures: Topics in Human Sexuality," 1971, folder "HEED Correspondence," box 10, TCP.

70. Crist, "Syllabus for HEED 33," n.d., folder "Committee on Human Sexuality," box 12, TCP.

71. Joe Stallings, "Friday Night at a Gay Bar," in *A Different Way of Life,* ed. Judie Friedman for HEED 33, Spring 1971, folder "HEED 33 Homosexuality," box 11, TCP.

72. Doug Hall, "Crist's Quest for Funds Getting No Commitments," *Daily Tar Heel,* 15 Sept. 1971, 1.

73. The School of Public Health donated $300, the Department of Health Education $250, the School of Nursing $250, and Student Health Services $390. Ibid.; Pam Phillips, "Sexuality Course Receives Funding," *Daily Tar Heel,* 22 Sept. 1971.

74. Bruce A. Baldwin and Robert R. Wilson, "A Campus Peer Counseling Program in Human Sexuality," *Journal of American College Health Association* 22, no. 5 (1974): 399–403.

75. Wilson interview.

76. Student Health Services, "Student Health Service: Information and Policies, 1972–1973," 1972, folder "Speech—1972, Aug. 25, UNC Orientation Program," box 25, TCP.

77. Carolyn S. Dixon to Bill Griffin, 28 Sept. 1971, folder "Human Sexuality—Committee for Human Sexuality, 1971," box 12, TCP.

78. Robert Reid Wilson, "First Annual Report: Human Sexuality Information and Counseling Service, University of North Carolina at Chapel Hill, Fall 1971 through Spring 1972," 24 Aug. 1972, folder "Human Sexuality Committee, 1972," box 12, TCP.

79. "Counseling Service Reports 1,091 Cases," *Daily Tar Heel,* 4 Sept. 1971, 1.

80. Wilson, "First Annual Report."

81. Margaret Scales and Takey Crist, interview by Johanna Schoen, Figure Eight Island, North Carolina, 25 May 2002.

82. Alice Carlton, interview with the author, Chapel Hill, North Carolina, 31 Mar. 2006; Daniel Leonard, interview with the author, Carrboro, North Carolina, 8 Feb. 2007.

83. Sara Spencer (pseudonym), interview with the author, Carrboro, North Carolina, 13 Feb. 2007.

84. "Hey Charlie," folder "Human Sexuality Committee, 1972," box 12, TCP.

85. Southern homophile organizations began in the 1950s, and the Gay Liberation Movement dates to at least 1971 in Atlanta. John Howard, *Men Like That: A Southern Queer History* (Chicago: Univ. of Chicago Press, 1999); John Howard, ed., *Carryin' On in the Lesbian and Gay South* (New York: NYU Press, 1997); John Howard, "Southern Sodomy; or, What the Coppers Saw," in *Southern Masculinity: Perspectives on Manhood in the South since Reconstruction,* ed. Craig Thompson Friend (Athens: Univ. of Georgia Press, 2009), 196–218.

86. Spencer interview.

87. Leonard interview.

88. Wilson interview.

89. Scales and Crist interview.

90. Robert Reid Wilson, "First Annual Report," emphasis in original.

91. Melinda Hickman, "Sex on Display: Union Display Interesting, Informative," *Daily Tar Heel,* 15 Feb. 1973.

92. Jeffery Kuhner, "Marriage Madness," *Washington Times,* 22 June 2008. See also Heather Mac Donald, "Are One in Five College Women Sexually Assaulted?" *National Review Online,* 5 Apr. 2011, available at www.nationalreview.com/articles/263834/are-one-five-college-women-sexually-assaulted-heather-mac-donald, accessed 6 Sept. 2011.

CHAPTER NINE

The Counterculture as Local Culture in Columbia, South Carolina

NICHOLAS G. MERIWETHER

In January 1966, former University of South Carolina graduate student and some-time Haight-Ashbury mail carrier Dale Alan Bailes was watching a Vietnam War protest march turn right off San Francisco's Market Street and begin the long nine-teen-block walk up Haight Street to Golden Gate Park. Rounding the corner, he encountered a flatbed truck with a band on it, playing a song whose refrain he could remember clearly 39 years later: "Bright before me / Signs implore / Help the needy / And show them the way / Human kindness is overflowing / And I think it's gonna rain today."[1] The lyrics were remarkable for their peaceful, humane hopefulness, especially given the increasingly violent antiwar demonstrations that had been erupting across the Bay in Berkeley and Oakland. But what impressed it-self on his memory even more were the flyers being handed out around the truck. They read, "A joyful alternative to war." To Bailes, that phrase echoed with mean-ing on multiple levels. It took several years for those meanings to unfold, but when they did, Columbia, South Carolina, had its first, full-fledged counterculture em-porium, cofounded by Bailes, a combination clothing boutique, bookstore, and head shop called The Joyful Alternative.

The story of the Joyful's establishment provides a window into several issues that historians of the sixties grapple with, from the antecedents of the countercul-ture to its labyrinthine connections to other defining phenomena of the sixties. But the story of the Joyful is more than just an example of national trends in the counterculture: it is also the story of the uniquely local resonances, incarnations, and antecedents of that broader national phenomenon. Indeed, the story of the Joyful represents an example of what historians have long called for: local studies of the counterculture. When we trace the story of the Joyful, we uncover powerful and perhaps surprising connections with national issues such as the civil rights movement and the Haight-Ashbury scene, but more importantly, how those cur-rents intersected with local institutions, people, and events that enacted and re-fined those broader currents in their own towns. As the founding of the Joyful

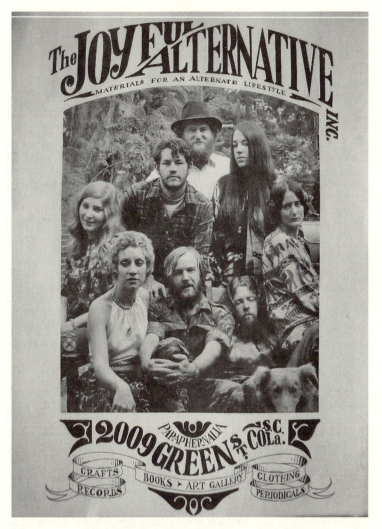

Figure 9.1. A Haight-Ashbury–style poster advertising Columbia, South Carolina's The Joyful Alternative in a way that made clear its countercultural allegiance. Dale Bailes is at top. Courtesy Merll Truesdale.

shows, the local contexts of the counterculture do more than just explain how it took root across the country in the "long sixties," but also how local people in turn reinterpreted the counterculture and made it an indelible part of the fabric of the nation.

Defining the counterculture today is difficult, but it was difficult then as well. Paul Goodman found this out in 1967 when he gave a lecture at New York's New

School for Social Research on the counterculture that did not go over well. Good-man, author of *Growing Up Absurd,* a seminal early exposition of the social forces that fueled the rise of the counterculture, was surprised at the hostility that he en-countered during this lecture.[2] "I had imagined that the worldwide student protest had to do with changing political and moral institutions," he recalled later, "and I was sympathetic to this. But now I saw that we had to . . . [deal] with a religious crisis. Not only all institutions but all learning had been corrupted by the Whore of Babylon, and there was no longer any salvation to be got from Works."[3] Pub-lished in 1970, his account of that evening makes plain the frustration he felt at the time and the anger he felt at the recollection even three years later. But what is most interesting about his assessment is his prescience in suggesting that there was something that bound the disparate phenomena that make up what historians now call the long sixties. Goodman's religious crisis would soon be dubbed the counterculture by others, but with no real consensus, then or since, about what the term really signifies.

That confusion began at the time: as David Farber notes, "The counterculture seemed insidious. It was everywhere and nowhere, hard to define and thus dif-ficult to stop."[4] Theodore Roszak, credited with having popularized the term with his 1968 book *The Making of a Counter Culture,* dryly opened that work by not-ing that "as a subject of study, the counter culture . . . possesses all the liabilities which a decent sense of intellectual caution would persuade one to avoid like the plague."[5] As David Burner suggests, "Beyond its antecedents among the Beats, the emergence of the counterculture has no single satisfactory explanation. . . . Even to call the counterculture a culture is to make the best of nomenclature."[6] However ill-defined, the specter of the counterculture still haunts our memory and compli-cates understanding of the sixties; as Nick Bromell has written, "It's the river that runs steadily and silently through American life these days, the river that welled out of the American psyche 30 years ago, spilling through the fissure blasted by rock 'n' roll and psychedelic drugs."[7]

But even if we disagree with Bromell, there remains the stubborn fact of its looming presence during the era that it helped define, its enduring significance in our cultural memory of those years. As Farber points out, "It was the counter-culture, more than the antiwar movement or Black Power groups, that seemed to many older Americans to be most threatening to their families and loved ones. And they were right to be worried; far more young people would experiment with illegal drugs and counterculture lifestyles than would ever participate in the civil rights, antiwar, or student movements."[8] His contention becomes all the more striking in the light of Alice Echols's observation that in the course of her research on the sixties, perhaps the most noteworthy lacuna was "the absence of good histories of the counterculture."[9] That gap in the literature goes deeper: W. J. Rorabaugh found an equivalent void in the archival record when he was research- ing his *Berkeley at War*. But it is Rorabaugh who, in passing, sets forth one of the driving arguments of this essay, for he not only stresses the degree to which the various aspects of the sixties that most concern him—the student movement, race relations, the New Left, and the counterculture—are entangled, he also makes the case for focusing on the local, not the national, in order to make sense of that entanglement.[10] As Farber has noted, "The counterculture took root in Atlanta's Fourteenth Street, Chicago's Old Town, the Lower East Side of New York, in Aus- tin, Texas, Lawrence, Kansas, and dozens of other places. The counterculture was about space, about taking over a few city blocks or a few acres of countryside and trying to make a world out of it, a place where all the old rules were up for grabs. . . . The counterculture was a way of life, a community, an infrastructure, and even an economy, not just a few lifestyle accoutrements like long hair and an occasional toke on an illegal substance."[11] Rorabaugh and Farber are both correct. As more local studies are done, we will likely begin to see how the counterculture and the other defining phenomena of that era, from the antiwar movement to feminism and gay rights, exhibit a complex entanglement that mimics the complexity of those movements' broader relationships to their national counterparts.

For Rorabaugh, "The social turmoil of the sixties was really a battle over power."[12] If he is right, then this essay provides a way of grounding his contention as well as addressing some of the challenges the counterculture poses for histori- ans by examining The Joyful Alternative as one site of resistance in that struggle. As Columbia's first real countercultural emporium, The Joyful Alternative was a hippie institution that survived for thirty years, evolving into one of the city's re- spected boutiques. The story of its founding illustrates not only a local incarna- tion of the counterculture but also one that exemplifies the tangled connections between the counterculture and other phenomena of the sixties. As such, it encap- sulates—and suggests a way of resolving—many of the challenges that have vexed counterculture historians.

Although the Joyful was a collective enterprise involving a group of friends, its genesis lies with Dale Alan Bailes and his experience of the sixties. His story personifies the interconnections between the national and the local, complicating those ties in ways that exemplify the broader national currents at work in the coun- terculture as well as the uniquely southern context that would adapt and modify the national as it was enacted regionally. Like many of his generation with liter- ary aspirations, Bailes saw himself as inheriting the mantle of the Beats. His early experiences in South Carolina cemented this awareness: arriving at the Univer- sity of South Carolina as a transfer student from the satellite campus USC-Aiken in 1962, he became a major contributor to the campus literary journal *The Crucible,* soon becoming its editor. A successful student double-majoring in English and psychology and member of the debate team, Bailes thrived at Carolina, developing a literary consciousness that would ultimately forge his identity as a writer. Likeable and charismatic, Bailes attracted people and made friends easily, traits that made him a natural leader and would later prove instrumental in founding the Joyful. A growing interest in civil rights added a political dimension to his writing and worldview, however: "This was '64, '65, and I was doing sit-ins, I was picketing George Wallace when he [visited Columbia]—I very much got into integration and [was] just a very political animal at that time. And so graduate school didn't really seem to matter in the light of world things."[13]

After only a year of graduate school at Carolina, he set out for New York "with a duffel bag full of books." He immersed himself in the post-Beat atmosphere of bohemian New York, living in the East Village and working at the famous jazz club the Village Vanguard before setting out for San Francisco with two friends, following what he remembered as "the Kerouac tradition and all that." In San Francisco, Bailes typified the early Haight-Ashbury experience, living an authentically post-Beat lifestyle, participating in poetry readings in the vestiges of the North Beach scene, and dancing at early rock concerts at the Fillmore Auditorium and the Avalon Ballroom, where bands such as the Jefferson Airplane and the Grateful Dead were building devoted local followings. His day job was another early Haight hippie mainstay, the post office: while peers like Phil Lesh, the bassist for the Dead, drove the mail trucks, Bailes carried the mail—and among his stops was the Grateful Dead's house at 710 Ashbury. It was during that time that he participated in the peace march whose flyer would provide him with the evocative phrase that so captured his imagination, the seed that, in the psychedelic sensibility of the counterculture, seemed to germinate of its own accord and blossom into the shop.

Bailes's travels changed him, and the America that he traversed changed along with him. The riots at the Democratic National Convention in Chicago in 1968 and the subsequent trial of the Chicago Seven sent shockwaves through the country, part of a perfect storm of political crises and traumas that seemed to herald an unraveling of the cultural fabric of the country, marked by the assassinations of Martin Luther King Jr. and Robert Kennedy, the trial of Bobby Seale in New Haven, the My Lai massacre, the Tet Offensive, and the Cambodian incursions. The crisis over the war, and in particular the Kent State killings and the nationwide campus strikes in response, struck Bailes especially forcefully when he returned to Columbia, home of Fort Jackson, a major army recruit training base. Much of the furor in the region centered around a local coffeeshop, derisively named "The

UFO" in response to the U.S.O., located a few blocks away. An avowedly antiwar establishment located prominently on Main Street, close to city hall, it was the major battleground in the fight for public space that defined counterculture battles from the Haight to Columbia, South Carolina. Shortly after Bailes's return in 1969, the UFO was padlocked and its owners tried for the common-law misdemeanor of maintaining a public nuisance. On 27 April 1970, the defendants were convicted and given six-year sentences, prompting local and even national outrage: the *Wall Street Journal,* while making clear its distaste for the defendants, decried the sentences in an editorial entitled "A Demeaning Disproportion" and noted that the decision "could erode respect for the [judicial process] far more effectively than any radical onslaught could hope to."[14] The *Journal* was correct, but the trial and the verdict also served as a catalyst for the local counterculture: the trial and the absurdly draconian verdict taught liberal Columbians, left-leaning professors, and hippies that what they had in common mattered far more than what separated them.

More tellingly, it showed some members of Columbia's long-oppressed African American community that these oddly dressed, long-haired, white dropouts shared a common worldview, a fact that would play an important role in the Joyful's founding. A young law school professor at Carolina who quietly assisted in the defense in the UFO trial later recalled: "For much of society there was a 'we/ they' mentality. President Nixon waged a successful campaign in 1968 by emphasizing the twin themes of victory in Southeast Asia and law and order at home. Crew cuts and American flags on one side, long hair and peace symbols on the other. While most of us were in fact somewhere in between, it often appeared that our world was split into two camps, and nowhere was this division more apparent than in the 1700 block of Main Street in Columbia, South Carolina."[15]

This was the scene that greeted Bailes on his return from San Francisco. Living on $58 a month unemployment from his time as a postal worker, Bailes immersed himself in the local scene, reconnecting with old friends in Columbia's burgeoning counterculture at places such as the Zoo, a ramshackle house that was home to two of Columbia's psychedelic rock bands, Christopher and Speed Limit 35, and J. B. Gantts, a coffeehouse on the edge of the university campus that he remembered as featuring "a great mixture of hippies and rednecks and folk singers." When a friend's brother came into town looking for a good time, he was sent to Bailes: "He wanted to have some fun, and she told him that I would be the person to talk to, that I partied a lot, that I would know what was going on." They hit it off, and when he asked Bailes what his plans were, he replied, "I'm thinking about this Joyful Alternative thing, and this store idea, sort of a bookstore or art-something." Years later he remembered the conversation clearly: "It was really that nebulous.

And he said, 'Well, that sounds good to me, I'll put $500 into it.' Five hundred dollars, when you're living on $58 a month. That went, 'click.' "[16]

Columbia may not have appeared to be the most likely site for such a venture, but like so many regional outposts of the counterculture, there was enough there to make the idea both appealing and feasible. Home to the University of South Carolina, Benedict College (a historically black college), and Columbia College (a women's college), Columbia had a small but vocal intelligentsia with a student population and professoriate whose demographics reflected more than just a local southern perspective. That perspective was also deeply conditioned by the experience of the civil rights movement, which had scarred the state; one of the protest rallies in support of the UFO defendants also marked the two-year anniversary of the Orangeburg massacre, in which three South Carolina State College students had been killed. The mingling of these causes was deliberate—and effective, if measured by the unease it provoked in the eyes of the establishment. The university's integration may have been more peaceful than that of other southern schools, but it was recent and far from settled; testimony in the UFO trial quoted a police officer as saying, "It was unprecedented in Columbia for white and black young people to be seen talking together across tables the way they were constantly doing at the UFO."[17]

In short order, Bailes assembled a group of like-minded friends, and the Joyful began to take shape. Renting an abandoned coal warehouse, the Joyful kept the former tenant's iconic sign, a touch that impressed locals and also made the quiet statement that this was as much a reclamation of the past as it was a reinvention of it. It was a gesture Columbians remembered decades later; as one wrote, "The Joyful Alternative left the old coal company signage on the sides of the building but fixed up the entrance and the display window (always full of freaky artwork) giving it that nice double-use patina. Turn-of-the-century Columbia side-walls meet early 1970s hippy storefront."[18] One friend supplied the art; two more scoured the countryside around Columbia, bringing back weathered planks from decaying barns and farm buildings they disassembled. Just as Bailes had seen hippies in the Haight recycle San Francisco's Edwardian past for their style, the Joyful's vision of the counterculture drew on the rich visual and artistic heritage of the South, from its Appalachian folk arts to its low-country crafts.

There was a time-honored heritage of eccentricity in the Carolina craft tradition, and Bailes and his friends could play to that with their wares. Just as hippie artisans in the Haight-Ashbury produced impressive revivals of needlecraft, leatherwork, and other handicrafts, the Joyful's founders were part of a community of Carolina hippies steeped in southern folk craft traditions as well as newer art forms such as tie-dye; they supplied the shop with beautiful hand-stitched clothes, objets d'art, and pipes.[19] Conversations among the partners mapped out a vision for the store. As Bailes related, "I came up with a slogan, 'Materials for an alternate lifestyle.' And we sort of branded—what they now call branding; I didn't know what I was doing then—we sort of branded ourselves with that."[20] Bailes's contribution focused on books and records that would support the southern incarnation of the counterculture, supplemented by art, handicrafts, and clothes made by his cofounders and their extended network of friends.

That branding was deliberate, grounded in Bailes's own experience in San Francisco, where he walked past the Haight-Ashbury institution, The Psychedelic Shop, run by the Thelin brothers, every day on his beat as a postal carrier. But Bailes and his friends also knew how they wanted to differentiate their shop from potential competitors, like the Purple Turtle, located a mile away, at 1110 Taylor Street. The Turtle predated the Joyful by a few months, opening in 1970, but it did not carry the same range of merchandise, nor did it market itself with the thoughtfulness of the Joyful's approach to a holistic hippie lifestyle. Other competitors followed. The next year, Maudy's Bosom opened at 709 Santee Avenue, also in the Five Points neighborhood, a few blocks away from the Joyful, but it, too, evinced a different, harder-edged ethos; as one Columbian recalled, "Though I never heard Dale say it, I always thought he chose the name of the shop to be in contrast with other stores like Maudy's Bosom, The Purple Turtle and AW Fully's. Instead of loud, blaring acid rock they played loud, blaring Grateful Dead."[21]

Given that band's oft-maligned image and their genre-bending expertise with not only the full-on psychedelia they helped pioneer (epitomized by the 1969 album *Live/Dead*) but also the stripped-down acoustic folk-rock of their 1970 albums *Workingman's Dead* and especially *American Beauty* (the cover of which can also be read as "American Reality"), Bailes's choice of this Haight-Ashbury institution as a mainstay of the store's soundtrack was both natural and telling. The Dead's music at the time demonstrated the ways that Appalachian and folk roots informed their creation of psychedelia; choosing that as a soundtrack cemented the Joyful's status as both a national conduit of the hippie experience and a uniquely southern-inflected instantiation of it. Nor was it forced: "I was a Deadhead. Two or three other people involved were Deadheads; we played the Grateful Dead a good bit in the store. Music was one of the main things happening in the Joyful."[22]

The music and incense, coupled with the merchandise and Bailes himself, avuncular and appealing, made the shop a center of Columbia's hippie scene, attracting like-minded souls—and effectively repelling those who weren't on board. When the Joyful closed in 2003, prompting reminiscences from a range of Columbians, one sniffed, "I never liked the place—I got some sort of very creepy vibe the first time I went; I mean the hair stood up on the back of my neck and I felt I had to leave right away. I never went back."[23] The counterculture, especially paraphernalia, could be scary, especially in places like South Carolina in the 1970s. But for those who were looking for it, the Joyful was the source of fond memories: "When I first discovered 'The Joyful Alternative' I was a freshman at Carolina in 1973. At that time it was located on Greene St. in an old warehouse looking building ... back then it was very much a 'head shop,' selling rolling papers, pipes, bongs, etc., along with the books and handicrafts. ... The place was full of all sorts of things, a kind of hippie emporium. But what I remember best about the place was the smell! The incense was almost overpowering."[24] As one former night watchman put it, the Joyful was "an upscale head shop. During the day, would-be hippies from the suburbs would drift in and buy their bongs and rolling papers and candles and Indian clothes. The chosen would sit around in rocking chairs, Dale holding court all the while listening to the Grateful Dead or Buffalo Springfield or Traffic or Spirit." To him, the shop was indeed the embodiment of Bailes's vision: "A little bit of San Francisco in the South."[25]

The Haight-Ashbury vibe was only half of Bailes's vision, however. The other half was the southern take on the counterculture, and implementing that took a lot of work. With almost three thousand dollars of startup capital, Bailes and his friends were entrepreneurial but not naive. One of Bailes's undergraduate friends had gone on to work for Dun and Bradstreet; he gave them a favorable D&B rating, crucial when they had to negotiate with New York distributors for goods on credit. Nor were they political naifs. Bailes and his partners had been especially impressed by local ACLU attorney Tom Broadwater, who had defended the UFO. To Bailes, Broadwater's courtroom performance was especially sympathetic, given Bailes's own experience in the mid-1960s with the civil rights protests. Fought before a judge who refused to remove the Confederate battle flag from its prominent place in the courtroom, with a prosecution whose strategy of attempting to demonize "outside agitators" as culprits echoed notorious tactics from civil rights cases, the UFO trial made it clear to the city's African American community that Broadwater's defense was very much in the tradition of their own struggles, a point underscored by Broadwater's prominence in the city's African American community. Bailes and his partners decided to ask Broadwater to handle the politically delicate task of the Joyful's incorporation.

Broadwater was no hippie, but he listened sympathetically to their presentation. Their vision was not subversive: the shop would be stocked with local, artisan-made wares, from clothing to art, catering to a segment of the community that shared a peaceful, artistic, and community-based vision of society. Those customers might not resemble what mainstream adult society thought was appropriate, but that touched a sympathetic chord in an African American lawyer whose personal experiences included harrowing incidents of discrimination, bigotry, and injustice. Nor did those experiences end when he entered court. Indeed, Bailes decided to approach Broadwater after reading about his performance in court:

> One reason I went to Tom was I read in the newspaper—and you can probably find this in the paper at the time—Tom Broadwater, I think he mispronounced a word, and John Foard mocked him, and said, "I think that word is" this or that. And Broadwater came back, "You will have to remember I am a product of separate but equal schools." [*Laughs.*] And that story alone made me want to meet Tom Broadwater.[26]

Bailes's reaction may have pleased Broadwater, or he may have been swayed by the sincerity of the young trio's dream, conveyed by Bailes's charisma and cofounder Barbara Howell's appealing earnestness. But Broadwater may also have recognized in their project an extension of what he had seen in the UFO trial: that the struggle of these young people, not just for public space but also for the right to live as they pleased, echoed ideals familiar from his own experiences in the civil rights movement. Broadwater completed the papers, registering the Joyful in 1971 as a corporation with Guy Padgett as president, Don McMahon as vice president, Dale Bailes as secretary, and Pamela McMahon as treasurer. It was classified as a "gift shop" and was located at 2009 Green Street.[27] The entrepreneurs were serious about being a business, but not at the expense of their countercultural vision: "We were a corporation legally but we were sort of a commune, not exactly a commune, in that there were eight or ten people, independent minds and artists and musicians."

Bailes's vision may have been the driving one, but the others' voices were no less instrumental. It meant that decision-making was consensual. That paradigm faced its first test before the shop opened, as the partners confronted their most difficult decision: whether to sell cannabis pipes and associated paraphernalia. "We talked amongst ourselves at length," Bailes remembers, "and there was serious discussion about whether or not to even sell paraphernalia. A couple of people just didn't want to do it, a couple of people said, 'Well shit, that's what the main thing is, you gotta get high!' And in the middle was a gray area. Some people thought, 'Well, we do it, so, you know.' And we made the decision to do it."[28] This had far-reaching implications, not only for the store's profitability—paraphernalia accounted for as much as a third of the shop's income in the first decade of its existence—but also for the role paraphernalia played, as a conduit between the national and the local. As his partners did with other local craftspeople, Bailes bought handmade pipes, bongs, and roach clips from local hippie artisans; he remembers wood, ceramic, blown glass, and buckhorn pipes along with the obligatory hardware store lamp-part efforts: brass and chrome metal parts that could be assembled into small, crude pipes, an enduring style in cannabis culture.[29] There were elaborate roach clips for those who preferred joints to pipes. Hippies who traveled to India, the Middle East, Northern Africa, and Central and South America also brought back pipes and other wares that complemented the hippie lifestyle, selling them to the Joyful. Though Bailes does not recall specific pipes, he is sure that "some of the people we bought from, some of the people that came in, had done that. There was so much travel going on then, and so many people were supporting themselves by doing this travel, by selling what they found."[30]

These wares and their sources also linked the Joyful to broader currents in the counterculture, from its general interest in lost, secret, or hidden knowledge to the ubiquity of travel along the famed hippie trail. When returning hippies showed off a small Peruvian clay pipe in the shape of a bird effigy, made in a style hundreds of years old, along with stories of cannabis use in cultures around the world, it provided a sense of historical connection and cultural groundedness that America's various prohibitions had severed. Former Merry Prankster (and later wife of the Grateful Dead's Jerry Garcia) Carolyn "Mountain Girl" Adams made that point in the preface of a book on cannabis cultivation that was published in 1973: "Marijuana is an ancient plant, cultivated for centuries all over the world for rope & papermaking, for its oil, resin & seeds. The Pre-Columbian cultures in North America certainly grew it, & time-honored techniques of cultivation have survived in India, Southeast Asia, & the Near East."[31] Beneath the mainstream media's focus on the nihilism and destructiveness of the counterculture lay a very real attempt to reconnect with older, submerged traditions that made the hippie quest for experience as much reclamation of a sundered heritage as it was a rejection of their immediate elders.

Bailes and his partners and the broader hippie community in Columbia allied themselves with the progressive, dissenting elements in southern history and Carolinian culture. For southern hippies such as Bailes, steeped in the injustices the civil rights movement battled, there was a particular need to rediscover and reclaim an admirable, usable heritage and make it the core of a southern countercultural orientation. Bailes was active in the ACLU and made sure that leaflets were prominently displayed in the store, a reminder that native-born dissent was as much a part of the southern political tradition as its more visible, repressive mainstream. Copies of Atlanta's underground newspaper *The Great Speckled Bird* shared counter space with *The Berkeley Barb*, making the point that the counterculture was just as southern as it was national. Local hippies appropriated the

American flag and redefined patriotism to encompass dissent like their national counterparts.

This cross-fertilization worked in both directions: just as the Dead's albums made plain their mastery of southern musical forms, the goods stocked by the Joyful showed how traditional southern crafts could not only inform and complement the national movement but in so doing also demonstrate that there was a distinctively southern way to enact the counterculture. Some crafts were incorporated seamlessly: beautiful needlework, for example, pleased both hippies and their grandmothers. Other crafts showed a certain countercultural subversion, such as pipes. Even there, though, the Joyful recontextualized southern craftsmanship. Long a staple of southern and South Carolina tobacco pipecraft, corncob pipes were also popular with hippies, especially the smallest size, nicknamed "nose warmers" or, more politely, "between-the-acts" pipes; Bailes remembers middle-aged salesmen picking up on their hippie popularity and adding the Joyful to their otherwise staid and respectable distribution routes.

The pipes and roach clips and bongs made possible Bailes's real interest, though, which was the book and record side of the store: "The paraphernalia made it possible for us to have a really good bookstore for as long as we did. I don't even remember how long we did, but when I was there, the seven or eight years I actively managed it, my main thing was the bookstore. . . . And there wasn't that much money in them to start with. But there was so much mark-up in paraphernalia, and it was much more popular than books; a lot more people were getting stoned than were reading. But my point was, for the store, it all goes together; it's all part of a new lifestyle, or a continuing lifestyle." With the books and records, Bailes was able to express his vision of the southern hippie even more fully, stocking a full range of southern writers and poets along with the Beats and other writers associated with the counterculture, even writing poet and novelist George Garrett to ask where some of his out-of-print titles could be found.[32]

His selection drew a wide readership, from hippies to college professors. One patron reminisced that "there was always a rather odd assortment of books there, and I remember very well the day I found the old Ace paperback editions of Jack Vance's 'Planet of Adventure' books there (*City of the Chasch, Servants of the Wankh, The Dirdir,* and *The Pnume*) . . . in those pre-Internet days, I never would have known of those volumes at all, not having seen them elsewhere."[33] Other patrons agreed, one recalling it as "the first place I saw books on alternative energy and people like Buckminster Fuller. They had the whole so-called New Age movement anticipated by at least 10 years in 1971 when I made my first visit. If you thought the book section in the Saluda Street store [the Joyful's second location] was quirky, you would have been truly fascinated with the selection in the original.

Much more variety, including more comics and sci-fi titles."[34] Other patrons recalled seminal sixties titles: "I've always enjoyed reading off the wall stuff, and The Joyful Alternative was loaded with it. The Whole Earth Catalog, Zap Comix, Oat Willy, [the Fabulous] Furry Freak Brothers. . . ."[35] Some customers had more refined tastes but still sought out Bailes's eclectic and unusual titles. Poet and Carolina professor James Dickey became one of the Joyful's best customers, in some months accounting for a majority of his poetry sales, and Bailes recalls selling him an obscure bluegrass LP whose signature banjo riff would feature heavily in the movie version of *Deliverance*. For Bailes, there was no contradiction between stocking Lawrence Ferlinghetti and Allen Ginsberg, James Dickey and George Garrett; to a southern hippie, it was not a stretch to go from Thomas Wolfe to Tom Wolfe. In the Joyful's eclectic bookshelf, we can see several hallmarks of the counterculture, including obligatory national texts by Beat writers as well as southern writers whose themes informed a distinctly regional inflection of the countercultural worldview.

Those books offered patrons a vital window into the counterculture as it unfolded, and they are still evocative, as historian Terry Anderson reminds us: "The most appropriate sources on the counterculture are the articles and books the freaks wrote in underground newspapers and published with obscure presses. Read what they were writing, and listen to their music."[36] Bailes continued to write and publish his own poetry during that time, and a poem he published in the *South Carolina Review* the same year that the Joyful opened echoed Beat themes of lost knowledge along with Garrettesque themes of homage to ancestors. A meditation on history and nature provoked by a cat's attack on a bird, the poem offers an allegory of Bailes's own experiences and impressions of the counterculture. It ends with a plea that "his new knowledge / will not throw him out of time."[37] Even for readers with no knowledge of Bailes's life at the time, it is difficult not to hear in it an echo of the hippie ideal of recapturing lost values and knowledge, of reconnecting with a buried past. It is a very southern view of the American countercultural mindset.

The Joyful Alternative changed over time, gradually abandoning pipes and most of its records and books in the 1980s and evolving into a boutique catering to a New Age and upscale clientele, just as many of its first customers settled into middle-class lifestyles that maintained some of the underlying values but only a few of the trappings of their countercultural youth. The emphasis on local, artisan-made items continued but quickly became a sideline, not a mainstay, of the stock they carried. Yet the shop stayed close to its ideals and its roots, despite a change in location, run by original cofounder Barbara Howells until she finally retired in 2003 and closed the store. Though not the Joyful's original site, the Joyful's old customers must feel a twinge when they pass by the old store and see its new tenant: Starbucks. Bailes ended his active involvement with the Joyful after eight years, moving to Los Angeles in 1979 to pursue a writing career; he now divides his time between Los Angeles and South Carolina. He remains friends with his fellow cofounders, visiting every year, and even returned to help Barbara Howells close the store in 2003. The longevity of those friendships, and of the store and its navigation from counterculture emporium to New Age boutique, also say something about the nature of the counterculture, and how that shaped the ways that this rich and complex aspect of the sixties eventually resonated into history, culture, and memory.

But in its early years, the Joyful was a quintessential hippie cultural establishment, and its founding reveals the ways that the counterculture spread throughout America—how the national was local, and how the local manifested and adapted the national. In so doing, what it can tell us about the counterculture and the sixties is how the founders of this shop, as local change agents, can be understood as part of a longer bohemian tradition that celebrates not only the art of defiance but also the possibility of art within defiance. And that is just a recasting of the grand old avant-garde belief, not in destruction, but in renewal and rebirth. In the creation of the shop, we can see the spirit of the counterculture: the determination to reclaim space, restore a real and imagined heritage, and renew the political strength of dissent. In the story of the Joyful's founding, we can gain insights into the counterculture on a number of levels, starting with the concern of the historian of ideas with the historical epistemology of the counterculture—what can be known about the term and its slippery relationship with the phenomenon it seeks to describe, and I would include here its deeper cultural antecedents. But the Joyful also demonstrates the term's elasticity, its capacity as an organizing rubric for the zeitgeist of the sixties: the way the word can embody its own kind of historical, conceptual ontology—how the counterculture fits into the broader matrix of the sixties. The building blocks of local, regional culture made and remade the counterculture into a rhizomatic movement that spread throughout America in the long sixties. The Joyful was one of those rhizomes.

Ultimately, the reason for examining this iconic Columbia institution is not only that it makes clear that the counterculture was indeed local but also that its connections with broader national currents are more complex than we have heretofore allowed. And when we do, we discover that the way the counterculture spread in Columbia—with the establishment of institutions such as the Joyful, the UFO, JB Gantts, and the Zoo, the suppression of institutions like the UFO, and even the careers (and recorded legacies) of local psychedelic rock bands such as Christopher and Speed Limit 35—manifests what Alice Echols has suggested, that "when the sixties are recast so that the New Left no longer occupies the privileged narrative core, the record of the late sixties is somewhat more mixed than the reigning interpretation of destructive disintegration would suggest."[38] In that mix, we can see defiance, certainly—but we can also see creativity and commitment, community and artistry. The story of the Joyful's founding shows how the counterculture took root across America, even in terrain that at first glance could not appear less like the Haight-Ashbury, and how that environment adapted and reinterpreted the zeitgeist that fueled and reflected the sixties. The Joyful not only enacted a southern vision of the hippie, it also reaffirmed its membership in the broader phenomenon: It was an expression of the counterculture as local culture, and visitors from New York or San Francisco could feel the same universal vibe when they walked into the store and saw Bailes holding court, surrounded by the accoutrements of the hippie lifestyle, southern-style. When Bailes padded over to the record player and followed a side of the Dead's Americana-inflected *Workingman's Dead* with a side of his uncles' band the Bailes Brothers, it made a point— tapping into what Greil Marcus once memorably called "the old, weird America" that hippies from faraway San Francisco, Chicago, New York, and Boston intuitively understood and could claim as their own.[39] For historians, that tableau captures the appeal, and the challenge, of the attempt to understand the counterculture, a profoundly tantalizing glimpse of the Dionysian spirit flickering beneath the Joyful's Dun and Bradstreet's rating.

NOTES

1. Dale Alan Bailes, interview by Nicholas G. Meriwether, 17 July 2005, 8. All further quotations from Bailes are from this interview unless otherwise noted. The lyrics are from the song with the same title, written by Randy Newman and first recorded on Newman's eponymous album released in June 1968. Bailes's memory may be correct: Not only did Newman write the song in 1966, he was part of a Bay Area/Los Angeles music scene that coupled Warner Bros. (which had purchased Reprise in 1963) with San Francisco–based Autumn Records, a label that recorded many local bands and musicians, several of whom could have known it and performed it; see "Randy Newman," www.randynewman.info/biography/a1.html. For more on the Autumn Records connection, see www.randynewman.info/biography/a0.html.

2. For Goodman's centrality to the counterculture, see the chapter "Exploring Utopia: The Visionary Sociology of Paul Goodman," in Theodore Roszak, *The Making of a Counter Culture* (Garden City, NY: Anchor/Doubleday, 1969), 178–204.

3. Paul Goodman, *New Reformation: Notes of a Neolithic Conservative* (New York: Random House, 1970), 48.

4. David Farber, *The Age of Great Dreams: America in the 1960s* (New York: Hill and Wang, 1994), 168.

5. Roszak, *Making of a Counter Culture*, xi.

6. David Burner, *Making Peace with the 60s* (Princeton, NJ: Princeton Univ. Press, 1997), 128.

7. Nick Bromell, *Tomorrow Never Knows: Rock and Psychedelics in the 1960s* (Chicago: Univ. of Chicago Press, 2000), 7.

8. Farber, *Age of Great Dreams,* 168.

9. Alice Echols, *Shaky Ground: The Sixties and Its Aftershocks* (New York: Columbia Univ. Press, 2002), 15.

10. W. J. Rorabaugh, *Berkeley at War: The Sixties* (New York: Oxford Univ. Press, 1989), x.

11. Farber, *Age of Great Dreams,* 168–69.

12. Rorabaugh, *Berkeley at War,* ix.

13. Bailes interview, 1.

14. "A Demeaning Disproportion," *Wall Street Journal,* 11 May 1970, 14.

15. William Shepard McAninch, "The UFO," *South Carolina Law Review* 46, no. 2 (Winter 1995): 365.

16. Bailes interview, 8.

17. Transcript of Testimony, State v. Hannafan, Court of General Sessions, Indictment No. 240, Fifth Judicial Circuit of South Carolina, 15–28 Apr. 1970, 972–73, quoted in McAninch, "The UFO," 373.

18. Michael Taylor, "The Joyful Alternative, Five Points: May 2003," 6 Dec. 2009, *Columbia Closings: What's Not in Columbia Anymore,* available at http://columbiaclosings.com/wordpress/?p=266, accessed 12 July 2011.

19. For more on Haight-Ashbury needlework crafts, for example, see Alexandra Jacopetti, *Native Funk and Flash: An Emerging Folk Art,* with photographs by Jerry Wainwright (San Francisco: Scrimshaw Press, 1974).

20. Bailes interview, 4.

21. "The Joyful Alternative, Five Points: May 2003," *Columbia Closings.*

22. Bailes interview, 6. It is an affinity he maintains to this day, and he is proud of having seen nearly 40 concerts before they formally disbanded in 1995.

23. "The Joyful Alternative, Five Points: May 2003," *Columbia Closings.*

24. Ibid.

25. "tomlove99," "Friday, May 30, 2003," *Welcome to My Reality,* available at www.tomlove99.blogspot.com/2003_05_25_tomlove99_archive.html, accessed 12 July 2011.

26. Bailes interview, 6. His memory is correct: during cross-examination, Broadwater pronounced "gross" as if it were "moss," prompting the exchange that Bailes recalled. See McAninch, "The UFO," 372.

27. *Hill's Columbia City Directory, 1971* (Richmond, VA: Hill Directory Publishers, 1971), 449.

28. Bailes interview, 4.

29. Ann Verberkmoes, "Folk Art—Hash Pipes," [1971], [1], Randall V. Mills Archive of Northwest Folklore, University of Oregon, Eugene, Oregon.

30. Bailes interview, 10.

31. Mountain Girl [pseud. for Carolyn Adams Garcia], *The Primo Plant* (Berkeley, CA: Leaves of Grass / Wingbow Press, 1977), 9.

32. Bailes interview, 5; Dale Alan Bailes to George P. Garrett, TS. George P. Garrett Papers. folder "The Joyful Alternative," box Alpha. Corr. B1, Alphabetical Correspondence Subseries: Group B, ca. 1957–1989 and undated. Rare Book, Manuscript, and Special Collections Library, Duke University, Durham, North Carolina.

33. "The Joyful Alternative, Five Points: May 2003," *Columbia Closings*; Bailes interview.

34. Ibid.

35. Ibid.

36. Terry H. Anderson, *The Movement and the Sixties: Protest in America from Greensboro to Wounded Knee* (New York: Oxford Univ. Press, 1995), 243, 245.

37. Dale Alan Bailes, "With a Cast of Thousands," *South Carolina Review* 4, no.1 (Dec. 1971): 64.

38. Echols, *Shaky Ground*, 66. Both Christopher and Speed Limit 35 had posthumous releases: Christopher's demo LP, *What'cha Gonna Do* (the band's pressing was labeled Chris-Tee Records in 1969) has been reissued several times on LP by various bootleg labels; there was an official, band-authorized reissue in 1999, *What'cha Gonna Do?* Scenescof SCOFCD1003. Speed Limit 35's eponymous LP was released by Swiss label RD Records in 1998 as RD 014LP.

39. Greil Marcus, "The Old, Weird America," liner note essay in *Anthology of American Folk Music*, comp. Harry Smith, CD reissue (Washington, D.C.: Smithsonian Folkways Recordings / Sony SFW 40090/A28750, 1997), 5–25. The Bailes Brothers, from West Virginia, were popular 1940s and 1950s close-harmony singers and accomplished stringed instrument performers known for their appearances on the *Grand Ole Opry* and *The Louisiana Hayride*.

CHAPTER TEN

Government Repression of the Southern New Left

GREGG L. MICHEL

In the spring of 1969, the Special Agent in Charge of the Federal Bureau of Investigation's Jackson, Mississippi, office devised a plan to undermine the local chapter of the Southern Student Organizing Committee. Comprising white college students involved in the civil rights, antiwar, and university reform movements of the era, SSOC was the most important group of white student activists operating in the South. The group was founded in Nashville in 1964 by students who sought to build support for the movements of the day among southern whites, particularly other white students. It adopted a moderate approach in its work; the group was committed to nonviolence, sought to win support through educational efforts and peaceful protests, and embraced the regional distinctiveness of the South, insisting that one could support reformist goals, such as opposing segregation, without compromising one's loyalty or devotion to the South.

With chapters on campuses across the region, the group's outspoken support for progressive causes, which often angered and embarrassed college authorities, played an important role in the long-term process of making predominantly white southern colleges and universities more open, tolerant, and politically diverse institutions.[1] In Jackson, a SSOC chapter had crystallized at Millsaps College in 1967, and over the next two years the small but hardy group of activists at this Methodist liberal arts school protested appearances on campus by Defense Secretary Robert McNamara, brazenly led civil rights marches through downtown Jackson, and published the irreverent alternative newspaper, *The Kudzu*.

Among the white students who led the Millsaps chapter was Natchez native Cassell Carpenter. The 1966 Queen of the Natchez Pilgrimage and daughter of a wealthy banker, Carpenter had grown up in the sheltered, segregated world of Dunleith, one of Natchez's famed antebellum mansions. Carpenter's segregationist views began to change when, after three years of boarding school in New York, she returned to Mississippi to attend college, first at the University of Mississippi and then at Millsaps. At Ole Miss, an activist who had participated in Freedom

Summer inspired Carpenter to reconsider her racial views and to join the Young Democrats Club. Soon after, she was deeply moved by the plight of striking black cotton workers outside Greenville when she visited their encampment, known as Strike City, in 1965.[2]

Carpenter's privileged upbringing among Natchez's elite brought attention to her activism, not least of all from Jackson's lead FBI officer. In the view of the Special Agent in Charge (SAC), Carpenter "has always boasted of her background and has had an effect on the youth in Mississippi in that they have tended to idolize her due to her wealth." Consequently, he designed a counterintelligence action to discredit her and sow discord in the SSOC chapter. Upon learning from confidential informants that some of the Millsaps SSOC activists supposedly believed that Carpenter's commitment to the cause had waned since she had developed an intimate relationship with one of the activists—they "sleep together and lie in bed all day"—the SAC proposed sending an anonymous letter to one of the disenchanted SSOC members attacking Carpenter and her lover. "We are for and very much interested in your New Left Movement, against the close [sic] society," the proposed letter began. "For the life of us we cannot understand what contributions [Carpenter] and [her lover] are making. Are they in it for free love? For their own personal motives, or what? Lets [sic] get rid of these two and get on with the program."[3] FBI Director J. Edgar Hoover endorsed the plan, though he did not think that the letter should be the extent of the field office's efforts against Carpenter. Given the SAC's characterization of Carpenter as especially influential among students, the FBI director encouraged his agent to "fully consider other measures for neutralizing her. Since her family appears to hold a position of social prominence in the Natchez area," Hoover helpfully suggested, "adverse publicity might be effective if such can be obtained securely."[4]

Hoover's FBI was not alone in its interest in SSOC. Throughout its five-year existence, law enforcement officials at all levels of government kept close watch on the group. Between 1964 and 1969, local, state, and federal authorities investigated, monitored, harassed, and intimidated white southern students who participated in SSOC. Some of the surveillance and harassment was direct, blunt, and out in the open, such as photographing students in demonstrations and threatening to arrest activists for fabricated offenses. More frequently, campaigns against SSOC, like the Bureau's effort against Carpenter, were surreptitious and covert, such as using informants to gather information or attempting to spread rumors about activists among their friends and families.

Whatever its form, government spying on SSOC was rooted in fears that the group would foment protest activity on southern campuses, a frightful possibility to officials well aware of campus unrest in western and northern states. That the

Figure 10.1. Mississippi Sovereignty Commission investigators often sought to intimidate student radicals by photographing them during demonstrations. Here, Millsaps
College student activist Cassell Carpenter is photographed during a civil rights demonstration in Jackson, Mississippi. Courtesy of the Mississippi Department of Archives
and History.

group had managed to form chapters at both large flagship institutions such as the
University of Virginia and the University of Florida and small colleges in remote
locales such as Furman University in Greenville, South Carolina, and Maryville
College in Maryville, Tennessee, only heightened government officials' unease
about SSOC's potential for creating unrest. SSOC's focus on southern whites,
unique among the New Left groups of the era, made it a ready target for authorities intent on clamping down on student protest in the South. And clamp down
they did. By the time SSOC dissolved in 1969, police authorities had spent more
than four years observing the group's activities, disrupting its protest actions, and
trying to sow discord among its members.

This government offensive against SSOC was an expression of the establishment's
siege mentality and antiradical paranoia. After all, SSOC was not the Students for
a Democratic Society (SDS) or the Student Nonviolent Coordinating Committee

(SNCC), let alone the Weather Underground or the Black Panthers. Compared to these more prominent groups, SSOC was a small, regionally focused organization that advocated nonviolent, moderate tactics in pursuit of the progressive goals it championed. That its advocacy of civil rights and its opposition to the war could inspire harassment by law enforcement agencies reveals the fears and insecurities of government authorities. To them, any challenge to racial conventions, any dissent from political orthodoxies, any opposition to the intensifying war in Southeast Asia was cause enough to unleash the powers of the state. The assault on SSOC thus highlights law enforcement's desperate efforts to suppress student protest in the region. As SSOC's experience shows, there was little room for dissent of any type in the South of the 1960s.

While anecdotal evidence of official harassment of civil rights and anti–Vietnam War activists existed throughout the 1960s, it was only after the demise of New Left organizations that historians have been able to document such allegations. Beginning in the mid-1970s, press reports and congressional investigations (aided by the Freedom of Information Act) gave the public access to government records showing that official harassment of progressive activists was pervasive, deeply secretive, and authorized by political and public safety officials at the highest levels of city, state, and federal governments.[5] The Federal Bureau of Investigation has received the most attention in the historical literature. Writing in the 1970s, Nelson Blackstock, Pat Watters, and Stephen Gillers authored the first significant studies of FBI surveillance of suspected subversives.[6] Subsequent works by Frank Donner, David J. Garrow, Kenneth O'Reilly, and Ward Churchill and Jim Vander Wall further exposed the sordid details of the Bureau's Counterintelligence Programs, known as COINTELPROs, against anti–Vietnam War protesters; black, Chicano, and American Indian civil rights activists; and others deemed a threat to domestic security.[7] These works on the FBI's campaign against movement activists helped draw attention to the issue, as did the work of other historians who uncovered government surveillance in their studies of the movements of the 1960s. Clayborne Carson's history of SNCC, Tom Wells's definitive study of the antiwar movement, and Taylor Branch's magisterial accounts of America during the King years all exposed covert government actions designed to disrupt and impede the efforts of activist organizations.[8]

In addition to the FBI, city and state agencies also expended resources to monitor and harass movement activists. Historians now have begun to explore these more localized efforts. "Red Squads," the domestic surveillance units in police departments across the country, are the focus of Frank Donner's pathbreaking work on police repression of civil rights and antiwar protesters. At the state level, the release in the 1990s of the records of the Mississippi State Sovereignty Commission, the most active state domestic surveillance unit in the South during this era, has enabled scholars such as Jenny Irons, Yasuhiro Katagiri, and Sarah Rowe-Sims to detail this agency's efforts to undermine activists working in the state.[9]

Thus far, however, government surveillance of outspoken white students in the South has escaped the attention of historians. This chapter calls attention to this oversight by spotlighting government surveillance and harassment of SSOC activists. The Red Squads kept close watch on the organization and frequently sought to disrupt its work. State police investigators tracked the group's activities and, most notably in Mississippi, infiltrated the organization's chapters. The FBI monitored and harassed the organization throughout most of its existence. By highlighting governmental efforts to spy on and repress the group, this chapter suggests that SSOC's experience with police power was not qualitatively different from that of its better-known contemporaries SNCC and SDS and thus further helps to reincorporate white southern progressive activists into the narrative of the movements of the 1960s.

The FBI played the most noteworthy role in monitoring social activism in the United States during the 1960s. SSOC was one of the Bureau's many targets; between SSOC's birth in 1964 and its collapse in 1969, the FBI collected more than eighteen thousand pages of material on the group—detailed reports from agents in the field on its activities, correspondence between local agents and Bureau leaders about counterintelligence actions, and copies of SSOC publications. SSOC first came to the FBI's attention in the early summer of 1964, most likely as a result of the group's work to organize white support for black rights during the Freedom Summer campaign in Mississippi. The Bureau's initial interest in SSOC, like so many of its investigations of this era, focused on whether the group was controlled by communists or was sympathetic to communist causes. In the FBI's first apparent internal memorandum about SSOC, the SAC in Atlanta examined SSOC's relationship with the Southern Conference Educational Fund, the civil rights organization that Hoover had long suspected of communist ties. Two days later Hoover ordered the Memphis office, which had jurisdiction in Nashville, SSOC's home base, to review information in its files and attempt to determine "the extent of influence of the SSOC by the members of the Southern Conference Educational Fund."[10] Ten weeks later, in September 1964, the Memphis office reported that its review could not definitively determine SSOC's political orientation, and it asked for approval to start a "discreet investigation" in order to make "an accurate determination of the organization's true character." Hoover consented, and the investigation began in October 1964.[11]

The Memphis office submitted its 62-page report, complete with appendices of SSOC publications, to headquarters and 17 other field offices in January 1965.

The report included a list of informants in Nashville, Atlanta, and New Orleans and offered a detailed discussion of SSOC's brief history. But it did not conclude that communists had infiltrated SSOC, a point Hoover noted in his response to the report.[12] Nonetheless, the continued uncertainty over SSOC's connection to communists led southern field offices to remain vigilant in their observations of the group throughout 1965 and 1966. From Richmond to Miami, Atlanta to San Antonio, agents worked with sympathizers who reported on SSOC meetings, monitored protest actions initiated by the group, and penned report after report, all aimed at determining if SSOC activists were allied with communists.

The Bureau's use of individuals sympathetic to its efforts highlighted the fact that the cultivation of informants was a critical tactic by which the FBI sought to monitor SSOC. The FBI maintained an active network of informants on campuses across the South. While some informants approached the Bureau with information on their own, Bureau agents recruited others. Field offices looked to faculty members and students for information on SSOC. In Virginia, the Richmond office reported to headquarters in 1968 that it "has had for sometime [*sic*] a program of developing confidential sources on college campuses." The SAC remarked that while the office had relied primarily on faculty informants, it was seeking to grow its network of student informants. "It is noted," the SAC wrote, "that sons and daughters of Bureau personnel are often students at pertinent colleges in the Richmond Division and would be very helpful in furnishing the desired information."[13]

Starting in late 1967, the FBI's coverage of SSOC intensified. Hoover instructed all 17 southern field offices to open investigations into the group and its members on the grounds that SSOC was in league with SDS and that "known Communist Party members are actively participating" in SSOC. He ordered each office to monitor local SSOC chapters and activists and to furnish his office with regular reports on the group. To assist in this work, Hoover made it clear that he expected the Bureau's offices to develop contacts with informants in their area, and he asked each office to explain its plan for cultivating "live informant coverage."[14] Over the next two weeks, southern field offices either began or stepped up investigations of the group. Shortly thereafter, SSOC was among the student groups the Bureau targeted in one of its COINTELPROs. Through the COINTEL-PROs, of which there were twelve over the years, the Bureau sought to neutralize a wide range of individuals and organizations that it deemed a threat to domestic security, from black nationalists and communists to white hate groups and Puerto Rican nationalists. Employing covert and often illegal tactics, including wiretapping, intercepting mail, planting false stories in the media, and working with the Internal Revenue Service to audit and challenge tax returns, the Bureau worked to undermine and disrupt legitimate and legal protest activity.[15] In May 1968, the FBI initiated COINTELPRO–New Left, a campaign specifically designed to under-mine activist student groups around the country. Hoover advised his agents that the "program must be approached with imagination and enthusiasm," suggesting that, among other things, they prepare fake leaflets, leak anonymous articles to friendly journalists, and spread rumors about activists' personal lives. Appalled by what he called the "scurrilous and depraved nature of many of the . . . activities, habits, and living conditions representative of New Left adherents," Hoover urged agents to publicize New Left behavior and "immorality" to parents and college administrators and to encourage local police to conduct drug raids as a means of attacking and weakening these organizations.[16]

COINTELPRO–New Left sharpened southern field offices' focus on SSOC. Over the next 13 months, until SSOC's dissolution, agents continuously monitored the organization and worked to disrupt its activities. It is difficult to overstate the level of surveillance the Bureau maintained on SSOC. Agents across the South regularly reported to headquarters about SSOC members' activities, discussions, and meetings. They gleaned some of this information from SSOC publications. But they also learned about developments in the group from informants, and the SACs commonly referenced these informants in the reports on SSOC that they filed with headquarters. Occasionally, the SAC's reports consisted almost entirely of verbatim remarks from informants, such as a February 1965 report from the SAC in Atlanta that shared his informant's summary of a recent SSOC meeting that he had attended in the city.[17] Field offices also developed propaganda to deter students from supporting the group. In Virginia in late 1968, the Richmond office sought to post a flyer on the University of Virginia and Virginia Commonwealth University campuses that attacked SSOC for being both un-American and too close to SDS. Attributed to a fictitious organization, "A Group for Liberal Student Government," the flyer warned students that SSOC, like SDS, has "never opposed a communist program" and "resorts to filth and obscenities to express its opposi-tion to American ways of life."[18]

Such anonymous attacks by the Bureau were common in 1968 and 1969. Less frequent but potentially more devastating were anonymous letters FBI agents sent to the families of activist students in the hope that the resulting familial turmoil would curtail the students' involvement in SSOC. In one case, the SAC in the Little Rock office reported that he had learned that a woman active in the local SSOC chapter was living with her boyfriend without her parents' knowledge. The SAC believed that an anonymous letter to the parents about their daughter's living arrangements might, in his words, prompt them to "take some action to disrupt [her] involvement in 'New Left' activities . . . and possibly disrupt other activities of the LR [Little Rock] SSOC." The letter, signed "A sincere and concerned friend," alerted the parents that their daughter and her boyfriend "have been going around Little Rock openly bragging about the fact that they are not married. . . . I feel that you would want to know about this sinful and immoral behavior." Though letters such as these did not dwell on students' political activities, their intent was to create family strife and thereby undercut the students' activism.[19]

Sometimes Hoover personally intervened to propose or, in some cases, disapprove such anonymous attacks. In 1968, for instance, the Bureau's Jackson office sought to sow discord between SSOC's leaders in Nashville and David Doggett, a student at Millsaps College and the group's most prominent activist in Mississippi. The Jackson SAC proposed sending an anonymous letter from a "Disenchanted Millsaps SSOC Member" to Tom Gardner, SSOC's chairman, complaining that Doggett was scared to join others in protesting the war at the Marine and Naval Reserve station. Hoover, though, thought the plan could backfire by leading to Doggett's "replacement by a stronger leader." He instead counseled that a "better approach to disrupt the Millsaps College Chapter of SSOC might be through a word-of-mouth campaign . . . pointing out his [Doggett's] timidity, thereby undermining his leadership and possibly causing the disbandment of the Chapter."[20]

Had the FBI been the only law enforcement agency to monitor and harass SSOC, the group would have faced enough of a challenge recruiting supporters, building a program, and preserving internal cohesion. That state and local officials also conducted surveillance of SSOC meant that the young activists were constantly under observation and forced to endure state-sponsored actions intended to debilitate their group. State domestic intelligence units employed tactics similar to the FBI's. In Alabama, a state in which SSOC struggled to find recruits and build support, the misleadingly named Alabama Commission to Preserve the Peace kept tabs on SSOC's work and maintained a clippings file on the organization.[21] Its neighbor to the west was more aggressive. The Mississippi State Sovereignty Commission tracked the group's activities in the Magnolia State and infiltrated SSOC meetings and activities in Mississippi.[22]

The legislation that created the MSSC in 1956 gave it the mission to "perform any and all acts deemed necessary and proper to protect the sovereignty of the state of Mississippi."[23] In practical terms this allowed the commission to function as part of a public-private effort to thwart civil rights advances in the state. Until its demise in the early 1970s, the MSSC worked closely with the Citizens' Council, the privately run organization dedicated to preserving white supremacy and segregation. With a staff of dedicated investigators and oversight from the governor's office—the governor, in fact, served as ex-officio chairman of the commission—the MSSC subjected activists to all manner of harassment and abuse. Its investigators traveled the state collecting information about civil rights activists and sympathizers and utilized a network of paid informants to monitor and disrupt the work of civil rights organizations.[24] It even deployed informants beyond the state's borders, in one instance purchasing information supplied by an informant in California on Berkeley students involved in the Free Speech Movement who also participated in civil rights campaigns in Mississippi.[25] Like the FBI, the commission first set its sights on SSOC in the summer of 1964 as a result of the group's work to build white support for the civil rights movement during Freedom Summer. The MSSC closely monitored the SSOC activists, collecting SSOC publications, compiling lists of SSOC activists working in the state, and researching the activists' backgrounds.[26] Though SSOC's work during Freedom Summer was over by August, the MSSC would remain focused on SSOC for the rest of the group's existence; information on nearly one hundred SSOC activists can be found in the commission's records. By 1967, the commission, wrote its executive director, Erle Johnston Jr., maintained a "very voluminous file on SSOC, its pamphlets, its policies, and its connections with subversive individuals and groups."[27]

The commission was particularly interested in trying to identify SSOC activists who were native Mississippians. After studying the group, investigator A. L. Hopkins worriedly noted that "a surprising number of Mississippians are involved in SSOC." State education and university officials also were worried. In March 1967, Erle Johnston Jr. noted that E. R. Jobe, the executive director of the Board of Trustees of Mississippi's Institutions of Higher Learning, requested that the commission "prepare some papers on activities and motives" of SSOC as well as SDS and the National Student Association that could be sent to "administrators of the colleges and universities" in the state.[28] Millsaps College's SSOC chapter, the most important in Mississippi, garnered particular attention from the MSSC. As the Millsaps activists began to speak out and organize demonstrations against the Vietnam War and for black rights, the commission quickly opened files on each of the students who participated in the group, including Diane Burrows, Everett Long, Lee Makemson, and Cassell Carpenter. David Doggett, the Millsaps student who spearheaded the SSOC chapter, especially irritated the MSSC; commission director Johnston labeled him the "chief agitator at Millsaps."[29] But Doggett, who had grown up in Mississippi, did not fit the segregationist image of the outsider who had come to campus to infect unsuspecting white Mississippians with his radical ideologies. Rather, his insider status made him especially dangerous in the commission's view, and its investigators sought to counter his efforts whenever they could. When Doggett, for instance, led a group of Millsaps students in a march through downtown Jackson in May 1967 to protest the recent killing of a bystander at a Jackson State student demonstration by National Guardsmen, MSSC investigators were there, taking the students' photos in an effort to intimidate them. When Doggett and several of the others began publishing the alternative newspaper *The Kudzu,* the commission assiduously collected each issue—in fact, the most complete collection of the newspaper resides in the MSSC's files—and worked with local officials to prevent its publication.[30]

Beyond working to observe and intimidate SSOC activists in Mississippi, the MSSC also infiltrated the organization. The extent of the commission's work in this regard is harder to document, since the staff took care to cover its tracks and protect its sources. SSOC veterans from Mississippi believe that the commission— as well as the FBI and local police—utilized informants as part of the effort to destroy the group.[31] Documents in the MSSC files confirm that the MSSC utilized informants to spy on the organization and undermine its work. The commission regularly paid an informant named Edgar Downing to spy on the organization.[32] Downing was most likely the informant whose 50-odd-page handwritten report offering a historical overview of SSOC served as the basis for commission investigator A. L. Hopkins's 1967 report on SSOC, which concluded that it is "the purpose of the SSOC and related civil rights groups, as well as the Communist Party, to cause a revolution in the USA as soon as possible." Erle Johnston Jr. then forwarded the report, with its list of Mississippians, including students, involved in "un-American activities," to E. R. Jobe, who had requested the report for school administrators in the state.[33] In the most significant example of the commission's infiltration of the group, an informant for the MSSC participated in the June 1969 meeting in Mississippi at which SSOC voted to dissolve itself. Though it is unknown how active a role the informant, David Davidson, played in the discussions, he filed a detailed report on the meeting with the commission's staff.[34]

Police officials in localities across the South matched their state and federal counterparts in the zeal they brought to investigations of suspected subversives. In this they had much in common with their colleagues in police departments throughout the nation. In the tumultuous political and social environment of the 1960s, special police intelligence and surveillance units—"Red Squads"—proliferated. As Frank Donner writes, "The lure of professionalization, the mastery of operational techniques, the accumulation of files, and the growth of a brotherhood of specialists . . . all led to the perception of radical hunting as an elite calling, charged with the awesome responsibility of protecting government and society from grave threats." By 1963, one law enforcement agency estimated that local police departments around the country deployed nearly three hundred thousand officers in work focused on identifying subversives. These units, typically walled off from the rest of the department, targeted individuals and groups considered a threat to the status quo. In the 1960s South, that meant civil rights activists, antiwar protesters, counterculturalists, and a variety of others who strayed from conventional norms or dissented from the politics of the day.[35]

Local Red Squads often acted in concert with state and federal officials to pursue leftist organizations and individuals with vigor. The Birmingham Police Department's Intelligence Unit concentrated its efforts on undermining the efforts of civil rights activists in the city. The unit had the backing of the city's notorious police commissioner, Eugene "Bull" Connor, and it was known to cooperate with the local chapter of the Ku Klux Klan. The police regularly, and openly, monitored the meetings of the Southern Christian Leadership Conference, the Alabama Christian Movement for Human Rights, and the movements and activities of Martin Luther King Jr., Hosea Williams, Ralph Abernathy, Fred Shuttlesworth, and other civil rights leaders. Nor did the police shy away from infiltrating the local movement, as it drew on a reliable network of informants and sympathizers. As a result, the police were rarely caught unawares by the groups' plans and actions. In Memphis, investigators in the police department's Domestic Intelligence Unit succeeded in infiltrating both black and white activist organizations in the city, such as the local chapter of the Vietnam Veterans Against the War and the Black Power–inspired Invaders. In New Orleans, the vice squad infiltrated the local SDS chapter as it sought to recruit high school students. The police officials in these cities, like their peers elsewhere in the South, considered white activists to be dangerous radicals who, in the words of a New Orleans detective, functioned as "an effective arm of the Communist Party working on the youth of America."[36]

In Jackson, the police routinely harassed the SSOC activists at Millsaps. Sometimes the abuse was petty, such as fabricated traffic infractions and the towing of activists' vehicles for supposed parking violations. At other times it was more consequential, such as when the police advised the owner of the office the activists rented to publish *The Kudzu* to evict them from the premises, advice the owner promptly heeded.[37] The police worked especially hard to prevent *The Kudzu*'s publication and curtail its distribution. In October 1968, for instance, twelve *Kudzu* staffers were arrested on trumped-up or fabricated charges ranging from vagrancy to assaulting an officer for attempting to sell the paper outside a local high school. Two months later, police arrested David Doggett, Everett Long, and two other staff persons for attempting to sell the paper—which authorities, in another effort to prevent its distribution, had branded "obscene literature"—at a high school and junior high school.[38]

Police officials frequently cooperated with state and federal law enforcement agencies in their investigations. Police departments commonly shared information that they had gathered on SSOC with the FBI and state domestic intelligence units, and they regularly acted on tips the other agencies provided them. In July 1968 an informant for the Little Rock FBI field office reported that a local SSOC activist was known to use and sell marijuana at her residence. The SAC relayed this information to the Little Rock Police Department, which subsequently executed a search warrant that led to the arrest of several SSOC activists for possession of marijuana.[39] In Richmond, local FBI agents and the investigative unit of the city police department built a strong collaborative relationship aimed at ousting SSOC and other New Left activists from the community. In a memo to FBI Director Hoover in early 1969, the Richmond Special Agent in Charge explained that his office had maintained "close and almost daily contact with the Intelligence Squad of the Richmond Police Department . . . [which] has a very active interest in disrupting New Left activities in Richmond."[40]

Sometimes the information the local police shared with other agencies proved inaccurate, but not before the FBI had intensified its surveillance of the group. On 20 May 1968 the assistant chief of police in Boca Raton, Florida, advised FBI officials in Miami that the SSOC chapter at nearby Florida Atlantic University was planning to protest an upcoming campus visit by Lewis B. Hershey, the director of the Selective Service System. With Hershey's appearance only three days away when the Miami agents learned of the planned protest, they quickly sprang into action. The SAC sent an urgent teletype to headquarters about the protest, passed the information on to military intelligence officials in Orlando, and asked the Jacksonville and Tampa field offices to investigate whether SSOC activists in their jurisdictions were planning to participate in the event. Three days later, the Miami SAC wrote headquarters that his office's investigation had determined that the United Campus Ministries group on campus, not SSOC, had planned the protest and that no protest had occurred because Hershey had cancelled his visit. Nonetheless, the inaccurate information had the effect of intensifying the Bureau's observations of SSOC throughout Florida.[41]

The Nashville Police Department's Red Squad paid special attention to SSOC since the group made its home in Music City. SSOC's chief nemesis was the Intelligence Division's head, Captain John Sorace. Only in his twenties when he took command of the newly created division in 1964, Sorace quickly developed a reputation for using questionable means to pursue his targets. As *The Tennessean* remarked, "If the mayor's idea of local law enforcement is a police force trained for political inquisition, snooping into the private affairs of local citizens and institutions, and creating a climate of suspicion . . . then Captain Sorace is his man."[42] Sorace's unit closely monitored SSOC activists in Nashville, spying on their meetings, photographing their comings and goings, and reporting their activities to federal officials. The Red Squad was more than likely aware of, if not directly involved in, the harassment SSOC activists had endured, including threatening phone calls, repeated break-ins at the SSOC office, and the occasional assaults at the hands of white toughs. In one instance in 1968, while SSOC leaders were away attending a meeting in Mississippi, the group's headquarters was burglarized. SSOC leaders suspected that Sorace's unit had played a role in the burglary since the items the thieves made off with included a typewriter, bank statements, cancelled checks, and the group's mailing list, the lifeblood of any activist organization.[43] In his most high-profile moment—one that highlighted the link between local and federal surveillance efforts—Sorace publicly accused SSOC, along with SNCC and the Southern Conference Educational Fund, of instigating the 1967 Nashville riot. These charges were made during Sorace's appearance before the Senate's Permanent Subcommittee on Investigations, headed by Arkansas's John McClellan. In his testimony, Sorace implausibly accused the white student group of being the driving force behind the demonstrations that had enveloped Nashville's black community. Calling SSOC, as well as SNCC, "so-called civil rights groups" that in actuality focused on "anti–U.S. Government themes," Sorace's testimony revealed that his unit, with full knowledge of the city's mayor, had conducted intensive surveillance of SSOC. Like Hoover's FBI, Sorace's unit considered the white activists to be subversives bent on destroying the accepted norms of race relations and undermining the American government. For Sorace and his counterparts in police departments throughout the South, the threat SSOC appeared to pose to the status quo justified any effort to defeat the group.[44]

Perhaps nothing better indicated the intensity of government scrutiny of SSOC than the fact that surveillance efforts continued even after the group's collapse in June 1969. Three weeks later, the Richmond SAC, noting the "need to take aggressive steps to disrupt SSOC," requested and received approval to send an anonymous letter to SSOC supporters complaining that SDS and Communist Party activists were gaining influence in the group. In October, Hoover approved a request from the SAC in Columbia, South Carolina, to work with a student sympathizer at Furman University to prevent the rechartering of the SSOC group on campus given the national office's closing. That same month, the much-feared Senate Subcommittee on Internal Security, chaired by Mississippi arch-segregationist James O. Eastland, subpoenaed SSOC's leaders and its organizational records, including membership rolls, financial records, and correspondence. In response, several former SSOC activists, resolved to protect the identity of the group's members and donors, gathered the records and made a late-night bonfire of them.[45]

The destruction of the group's records was the coda to the organization's demise. Not only had the group disappeared, its paper trail had now almost entirely vanished as well. The government, which had harassed SSOC throughout its brief life, was now pursuing it even after its death. But tempting as it may be to blame the group's death on government repression, one should be careful not to overstate the role of law enforcement in SSOC's demise. Certainly, government spying and harassment regularly distracted and disrupted the group. Yet SSOC also struggled with numerous other challenges, from continually refining the organization's goals to managing its relations with SDS and other groups skeptical of its regional focus. Ultimately, these other issues played a larger role in SSOC's eventual demise than did government harassment. At most, this harassment heightened tensions within the group and amplified its weaknesses, but these tensions and weaknesses existed apart from any actions taken by law enforcement authorities. Nonetheless, it is the existence of a government campaign against SSOC rather than its impact that deserves attention. Federal, state, and local authorities actively worked to undermine an organization that advocated peaceful protest and racial reform in the South. Their efforts, rooted in fears of campus uprisings and the collapse of the region's white supremacist racial order, make it clear that, in the southern context, any type of dissent would bring down the heavy hand of state authority.

The growing body of evidence regarding government surveillance of activists in the 1960s has provided historians with crucial new sources for documenting the harassment these activists faced. Much, however, about this government activity remains unknown. Despite the voluminous COINTELPRO files, not all records of the Bureau's work have survived or been made public. While the Mississippi State Sovereignty Commission files are now readily accessible, the files for other state agencies are not. And southern police departments have been unwilling to make the records of their Red Squads public or even to acknowledge the existence of such materials. Of course, law enforcement agencies' reluctance to open their files to outsiders is not surprising, especially since such files likely contain evidence of illegal or unethical actions. The challenge for historians is to locate these files and records. It is an especially important task for historians of New Left activism in the South of the 1960s and 1970s, for documenting such abuses of government power will be critical to demonstrating that these activists, such as those in SSOC, endured extensive surveillance and harassment by federal, state, and local authorities.

NOTES

1. For a history of SSOC, see Gregg L. Michel, *Struggle for a Better South: The Southern Student Organizing Committee, 1964–1969* (New York: Palgrave Macmillan, 2004).

2. *Southern Patriot*, Mar. 1969.

3. SAC, Jackson to Director, FBI, 28 May 1969, Federal Bureau of Investigation Files and Records, "Southern Student Organizing Committee," in the author's possession (hereafter cited as FBI-SSOC). The names of both Carpenter and her boyfriend are redacted in

the FBI papers. Carpenter's identity, though, was easy to discover given other information contained in the SAC's report, such as that the woman in question came from a prominent Natchez family.

4. Director, FBI to SAC, Jackson, 16 June 1969, FBI-SSOC. See also *Southern Patriot,* Mar. 1969. FBI documents do not reveal if the SAC devised other actions against Carpenter, though he did subsequently report to the director that the chapter "had received complaints concerning too much promiscuous activity"—presumably by Carpenter—and that Carpenter had separated from her boyfriend and moved to Colorado. SAC, Jackson to Director, FBI, 25 July 1969, FBI-SSOC.

5. The work in the mid-1970s of the U.S. Senate Select Committee to Study Governmental Operations with Respect to Intelligence Activities—known as the "Church Committee," for its chairman, Senator Frank Church of Idaho—gave the first broad, public exposure to the extralegal tactics that government authorities utilized against political activists. The Church Committee published six books of findings and seven volumes of hearing transcripts and exhibits (as well as an interim report on allegations that the Central Intelligence Agency had plotted to assassinate foreign leaders). On domestic intelligence activities, see U.S. Senate, Select Committee to Study Governmental Operations with respect to Intelligence Activities, Final Report, 94th Cong., 2nd Session, 1976, Book II (Intelligence Activities and the Rights of Americans) and Final Report, 94th Cong., 2nd Session, 1976, Book III (Supplementary Detailed Staff Reports on the Intelligence Activities and the Rights of Americans); and U.S. Senate, Select Committee to Study Government Operations with Respect to Intelligence Activities. 94th Cong., 1st Session, 1975 *Hearings on Intelligence Activities,* vol. 6 (Federal Bureau of Investigation).

6. Pat Watters and Stephen Gillers, *Investigating the FBI* (New York: Doubleday, 1973); Nelson Blackstock, *COINTELPRO: The FBI's Secret War on Political Freedom* (New York: Vintage, 1975).

7. Frank J. Donner, *The Age of Surveillance* (New York: Knopf, 1980); David J. Garrow, *The FBI and Martin Luther King, Jr.: From "Solo" to Memphis* (New York: W.W. Norton, 1981); Kenneth O'Reilly, *Hoover and the Un-Americans: The FBI, HUAC, and the Red Menace* (Philadelphia: Temple Univ. Press, 1983); Ward Churchill and Jim Vander Wall, *Agents of Repression: The FBI's Secret Wars against the Black Panther Party and the American Indian Movement* (Boston: South End Press, 1990); Kenneth O'Reilly, *"Racial Matters": The FBI's Secret File on Black America, 1960–1972* (New York: Free Press, 1989); and Ward Churchill and Jim Vander Wall, *The COINTELPRO Papers: Documents from the FBI's Secret Wars against Domestic Dissent* (Boston: South End Press, 1990).

8. Clayborne Carson, *In Struggle: SNCC and the Black Awakening of the 1960s* (Cambridge, MA: Harvard Univ. Press, 1981); Tom Wells, *The War Within: America's Battle over Vietnam* (Berkeley: Univ. of California Press, 1994); Taylor Branch, *Parting the Waters: America in the King Years, 1954–1963* (New York: Simon and Schuster, 1988); Taylor Branch, *Pillar of Fire: America in the King Years, 1963–1965* (New York: Simon and Schuster, 1998); Taylor Branch, *At Canaan's Edge: America in the King Years, 1965–1968* (New York: Simon and Schuster, 2006). See also James Kirkpatrick Davis, *Assault on the Left: The FBI and the Sixties Antiwar Movement* (Westport, CT: Praeger, 1997); and David Cunningham, *There's Something Happening Here: The New Left, the Klan, and FBI Counterintelligence* (Berkeley: Univ. of California Press, 2004).

9. Paul G. Chevigny, "Politics and Law in the Control of Local Surveillance," *Cornell Law Review* 69, no. 4 (1984): 735–83; Frank J. Donner, *Protectors of Privilege: Red Squads and*

Police Repression in Urban America (Berkeley: Univ. of California Press, 1990); Dwight Watson, *Race and the Houston Police Department, 1930–1990: A Change Did Come* (College Station: Texas A&M Univ. Press, 2005), Sarah Rowe-Sims, "The Mississippi State Sovereignty Commission: An Agency History," *Journal of Mississippi History* 61, no. 1 (1999): 29–58; Yasuhiro Katagiri, *The Mississippi State Sovereignty Commission: Civil Rights and States' Rights* (Jackson: Univ. Press of Mississippi, 2001); Jo Freeman, "The Berkeley Free Speech Movement and the Mississippi Sovereignty Commission," *Left History* 8, no. 2 (2003): 135–44; Jenny Irons, *Reconstituting Whiteness: The Mississippi State Sovereignty Commission* (Nashville, TN: Vanderbilt Univ. Press, 2010).

10. SAC, Atlanta to Director, FBI, 10 July 1964, and Director, FBI to SAC, Memphis, 28 July 1964 (quotation), FBI-SSOC. On the Southern Conference Educational Fund and its long-time leaders, Anne and Carl Braden, see Catherine Fosl, *Subversive Southerner: Anne Braden and the Struggle for Racial Justice in the Cold War South* (New York: Palgrave Macmillan, 2002).

11. SAC, Memphis to Director, FBI, 25 Sept. 1964 (quotation) and Director, FBI to SAC, Memphis, 14 Oct. 1964, FBI-SSOC.

12. SAC, Memphis, Report, "Communist Infiltration: Southern Student Organizing Committee," 8 Jan. 1965 and Director, FBI to SAC, Memphis, 28 Jan. 1965, FBI-SSOC.

13. SAC, Richmond to Director, FBI, 2 July 1968, FBI-SSOC.

14. Director, FBI to SACs, 15 Dec. 1967, FBI-SSOC.

15. On the number of COINTELPROs, see Alexander Charms, *Cloak and Gavel: FBI Wiretaps, Bugs, Informers, and the Supreme Court* (Urbana: Univ. of Illinois Press, 1992), 134n16. Among the works that focus on the COINTELPROs are Blackstock, *COINTELPRO*; William C. Sullivan with Bill Brown, *The Bureau: My Thirty Years in Hoover's FBI* (New York: W.W. Norton, 1979); Donner, *Age of Surveillance*; Garrow, *FBI and Martin Luther King, Jr*; Churchill and Vander Wall, *Agents of Repression*; O'Reilly, *"Racial Matters"*; Churchill and Vander Wall, *COINTELPRO Papers*; Davis, *Assault on the Left*; David Cunningham, "State Versus Social Movement: FBI Counterintelligence Against the New Left," in *States, Parties, and Social Movements*, ed. Jack A. Goldstone (Cambridge, U.K.: Cambridge Univ. Press, 2003), 45–77; and Cunningham, *There's Something Happening Here*.

16. Athan Theoharis, *Spying on Americans: Political Surveillance from Hoover to the Huston Plan* (Philadelphia: Temple Univ. Press, 1978), 148; Donner, *Age of Surveillance*, 232–37, quotation 235; Churchill and Vander Wall, *COINTELPRO Papers*, 175–77; Cunningham, *There's Something Happening Here*, 33–34, 50–51.

17. SAC, Atlanta to Director, FBI, 26 Feb. 1965, FBI-SSOC.

18. SAC, Richmond to Director, FBI, 5 Nov. 1968, FBI-SSOC.

19. SAC, Little Rock to Director, FBI, 14 Oct. 1968, FBI-SSOC.

20. SAC, Jackson to Director, FBI, 29 May 1968; Director, FBI to SAC (quotation), Jackson, 7 June 1968, FBI-SSOC.

21. Alabama Commission to Preserve the Peace, Alabama Department of Archives and History, Montgomery, Alabama. The Alabama State Sovereignty Commission also tracked civil rights activists in the state. Its files, though, most likely were purged before the state Department of Archives and History took possession of them. Aldon Monroe, telephone conversation with the author, Feb. 2006.

22. On the Mississippi State Sovereignty Commission, see Irons, *Reconstituting Whiteness*; Katagiri, *Mississippi State Sovereignty Commission*; Rowe-Sims, "The Mississippi State Sovereignty Commission: An Agency History"; and Christopher Paul Lehman, "Mis-

sissippi's Extraordinary Month: The Demise of the Sovereignty Commission and of Unprofessional Leadership at the Mississippi State Penitentiary, November 1973," *Journal of Mississippi History* 68, no. 4 (2006): 287–306. Alabama's and Mississippi's investigative units, along with Louisiana's, joined forces to create the Southern Association of Investigators in the mid-1960s. In 1967, an Alabama Commission to Preserve the Peace report on "organizations operating in the Southeastern United States whose purpose or programs might cause breach of the peace or pose problems for law enforcement" and which called SSOC "a motley crew of leftists," can be found in the Mississippi State Sovereignty Commission files. SCR no. 2-158-1-12-1-1-1 to 2-158-1-12-7-1-1 (quotation from 2-158-1-12-1-1-1 and 2-158-1-12-7-1-1), Series 2515: Mississippi State Sovereignty Commission Records, 1994–2006, Mississippi Department of Archives and History, Jackson, Mississippi. On the Southern Association of Investigators, see Jeff Woods, *Black Struggle, Red Scare: Segregation and Anti-Communism in the South, 1948–1968* (Baton Rouge: LSU Press, 2004), 243–44; and Tiffany Joseph, "White Resistance," available at www.stg.brown.edu/projects/FreedomNow/themes/resist/index.html, accessed 14 June 2012.

23. House Bill 880, Mississippi State Legislature, 1956, Sovereignty Commission / Citizens' Council, folder 2, T-90.25, Tougaloo College Archives, available at www.stg.brown.edu/projects/FreedomNow/scans/TJ0014-01.jpg and www.stg.brown.edu/projects/FreedomNow/scans/TJ0014-02.jpg, accessed 14 June 2012.

24. See, for example, Erle Johnston Jr., "Memorandum to File," 18 May 1964, SCR no. 9-32-0-4-1-1-1, Mississippi State Sovereignty Commission Records.

25. Freeman, "Berkeley Free Speech Movement."

26. See, for instance, lists of SSOC volunteers during the summer project. SCR no. 2-158-3-14-2-1-1; SCR no. 2-158-3-37-11-1-1 and SCR no. 6-44-0-13-11-1-1, Mississippi State Sovereignty Commission Records.

27. Erle Johnston Jr., "Memorandum to File," 4 Apr. 1967, SCR no. 2-158-1-14-1-1-1, Mississippi State Sovereignty Commission Records.

28. Erle Johnston Jr., "Memorandum to File," 9 Mar. 1967, SCR no. 2-158-1-13-1-1-1, Mississippi State Sovereignty Commission Records.

29. A. L. Hopkins to Erle Johnston Jr., 14 Apr. 1967, SCR no. 2-158-3-2-1-1-1 to 2-158-3-7-1-1 (quotation from 2-158-3-2-4-1-1); Erle Johnston Jr., "Memorandum to File," 20 June 1967, SCR no. 3-11-0-26-1-1-1, Mississippi State Sovereignty Commission Records.

30. Lists and discussion of students involved in the 1967 protest march can be found in SCR no. 3-11-0-27-1-1-1, Mississippi State Sovereignty Commission Records. Cassell Carpenter, Gary Brooks, David Doggett, and Sue Barnes were among the protesters at the demonstration whose photographs were taken by Sovereignty Commission investigators. See, for example, SCR no. 3-11-0-25-2-1-1 and SCR no. 3-11-0-25-3-1-1, Mississippi State Sovereignty Commission Records. On *The Kudzu*, see David Doggett, "*The Kudzu*: Birth and Death in Underground Mississippi," in *Voices from the Underground: Insider Histories of the Vietnam Era Underground Press*, vol. 1, ed. Ken Wachsberger (Tempe, AZ: Mica Press, 1993), 213–32; David Doggett, "*The Kudzu* Story: Underground in Mississippi," *Southern Exposure* 2, no. 4 (1975): 86–95; *Southern Patriot*, Dec. 1968; Donald Cunnigen, "Standing at the Gates: The Civil Rights Movement and Liberal White Mississippi Students," *Journal of Mississippi History* 62, no. 1 (2000): 1–19; and Stephen Flinn Young, "*The Kudzu*: Sixties Generational Revolt—Even in Mississippi," *Southern Quarterly* 34, no. 3 (1996): 122–36.

31. David Doggett, interview by the author, 30 Aug. 1994, Philadelphia, Pennsylvania.

32. Edgar Downing to Earl [*sic*] Johnston, 28 Feb. 1965, SCR no. 2-158-3-13-1-1-1 to 2-158-

3-13-3-1-1, Mississippi State Sovereignty Commission Records; Tom Scarbrough, Investigator to Honorable Erle Johnston Jr., Director, 9 Mar. 1965, SCR no. 2-36-2-46-1-1-1, Mississippi State Sovereignty Commission Records.

33. Untitled Report, SCR no. 2-158-3-14-2-1-1 to 2-158-3-57-1-1, Mississippi State Sovereignty Commission Records; A. L. Hopkins to Erle Johnston Jr., 14 Apr. 1967, SCR no. 2-158-3-2-1-1-1 to 2-158-3-7-1-1 (quotation from 2-158-3-2-7-1-1), Mississippi State Sovereignty Commission Records; Erle Johnston Jr. to Dr. E. R. Jobe, 18 Apr. 1967, SCR no. 2-158-3-1-1-1-1, Mississippi State Sovereignty Commission Records.

34. David Davidson to Kenneth W. Fairly, 9 June 1969, SCR no. 2-158-4-20-2-1-1 to 2-158-4-20-8-1-1, Mississippi State Sovereignty Commission Records.

35. Donner, *Protectors of Privilege,* 66–67, 81–82.

36. Ibid., 305–19; Memphis *Commercial Appeal,* ca. 8 Sept. 1976; Gerald D. McKnight, "The 1968 Memphis Sanitation Strike and the FBI: A Case Study in Urban Surveillance," *South Atlantic Quarterly* 83, no. 2 (1984): 138–56; Gerald D. McKnight, *The Last Crusade: Martin Luther King, Jr., the FBI, and the Poor People's Campaign* (Boulder, CO: Westview Press, 1998); Clarence Doucet, "Detective Says SDS Does Work for Communist Party," *New Orleans Times-Picayune,* ca. 1963, SCR no. 13-8-2-92-1-1-1, Mississippi State Sovereignty Commission Records.

37. *The Kudzu* 1, no. 9 (ca. 26 Feb. 1969).

38. Doggett, "*The Kudzu,*" 219–21, 224–29; Doggett, "*The Kudzu* Story," 90–91; *Southern Patriot,* Dec. 1968; Doggett interview; Everett Long, interview by the author, 12 Nov. 1994, Nashville, Tennessee; Cassell Carpenter to author, 27 July 2002; *Purple and White* (Millsaps College), 18 Oct. 1968, Millsaps College Archives, Millsaps-Wilson Library, Millsaps College, Jackson, Mississippi; *The Kudzu* 1, no. 3 (23 Oct. 1968), and 1, no. 9 (ca. 26 Feb. 1969); *Jackson Daily News,* 18 Oct. 1968; Jackson *Clarion-Ledger,* 10 Oct. and 20 Dec. 1968; and *The Reflector* (Mississippi State Univ.), 17 Dec. 1968.

39. SAC, Little Rock to Director, FBI, 20 Aug. 1968, FBI-SSOC.

40. SAC, Richmond to Director, FBI, 11 Jan. 1969, FBI-SSOC.

41. Miami to Director, FBI, 20 May 1968, 23 May 1968, and 24 May 1968, FBI-SSOC.

42. Quoted in *Southern Patriot,* Jan. 1968. See also *New South Student* 4, no. 7 (Dec. 1967); and *Nashville Banner,* 24 Aug. 1966.

43. Mike [Welch] to Ed Hamlett, 12 July 1968, Hamlett Ed White Folks Project Collection, [1963?]–2001, McCain Library and Archives, University Libraries, University of Southern Mississippi, Hattiesburg, Mississippi.

44. Hearings Before the Permanent Subcommittee on Investigations of the Committee on Government Operations. United States Senate, Part 2, Nashville (Washington, D.C.: U.S. Government Printing Office, 1967), 638–708 (quotation 706).

45. SAC, Richmond to Director, FBI, 26 June 1969, and Director, FBI to SAC, Richmond, 7 July 1969, FBI-SSOC; SAC, Columbia to Director, FBI, 8 Oct. 1969 and Director, FBI to SAC, Columbia, 20 Oct. 1969, FBI-SSOC; Subpoena of Joe Bogle, Subcommittee on Internal Security of the Committee on the Judiciary, United States Senate, 1 Oct. 1969, in the author's possession.

PART IV

Black Power and the Legacy of the Freedom Movement

North Carolina A&T Black Power Activists and the Student Organization for Black Unity

JELANI FAVORS

During the fall of 1969, students at North Carolina A&T crowded into a gymnasium to hear Howard Fuller, a young firebrand and nationally known community activist who addressed rising black discontent and demands for justice. "We . . . should get the feeling that seemingly exists at A&T," Fuller exclaimed. "Students here not only talk, but act. Their rhetoric is that of revolution . . . a rhetoric of action."[1] Historically black colleges, the epicenters of the insurgency that had defined the decade, continued to serve as flashpoints for confrontations with the white power structure as the 1960s drew to a close. Colleges across the country experienced a surge in mobilization, violent exchanges with local and federal authorities, and a robust ideological debate that probed the varying and often conflicting theories regarding the liberation of black people.

Greensboro, North Carolina, was like most other American cities in the throes of the civil rights movement. While visible barriers to equality were slowly receding, institutionalized white supremacy was becoming more deeply entrenched, a fact that did not go unrecognized by a growing number of student activists. Five months before Howard Fuller's visit, a group of students from across the country flocked to A&T's campus to launch a new student organization called the Student Organization for Black Unity.

Generations of Insurgency: Black Colleges as Seedbeds of Activism

The flowering of Black Power ideology, particularly as it was represented on historically black colleges and universities (HBCUs), has received limited attention and narrow analysis by civil rights scholars. Indeed, most studies focus on the evolution of the Student Nonviolent Coordinating Committee (SNCC) or the emergence of Black Studies departments on predominantly white campuses. While there are a variety of biographies, monographs, and articles that discuss activism connected to black colleges, very few characterize student protest as a direct product of the environment in which students lived, learned, and socialized. Black colleges are often described as an environment where activism was generated in spite of the setting, not as a direct result of it. The general depiction consists of conservative administrators, disengaged and apathetic faculty, and an independent student base that found the resolve to challenge white supremacy on their own or with the assistance of sympathetic campus outsiders. While it is certain that a great deal of personnel directly connected to HBCUs attempted to ward off the rising insurgency of the civil rights movement, the suggestion that black student activism was not directly and indirectly produced through the inner workings of black college life demands deeper inquiry and revision.

This limited scope fails to elevate our understanding of institutions that served as seedbeds of activism, producing a wave of militant black youth who helped to reshape the political landscape of America. It was within the space of black universities that prominent contributors to the Black Power era such as H. Rap Brown, Jesse Jackson, Nikki Giovanni, Stokely Carmichael, Ruby Doris Smith-Robinson, and Courtland Cox first found their voices; the Atlanta University Center, comprised of Morehouse, Spelman, and Clark Atlanta University, housed what was arguably the era's most important think tank, the Institute of the Black World; and although campus violence in this era is most often associated with the shootings at Kent State, National Guardsmen and local authorities stormed the campuses of numerous HBCUs and tragically claimed the lives of several students.

As the movement unfolded in Greensboro, it was clear that A&T was the engine that generated local activist energies. The institution produced most of the local leadership, served as a rallying point for insurgents, was a frequent host to nationally known dissidents, and served as a beacon of pride for the local black community. But A&T's history as a source of activism had in fact reached back into the earliest years of the twentieth century.[2] Thus, by the time 1 February 1960 arrived, the student body of North Carolina A&T was primed by a tradition of resistance that the sit-in movement took to unprecedented levels. These famous protests, which historian Taylor Branch referred to as "schoolboyish deed[s]," were more complicated than spontaneous feats of bravado.[3] Throughout the halls of black academia, race consciousness had been deliberately embedded in the minds of black youth in an attempt to counter systemic efforts to erode their self-confidence. Generations of youth, sheltered from the full brunt of such oppressive messages, consequently generated enough confidence to examine critically the American paradox of race relations and eventually make the perilous move to challenge white supremacy head on. Jibreel Khazan (Ezell Blair), a member of the Greensboro Four, recalled: "They were living a lie in their thinking that because of our color, we were unintelligent and we knew nothing. But these things were taught to us by the time we were in grade school. . . . Our teachers in the segregated school system told us they were preparing us for the day that we would be free and that we were going to be the leaders of that freedom. This is before Martin Luther King and Rosa Parks came along. This is what I was taught in my school system in Greensboro."[4]

By 1960 many of the students that engaged in the crusade to dismantle Jim Crow had been empowered by their interactions with teachers, mentors, and community leaders, many of whom were trained at black colleges. This relationship would prove critical as the decade unfolded. Unlike other settings in the civil rights movement, the struggle for liberation in Greensboro received support from a diverse cross-section of the black community.[5] This broad coalition, inspired by new tactics from the Congress of Racial Equality, led to the mass jail-ins of 1962 and 1963.[6] Claude Barnes recalled that during this stage, "We had masses of people. Ordinary people. Maids like my mother. Store clerks like my aunt. Teachers, janitors, young people like myself. Across the gamut and across class lines. . . . They were attracted to the strength of this movement."[7]

Despite the growing numbers of rank-and-file citizens being enticed to join the struggle, it was the resolve of the local white power structure that set the tone for future protests that later caused the emotions of young activists to race through hope, doubt, frustration, and anger.[8] While "white only" signs had been mostly removed throughout "Gate City" by 1965, the policies that defined the day-to-day struggles of common black folk went largely unaffected. Housing, health care, wealth disparities, and police brutality were issues that universally affected poor communities from the rural shanties to the urban slums. Across the country, local and federal officials fortified their positions under the banner of "all deliberate speed" while remaining ambivalent to the needs of people marginalized by the color line. Greensboro was no different. Historian William Chafe noted, "The failure of white leaders to initiate more substantive programs toward racial equality carried a dual message: not only would renewed direct-action protest be necessary for further change; the next time such protests would be fueled by the anger that came from knowing how little past rhetoric had accomplished."[9]

The definitive conditions that led to the creation of the Student Organization for Black Unity (SOBU) were thus well in place by 1968. The most prominent factor that led to the creation of this organization was the desire to recapture the potential of radical youth as instruments for transformation. SNCC was crumbling. Despite attempts to continue what sociologist Charles Payne referred to as the "organizing tradition," the majority of field projects sponsored by the organization had all but ceased by 1968. As the various projects of SNCC were coming to a close, the activist energies of Greensboro were still simmering, as they had been since 1 February 1960. Greensboro was not SNCC territory, nor was it characterized by the rising class divisions that many SNCC organizers were finding in the field.[10] These realities and the continued discriminatory practices of the Greensboro power structure provided the foundation for an organization that was directly connected to the early rise of SOBU: the Greensboro Association of Poor People.

Poverty and Power: The Merger of the Poor People Campaign and the Student Movement

In 1964, President Lyndon Baines Johnson officially declared a "War on Poverty." While LBJ's new programs set out—with mixed results—to break the cycle of poverty, local black neighborhoods still struggled against discriminatory housing, denial of key resources, and obstinate white political and business leaders who were insensitive to black concerns. The united and massive response to Jim Crow policies in Greensboro during the first half of the decade all but ensured that as the focus of the movement shifted to more institutionalized issues after 1965, a concerted effort from the black community would follow. "We will no longer be intimidated by 'gun toting' landlords, and non-acting city officials," exclaimed Lula Pennix, a local community leader. "We are demanding immediate actions be taken."[11]

This spirit of self-determination was captured by the Greensboro Association of Poor People (GAPP) in the summer of 1968. Building on the collective experiences of Greensboro's impoverished communities and the failures of local agencies to address their concerns, GAPP was launched by the merging of several interests and previously existing organizations. Residents of the city's public housing had formed the United Neighborhood Improvement Team to focus on inequities in housing and created an intern program by partnering with twelve black professional men within the city and the Foundation for Community Development in Durham. The goal was to channel the energy of the earlier student movement directly into a new initiative by offering six community organizing internships to students.[12] By the end of the summer, all involved parties decided to continue their collective efforts, thus launching GAPP.

GAPP quickly expanded its agenda beyond issues of fair housing and tenants rights to include labor concerns, police brutality, public schools, and cooperative economics within the black community. The GAPP paradigm was "designed to organize black people around their immediate problems and material concerns in such a way as to create a sense of power and determination sufficient to effect change on the policy level."[13] GAPP's presence within the black community now set the stage for a vital support network ready to sustain the activism of militant youth. Greensboro had no shortage of young radicals as the presence of A&T continued to serve as a rallying point for the black freedom movement.

For many A&T students, Black Power was an idea whose time had come. If the political landscape of Greensboro and the nation shifted slowly, the ideologies that informed and directed the civil rights movement most certainly did not. Black Power ideology flowed through the halls and dormitories of black colleges. Capturing the growing social, political, and economic frustration of marginalized communities, Black Power was an alluring concept. It possessed the boldness and bravado that nonviolent rhetoric did not. It offered the opportunity to "stick it to the Man," a sentiment that many black youth had secretly desired to do all their lives, making the political climate conducive to mass mobilization on campus. Student activist Claude Barnes recalled: "During that time, I can remember the SGA [Student Government Association] would call a meeting. I don't care if they called it at 2:00 a.m., Harrison Auditorium would be filled up. People would come out of their dormitories with rollers in their hair. It was that kind of attention. It was that kind of concern among the student body at that time about what's going on in this community and what role could A&T play."[14]

The synergy that existed between students and GAPP was displayed in a strike of cafeteria workers on A&T's campus during the spring of 1969. The workers demanded better wages and working conditions. The strike, which lasted three days, received 90 percent support from the student body. Students formed an ad hoc committee to eat off campus while the cafeteria was closed. Three days after the inception of the strike, the administration of A&T reached a settlement with the cafeteria workers, bringing quick resolution to the matter. However, without the pressure and support of the student body, it is uncertain how successful the workers' efforts would have been. Student leader Vincent McCullough exclaimed, "The will of black people can never be suppressed."[15] McCullough not only reflected the sentiment of his fellow Aggies but additionally conveyed the communal support that made the Greensboro model a standout among other "movement centers."[16]

Since the mass jail-ins of 1962–63, the relationship between community and students had remained strong. Those connections were strongest among community members who earned their living by working on and near campus. But it was an exchange with local law enforcement that set the tone for the violent struggle that would define the end of the academic year. On 13 March 1969, twenty-five hundred students decided to show their support for the striking workers by marching to the home of President Lewis Dowdy. Tensions increased when the predominantly white police force arrived on the scene to disperse the crowd.

A struggle ensued as police attempted to escort students back to campus. Cohen Greene, a student at A&T, reported: "The students then marched to East Market Street where cars were stoned, traffic was held up, and windows were broken. The rock-throwing crowd concentrated at Sid's Curb Market until the police arrived later. George Bain, owner of the curb market, was confronted earlier on Wednesday and asked to contribute food during the strike, but refused . . . this curb market was probably singled out because 'it is the only white owned business in that area and most students feel it shouldn't be there.'"[17]

The tenets that served as the underpinning of Black Power manifested themselves in the streets of Greensboro during the 1969 strike. Students who believed that their rights had been marginalized lashed out at anything they regarded as symbolic of white authority. A college administration that exploited its workers, police that harassed and abused students, and white-owned businesses that were not supportive of student causes and exploited students' dollars were the focal point of student anger. In the aftermath, three students suffered gunshot wounds, and several more were injured when local law enforcement attempted to "handle" the incident.

In the days following the riot, many students called for retaliation and revenge. The police violence in Greensboro was part of a national trend, as gun-wielding National Guardsmen and police officers were called in to suppress ghetto rebellions, wounding and killing innocent African Americans in the name of law and order. Rather than deal with black grievances, conservative white politicians built a backlash against black militancy by acting as if all the protest had been caused by unruly and lawless youngsters who needed to be taught a lesson. Law enforcement endorsed hard-line tactics to force dissidents to comply, setting up a rash of violence that would sweep across inner city streets and college campuses alike. Showing that A&T students would not back down, the *A&T Register* proclaimed, "The business community of Greensboro must pay for police brutality. The simulated battleground, for which police used A&T's campus, should be responded to by the Aggie family with redress and insurrection."[18] Tensions were building in Greensboro that did not go unnoticed in the local community and beyond. The city's black high school youth, adult community activists, and black militants across the country had their eyes on A&T. In just two months after the fallout from the cafeteria, all of them would converge on the institution to create SOBU, raise the call for Black Power, and witness one of the most violent campus exchanges in student movement history.

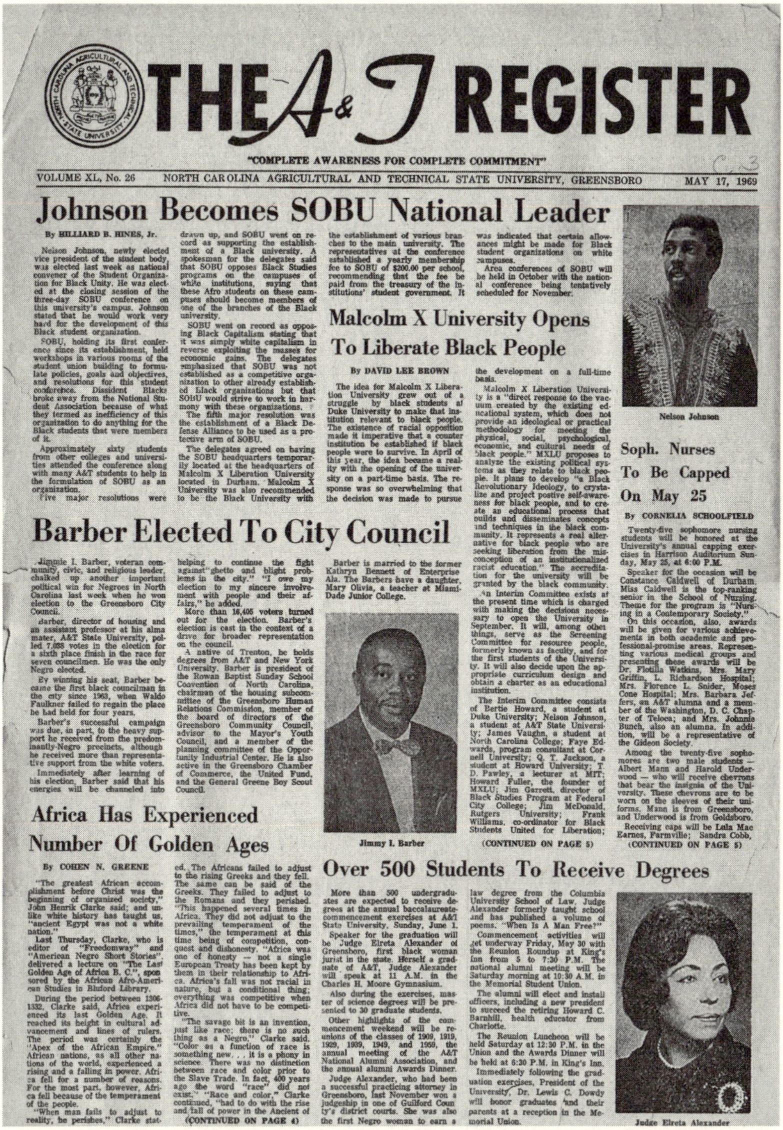

THE A&T REGISTER

"COMPLETE AWARENESS FOR COMPLETE COMMITMENT"

VOLUME XL, No. 26 NORTH CAROLINA AGRICULTURAL AND TECHNICAL STATE UNIVERSITY, GREENSBORO MAY 17, 1969

Johnson Becomes SOBU National Leader

By HILLIARD B. HINES, Jr.

Nelson Johnson, newly elected vice president of the student body, was elected last week as national convener of the Student Organization for Black Unity. He was elected at the closing session of the three-day SOBU conference on this university's campus. Johnson stated that he would work very hard for the development of this Black student organization.

SOBU, holding its first conference since its establishment, held workshops in various rooms of the student union building to formulate policies, goals and objectives, and resolutions for this student conference. Dissident Blacks broke away from the National Student Association because of what they termed as inefficiency of this organization to do anything for the Black students that were members of it.

Approximately sixty students from other colleges and universities attended the conference along with many A&T students to help in the formulation of SOBU as an organization.

Five major resolutions were drawn up, and SOBU went on record as supporting the establishment of a Black university. A spokesman for the delegates said that SOBU opposes Black Studies programs on the campuses of white institutions, saying that these Afro students on these campuses should become members of one of the branches of the Black university.

SOBU went on record as opposing Black Capitalism stating that it was simply white capitalism in reverse exploiting the masses for economic gains. The delegates emphasized that SOBU was not established as a competitive organization to other already established Black organizations but that SOBU would strive to work in harmony with these organizations.

The fifth major resolution was the establishment of a Black Defense Alliance to be used as a protective arm of SOBU.

The delegates agreed on having the SOBU headquarters temporarily located at the headquarters of Malcolm X Liberation University located in Durham. Malcolm X University was also recommended to be the Black University with the establishment of various branches to the main university. The representatives at the conference established a yearly membership fee to SOBU of $200.00 per school, recommending that the fee be paid from the treasury of the institutions' student government. It was indicated that certain allowances might be made for Black student organizations on white campuses.

Area conferences of SOBU will be held in October with the national conference being tentatively scheduled for November.

Nelson Johnson

Malcolm X University Opens To Liberate Black People

By DAVID LEE BROWN

The idea for Malcolm X Liberation University grew out of a struggle by black students at Duke University to make that institution relevant to black people. The existence of racial opposition made it imperative that a counter institution be established if black people were to survive. In April of this year, the idea became a reality with the opening of the university on a part-time basis. The response was so overwhelming that the decision was made to pursue the development on a full-time basis.

Malcolm X Liberation University is a "direct response to the vacuum created by the existing educational system, which does not provide an ideological or practical methodology for meeting the physical, social, psychological, economic, and cultural needs of black people." MXLU proposes to analyze the existing political systems as they relate to black people. It plans to develop "a Black Revolutionary Ideology, to crystalize and project postive self-awareness for black people, and to create an educational process that builds and disseminates concepts and techniques in the black community. It represents a real alternative for black people who are seeking liberation from the misconception of an institutionalized racist education." The accreditation for the university will be granted by the black community.

An Interim Committee exists at the present time which is charged with making the decisions necessary to open the University in September. It will, among other things, serve as the Screening Committee for resource people, formerly known as faculty, and for the first students of the University. It will also decide upon the appropriate curriculum design and obtain a charter as an educational institution.

The Interim Committee consists of Bertie Howard, a student at Duke University; Nelson Johnson, a student at A&T State University; James Vaughn, a student at North Carolina College; Faye Edwards, program consultant at Cornell University; Q. T. Jackson, a student at Howard University; T. D. Pawley, a lecturer at MIT; Howard Fuller, the founder of MXLU; Jim Garrett, director of Black Studies Program at Federal City College; Jim McDonald, Rutgers University; Frank Williams, co-ordinator for Black Students United for Liberation;

(CONTINUED ON PAGE 5)

Soph. Nurses To Be Capped On May 25

By CORNELIA SCHOOLFIELD

Twenty-five sophomore nursing students will be honored at the University's annual capping exercises in Harrison Auditorium Sunday, May 25, at 6:00 P.M.

Speaker for the occasion will be Constance Caldwell of Durham. Miss Caldwell is the top-ranking senior in the School of Nursing. Theme for the program is "Nursing in a Contemporary Society."

On this occasion, also, awards will be given for various achievements in both academic and professional-promise areas. Representing various medical groups and presenting these awards will be Dr. Flotilla Watkins, Mrs. Mary Griffin, L. Richardson Hospital; Mrs. Florence L. Snider, Moses Cone Hospital; Mrs. Barbara Jeffers, an A&T alumna and a member of the Washington, D. C. Chapter of Teloca; and Mrs. Johnnie Bunch, also an alumna. In addition, will be a representative of the Gideon Society.

Among the twenty-five sophomores are two male students — Albert Mann and Harold Underwood — who will receive chevrons that bear the insignia of the University. These chevrons are to be worn on the sleeves of their uniforms. Mann is from Greensboro, and Underwood is from Goldsboro.

Receiving caps will be Lula Mae Earnes, Farmville; Sandra Cobb,

(CONTINUED ON PAGE 5)

Barber Elected To City Council

Jimmie I. Barber, veteran community, civic, and religious leader, chalked up another important political win for Negroes in North Carolina last week when he won election to the Greensboro City Council.

Barber, director of housing and an assistant professor at his alma mater, A&T State University, polled 7,038 votes in the election for a sixth place finish in the race for seven councilmen. He was the only Negro elected.

By winning his seat, Barber became the first black councilman in the city since 1963, when Waldo Faulkner failed to regain the place he had held for four years.

Barber's successful campaign was due, in part, to the heavy support he received from the predominantly-Negro precincts, although he received more than representative support from the white voters.

Immediately after learning of his election, Barber said that his energies will be channeled into helping to continue the fight against "ghetto and blight problems in the city." "I owe my election to my sincere involvement with people and their affairs," he added.

More than 16,405 voters turned out for the election. Barber's election is cast in the context of a drive for broader representation on the council.

A native of Trenton, he holds degrees from A&T and New York University. Barber is president of the Rowan Baptist Sunday School Convention of North Carolina, chairman of the housing subcommittee of the Greensboro Human Relations Commission, member of the board of directors of the Greensboro Community Council, advisor to the Mayor's Youth Council, and a member of the planning committee of the Opportunity Industrial Center. He is also active in the Greensboro Chamber of Commerce, the United Fund, and the General Greene Boy Scout Council.

Barber is married to the former Kathryn Bennett of Enterprise Ala. The Barbers have a daughter, Mary Olivia, a teacher at Miami-Dade Junior College.

Jimmy I. Barber

Africa Has Experienced Number Of Golden Ages

By COHEN N. GREENE

"The greatest African accomplishment before Christ was the beginning of organized society," John Henrik Clarke said; and unlike white history has taught us, "ancient Egypt was not a white nation."

Last Thursday, Clarke, who is editor of "Freedomway" and "American Negro Short Stories", delivered a lecture on "The Last Golden Age of Africa B. C.", sponsored by the African Afro-American Studies in Bluford Library.

During the period between 1306-1332, Clarke said, Africa experienced its last Golden Age. It reached its height in cultural advancement and lines of rulers. The period was certainly the "Apex of the African Empire." African nations, as all other nations of the world, experienced a rising and a falling in power. Africa fell for a number of reasons. For the most part, however, Africa fell because of the temperament of the people.

"When man fails to adjust to reality, he perishes," Clarke stated. The Africans failed to adjust to the rising Greeks and they fell. The same can be said of the Greeks. They failed to adjust to the Romans and they perished. "This happened several times in Africa. They did not adjust to the prevailing temperament of the times," the temperament at this time being of competition, conquest and dishonesty. "Africa was one of honesty — not a single European Treaty has been kept by them in their relationship to Africa. Africa's fall was not racial in nature, but a conditional thing; everything was competitive when Africa did not have to be competitive.

"The savage bit is an invention, just like race; there is no such thing as a Negro," Clarke said. "Color as a function of race is something new. . . it is a phony in science. There was no distinction between race and color prior to the Slave Trade. In fact, 400 years ago the word "race" did not exist." "Race and color," Clarke continued, "had to do with the rise and fall of power in the Ancient of

(CONTINUED ON PAGE 4)

Over 500 Students To Receive Degrees

More than 500 undergraduates are expected to receive degrees at the annual baccalaureate-commencement exercises at A&T State University, Sunday, June 1.

Speaker for the graduation will be Judge Elreta Alexander of Greensboro, first black woman jurist in the state. Herself a graduate of A&T, Judge Alexander will speak at 11 A.M. in the Charles H. Moore Gymnasium.

Also during the exercises, master of science degrees will be presented to 30 graduate students.

Other highlights of the commencement weekend will be reunions of the classes of 1909, 1919, 1929, 1939, 1949, and 1959, the annual meeting of the A&T National Alumni Association, and the annual alumni Awards Dinner.

Judge Alexander, who had been a successful practicing attorney in Greensboro, last November won a judgeship in one of Guilford County's district courts. She was also the first Negro woman to earn a law degree from the Columbia University School of Law. Judge Alexander formerly taught school and has published a volume of poems, "When Is A Man Free?"

Commencement activities will get underway Friday, May 30 with the Reunion Roundup at King's Inn from 5 to 7:30 P.M. The national alumni meeting will be Saturday morning at 10:30 A.M. in the Memorial Student Union.

The alumni will elect and install officers, including a new president to succeed the retiring Howard C. Barnhill, health educator from Charlotte.

The Reunion Luncheon will be held Saturday at 12:30 P.M. in the Union and the Awards Dinner will be held at 6:30 P.M. in King's Inn.

Immediately following the graduation exercises, President of the University, Dr. Lewis C. Dowdy will honor graduates and their parents at a reception in the Memorial Union.

Judge Elreta Alexander

Figure 11.1. The front page of the North Carolina A&T *Register* on 17 May 1969 depicts a college on the front lines of "Black Power" at the height of the movement. Courtesy F. D. Bluford Library Archives, North Carolina Agricultural and Technical State University.

The Syndicate: A&T and the Creation of SOBU

They called themselves "The Syndicate." Calvin Matthews, Leander Forbes, Vincent McCullough, W. Avon Drake, and Robert "Tazz" Anderson made up a small, informal fellowship of young, cool, and conscious "brothers" who had all arrived on A&T's campus in 1965 as freshmen. By the time they became upperclassmen, the young men had developed leadership skills as Student Government officials. McCullough, who later become SGA president, jokingly carried a folder marked "TOP SECRET" just to give the impression that he and his comrades were "in the know." But student life on A&T's campus in the latter half of the decade had produced a number of serious events that were no laughing matter, and the young men were determined to embrace the burgeoning movement.

College students across North Carolina were becoming more involved in activism, but by 1968 SNCC had lost its campus presence and there was no mass-based national black student organization. In January 1969, A&T students sent a delegation to the State Student Legislature, a statewide forum for college youth, with the hope of assuming a greater leadership role in the organization. It worked. John Tabb, an A&T student, was selected as the delegate to the National Student Association meeting later in February. Accompanied by members of "The Syndicate," the students arrived at the NSA meeting prepared to sharpen their focus on the concerns of black college students nationally. Black students at the NSA meeting listened intently as the Greensboro representatives advocated pulling out of the NSA altogether and forming their own organization, an idea that other students with black nationalist leanings embraced. "Before the discussion progressed further, Drake told the gathering that we already had an organization started at A&T and were planning a conference in the spring," recalled Syndicate member Leander Forbes. "When asked what was the organization's name, without hesitation, he blurted out, 'SOBU—Student Organization for Black Unity.' Though no such organization existed at the time, Drake asked Tazz, Vincent, and myself to go back to A&T and try to set things in place for the first meeting."[19]

This impromptu attempt of "The Syndicate" to make A&T the launching point for a new national organization could have backfired, had it not been for the fact that the black community of Greensboro had a tradition of organizing militant black youth. The conference was scheduled for May, and a number of Aggies were eager to welcome this new wave of like-minded young radicals to campus. Chief among them was Nelson Johnson, a young but experienced activist who had served as a "master organizer" with GAPP and was the incoming vice president of A&T's SGA. Johnson entered A&T as a student in 1965, the same year that the young men of "The Syndicate" first arrived on campus. But as an Air Force veteran, he was a nontraditional student who possessed a higher level of maturity and had been more politically astute than most campus activists. "What we need is a Black university to serve the needs of Black people," declared Johnson. "Such should be the goal and destiny of A&T State University."[20]

Designed to recapture and reimagine the fractured remains of SNCC, SOBU gathered on A&T's campus on 8 May 1969. Sixty black students from both predominately white and historically black colleges arrived at the first convening of SOBU. Echoing what Johnson had advocated, the students developed a platform infused with Black Power and black nationalism. SOBU moved quickly beyond the ideological debates surrounding purpose and membership that had so limited SNCC's campus presence in the mid-1960s. Student correspondent David Lee Brown reported that "SOBU was founded because there has been a growing desire and need on the part of students of Afro-American heritage to form a student organization that would be solely Black—physically, mentally and spiritually."[21] Brown's comment underscored the prevailing sentiment shared by frustrated black students who were prepared to define the future of the race without the involvement or input of white liberals. Greensboro was clearly an ideal setting for the militant youth, a fact that was not lost on the student organizers whose idea it was to bring the initial conference there. As the students began sorting out the future path of the organization, the city teetered on the verge of its most explosive round of racial violence yet.

Dudley High School stood as a beacon of pride for Greensboro's black community. It was the oldest black high school in the city and was less than four miles from A&T. Its close proximity to A&T helped forge bonds with college students who served as tutors, mentors, and role models for the high school students. Subsequently, when students at Dudley protested the student government election results, they found a sympathetic ear on campus. At issue was Claude Barnes, a young militant barred from assuming the presidency despite having enough write-in votes from his peers. The Dudley incident reflected one of the first generational divides in a community that had essentially been in lockstep throughout the turbulent decade. Not only did a number of older blacks struggle to embrace the aggressive political stance adopted by the youth, but a great many failed to warm up to the cultural stylings of a generation that appeared not to look the part. Historian William Chafe noted that four months prior to the election, "a male student had been suspended for wearing bib overalls to school. Before that the same punishment had been meted out to girls who wore 'Afros.'"[22]

What had begun as a cultural impasse between high school administrators and young people reflecting the dress and rhetoric of the times continued to smolder during the opening weeks of May. Beginning with Barnes's suspension on 7 May, students staged a walkout that garnered the support of A&T students. When the report of tension and trouble at Dudley arrived in the midst of the founding SOBU meeting, students reacted swiftly. Nelson Johnson shuttled a group of the SOBU conference attendees down to Dudley in an attempt to cool off what was becoming an increasingly tense setting. By May of 1969, Johnson had become the face of the movement in Greensboro and public enemy number one to the local white power structure. He was the chief coordinator for GAPP, a key player in the creation of SOBU, and the vice president of student government at A&T. The blame for the Dudley uprising quickly shifted to Johnson, leading to his arrest on trespassing charges. In assessing the direction of the liberation movement in the days after his trial, Johnson wrote, "To the degree that our analyses and interpretations are incorrect, we hope that our motives exonerate us to the generations that have gone before and those which must follow. To the degree that we are forced to use means of that we would not rather use, may God forgive us. The torch of liberation burns on for our people."[23] The commotion over Barnes's election was only the opening salvo. In the coming days, SOBU attendees, citizens of Greensboro, and the entire nation would witness a town under siege.

Ed Whitfield was a student at Cornell University when he arrived at the SOBU conference prepared to become further engaged in the movement. He was among many youth who had left the conference politically stimulated by what he had witnessed. As president of the Black Student Organization at Cornell, Whitfield helped to pioneer the Africana Studies program there, but Greensboro provided a laboratory for Whitfield to put theory into practice, a fact that would soon draw him back to the city. As SOBU participants returned to their respective campuses, they received the startling news of how violently Greensboro authorities had reacted to the escalating Dudley/A&T revolt. Whitfield recalled, "When I went back to school a few days later I looked in the newspaper, and on the front page of the *New York Times* here I see a picture of North Carolina A&T State University, Scott Hall with some National Guardsmen crouched down behind some barricades and I was telling people, you know I was just there a couple of days ago."[24]

Whitfield was describing the state's tactics to force the dissidents from A&T into line. On 23 May, two weeks after the initial melee at Dudley, A&T came under attack. Governor Bob Scott, whose name was affixed to the main male dormitory on campus, ordered National Guardsmen to sweep the university, thus "routing hundreds of students with gunfire and tear gas."[25] Targeting A&T seemed to be the logical strategy for state officials since the institution had been an enclave for young activists, a dominant source of insurgency in the city, and an influential locus for movement activity throughout the state. Steady protests at Dudley High School between 7 May and 23 May were fueled by activist energies emitted from the nearby university. Scott was determined to extinguish those energies by using the full resources of the state. Guardsmen stormed the male dormitories of Cooper and Scott Halls in an attempt to confiscate weapons that had been allegedly used by snipers. Dr. George Simpkins, former president of the local chapter of the NAACP, recalled, "You could hear the tanks coming up the street at 5:00 in the morning to move on to the campus."[26] University president Lewis Dowdy had already ordered students to leave by 6:00 p.m. that evening due to the brewing conflict. However, male students awoke that morning to the sounds of gunfire as rounds penetrated the walls of the dormitory. Vernice Wright, a student writer for the *A&T Register,* reported: "Dowdy made it quite clear that no authority, referring to Mayor Elam and Police Chief, Paul Calhoun, notified him of the intended 'sweep' of Cooper and Scott Halls. . . . Consequently, male students there were subjected to tear gas and were marched from their living quarters in towels thrown around the waist and in pajamas. . . . Dowdy added that upon completing the search of the two male dormitories, only two operable weapons were found by the guards."[27]

In the wake of the attack, students were stunned to discover that Willie Grimes, a freshman from Greenville, North Carolina, had been shot and killed by unknown assailants; several more were injured. What started as the demands of high school students to be dealt with fairly had transformed A&T's campus into a war zone. The federal government called for congressional hearings, thus providing a national forum to expose the root cause of the revolt. The State Advisory Committee issued a report entitled *Trouble in Greensboro,* which concluded that "law and order must be accompanied by justice. . . . The State of North Carolina and the city of Greensboro must show to all, but especially to black students, that the law is neutral and race plays no part in its enforcement. The North Carolina National Guard cannot take pride in its actions at A&T State University."[28] Despite these findings, the state did virtually nothing to make amends for its assault on A&T, and the murder of Grimes continues to go unsolved.

The violent end to the academic year at A&T left the campus physically and emotionally scarred, but it did not break the students' resolve to remain committed to the principles of Black Power. In its fledgling state, SOBU also remained dedicated to the cause upon which the organization was founded and continued to look toward Greensboro and North Carolina more broadly as a foundation for new efforts. The group's first conference had hosted 60 students and even during its inception fittingly took place in the middle of a civil insurrection centered on the rights of black youth. Members returned to North Carolina in November 1969 for their second conference, this time converging on Durham. Their numbers had increased tenfold. Six hundred students attended from across the country and appointed Nelson Johnson as their national convener. In their second meeting, students further outlined their goals and vision. A correspondent from A&T reported, "As a result of the SOBU conference, a better communication between Black campuses is being developed. A SOBU newspaper will be started with plans for bi-monthly publication."[29]

SOBU was becoming a national organization, but it would remain linked to the Greensboro community in which it was born. This was due in large part to the continued presence of Nelson Johnson, who now assumed leadership roles on campus, in GAPP, and in SOBU. Despite the tragedy of the events in Greensboro, the Dudley/A&T revolt and the founding of SOBU in the city demonstrated that the civil rights movement was very much alive in North Carolina. Within activist circles, A&T was becoming a proving ground for a more radical form of protest, a fact that was championed by many of its students. Some students interpreted the standoff with law enforcement as a victory. As the *A&T Register* reported, " 'The image of A&T is an all time high as far as Blacks are concerned,' emphasized Johnson. 'If the enrollment is down,' he commented, 'the students at A&T are not to blame. If whites are afraid to attend sports events on this campus, that too was unfortunate. But the blood Willie E. Grimes shed was noble blood and he died in this country for his people.' At this time the audience again interrupted Johnson with applause."[30]

Tensions in the city remained elevated as students returned. Much to the chagrin of Greensboro's city leaders, SOBU dropped a permanent anchor in Greensboro and was prepared to carry on the organizing tradition that had made SNCC legendary in civil rights circles. Unlike other southern cities such as Birmingham or Jackson, the movement in Greensboro was escalating by the end of the decade, a fact that drew even more proponents of Black Power. Both GAPP and the Foundation for Community Development had intimate experience in working with students. GAPP itself was comprised of many current and former students from A&T, and the FCD had created the student internship program that led to the establishment of GAPP. Howard Fuller, who served as the head of the FCD, believed that education was the most important front in the war against white supremacy. As a witness to the spirit of insurgency that was swirling around A&T and Greensboro, Fuller brought a new and innovative African American educational institution to Greensboro that continued to raise the city's profile among Black Power proponents.

Founded in the wake of black student protests at Duke University in 1969, Malcolm X Liberation University was the radical outgrowth of a new argument for independent schools that advanced a curriculum designed to liberate the minds and communities of black people. In its second year of operation, founder

Howard Fuller relocated MXLU to Greensboro and staffed the school with community volunteers and members of SOBU. Among them was Ed Whitfield. Whitfield represented the type of young, idealistic black nationalist who was committed to the work of SOBU. "All I knew for sure was that I was dedicated to spending my life trying to improve the condition of the community of which I was a part," Whitfield recalled, "and to be a part of the struggle that had been part of my consciousness since childhood. And that's what brought me to Greensboro."[31]

With GAPP, MXLU, and SOBU all maintaining a heavy presence in the city, it was clear that by 1971, Greensboro had become, as William Chafe noted, "the center of Black Power in the South."[32] The mobilization and organizing that characterized the black political landscape of Greensboro was punctuated by the ideology of black nationalism. As A&T alumnus Jesse Jackson reminded black America at the 1972 National Black Political Convention in Gary, Indiana, it was "nation time."[33] Howard Fuller's effort to launch MXLU was being duplicated through other channels in Greensboro. GAPP and SOBU also supported the efforts of disenchanted Dudley High School students in developing the Willie Ernest Grimes Freedom School for secondary and primary training, whose goal it was to establish "authentic independent Black education institutions for themselves."[34] In a 1970 *Ebony* magazine article, leading black scholar Vincent Harding captured the evolution of these new educational endeavors: "Although the movement towards a Black University has often been misunderstood, misinterpreted, and sometimes misguided, it has touched every one of the traditionally black campuses, and in some cases has pressed faculties, administrations, and trustees into black oriented directions which were unforeseen a few years earlier."[35]

Harding's characterization of reform efforts as "misunderstood, misinterpreted, and sometimes misguided" was not reserved for black education alone. The Black Power era suffered from external and internal factors that threatened its longevity. These factors would soon arrest the development of the movement and create major problems for both GAPP and SOBU.

Rifts and Schisms: The Fracturing of SOBU and Black Power in Greensboro

For young activists who subscribed to black nationalism, Pan-Africanism represented the next logical step in their ideological transformation. If the concept of nation-building began as an effort to go block by block and school by school in an attempt to construct self-determination and empowerment, then the decision to cast a wider net across the diaspora seemed a rational transition. In discussing the objectives of SOBU, Ed Whitfield recalled, "Before there was an African

Liberation Support Committee and African Liberation Day, we organized at the United Nations in the spring of 1970 in commemoration of the Sharpeville massacre."[36] SOBU's decision to sharpen its focus on worldwide struggles against white supremacy was the beginning of an increasingly divisive debate over the proper path to liberation.

From pool halls to dorm rooms, black youth debated and discussed the ideas of Marxism, cultural nationalism, and Pan-Africanism, all the while fixated on the overarching theme of liberation. What developed in the midst of these discussions was what Nelson Johnson would later refer to as a sort of "blacker than thou" mentality.[37] A&T offered itself as an ideal repository for these competing beliefs, as young intellectuals matched wits and arguments into the wee hours of the morning. Stokely Carmichael arrived on campus in 1971 (one of several visits Carmichael made to A&T) outlining the problem that would continue to afflict the movement for years to come. "Now from South Africa to Nova Scotia, the Black world finds itself in political chaos," Carmichael declared to the overflowing gymnasium. "We are in political chaos simply because we do not have a common ideology which represents our common interests. . . . Thus, it is necessary for us to seek an ideology around which we can be unified."[38] Although Carmichael was a committed Pan-Africanist, it remained to be seen what, if any, theory would unite and guide the development of black empowerment in Greensboro and beyond.

This debate was not new. The struggle for black liberation in America is replete with cases of theoretical disunity. The inability to coordinate efforts of competing organizations had in many ways impeded black progress in the past, and it threatened to do so in Greensboro during the Black Power era. Ed Whitfield's journey to Greensboro as an activist with MXLU and SOBU was a rocky one. He came to realize that in a growing number of political circles, diverging points of view and competing theories were not welcome. A growing critique of classism garnered the attention of many radical youth who sought to broaden the civil rights movement beyond its concerns with the color line as defined by W. E. B. Du Bois. Whitfield wrote a controversial editorial in SOBU's national newspaper, *The African World*, declaring that the civil rights movement "was dead." He argued instead for a sea change in the struggle for liberation that would embrace broader proletarian concerns. His peers were not supportive. Whitfield recalled, "I remember people looked at it and got angry because they thought I was saying everything was okay. I was one of the people that was struggling a lot inside of SOBU for . . . trying to look at how the workers' movement was developing, and the extent that that's going to begin to address . . . economic issues."[39]

SOBU reflected a paradigm shift that was causing tension throughout the Black Power movement. Militants influenced and persuaded by the grassroots antipoverty campaigns of the late 1960s debated the efficiency of movements predicated on race-based analysis. For a growing number of activists, the mantra of "power to the people" now expanded beyond race to include the struggle against capitalist exploitation. This new discourse encompassed poor whites victimized by the class line, though it tended to ignore the cultural roots of African people, a fact that was unsettling to many black nationalists. Reflecting this shift, in 1972 SOBU shed its singular identification with students and renamed itself the Youth Organization for Black Unity, a move that signaled a broader concern with capitalism, political economy, and class analysis. Greensboro and A&T seemed to be a perfect setting to inject Marxian principles. Students there had joined with cafeteria workers in the months before the Dudley uprising, and there were black workers in Greensboro who aligned themselves with GAPP's agenda by serving as volunteers. However, it was difficult to sell an anticapitalist message to many first-generation college students who had been sent off to school to make their parents proud by gaining entrance to an expanding middle class. "The initial perspective of the young student activists was that of militant reformers," wrote sociologist Rod Bush. "They wanted to make a place for themselves in the system."[40] Thus the transition to youth workers from students alienated a great many Aggies—A&T alumni—a factor that weakened the Black Power movement on campus in the 1970s.

As the 1970s dawned, GAPP and SOBU were confronted with the same issues that other civil rights groups were struggling with. Cooptation, surveillance, and repression from government officials and local authorities presented a litany of problems for committed black radicals, but several organizations and institutions were additionally burdened with a leadership crisis stemming from a seemingly growing field of opportunists. Limited access to the financial resources needed to keep their agendas afloat and their doors open presented yet another challenge, undermining the effectiveness and longevity of grassroots efforts. However, the flames of internal discord were most often fanned by the controversy over the direction of the movement.

But before this decline occurred, GAPP and SOBU made an impact on Greensboro. With former students from A&T at the helm, GAPP successfully organized strikes among public school cafeteria workers, sanitation workers, blind workers employed with Industries of the Blind, and exploited tenants in public housing. For people living in condemned homes and renting substandard property in Greensboro, GAPP's protest for immediate reform and restitution resonated far more strongly than ideas of black nationhood.

The black tenants of Greensboro's public housing might be able to relate to the struggles of black people in the slums of Soweto and the shanty towns of Brazil or the dreams of complete black autonomy as expressed within the tenets of black nationalism. Yet the more pressing matter was pragmatism. Organizers needed feasible and accessible methods of protest that would deliver basic services and human rights to their constituents. In their estimation, Marxism increasingly became a more attractive philosophy than the Pan-Africanist theories embraced sometimes by SOBU and exclusively by the leadership of MXLU. As SOBU leader Nelson Johnson recalled, "Community people in Greensboro also criticized pan-Africanists for doing nothing but talk. They told us that waiting for African revolution is no solution for everyday folks."[41]

While Marxism failed to attract aspiring middle-class students, Pan-Africanism and cultural nationalism most certainly did. Several students on A&T's campus relished intimidating older professors with the aggressive rhetoric of Black Power and vowed to defend the black community against the imperialist forces of America. Their language was bold and brash, attracting students who were both committed to the rhetoric and those who were simply curious to see what defiant move they would take next. Although there was no credible threat of Black Panther Party organizing within Greensboro, a handful of students did gravitate toward the idea of self-defense.[42] A group of A&T students calling themselves the Black Liberation Front promoted a more aggressive stance on campus by stashing weapons and declaring their intention to use them against white aggressors, echoing Black Panther rhetoric and tactics. One student characterized them as "walking around with their tams and black shirts and pants—everything was black—urging students to join the Panthers."[43] While the BLF's violent tone attracted the curiosity of their fellow students, it failed to resonate en masse, rendering BLF a spectacle and not a mass-based campus movement. What the organization did accomplish was establish itself as a touchstone for defiant black manhood and womanhood, an important ideological current that was well represented in various elements of the Black Power era. However, there was method to what many conservatives perceived to be the madness of Black Power.

The spirit of nation-building and Pan-Africanism blossomed on A&T's campus. Pressure was mounting against HBCUs to move from veiled expressions of their racial identity to explicit endorsement of all things black. Debates over the infusion of white liberalism greatly impacted the longevity of SNCC, a fact that SOBU leaders appeared determined not to repeat by unequivocally embracing the rhetoric of Black Power. Building on SNCC's post-1966 agenda, SOBU created significant inroads that linked them with the global struggle for black liberation. Historian Anthony James Ratcliff noted: "Just as SNCC activists had developed the Pan-African Skills Project and Drum and Spear Bookstore, which built direct links with progressive African governments, SOBU established a Pan-African Medical Program providing Southern African liberation movements, as well as community health centers in the U.S., with vitally needed medical supplies, tools, and money."[44]

In addition to the Pan-African Medical Program, SOBU adopted several more programs that were framed by the concepts of black nationalism. Among them were the Save and Change Black Schools Program, the National Community Work Program, and participation in the formation of the African Liberation Support Committee. Their main source of pride also operated as their main source of communication and was firmly in the shadows of the Universal Negro Improvement Association: *The African World*. SOBU's newspaper clearly mirrored itself after Marcus Garvey's *The Negro World* and enjoyed a wide readership, considering its limited financial resources. By 1974, they boasted a circulation including 49 states and 30 countries.[45]

SOBU's expansion on a national level was due in no small part to intense organizing by a cadre of dedicated student activists. Black students exchanged ideas through *The African World* and campus newsletters. But they also fragmented with considerable speed, as various leaders and ideologies jockeyed for position. The spirit and idea of SOBU quickly split into new Black Power cells. The National Association of Black Students, the Pan African Students Organization in the Americas, and the Congress of African Students soon joined SOBU on the political landscape of student activism. These new outgrowths became engaged in robust ideological debates, with NABS and CAS soon adopting the same Marxist paradigm that SOBU eventually embraced, a transformation that did not go untested by those who disagreed with the move.

Battling for ideological hegemony did not immediately impede SOBU's early growth or influence. SOBU, like most other civil rights organizations, found its strength in coordinating local people and dispatched a number of student activists into the field to draw new youth to its cause. Ed Whitfield, who served as the Northeast Regional Coordinator, mobilized students from the New York area before dedicating his full energies to Malcolm X Liberation University after 1970. Gene Locke, a dedicated student activist from Houston, directed organizing efforts in Texas. Tim Thomas coordinated SOBU efforts in Washington, D.C., and Ron "Slim" Washington, a standout basketball player turned fulltime activist, led a group of black radicals who organized students in Colorado, Kansas, and throughout the Midwest.

But the heart of SOBU was Greensboro. Even as the organization began to cast a wide net throughout the country and throughout the diaspora, the work and mobilizing taking place in North Carolina directed SOBU's agenda. Besides the fact that the national headquarters were located in Greensboro, SOBU's working relationship with MXLU and GAPP and close proximity to A&T gave them the

drive and direction to lead both local and national efforts. Underscoring Howard Fuller's attraction to Greensboro, historian Cedric Johnson noted, "Ever since
the historic 1960 lunch counter sit-ins, the Greensboro area had been a locus of
militant black political activity and was, therefore, home to dense local network
of organizations and activists."[46] When Fuller (who by the beginning of the 1970s
was going by the name Owusu Sadaukai) promoted the idea of African Liberation
Day in 1972, he requested that SOBU members Nelson Johnson and Jerry Walker
serve as the North Carolina state coordinators of the national effort. Johnson and
Walker recruited campus leaders from Shaw University, Bennett College, North
Carolina Central, Winston Salem State, and UNC-Charlotte to support the new
initiative.[47] The efforts of SOBU and other nationally prominent civil rights organizations resulted in the convergence of over sixty thousand demonstrators in San
Francisco, Washington, D.C., and Toronto on 27 May who defiantly called for an
end to Africa's occupation by foreign powers. In doing so, activists linked themselves with freedom fighters across the global diaspora who were also engaged in a
struggle against imperialism and white supremacy.

Reflections: The Legacy of Student Activism within the Black Power Era

The politicization of black youth elevated the discourse surrounding the struggle
for black liberation. One of the lasting effects of these student/youth formations
was the establishment of black student unions and centers at several predominantly white universities. As the Black Power movement sputtered and stalled
from the 1970s on, new enclaves for black youth ensured that the injection of racial
consciousness that had long been a mission of the black colleges that produced the
activism of the sixties would remain an empowering and transformative force.

Black college students also embraced forms of cultural nationalism to counter-
act an inferiority stigma that had lasted for generations. The flourishing of black
culture in art, fashion, and music cannot be overstated for the indelible impact it
had in defining the late 1960s and much of the 1970s. Recalling such a moment he
experienced on campus as a student at A&T, former activist Claude Barnes noted:
"It was a hell of a thing to watch Nina Simone come on stage in her combat boots
and talk about how she had heard so much about A&T. And this was not just an
act, she had heard about the students at A&T and they had a reputation that was
well deserved because again anytime there was any issue that the Black community was concerned about, the A&T students were there."[48]

Perhaps the most lasting impact of Pan-Africanist theory as it was generated
during the modern civil rights movement was the creation of Black Studies as a

discipline, which in turn spawned a plethora of ethnic and gender studies departments throughout the country. The arrival of Black Studies was an unprecedented shift for the intellectual world. Never before had the academy been held hostage (figuratively and literally) or witnessed the vehement demands from students to recognize their heritage and culture as a legitimate field of study. Although A&T failed to create a Black Studies department, race consciousness remained vibrant on campus as the university responded to student concerns by instituting the African/Afro-American House, now known as the Mattye Reed African Heritage Museum. A&T also provided courses on race that were offered throughout the academic year and continued to bring high-profile activists to campus for students to engage.

While the struggle in Greensboro offered several illustrations of the generational divide that characterized the counterculture movement, it also demonstrated an existing partnership not witnessed in most other places. Administrators and several faculty members at both A&T and Bennett served as both official and unofficial advisors to their students engaged in the movement. The old guard of Greensboro's black community developed a working relationship with young radicals with whom they often sympathized, particularly when the white power structure used violent coercion against black youth. As Chafe noted, when Malcolm X Liberation University relocated to Greensboro, "virtually the entire roster of established black leaders turned out to welcome the new facility."[49] Nevertheless, Black Power politics was distasteful to many members of the old guard black elite. Regardless of the increased movement activity that pushed Greensboro to the forefront of the black freedom struggle and created positive outlets for marginalized African Americans throughout the city, there was a growing sentiment of contention from those who held fast to the goals that had defined the early civil rights movement. Historian Devin Fergus noted, "In many ways MXLU's institutional existence was increasingly recognized as a paradigmatic repudiation of the integrationists agenda mobilized during the Greensboro sit-ins in 1960."[50]

Despite the general distrust that divided the young against the old during the Black Power era, the relationships forged in the Greensboro community reflected deep and abiding African traditions. The general respect afforded to their elders who often provided them counsel was clearly displayed in a leaflet disseminated in Greensboro by SOBU entitled "To Our Moms and Pops from the Black Radicals." In part it read, "It may seem to you sometimes that we act too swiftly or dangerously," said the youth of SOBU. "The whole matter boils down to an honest and dedicated effort to improve the lot of our people in this city and indeed the world. We ask that you consider this point strongly. Think of the situation as if your own son or daughter were talking with you."[51] SOBU's attempt to reach out across the generational divide reflected a genuine effort to build bridges to sustain a movement that was faltering on various fronts. Young black activists concretely understood the need to foster relationships with those who had constructed earlier inroads toward freedom. Efforts to patch broken relationships and build a unified coalition proved fruitless, as compromise between the young and the old soon became the least of the worries confronting dissidents in Greensboro.

The idealism that swept colleges, churches, shotgun houses, and ghettoes convinced countless black folks that full liberation would soon be within reach. However, with external factors mounting against the movement, internal divisions frustrated activists committed to the struggle. Infighting, splinter groups, disaffection, and even sabotage muffled intellectual exchange and damaged opportunities to achieve mutual understanding. Debates over Marxism, cultural nationalism, and Pan-Africanism formed a triangulation of ideological discord that fueled animosity between friends and warring factions. On a national scale, the Black Panther Party provided the best illustration of the disharmony that was consuming various outlets for Black Power politics. "In the end, neither side scored a victory and the biggest loser turned out to be the party itself," wrote Panther historian Curtis Austin in documenting the split between the Newton and Cleaver camps. "The open warfare compelled members to leave the organization in droves."[52] Complete denunciation and repudiation of diverging theories kept many organizations in static positions, unable to find common ground with those who professed a desire to advance the freedom movement.

In Greensboro, these polarizing forces crippled the efforts of both SOBU and GAPP. The divisions within SOBU over ideological direction led many of the officers who resided in Greensboro to direct their time and energy into local organizing as spearheaded by GAPP, thus leaving SOBU with little direction from the national headquarters. However, the organization whose efforts had transformed Greensboro into a stronghold of the Black Power movement and served as a springboard for SOBU was on its last legs by 1974. Comprised of a broad cross-section of the black community, GAPP's struggles demonstrated how the movement was dissipating on all fronts. Many youth were becoming disenchanted, committed adult activists clung to limited resources, and the white power structure strengthened its efforts to suppress the demands of the once-formidable organization. "GAPP is at a low point: we have no money; there is no program; the board is confused, disorganized and weak; the staff is virtually non-existent," wrote Nelson Johnson. "We have reached a point where a clear decision must be made. We must declare whether we are going to close shop and go home or whether we are going to reorganize, reconstruct, and, indeed rebuild."[53] GAPP's legacy is one that deserves greater study. Despite its brief life, GAPP was not only one of the most effective local organizations, it also left a wide national imprint. SOBU and its offshoots can all trace their developmental roots back to the mobilization that occurred on behalf of the North Carolina nationalists, chiefly residing in Greensboro.

The internal divisions that characterized the Black Power era are part of a historical pattern that defined the struggle for black liberation long before the civil rights movement. In documenting the history of the Negro Sanhedrin, a confederation of six major civil rights organizations formed in 1923, historian C. Alvin Hughes chronicles the disbandment of the organization in 1925 due in large part to the arrest and removal of the group's chief adversary, Marcus Garvey. Hughes wrote, "Thus, the United Front Movement, which did not include Garvey . . . no longer pressed toward its goal of national unity."[54] In his seminal work *The Golden Age of Black Nationalism,* Wilson Jeremiah Moses suggested: "Du Bois's public exchanges with Garvey were healthy for the black community. They made it clear to white America that all black people are not stamped out of the same mold, that all do not have the same aspirations or the same values. . . . While some may wring their hands and lament the disunity that was publicly displayed, others may be inclined to argue that this was the essence of the Harlem Renaissance, an organic flourishing of emotion."[55] Moses' analysis is partly right. There is, however, a thin line between the "flourishing of emotion" and the diminished opportunity to exchange freely in healthy debate over common goals. A number of student activists surrendered to divisions that were both political and personal in nature. Perhaps looking back on opportunities missed, a 1975 editorial from *The African World,* the voice of SOBU, poignantly stated, "Remember, those who deprecate theory in fact, deprecate revolution."[56] The ideological divisions that impaired efforts to form a united front in the first half of the twentieth century were largely organic in nature. However, the rifts between numerous civil rights organizations during the 1960s and 1970s were often orchestrated and exacerbated by external forces, weakening overall efforts and hastening the demise of the movement. Nevertheless, veterans of the movement often reflect on the triumph over what was and disappointedly wonder what could have been.

Black colleges were central to the flowering of the Black Power movement, as they were to the wave of national insurgency that first unfolded in 1960. The race consciousness that was infused into their curriculum benefited students who in turn learned identity, purpose, and mission. They were steeped in a racial and pedagogical tradition that translated into more assertive demonstrations for justice, profoundly shaping who they were as students and as activists. As the movement began to unravel due to various causes, colleges like A&T were still making valuable contributions to the struggle and advancing a Black Power agenda that was transformative for the consciousness and communities of African Americans.

It is no surprise, therefore, that organizations like SOBU were directly linked to educational institutions such as A&T that served as political enclaves and helped to revitalize the concepts of freedom and democracy for all Americans.

NOTES

1. "Howard Fuller Addresses Black Student Conference," *A&T Register*, 10 Oct. 1969, North Carolina A&T State Univ. Archives.

2. William Chafe has written the authoritative work on the civil rights movement in Greensboro. Chafe traces student activism in Greensboro back to the 1930s and gives several examples of students from Bennett College and North Carolina A&T actively participating in demonstrations against Jim Crow long before the famous sit-ins of 1960. However, Chafe's community study of Greensboro presents a partial view of campus life as it related to activism at A&T. His attention to cultural patterns, protest traditions, and community institutions throughout the city provides room for more detailed analysis of student life and the progenitors of insurgency at A&T. See Chafe, *Civilities and Civil Rights: Greensboro, North Carolina, and the Black Struggle for Freedom* (New York: Oxford Univ. Press, 1980).

3. Taylor Branch, *Parting the Waters: America in the King Years, 1954–1963* (New York: Simon and Schuster, 1988), 276.

4. Jibreel Khazan, interview with the author, 8 July 1999, tapes in author's possession.

5. This unique coalition across class lines in Greensboro diverges from the narrative of most other communities on the front lines of the civil rights movement. For example, historian Hasan Jeffries documents that the SNCC campaign in Lowndes County, Alabama, illustrates black professionals who failed to embrace a political agenda that included the plight of working-class and poor blacks. For more on SNCC and Lowndes County, see Jeffries, *Bloody Lowndes: Civil Rights and Black Power in Alabama's Black Belt* (New York: NYU Press, 2009).

6. For more on the mass jail-ins in Greensboro, see August Meier and Elliot Rudwick, *CORE: A Study in the Civil Rights Movement, 1942–1968* (Urbana: Univ. of Illinois Press, 1975); Chafe, *Civilities and Civil Rights*; and Tom Dent, *Southern Journey: Return to the Civil Rights Movement* (New York: William Morrow, 1997).

7. Claude Barnes, interview with the author, 23 Dec. 1998, tapes in author's possession.

8. The term *white power structure* is used often in civil rights discourse. In Greensboro, like many other American cities, the power structure included city hall, housing authorities, law enforcement, and financial institutions. Additionally, these various forms of more institutionalized racism were both explicitly and tacitly supported by a number of average white citizens, some of whom resorted to more violent forms of coercion. There are numerous studies that examine the transformation to Black Power within SNCC. For more on this ideological evolution, see Clayborne Carson, *In Struggle: SNCC and the Black Awakening of the 1960s* (Cambridge, MA: Harvard Univ. Press, 1981); John Dittmer, *Local People: The Struggle for Civil Rights in Mississippi* (Urbana: Univ. of Illinois Press, 1995); Charles Payne, *I've Got the Light of Freedom: The Organizing Tradition and the Mississippi Freedom Struggle* (Berkeley: Univ. of California Press, 1995); Cynthia Griggs Fleming, *Soon We Will Not Cry: The Liberation of Ruby Doris Smith Robinson* (Lanham, MD: Rowman and Littlefield, 1998); Stokely Carmichael, *Ready for Revolution: The Life and Struggles of Stokely Carmichael* (New York: Scribner, 2003); Christopher Strain, *Pure Fire: Self Defense as Activism in the Civil Rights Era* (Athens: Univ. of Georgia Press 2005); Wesley Hogan, *Many Minds, One Heart:*

SNCC's Dream for a New America (Chapel Hill: Univ. of North Carolina Press, 2007); and Jeffries, *Bloody Lowndes.*

9. Chafe, *Civilities and Civil Rights,* 213.

10. For more on the class divisions SNCC activists uncovered, see Jeffries, *Bloody Lowndes.*

11. The author has been given access to the unprocessed papers of the Greensboro Association of Poor People (GAPP), a vital organization to the civil rights movement in Greensboro. Lewis Brandon, a former student at A&T and a longtime activist in Greensboro, has collected the GAPP papers over time. The GAPP papers are four boxes that contain memoirs, minutes, flyers, essays by local and national activists, and correspondence related to GAPP activity. They also contain papers relating to the Student Organization for Black Unity (SOBU). These papers contain copies of the SOBU newspaper, *The African World,* correspondence between activists, flyers, newsletters, and newspaper clippings. These papers are currently in the possession of the author. Lula M. Pennix to Scarborough Realty Company, 22 Jan. 1969, Greensboro Association of Poor People Papers, personal archive of Mr. Lewis Brandon.

12. Students enrolled in the internship program represented a cross-section of North Carolina colleges. Those students included: Rosalyn Woodward (North Carolina A&T State University), Catherine Watson (Duke University), Peggy Richmond (Bennett College), Larry McCleary (Fayetteville State College), Charles Hopkins (Duke University), and Lacy Joyner (North Carolina College). All students were placed in Greensboro for their internship in community organizing, a factor that strengthened the possibility for continued use of Greensboro as a laboratory for social activism. See A. S. Webb to Paul Gezon, 22 July 1968, Greensboro Association of Poor People Papers, personal archive of Mr. Lewis Brandon.

13. Greensboro Association of Poor People Fact Sheet, Greensboro Association of Poor People Papers, personal archive of Mr. Lewis Brandon.

14. Claude Barnes interview, 23 Dec. 1998.

15. Lillie Miller, "Students Aid Workers in Obtaining Demands," *A&T Register,* 20 Mar. 1969, North Carolina A&T State Univ. Archives.

16. Sociologist Aldon Morris defined the concept of "local movement centers," which refers to the generation of activism amongst an aggrieved population by a specific organization or entity. See Aldon Morris, *The Origins of the Civil Rights Movement: Black Communities Organizing for Change* (New York: Free Press, 1984).

17. Cohen N. Greene, "Police Open Fire on Students in Wake of Campus Disturbance," *A&T Register,* 20 Mar. 1969.

18. Horace Ferguson, "From Plantation to Hunting Ground," *A&T Register,* 28 Mar. 1969.

19. Leander Forbes, "Reflective Notes on May 1969 at North Carolina A&T State University," Greensboro Association of Poor People Papers, personal archive of Lewis Brandon.

20. Nelson Johnson, "Projection in Blackness," Greensboro Association of Poor People Papers, personal archive of Lewis Brandon.

21. David Lee Brown, "University to Be Site of First Conference for Black Students," *A&T Register,* 2 May 1969.

22. Chafe, *Civilities and Civil Rights,* 185.

23. Nelson Johnson to Lewis Brandon, 1 Nov. 1969, Greensboro Association of Poor People Papers, personal archive of Mr. Lewis Brandon.

24. Ed Whitfield, testimony to the Greensboro Truth and Reconciliation Commission, Public Hearing no. 1, 16 July 2005.

25. "650 Troops Sweep A&T," *Greensboro Daily News,* 23 May 1969.

26. Dr. George Simpkins interview, 12 July 1999.

27. Vernice Wright, "Hearing Indicates Racist City," *A&T Register,* 10 Oct. 1969.

28. North Carolina Advisory Committee to the U.S. Commission on Civil Rights, *Trouble in Greensboro: A Report of an Open Meeting concerning Disturbances at Dudley High School and North Carolina A&T State University* (1970) (CR1.2:T75), 14.

29. "Over 600 Attend SOBU Conference," *A&T Register,* 7 Nov. 1969.

30. "Johnson Assails Student Press," *A&T Register,* 26 Sept. 1969.

31. Ed Whitfield testimony to the Greensboro Truth and Reconciliation Commission, Public Hearing no. 1, 16 July 2005.

32. Chafe, *Civilities and Civil Rights,* 220.

33. Peniel Joseph, *Waiting 'Til the Midnight Hour: A Narrative History of Black Power in America* (New York: Henry Holt, 2006), 280.

34. Position Paper no. 1, July 1970, Greensboro Association of Poor People Papers, personal archive of Mr. Lewis Brandon.

35. Vincent Harding, "Toward the Black University," *Ebony,* Aug. 1970, 156–59.

36. Ed Whitfield testimony to the Greensboro Truth and Reconciliation Commission, Public Hearing no. 1, 16 July 2005.

37. Chafe, *Civilities and Civil Rights,* 181.

38. Transcription of speech delivered by Stokely Carmichael, 21 Mar. 1971, Greensboro Association of Poor People Papers, personal archive Mr. Lewis Brandon.

39. Ed Whitfield, testimony to the Greensboro Truth and Reconciliation Commission, Public Hearing no. 1, 16 July 2005.

40. Rod Bush, *We Are Not What We Seem: Black Nationalism and Class Struggle in the American Century* (New York: NYU Press, 1999), 160.

41. Sally Bermanzohn, *Through Survivors Eyes: From the Sixties to the Greensboro Massacre* (Nashville, TN: Vanderbilt Univ. Press, 2003), 121.

42. Only 24 miles away from Greensboro was one of the strongest Black Panther Party (BPP) chapters in the southeast. The Winston Salem BPP blossomed under the leadership of Nelson Malloy and created a number of local initiatives that benefited the local black population. Despite the fact that the BPP never took a strong root in Greensboro, the presence of the BPP in Winston Salem made the Triad Area a formidable stronghold for Black Power politics. For more on the Panthers in Winston Salem and the history of the organization's efforts to coordinate at the local level, see Curtis Austin, *Up against the Wall: Violence in the Making and Unmaking of the Black Panther Party* (Fayetteville: Univ. of Arkansas Press, 2008); Judson L. Jeffries, *Comrades: A Local History of the Black Panther Party* (Bloomington: Indiana Univ. Press, 2007); Judson L. Jeffries, *On the Ground: The Black Panther Party in Communities across America* (Oxford: Univ. Press of Mississippi, 2010); Peniel Joseph, *Neighborhood Rebels: Black Power at the Local Level* (New York: Palgrave Mcmillan, 2010); and Donna Jean Murch, *Living for the City: Migration, Education, and the Rise of the Black Panther Party in Oakland, California* (Chapel Hill: Univ. of North Carolina Press, 2010).

43. Chafe, *Civilities and Civil Rights,* 181.

44. Anthony James Ratcliff, "Liberation at the End of a Pen: Writing Pan-African Politics of Cultural Struggle" (PhD diss., Univ. of Massachusetts Amherst, 2009).

45. Youth Organization for Black Unity, "Proposal for Expansion of Printing Capabilities and the Establishment of a 'Marketplace' Operation," Greensboro Association of Poor People Papers, personal archive Mr. Lewis Brandon.

46. Cedric Johnson, *Revolutionaries to Race Leaders: Black Power and the Making of African American Politics* (Minneapolis: Univ. of Minnesota Press, 2007), 137.

47. "African Liberation Day Coordinating Committee in Greensboro," Greensboro Association of Poor People Papers, personal archive of Mr. Lewis Brandon.

48. Claude Barnes interview, 23 Dec. 1998.

49. Chafe, *Civilities and Civil Rights,* 219.

50. Devin Fergus, *Liberalism, Black Power, and the Making of American Politics, 1965–1980* (Athens: Univ. of Georgia Press, 2009), 80.

51. "To Our Moms and Pops, From the Black Radicals," Greensboro Association of Poor People Papers, personal archive of Mr. Lewis Brandon.

52. Austin provides an excellent analysis of the division that existed between Huey P. Newton and Eldridge Cleaver, one that was manipulated by the FBI. The former vowed to bring the Panthers above ground and fight discrimination through more traditional means, while the latter favored the armed self-defense strategies broadly associated with early Panther tactics. See Austin, *Up against the Wall,* 326.

53. "A Proposal for a New Thrust—1974 and Beyond," Greensboro Association of Poor People Papers, personal archive of Mr. Lewis Brandon.

54. C. Alvin Hughes, "The Negro Sanhedrin Movement," *Journal of Negro History* 69, no. 1 (Winter 1984): 11.

55. Wilson Jeremiah Moses, *The Golden Age of Black Nationalism, 1850–1925* (Oxford, U.K.: Oxford Univ. Press, 1978), 249.

56. "The Importance of Theory," *The African World* 4, no. 11 (July 1975), Greensboro Association of Poor People Papers, personal archive of Mr. Lewis Brandon.

CHAPTER TWELVE

Black Power and the
Freedom Movement in Retrospect

CLEVELAND L. SELLERS JR.

My experience as a student and activist in the freedom struggle afforded me the unique opportunity to be a part and product of history. A member of the Student Nonviolent Coordinating Committee and its program director from 1965 to 1967, my résumé reads like an account of the movement. I participated in the protests at Selma, the March on Washington, and the Mississippi Freedom Summer campaign. I heard the call for Black Power and refused to be drafted into the Vietnam War. I was there when officers of the South Carolina State Patrol turned their guns on the state's own young citizens in Orangeburg and then blamed me for inciting the riot. I was at Cornell University when the second African American Studies program was started. Like many students in the struggle, I was arrested, jailed, and surveilled by the FBI and its counterintelligence program. I was mocked and maimed, made victim and victor, hero and villain. Despite the obstacles and opposition, like many others, I sang and survived; I organized and I cried out. I rallied and I watched the ugly process of progress. I didn't just grow up with the movement—its phases of change mirrored my own.

Given my history, I've seen and been a lot of things, but I have rarely been as perplexed as I was when I had the opportunity to go into a history classroom in the early 1990s. I asked my wide-eyed students questions about Birmingham in 1963 and the 1965 Voting Rights Act. I asked the class to name three women active in the civil rights movement who were not Rosa Parks, Coretta King, or Angela Davis. Being that the class was in South Carolina, I also asked about the Orangeburg massacre, the most tragic terror attack on students in the annals of civil rights history. I couldn't get a satisfactory response to any of those questions. All of these years later, little has changed. I've heard the middle school version of our history. *How black people were in slavery until Martin Luther King Jr. came and freed them.* Or the more sophisticated version of the college freshman who can tell you *how "it" all started when Rosa Parks simply got tired one day and decided she would not give up her seat on the bus to a white person, regardless of what the sign*

Figure 12.1. Stokely Carmichael at the 1966 Mississippi March Against Fear, announcing the concept of "Black Power." Cleveland Sellers stands at center rear of the group on the truck platform. © Bob Fitch Photo.

said. How some students stood up, sat-in, got sprayed with hoses, filled the jails, took a ride on a bus, marched on Washington, and then, amid calls complemented with raised fists and cultural consciousness, the story ends—as mysteriously and suddenly as it began.

But our movement was not a spontaneous rebellion, a revolution spearheaded by a single charismatic leader. It was rather a collective action refueled and reinvented continually in an effort to fight for freedom for all people. The schoolhouse paraphrase is more than unfortunate. It is dangerous, a children's tale that blots out the historical generations and regenerations of the movement and cuts off its roots and limbs, its links to before, after, and today—leaving it as unattached, chopped timber in the fires of memory. Easily burned, its fire spent, its warmth forgotten, the "ashes" of our story nevertheless hides sparks and embers of its truer self.

It would be easy to blame the mistaken origins and legacy of the civil rights movement and the black student movement in particular on the American educational system. Standardized testing, No Child Left Behind, budget cuts, and "races to the top" on the back of math and science courses (as opposed to classes in history and humanities) have made it harder to fit our story into a semester's worth of American history. How can students get that story when the only measure of what they know—and dare I say what is made important—on the hundred-question final exam must cover the whitewashed versions of American discovery, Manifest Destiny, and the decontextualized ideas of the New Deal? It would be easy, as well, to point to the inattention of those in the movement who have been too busy continuing the struggle to worry about how it is recorded. Or commiserate with those who suffered so much pain and suffering, torment and trauma, that they have been silenced by their experiences. But there is something much larger going on. I won't say sinister, but definitely larger. At the hands of writers who have added volumes to the annals of the civil rights literature, some with good intentions and others without, the movement has been condensed to 13 glorious years from 1955 to 1968. We get Rosa's assertion of her rights and Martin's assassination; the boycott that sounded the start of it and the bullet that signaled its end. In moving icon to icon, our movement has been cut up into bite-sized portions, packaged into an easily digestible version, vacuum-sealed, and made ready for quick consumption. Those writers have nearly succeeded in making our nuanced nexus, our lengthy suffering, and our "movement of movements" prim, proper, palatable.[1] And, in doing so, have made it paraplegic.

The narrative that we get, even from top intellectuals and scholars, too often begins *in medias res,* reduces the foot soldiers to footnotes, creates climax and false resolution, prefers flat characters to dynamic, fully developed (and fully flawed) humans, muddies our morals, constricts our themes. The narrative compacts the story so much that what we get is a literature that canonizes Dr. King, leaves out women and students, and marginalizes the spunk that pulled the movement out of dormancy. The popular narrative goes for the big events and big names while leaving out the small efforts that built up collective action, and ultimately, summarizes—badly—what is profound and complex.

In recent years, this traditional narrative, with its aerial view of the movement—looking from the top down instead of from the ground up—has come under scrutiny. Historian Charles Payne, in his widely respected work, criticizes the traditional narrative for minimizing the importance of local struggle. Payne explains that

> placing so much emphasis on national leadership and national institutions minimizes the role "ordinary" people played in changing the country and the enormous costs that sometimes entailed for them. It implicitly creates the impression that historical dynamism resides among elites—usually white, usually male, usually educated—and that non-elites lack historical agency. The gender bias of traditional history is especially inappropriate in this case since at the local level, women provided a disproportionate share of the leadership in the early

1960s. . . . [This top-down perspective] misses the complexity of the African-American community—its class, gender, cultural, regional, and ideological divisions—and how that complexity shaped responses to oppression. . . . [It leaves us remembering] a few well-defined leaders. . . . [but forgetting] the undifferentiated masses. . . .

Concentration on the period between the mid-1950s and the mid-1960s—the Montgomery to Memphis framework—underplays the salience of earlier periods of struggle. All apart from their significance for understanding the modern civil rights movement, those earlier struggles are important in their own right as revealing the evolving self-consciousness of African Americans and the shifting constraints that confronted them. . . .

A top-down perspective presumes that the most appropriate historical markers have to do with legislative/policy changes. This position makes it very difficult to understand the movement as a transforming experience for individuals or as an evolving culture, which in turn makes it very difficult to understand the radicalization of the Movement. . . . [Top-down history also tends to imply] that the movement can be understood solely through large-scale, dramatic events, thus obscuring the actual social infrastructure that sustained the movement on a day-to-day basis.[2]

By flattening timelines, intricacies, and details, the traditional narrative distorts and oversimplifies the freedom struggle. There is no community-based view of how individual localities produced indigenous, homegrown action—with as much local flair as rice dishes or barbecue—that was able to merge with the larger movement taking shape across the South. We don't get enough of the stories such as St. Augustine and Tuskegee, where local people developed local tactics and had their own local leadership, including those "race leaders" who would have been invisible to the white power structure yet were at the forefront of handling issues of discrimination and injustice at home. These race leaders were the frontline problem-solvers and acted as the local connectors to the larger intra- and interstate networks of social justice organizations. Because of the traditional narrative's neglect, we lose context for how Fannie Lou Hamer and Ella Baker tapped into activists in the communities they served, how the NAACP and the Brotherhood of Sleeping Car Porters built links within and outside of their organizations, and how the Congress of Racial Equality could complete a series of sit-ins in the early 1940s. By ignoring the dynamic local terrain of the freedom struggle, the traditional narrative creates a movement of immaculate progression. Somehow, some way, action was synthesized and presented as effective without there being any mention of the infrastructure activists built over time to bolster and sustain progress.

This traditional narrative leaves out the magnitude of the white backlash against the freedom struggle. We get little on how the efforts of minorities to secure their constitutional rights were undermined. There's the lack of emphasis put on the Southern Manifesto, the written condemnation of the *Brown v. Board of Education* school desegregation decision by 19 members of the U.S. Senate and 77 members of the House of Representatives, what it said about the power structure's racism and refusal to obey the law of the land when it outlawed segregation. There's even less mention of how the white South did everything possible to abandon and dismantle public education rather than integrate or equalize it.

As historian Jacquelyn Dowd Hall explains, the "dominant narrative of the civil rights movement . . . distorts and suppresses as much as it reveals."[3] If we want to understand the legacy of the student movement, we must get its origins right. We can't begin in Montgomery or even with *Brown v. Board of Education,* as the popular narrative would suggest. We have to start decades earlier and end decades later to get the fullest picture.[4] Hall asserts the "*truer* story—the story of a 'long civil rights movement' that took root in the liberal and radical milieu of the late 1930s, was intimately tied to the 'rise and fall of the New Deal Order,' accelerated during World War II, stretched far beyond the south, was continuously and ferociously contested, and in the 1960s and 1970s inspired a 'movement of movements' that defies any narrative of collapse." Black students played a vital and often underexamined part in that epic. As Hall and other scholars have suggested, it's time to lengthen the timeline in order to reclaim the movement's foundations and early successes.[5] By lengthening the timeline, stretching it backward and forward, we can see where and how the student-driven movement expanded, spread its roots, and let its branches provide shade and lookouts toward other revolutionary actions.

Student Activity/Activism

The civil rights movement emerged from the efforts of young black people to break the back of Jim Crow, *Plessy v. Ferguson*'s legacy of racial discrimination and segregation—both de facto and de jure. The protest traditions, culture, and tactics that these students used were passed down from one generation to another through black institutions—our churches, press, schools, organizations, and race leaders. It is the same protest tradition that has been employed since Africans first encountered Europeans, but somehow the students' role as torchbearers of that legacy has remained largely in shadows.

Mention the start of the student movement, and there is the iconic image of Ezell Blair, Joseph McNeil, Franklin McCain, and David Richmond seated at the lunch counter in Greensboro, North Carolina. These North Carolina A&T students, clad in their overcoats on that February day in 1960, seemed stoic and resolved. No fear appeared on their faces. No anger. Just determination to sit down until justice was served. Popular histories demote the Greensboro Four's actions to a moment of frustration. They herald the appearance of the sit-in as a national tactic in the fight for rights but fail to recognize that, in the words of Ella Baker, this was "not just about a hamburger." Instead, that sit-in represented the emergence of a new generation of activists who believed that at the cornerstone of our resistance was the "right to directly protest for rights."[6] We students felt it our moral obligation to act against the forces that reduced our families and friends to second-class citizens because of our race. We students were leading ourselves, contrary to the King-centered history that makes it appear that the movement was organized and led by black, male preachers who merely wanted to secure those civil rights guaranteed by the U.S. Constitution.

We students sought to change three specific trends in the fledgling movement: (1) the traditional Negro leadership of preachers who sought salvation, justice, freedom, and peace in the ever-after; (2) the movement's traditional legal tactics that redressed grievances through the courts and legislation; and (3) the leadership of old men who were hesitant to employ more radical action and were willing to extend time for compromises or negotiation. Students wanted a timely resolution, not some long, drawn-out series of solutions that amounted to "justice long delayed [equaling] justice denied."[7] We students preferred mass action over legalism. We wanted our freedom and we wanted it "now." So we insisted that the leadership become indigenous and include young people, old people, women, all those who believed in justice.

To understand the student movement's roots, we can't start with the Greensboro sit-in. Although 1960 was a pivotal moment, it was preceded by decades of student activism. The use of students as catalysts and organizers for social action has a rich history. Student activism goes back to Howard University's Law School Class of 1933, of which Thurgood Marshall and Oliver Hill were notable graduates. These protégés and students of Charles Hamilton Houston, regarded as the law school's "architect," constitute a wave of activists forged in the halls of legal academe that was then set loose on the community and courts.[8] Houston built and won the accreditation for Howard's law program and set the legal agenda of the NAACP. As a mentor and instructor, Houston made his agenda plain to the students. He was not merely educating future lawyers but creating a cadre of "social engineers" who had the consciousness to reconstruct society, to make a tremendous commitment of time, talent, and resources and create enough legal precedents to establish that under *Plessy* blacks did not enjoy equal protection under the law, as was required by the 14th Amendment. Later, that focus shifted to the overturning of the "separate but equal" doctrine altogether.

The work of Houston and his students began in 1935 with their court battles to root out the inequities caused by Jim Crow public institutions of higher education. Later, Houston traveled to the South and was appalled by the vast disparity in school funding between black and white public schools in South Carolina. His outrage became his students' mantle. Houston's student/lawyer/activists, including Thurgood Marshall, uncovered inequity in South Carolina, Virginia, Delaware, Washington, D.C., and Kansas and appealed these cases to the U.S. Supreme Court. These five cases aligned for the *Brown v. Board of Education of Topeka, Kansas,* school desegregation case in 1954. Although Houston didn't live long enough to see the *Brown* ruling, he planted the seed in his students. And like many student activists, Marshall built on the pedagogy of his mentor. Marshall, as the counsel for the NAACP Legal Defense Fund, began taking cases across the South that chipped away at "separate but equal." When Marshall signed on to a Clarendon County, South Carolina, suit, which became the *Briggs v. Elliott* case (1951), he was counseled by South Carolina judge J. Waties Waring to reject school equalization in favor of full desegregation. This case, the first to argue for an end to segregated policies in public schools, provided the underpinning of the *Brown* ruling. Judge Waring's dissent in the *Briggs* case would become a cornerstone of the *Brown* decision.

Houston's protégés were not the only African American student activists associated with the *Brown* ruling. Scott's Branch High School students in Clarendon County were integral in rallying their community's support against segregation. They challenged their school system's white leadership and signed on as petitioners, witnesses, and claimants in the lawsuit that dared the state of South Carolina and later the United States to square the reality of equality in schooling with the promise of it. In each of the separate cases of the *Brown* decision, student activists can be found. In Farmville, Virginia, that student was Barbara Johns, age 16, who led her schoolmates in a walkout and strike protesting their high school's severe overcrowding and inferior facilities. Johns's leadership and her classmates' activism compelled the community and courts to rethink whether shoddily constructed school additions or a few buses could make up for inherently unequal schooling. The *Brown* cases, argued by Houston's social engineers, dismantled Jim Crow while inspiring the students in those black schools, confirming that theirs was a valuable presence in the movement, both in and out of court. These students, in law and the public schools, comprised an initial wave of student activists who used their network of like-minded classmates to exact change.

In the wake of *Brown,* student activism continued to build as black students across the country spoke out against discrimination. In 1956, Fred H. Moore led fifteen hundred students at South Carolina State College and Claflin College in campus strikes and other protests against racism.[9] Black parents in Orangeburg, South Carolina, had petitioned for integrated schools, in accord with the *Brown* decision. This was met with swift reprisals from the white supremacists, who chartered their own White Citizens' Council branch. Parents who had signed the integration petition were—using the typical "Big Squeeze" tactic of whites in opposition—fired from their jobs, denied loans, and evicted from their homes or had their mortgages foreclosed.

Moore, the president of the student government at S.C. State, wanted to fight back against this white repression by organizing a boycott, but when the president of S.C. State refused to support it, a student strike resulted. The protests went on for days; the school's president was hanged in effigy. Moore and several of his co-organizers were expelled, but their activist spirit was not squelched. Students in Nashville planned a similar protest in late 1959. In their organizing they decided to wait until after the Christmas break and were just weeks behind the Greensboro students in successfully sitting in.

Just as vital to the story of student activism as these individual cases were the NAACP student chapters. These groups worked boldly and courageously to combat racism. Their myriad stories illustrate the long history of student activism. The historical roster is packed with names of students who created or were propelled by the struggle for social justice, yet few make it to the registry of fame when the freedom struggle's long story is abridged into the short Montgomery-to-Memphis narrative.

One early student activist helped create the move for social justice post-mortem. In the late summer of 1955, Emmett Till, a 14-year-old black boy, was kidnapped from his uncle's home in Money, Mississippi, beaten beyond recognition, and shot. His young, lifeless body was weighted down and thrown into the river—a gruesome tradition of Mississippi white terrorists. Rev. Fred Shuttlesworth once commented that "no one but the Almighty knows how many black men are in the rivers of Mississippi." An all-white jury freed the men who murdered the child. When Emmett's mother held an open-casket funeral for her son, showing the world his bloated, battered body, he became more than an example of how Mississippi, one of the most recalcitrant and violent states, treated blacks; Emmett became a catalyst for change. Rebecca de Schweinitz writes that "Till's murder and the travesty of justice that followed figured prominently in the testimonies of six witnesses who appeared before the Senate Subcommittee on Civil Rights two years later." Their testimony helped pave the way for the Civil Rights Act of 1957, which "included specific provisions for federal involvement in the southern justice system."[10] Emmett became a symbol for the movement. People protested his murder, pooling money for the NAACP's victim fund and adding voice to the furor over southern injustice and cruelty. At 14, a student, cut down in his youth for being black and bold in a time where both could have fatal consequences, Emmett was a martyr. Emmett was our peer. Those of us in our teens and early twenties viewed Emmett Till's murder as the trigger for our heightened social consciousness. My generation of young African Americans vowed to vindicate the death of our brother by changing the world and the racial climate.

By the end of 1956, many young black students were primed to take action and spark the fledgling freedom movement. Yes, there had been those legal victories thanks to the work of Charles Houston's student-activists. But a new movement was needed. Organizations such as the Southern Christian Leadership Conference began in 1957. And on 1 February 1960, those four students at North Carolina A&T went to downtown Greensboro's Woolworth's and sat-in, demanding service from the whites-only lunch counter. That action unleashed energy in the movement. The sit-in as a means of nonviolent direct action spread like wildfire. More and more students were willing to risk jail, hostile attacks, alienation, expulsion, even death.

Some presidents of historically black colleges and universities (HBCUs) supported their students, while others closed their institutions and expelled students who participated in any type of demonstration. To his credit, James Nabrit, president of Howard University and peer of Marshall and Houston, opened up his university to students expelled from other institutions for their involvement in the struggle. The threat of expulsion from college made it a tremendous risk for student organizers and activists. Most of these protesters were first-generation college students who had all of their families' resources invested in their educations. Yet the commitment of these young people to justice and to their community outweighed the personal concerns.

In just three months, more than forty thousand students had engaged in some form of sit-in protest. White students joined hands with their protesting brothers and sisters. The challenge for the student movement was finding a way to unify the student protesters and harness the collective energy of the young activists. Ella Baker secured funds from the Southern Christian Leadership Conference (SCLC) to bring the sit-in protesters together to coordinate their efforts. In April 1960, protesting students assembled at Shaw University in Raleigh, North Carolina, to form a coordinating committee.[11] Many of the civil rights organizations sent representatives to the Shaw meetings. Jim Lawson, a seasoned protestor, would lead nonviolence workshops. Baker would be the single most important person who helped shape SNCC, the organization that changed the social and political landscape of America. Baker, aware that the students needed to be organized, also fully comprehended the concept of political empowerment and knew that the students must first come to the realization of their own empowerment. After many subsequent meetings and with Baker's sage advice, the Student Nonviolent Coordinating Committee, colloquially abbreviated to SNCC and vocalized as "snick," was born.

Although initially funded by the SCLC, which wanted to create a student arm of its organization, SNCC was an autonomous organization. The students of SNCC agreed to expand mass action. We decided on a nontraditional leadership model—rejecting a top-down or charismatic leadership style—adopting instead a Quaker-style, group-centered decision-making process. Dedicated to social change without resort to force or brutality, the commitment to avoiding violence came to some as a religious conviction and to others as the best tactic for avoiding disastrous confrontations with mobs and police. Born of these novel morals and tactics, SNCC prided itself on building a movement rather than a mere organization. It determined to draw its strength and wisdom, inspiration and spiritual depth, from the souls of black people of the South. As historian Erin Chung put it, with "an eclectic array of ideas adopted from Gandhian theories of nonviolent direct action and from the traditions of pacifism formulated by the Congress of Racial Equality (CORE), the Fellowship of Reconciliation, and SCLC, SNCC was dedicated primarily to coordinating the new student militancy in the South with the national Civil Rights Movement."[12]

The *story* of SNCC, although unique in how it developed and approached the movement, is essential to understanding the *history* of the student movement. The phases of SNCC point to and intersect with the overarching issues and tactics that were used in student activism. SNCC spearheaded, in Chung's words, the "transition from legal intervention to direct action, and finally to black power in the civil rights movement." Part-time protesters, part-time students, SNCC moved through four phases over its decade-long struggle.

Phase I: Launching Mass Action and Voter Registration / Voter Education, 1960–62

Beginning with the 1 February 1960 sit-in, students across the South took part in nonviolent direct action against segregated public facilities including lunch counters, buses and bus terminals, hotels, parks, libraries, and even churches. SNCC would organize and publicize the protests of these student groups in the activist newsletter *The Student Voice* edited by communications chair Julian Bond. By 1961, SNCC workers such as Diane Nash, Charles Sherrod, Ruby Doris Smith, and Charles Jones were moving to more extensive public demonstrations and using the "jail, no bail" tactic that quickly gained prominence in the student movement. 1961 also included SNCC's involvement in the CORE Freedom Rides, wherein black and white activists rode from Washington, D.C., to New Orleans as a test of the desegregation of local bus and transportation facilities. While the first leg of the trip was relatively peaceful, other than an incident in Rock Hill, South Carolina, where a mob of white men beat two of the black male riders, the stops in Alabama proved a turning point. First a bus was firebombed outside Anniston; then a busload of riders was beaten severely, some nearly to death, by a Klan-led mob in Birmingham. It looked as if the rides might be ended by this brutality. But in the face of great physical danger, student representatives from SNCC, organized by Diane Nash, volunteered to finish the Freedom Rides. Several of the SNCC volunteers were beaten and jailed when the rides reached Montgomery and were later imprisoned in Mississippi's notorious Parchman Penitentiary. Despite hostility and even resistance from the Kennedy administration, which asked that the rides be halted because they were provoking violence, SNCC's courageous action to continue the Freedom Rides sent out the message that nonviolent direct action would not be stopped even by brutal white supremacist mobs.

By late 1961, a new initiative on voting rights had begun. Robert Kennedy wanted to have the civil rights leadership adopt a voter registration program. Later, private sector foundations provided resources to establish the Voter Education Project. While some members of SNCC were reluctant to take part in an initiative begun and sponsored by the Kennedy administration, other workers saw voter registration as the logical next step in the struggle. Within SNCC, a split occurred between the direct action wing, which was hindered by what its activists saw as "divine" Washington's intervention, and the voter registration wing headed by Jones and Sherrod.

Voter registration and education projects were organized throughout the South with the VEP donors responsible for funding many indigenous efforts. SCLC adopted the Citizenship School founded by Septima Clark and Esau Jenkins and designed to help potential voters pass the literacy test as part of its Voter Registration Program. SNCC had already been working on voter registration in Mississippi. The group orchestrated Freedom Days where organizers mobilized local black residents to travel to county courthouses to register to vote. SNCC later organized the Freedom Vote: mock elections that paralleled regular elections but with black candidates campaigning and blacks voting to demonstrate that African Americans would vote and participate in the political process, en masse, if they had the opportunity. This was particularly necessary given much of the South's hostile reaction to black voters, which manifested itself in all kinds of intimidation tactics. Years before the VEP projects were funded, for example, Fannie Lou Hamer had her home shot up with 21 bullets and was evicted when she registered to vote in Mississippi. In 1961, early efforts to register voters in Mississippi triggered the

murder of Herbert Lee, who was active in the NAACP and SNCC voter registration project. Lee was shot twice by E. H. Hurst, a white state representative. Louis
Allen, the black witness to this crime, was also murdered before he could testify
about Lee's murder.

This tragedy ended the early debate over which course to take; it really didn't
matter where you stood—voter registration or direct action—they both challenged the status quo and the institution of segregation. Herbert Lee was the first
fatality of this kind for SNCC. We all now knew that we had taken on much more
responsibility than we initially envisioned when we became organizers, since we
saw firsthand that racists would not hesitate to murder blacks who—as a result of
our organizing—asserted their constitutional rights.

In 1962, SNCC began to organize in Albany, Georgia. The goal was to organize
the community around protests against segregation and establish a voting rights
drive. In reaching Albany, many students withdrew from school to work fulltime
for SNCC and the freedom struggle. It was in Albany that the student organizers
popularized mass meetings and started using the freedom songs as a viable tool
of the movement. Four months into SNCC's organizing in Albany, the SCLC and
Dr. King were invited in when the protests slowed. In comparison with earlier
and later campaigns, Dr. King and the SCLC came and, lacking a plan or program
for how to build on the work of SNCC in the city, suffered their first "defeat" in
the Albany campaign. Dr. King and the SCLC's usual focus on mobilization made
them unprepared for how to respond to the Albany police's tactics for dealing with
demonstrators. The Albany police, unlike elsewhere in the South, didn't resort
to brutality to squelch protest but instead escalated the charges. Protestors were
charged with crimes like sedition instead of being bitten by police dogs or beaten
by baton-wielding cops. Dr. King and the SCLC's practice of nonviolent direct action had little traction in the face of the seeming civility in Albany. Dr. King and
the SCLC eventually withdrew from Albany, leaving SNCC's Charles Sherrod to
remain and continue working to empower the black community there.

Phase II: Extending Mass Action and Voter Registration /
Voter Education, 1963–65

Following Albany, the SCLC launched a new campaign, a plan called Project C
(for Confrontation) in Birmingham, challenging the city's segregationist policies. After a few weeks of protest, the number of adult protesters divided. At a
rally Dr. King asked for new volunteers for the protest. Lines of young students
volunteered. Over the course of the Birmingham movement some four thousand
student protesters were arrested, ranging in age from 5 to 18. This first experience

with mass political action and consciousness-raising among black youths broke the composure of Sheriff Eugene "Bull" Connor, who responded by turning water hoses and police dogs on the nonviolent protesters. When the Birmingham City Council voted to desegregate, Rev. Fred Shuttlesworth concluded that "the city of Birmingham has reached an accord with its conscience."

But four months later the Ku Klux Klan, along with an FBI informant, planted bombs in the basement of the 16th Street Baptist Church, killing four little girls (ranging from 11 to 13 years of age) and wounding the consciousness of black America. In the summer of 1963 terror would strike again, with the murder of Mississippi NAACP leader Medgar Evers. Evers's voice was silenced by those who didn't support the notion that all men were created equal.

The March on Washington, in August 1963 (which came between the Medgar Evers murder and the Birmingham Church bombing) proved another decisive moment for both the movement and SNCC. The March on Washington stood as an effort to build a new coalition of liberals, labor organizations, the church, and the civil rights organizations. While these groups had goals that should intersect, the four had never quite worked well together. The March on Washington targeted an end to segregation and made known the need for civil rights legislation. But even before the march had begun, the church representative wanted the students' message to be tempered. National Council of Churches President Eugene Carson Blake objected to the words *masses* and *revolution* in the draft of SNCC leader John Lewis's speech. Archbishop Patrick O'Boyle said that he would not appear on the platform if John denounced gradualism, as he had in the draft of his speech, where he termed *patience* "a dirty and nasty word." Other march organizers objected to the draft's fiery pledge that "we will march through Dixie like Sherman, leaving a scorched earth with non-violence." A. Philip Randolph asked SNCC to make the changes. This was his day, after some 20 years planning a March on Washington movement. Lewis changed the language. But this was a learning moment for the Snickers: They must always stick to their principles and not compromise the voice of SNCC. Afterward, Malcolm X referred to the March as the "Farce on Washington." While the Grand Coalition of the church, liberals, labor, and civil rights organizations had been lauded, after this first public function, much of the key parts began to dissolve.

During the summer of 1964, with the rising recognition that black political power and access to that power were paramount goals, SNCC's Bob Moses spearheaded the massive Mississippi Freedom Summer Project. The vision was that if we could open the "closed society in Mississippi" and break the back of white supremacy in one of the deep South's toughest and most racist states, we would be able to end segregation for good. Some one thousand volunteers (lawyers, teachers, nurses, doctors), including students from America's most prestigious colleges and universities, flocked to Mississippi. Many of the volunteers lived in the homes of black Mississippians, where they learned fresh lessons in history, diversity, and courage. The goals of Mississippi Freedom Summer were to expand the freedom vote project, create freedom schools (summer school classes), build community centers, and, above all, organize the Mississippi Freedom Democratic Party to challenge the seating of the lily-white Mississippi delegation at the national Democratic Party Convention.

Some SNCC organizers assumed that the March on Washington's Grand Coalition of the church and liberal, labor, and civil rights groups would support an effort by the MFDP to unseat the party regulars, white supremacist "Dixiecrats," who were not loyal to the national party and had voted in 1960 for Richard Nixon, the Republican Party's presidential candidate. It was power politics at its rawest. The Democratic Party treated the MFDP in the most dismissive way. The MFDP candidates—many of whom had never left the state of Mississippi; many more may have never left their home counties—traveled to Atlantic City to justify why they deserved to be seated. That seating, however, did not happen.

After the MFDP indigenous leadership and the Mississippi activists' failure to secure the support of the Democratic Party, it became clear even to Dr. King, Bayard Rustin, Roy Wilkins, and others that indigenous freedom movements were not welcome within the Democratic Party. It was a very bitter pill to swallow for the Mississippi Summer volunteers whose idealism had made them believe in national party politics.

Phase III: Independent Political Action, 1965–67

The dates of SNCC's entrée into its third phase overlap with the second primarily because of the twin needs of voter registration / voter education and independent political action. Almost immediately after the defeat of the MFDP, SNCC's research office began to stake out policies and regulations for the creation of independent political organization, in other words a third party. The backlash against incorporating local black candidates into the already established parties made clear the necessity of constructing a new and separate party that would represent the needs of and build platforms around indigenous concerns. Jack Minis, SNCC research director, found an old Alabama law that allowed for independents to create their own county party. SNCC's Stokely Carmichael seized on this while organizing the rural population of Alabama's Dallas, Lowndes, and Green counties. As part of the effort to create an independent political organization, Carmichael developed tactics and educational materials to help guide the local population's empowerment. This material, published as advertisements by SNCC, was enough to get volunteers from major urban communities to monitor the entire party-building process. The community was involved in picking a mascot for the new freedom organizations. Their choice: a black panther, because it looked like them—sleek, fast, fierce. There was tremendous grassroots support for the new political party. Still, their endorsement had consequences. Many people were displaced or thrown off their land because of their involvement with what was called the Lowndes County Freedom Organization. At the same time, Alabama's white Democrats were continuing to oppose the black freedom struggle.

Throughout the formation of the Lowndes County Freedom Organization, the Democratic Party embarked on a misinformation campaign and talked about the antiwhite "Black Panther Party," which they had renamed for subversive purposes. Their focus on the black-empowerment aspect of the party was a scare tactic and a means of discrediting the organization. Later, as a means of bringing truth and attention to the party, when the first major election campaign occurred black youth were recruited from Philadelphia, New York, and Los Angeles to help get people to the polls. These groups were called "Friends of the Black Panthers Party." The effort proved successful, and the Lowndes County Freedom Organization candidates became the first real candidates to be elected from within their own poor, black, and indigenous populations.

From the Lowndes County experience, SNCC developed a portable model for use in urban centers. SNCC was able to work outside of the South to harvest some of the energy that was so evident during the urban rebellions in places such as Harlem and Philadelphia in 1964, Watts in 1965, and Detroit in 1967. SNCC efforts to organize in urban areas, using tactics that had worked in the South, were not effective. The demographics were very different. SNCC was trying to organize in urban centers, but SNCC did not foster urban rebellion, as the Kerner Commission (the National Advisory Commission on Civil Disorders), called in to investigate the riots, found. The rebellions, although blamed on the Black Panther Party and the mobilization of black masses to create their own political movements, were the result of these communities' encounters with police brutality, unemployment, lack of recreational activities, substandard schools, and poverty. This portion of SNCC highlighted its entrance into a new era of exploring culture and identity. And it proves, definitively, that the Black Power (Black Panther Party) organizing model was first launched in Alabama.

History validates that the Black Power model was the correct and appropriate direction for the black freedom struggle. The origins of the term derived from the spontaneous chant-like response of local black listeners in Greenwood, Mississippi, to a passionate nighttime speech on 16 June 1966 by Stokely Carmichael after his release from jail on trumped-up charges on James Meredith's 210-mile "March Against Fear." I was there.

The turn to "black" power, organizing based on the independent political model, was a necessary step that required us to break ranks with white SNCC workers. Their dismissal was not intended as an expulsion but as a reassignment to move into poor white communities to foster collective action and organize there. This move caused internal splits and external condemnation. John Lewis left the organization shortly thereafter. Many, but not all, of those remaining white SNCC workers left the movement altogether. Lewis, today a senior U.S. congressman, ironically is the epitome of success of Black Power tactics.

We found it necessary first to counter the mindset that dehumanized the black man to himself. SNCC's focus on Black Power legitimized the need of black consciousness as an aspiration of the movement. From 1960 through 1966, the freedom struggle / civil rights movement was concentrated in the black community only, because it was the only community where organizing for change, protest, and resistance occurred. People such as Fannie Lou Hamer wanted to take control of their own destinies. She wanted self-determination even though she had received the right to vote (thanks to the 1965 Voting Rights Act) and the end to legal (de jure) segregation.

John Lewis, spinning from his defeat for wanting to be SNCC's "chairman for life," called Black Power "empty rhetoric"—but all slogans are rhetoric. "FREEDOM NOW" and "WE'LL BE FREE BY 1963" were rhetoric. "Black Power," however, was a definitive turn to think about the possibilities available to the black masses once they were able to shake off the psychological damage to their identities and self-worth caused by centuries of slavery, discrimination, oppression, and violence. As a specific example, from the concept has emerged the incorporation of African American Studies today as an accepted field of study in American higher education—one that a half-century ago did not exist. Mississippi now has more black elected officials than any other state. In 1960 there were none.

By 1966, along with becoming a predominantly black organization again, SNCC was poised to take on more international concerns. SNCC issued a statement against the Vietnam War in January 1966, a few days after the murder of Sammy Younge. Younge, a recipient of the U.S. Navy's Purple Heart for his service during the Bay of Pigs invasion, was killed in Tuskegee, Alabama, while working on SNCC's voter registration campaign and trying to integrate a local restroom in a gas station owned by an avowed racist. This was the first of SNCC's members killed doing civil rights work. The irony that Younge was killed trying to secure the right to vote after serving to bring democracy to the world presented a dilemma that SNCC could not ignore. SNCC initiated black anti–Vietnam War and anti-draft protests because it believed that the government-stated war goals were deceptive and that the United States did not intend to expand democracy, freedom, and justice in Southeast Asia. The SNCC research department published numbers that the casualty rates for African American and Latino soldiers in Vietnam were disproportionately high in comparison to their white counterparts.[13] Thus four grievances made up SNCC's condemnation of the war: (1) the disproportionate numbers of black males in combat units; (2) the belief that civil rights work should be considered an alternative to the military draft; (3) the knowledge that medical and educational deferments were not available to blacks and Latinos; and (4) the fact that draft boards across the South used discriminatory hiring practices to create all-white selective service systems that unfairly put the onus on minority draftees. SNCC would be the first and only civil rights organization to make a statement against the war. It would be a full year later, after constant encouragement by the Snickers, that Dr. King would make his iconic speech at Riverside Church condemning the war. Dr. King stated that the Vietnam War was "rapidly degenerating into a sordid military adventure." Eventually Floyd McKissick of CORE and SCLC followed SNCC's lead and became one of the leaders in the antiwar movement.

Phase IV: Human Rights, 1967–69

The transformation of SNCC into an organization interested in human rights not just in the United States but throughout the world was clear in its May 1967 official statement that SNCC "encourages and supports liberation struggles against colonialism and economic exploitation wherever these conditions exists. It supports those nations that assume a position of positive non-alignment, and express a point of view most consistent with its own views." Jim Forman rightly observed that since "its inception in 1960, SNCC has always been interested in the African Phase of the struggle against racism." Indeed, in 1963, SNCC members persuaded the minister of home affairs in Kenya, Oginga Odinga, to join in the Atlanta protest against segregation. After the 1964 summer project, Harry Belafonte arranged for a SNCC delegation including Fannie Lou Hamer, John Lewis, and Julian Bond to visit Kwame Nkrumah's Ghana and Ahmed Sékou Touré's Guinea. The trip provided an opportunity for the delegates to begin the discussion of the right to vote and what that meant in terms of self-determination, slavery, culture, identity, and heritage between Africans and black Americans. For the delegates, traveling abroad and seeing an entire country where black people were doing things the segregated South said they could not—flying planes, operating banks—was revolutionary. The delegation also had an opportunity to meet Malcolm X. In 1965, on the anniversary of South Africa's Sharpeville Massacre, SNCC mobilized against apartheid. Within two weeks, I was arrested in Washington, D.C., and New York for sit-ins at the South African Embassy and Consulate Office to the United Nations.

SNCC's commitment to the African and international freedom struggle continued as it approached the end of the decade with a vast network of alliances and support groups. The post–civil rights Black Power initiatives provided the most important legacy that has supported the existence of hundreds and thousands of Black, African, Latino, and Asian American and women's organizations, caucuses, politicians, and educational boards in the country to this day. SNCC's legacy, like that of the student movement at large, was not just about public accommodations or voting but rather about the power of young people to become agents and organizers in communities to bring about change. Our intention was to work ourselves out of existence by building local organizations that would let the indigenous populations gain control of their destiny as well as build on educational, health, and economic concerns. When SNCC began, we never intended to be just another civil rights organization working in the South but aspired to become a group entrenched in a borderless freedom struggle. SNCC's many political and social affiliates made it a natural ally and blueprint for causes as varied as the movement for Puerto Rican Independence, the Organization of Latin American Solidarity in Cuba, the American Indian Movement, and liberation efforts in Angola and Mozambique.

Student Energy and Exhaustion

All of these alliances brought external retribution to SNCC. Covert government programs such as COINTELPRO used surveillance and lies to sabotage the organization and its members. The mainstream media changed for the worse as the decade progressed. The media had been effective in covering the movement in the early days of mass resistance, broadcasting and reporting for the entire world the atrocities committed against black children, citizens, and activists. But between 1965 and 1968, major newspapers such as the *New York Times* and the *Atlanta Journal-Constitution* experienced a transition in the reporters who were covering the movement. Those who had started out covering boycotts and bombings, action and agitation—reporters who had known the players and organizations of the previous years—were replaced by those less comfortable and less familiar. With that came a tenor in the coverage that offered fear and willful misrepresentations. For example, in 1967 the *New York Times* published a distorted lead story on Black Power. The paper's position came from a rogue group called the Atlanta Project—an organization that we had dismissed from SNCC because they were not adhering to SNCC rules and policy. Here was a group touting a separatist viewpoint, an erroneous representation of Black Power, but no one from the *Times* checked with us in SNCC. SNCC's position on Black Power was *never* published. We wanted the community to decide what Black Power meant to them separately, as it would and should mean different things in different locales. Around that same time, the black clergy took out an advertisement in the *New York Times* asserting that there was a lot of good going on with Black Power. Few outlets, if any, reported that reaction to Black Power, but they did report heavily on the "expulsion" of white members. That publications as reputable as the *New York Times* were getting it wrong is indicative of the media climate in those times.

But let's also add the external impacts on the movement. American attitudes and focus changed with the escalation of the war on Vietnam. The Tet Offensive, the draft, each of these moved the agenda from civil rights to civil liberties. Formal opposition to the students and their activism also took precedence as the conservative agenda promoted the election of Richard M. Nixon. His "Southern Strategy," which heightened controversy over desegregation, busing, and the need for "law and order," created wedge issues to win more votes from conservative, southern whites. This shift in national conversation elevated Nixon's political agenda above the struggle's agenda in the public eye. SNCC and much of the student movement lost support, owing to the curb on civil liberties and the declining effectiveness of moral suasion as a vital tactic to rally the nation behind the movement.

These external factors created a weight on the student movement, but internal issues also compromised its pace. To follow the common narrative, after the "success" of the adoption of the Civil Rights Act and the Voting Rights Act of the mid- to late 1960s, absent the charismatic leadership of Dr. King and amid the cries for Black Power, the revolutionary youth relinquished their platforms and pickets and gave up their politics and passion either to self-destruct or to simply defect. That's far from the case. Instead, one of the reasons for some waning (not all of it, by a long shot) was the movement's successes. Since students had begun advocating for change across the South and across America, they had met many of their outlined goals. Among them: the 1954 U.S. Supreme Court ruling in *Brown v. Board of Education*, the 1957 Civil Rights Act, the 1964 Civil Rights Act, the 1965 Voting Rights Act as well as the Interstate Commerce Commission's ruling against segregation on interstate carriers and terminals. There was the widespread desegregation of public facilities, mass voter registration, and the mobilization of people who had been marginalized or kept outside of the social and political process. Students in the movement had focused attention on the war in Southeast Asia, exposing its bias and hypocrisy. They had laid the organizational basis that could be used as a tactical model for further social change.

Another factor affecting the student movement was fatigue. The physical stress of being put in harm's way in the hostile climate of Jim Crow segregation can only inadequately be put into words. To behave nonviolently in the face of threats, assault, and terror; to fear constantly for the safety of one's self, family, and other loved ones; to deal each day with the memory of oppression and violence; to bear the emotional burden of dehumanization and demonization as well as the mental strain of strategizing, organizing, and empowering a repressed population and trying to outwit a suppressive population was a burden akin to few others. Student activists, at best, could expect to spend two years doing fieldwork, particularly in hostile states such as Mississippi, and still maintain their health. Add to this the combat-like conditions in the war for rights of all kinds, and it is little wonder that many student activists did not have long "tours of duty."

With such extreme conditions and high turnover rate, the lack of a system for recruitment, screening, and education of new student organizers took its toll. There was a brain and body drain within the movement, and the internal education processes necessary to sustain the movement at its previous high levels just were not there. In SNCC alone, there were only 160 members when the group was at its largest. By the time SNCC's focus had changed to human rights, 18 of its approximately 60 remaining members were under investigation by the FBI or were being held in jail for refusing to be drafted. Moving from southern to northern organizing also slowed down the movement. Rural southern organizational and tactical models were inappropriate for northern communities that faced very different sets of problems and indigenous setups. A changing ideology was also necessary. Student organizers had to contend with the move from idealism to a more materialist philosophy.

Legacy

A full retrospective on the freedom struggle should raise questions about what has truly changed, how things can continue to improve, what can be done to repair the past. Yet the questions that get asked over and over again, like chords replayed so much they have warped the record, are: "What happened to the student movement?" "Where did the activists go?" "What happened to the energy?" The slowdown of the student movement after the late 1960s should not be construed as a breakdown of the movement under the pressure of external forces, nor wrongly attributed to the assassination of Dr. King. We need to validate the movement after 1968 and Dr. King and confirm the successes that followed instead of just surmising, disdainfully, how Black Power ruined the movement. We wouldn't have been singing *kumbaya* if we had done otherwise and never raised the bar of cultural identity as a means of creating social change.

No, what happened with the student movement is what has historically happened to all movements. It morphed. Adhering to the laws of the universe, just as matter cannot be created nor destroyed but can change form, so too can the collective, combined spirit of activism. Movements cannot be created nor destroyed, but they can change form. Which is why to understand the fate of the black student movement, we must first talk about the evolution present in social change. In starting with slavery, although we can definitely go back much further, we begin with the abolitionist movement that sought ways economic, moral, and literary to release a population from bondage. When slavery ended, the protest tradition did not. Instead we move into the period of Reconstruction and its fights for equality, reparations, and public education only to face the rise of the Redeemers of the Confederacy. Then the anti-lynching movement sprang up to protect a people from the horrors of early Jim Crow. There's the Harlem Renaissance and the call of the New Negro movement, each pulling and uniting folk to demand better conditions and more race pride, questioning how the government was meeting the needs of its darker brothers and sisters. These same quests, calls, and concerns echo through to our modern civil rights struggle, which, as I have shown, pushed itself forward into a concern about national and global human rights.

Given this transformative nature of movements and activists, the fluidity of how causes connect, why is it that historians decide that the black student movement ended with Dr. King, that after the 1965–68 period, there is nothing else? In fact, one of the richest periods for activism was the time from 1968 to 1975. It was then that students were driven to win rights of all kinds. Jacquelyn Dowd Hall casts our struggle as an "undefeated but unfinished revolution, a world-defining social movement that has experienced both reversals and victories and whose victories are now, once again, being partially reversed."[14] But much of that is because we have not cast the forward momentum in the correct light.

Black Studies

Black student activists developed a searching critique of institutions of higher education.[15] Many black students at majority-white institutions began to organize black student unions and demand black studies programs. I was there when, in response to student pressure, Cornell University established the second Black Studies program in the country, the first at an Ivy League school. They wanted African American history, African history, and a host of other courses that would take seriously the origins and legacy of black Americans. If there was going to be a discussion about access and equity, student activists figured that they must move toward curricula and classes that taught black culture and the black community the full accounts necessary to prepare citizens. They called for increasing the number of black students and professors. At historically black institutions, the rallying cry was that the students have more say in the operations of their schools. This activism, too, has stretched forward to the present day in defense of affirmative action and other movements that sought to have culturally responsible curriculum and pedagogy entrenched in education. Black HBCU athletes swelled the ranks of the NFL with their speed and quickness. John Carlos and Tommie Smith staged a Black Power protest at the Mexico City Olympics in 1968 against racism in America. Harry Edwards organized a boycott of black athletes against the 1968 Olympics. Young student-athletes became political and got involved in securing changes in college and professional athletics.

African Activism and Beyond

Those involved in the student movement called it a "freedom struggle," not a civil rights movement, because they were already connecting it to issues beyond race and to the world outside the United States. This is the same thread that William Minter pulls in his essay collection *No Easy Victories*. Minter, citing the work of Lisa Brock, noted that "despite the internationalist perspective of almost all the principal civil rights figures, the standard narrative focuses exclusively on civil rights at home. There is little consciousness of that stream of American internationalism that identifies not with American preeminence but with the demand for full human rights both at home and abroad."[16] By the time white protesters in the 1980s began to demand an end to apartheid in South Africa, there had already been a legacy of student activists demanding that same idea. During and since the movement, there have been those student activists who relate our struggle to the wars being waged by third world revolutionaries in Africa, Asia, and Latin America to help understand domestic racism.

Black Arts

The search for tactics to empower the poor black community led to a discussion of black consciousness. With black consciousness began intense efforts to reconstruct the black value system toward the unique cultural experiences of blacks in the diaspora. The reclaiming of identity in the label "African American," to replace the imposed "Negro," is one highly visible aspect of that reconstruction. Parents began giving their children African names, people began speaking Swahili, celebrating Kwanzaa, hosting black family reunions, and participating in genealogical studies, all evidence of profound shifts in black consciousness and black identity that students had championed for years. As activists led their communities into studies of how culture plays a central role in the African American experience, the discussion branched out. People in the arts community began thinking about culture's effect on community and vice versa, inspiring a new Black Arts Movement. Artists such as Amiri Baraka, Gil Scott-Heron, Don Lee, Nikki Giovanni, and others built on art forms that rebirthed the notion that black is beautiful and revived the talents and artistry of black people. The Black Arts Movement spawned black publishing houses, literary journals, and other cultural institutions to promote the stories and art of black Americans without having to go through the mainstream. In music we witnessed the Freedom Singers and Freedom Songs telling the stories of courage and sacrifice of many unsung Sheroes and Heroes (Fannie Lou Hamer, Ella Baker, Ruby Doris Robinson, Amzie Moore, E. W. Steptoe, and Jessie Harris). The Freedom songs from the Freedom Struggle impacted popular culture first with Joan Baez and Bob Dylan. During the Black Power phase, anthems such as James Brown's "Say It Loud—I'm Black and I'm Proud"; Martha and the Vandellas' "Dancing in the Street"; Aretha Franklin's "Respect"; Curtis Mayfield's "We the People Who Are Darker than Blue"; and Marvin Gaye's "What's Going On" rang out with the rage, questioning, pride, and passion of raised consciousness; the impulse continued with Bob Marley, Hugh Masekela, and Miriam Makeba.

Black Politics

Beginning with the National Black Political Convention in Gary, Indiana, in 1972, the same spirit that inspired action toward the MFDP and the Lowndes County Freedom Organization has come forward. From as early as 1967, conferences and planning committees have sought to find out how to build on independent political organization and how to gain more power for the black community in all areas, including school boards, mayoralties, state legislatures, and Congress. In 1966, two veterans from the Atlanta Student Movement and SNCC, Julian Bond and Ben Brown, won seats in the Georgia State Legislature. Julian was initially denied his seat because he supported SNCC's anti–Vietnam War statement; the U.S. Supreme Court seated him on the basis of denial of free speech. In the 1970s and 1980s, the election of mayors in southern black towns presented local change, while the gaining of black seats in the U.S. House of Representatives and historic presidential campaigns signaled an end to a century of having very few blacks in national political office. Successful campaigns, such as the 1973 election of Maynard Jackson as Atlanta's mayor—the first black man to lead a major city in the South—or Charlotte's election of Harvey Gantt as mayor in 1983, reveal the trend as much as Jesse Jackson's historic yet unsuccessful campaign for the Democratic presidential nomination in 1988. Today, because of the forward thrust of those leaving the civil rights movement, we have been able to get out the vote, educate black voters, and, in 2008, elect the first black president, Barack Obama.

Some might think it disingenuous to take credit for the whole of the student movement but in talking about representing the conscience/consciousness of it, SNCC must not let itself go unsung. We don't have a copyright on protest, but we made it popular. We made it possible. In reviewing the forward history, it is undeniable that during the decades that followed, SNCC's DNA is in the lifeblood of all of the successful organizations that moved forward into new progressive movements. These include those newly fighting to end the war; the advancement of environmentalism; the recognition of women's rights; gay, bisexual, and transsexual liberation; black studies; promotion of fair trade; movements for farm workers and immigration reform; full employment and jobs; universal health care; animal rights; the Black Panthers and Gray Panthers; tenants rights; the protection of the handicapped and homeless; and, lately, the defense of public property from privatization; as well as access to quality education as a human right. All have the telltale fingerprints of SNCC's direct action, teach-ins, and civil disobedience methods, language, tactics, ideology, and rejection of silent suffering and political correctness as the preferred strategies for survival. Do we not hear from all their lips our anthem, "We Shall Overcome"?

The work is not done. Dr. King's goal was the "Beloved Community." SNCC was able to create a sense of that Beloved Community during its tenure. Most of us came in to the movement with someone, yet when most of us left, it was on our own. That loss of community and camaraderie has not always been easy to bear. Some of us left pursued by the FBI and the draft boards. Others of us, particularly some of the white activists, left feeling underappreciated and forced out. Still others of us left to expand the movement in directions that we felt it needed to go, casting our nets far and wide to reap a greater harvest. All of us left SNCC understanding that things were still unfinished. Because until racism is undermined and destroyed and the poor are organized and empowered, there will never be the Beloved Community. We are well into the twenty-first century, and we are not yet a "postracial" America. Like the protest tradition's history, we continue to pass it along. The energy has been forwarded and harnessed and awaits being joined by other forces. The next generation of students will take the torch and demand that *all* of humanity continue the *struggle* for *justice, equality,* and *peace.* As Dr. King said, "Our lives begin to end the day we are silent about things that matter."

NOTES

1. Van Gosse, *Rethinking the New Left: An Interpretative History* (New York: Palgrave Macmillan, 2005).

2. Charles Payne, "Debating the Civil Rights Movement: The View from the Trenches," in *Debating the Civil Rights Movement, 1945–1968,* ed. Steven F. Lawson and Charles Payne (Lanham, MD: Rowman and Littlefield, 1998), 125–26.

3. Hall, "The Long Civil Rights Movement and Political Uses of the Past," *Journal of American History* (Mar. 2005): 1233–65.

4. Hall writes that "by confining the civil rights struggle to the South, to bowdlerized heroes, to a single halcyon decade, and to limited, noneconomic objectives, the master narrative simultaneously elevates and diminishes the movement. It ensures the status of the classical phase as a triumphal moment in a larger American progress narrative, *yet* it undermines its *gravitas.* It prevents one of the most remarkable mass movements in American history from speaking effectively to the challenges of our time." Hall, "Long Civil Rights Movement," 1233.

5. For additional writing on the "long" civil rights movement, see Adam Fairclough, *Race and Democracy: The Civil Rights Struggle in Louisiana, 1915–1972* (Athens: Univ. of Georgia Press, 1995); Greta de Jong, *A Different Day: African American Struggles for Justice in Rural Louisiana, 1900–1970* (Chapel Hill: Univ. of North Carolina Press, 2002); Payne, "Debating the Civil Rights Movement," 108–11; and Jacquelyn Dowd Hall, "Mobilizing Memory: Broadening Our View of the Civil Rights Movement," *Chronicle of Higher Education* (27 July 2001), B7–B11.

6. Cleveland Sellers and Robert Terrell, *The River of No Return: The Autobiography of a Black Militant and the Death of SNCC* (Jackson: Univ. of Mississippi Press), 1990.

7. Martin Luther King Jr., "Letter from a Birmingham Jail."

8. Genna Rae McNeil, *Groundwork: Charles Hamilton Houston and the Struggle for Civil Rights* (Philadelphia: Univ. of Pennsylvania Press, 1984). For a more thorough discussion of Houston, see "In Tribute: Charles Hamilton Houston," *Harvard Law Review* (June 1998).

9. Cecil Williams, *Freedom and Justice: Four Decades of the Civil Rights Struggle as Seen by a Black Photographer of the Deep South* (Macon, GA: Mercer Univ. Press, 1995).

10. Rebecca de Schweinitz, *If We Could Change the World: Young People and America's Long Struggle for Racial Equality* (Chapel Hill: Univ. of North Carolina Press, 2009), 102.

11. On Ella Baker and her influence on the student movement, see Belinda Robnett, *How Long? How Long?* (New York: Oxford Univ. Press, 1997); Gloria Richardson, *Freedom Is Constant Struggle* (film); Faith Holsaert et al., eds., *Hands on the Freedom Plow: Personal Accounts by Women in SNCC* (Champaign: Univ. of Illinois Press, 2011); and Clayborne Carson, *In Struggle: SNCC and the Black Awakening of the 1960s* (Cambridge, MA: Harvard Univ. Press, 1996).

12. Erin Chung, "Student Nonviolent Coordinating Committee (SNCC): Young Soldiers of the Civil Rights Movement," Institute of Diaspora Studies, Northwestern University, Evanston, Illinois.

13. Using numbers from the SNCC Research Department, Julian Bond, in his comic book *Vietnam,* included statistics that 2 out of 5 soldiers (40%) killed in Vietnam were black. See Julian Bond and T. G. Lewis, *Vietnam: An Anti-War Comic Book,* 1967. See "The Sixties Project," available at http://lists.village.virginia.edu/sixties/HTML_docs/Exhibits/Bond/Bond.html, accessed 14 June 2012. Since then, others have placed black casualty rates

at as high as 16% (in the year 1966) with decreases afterward. James Westheider, *Fighting on Two Fronts: African Americans and the Vietnam War* (New York: NYU Press, 1996), 12–13.

14. Hall, "Long Civil Rights Movement," 1233.

15. Cynthia Bobo, Cynthia Hudley, and Claudine Michel, eds., *The Black Studies Reader* (New York: Routledge, 2004).

16. In the same volume, Brock notes that as she began to "explore the 1950s, probably the most revelatory for me was the discovery that virtually all U.S.-centered activists and scholars whom we identify with civil and human rights movements consciously saw themselves as working in solidarity with the peoples of Africa."

Historiographical Reflections

DOUG ROSSINOW

Well, I have been waiting some time.

I'm being a bit tongue-in-cheek here. However, I really am gratified to see the important work gathered in this volume. It is 2012 as I write these words. When I published my book *The Politics of Authenticity* in 1998, I did not have specific expectations concerning future scholarship on student activism and radicalism in the American South during the era of the 1960s. But I did think that more work would be forthcoming on specific, local settings, whether focused on campuses or on broader metropolitan areas. And I expected more work to come on areas outside the "northern rim," stretching from Morningside Heights to Cambridge, across to Ann Arbor and Madison and then to Berkeley, that had, up until the 1990s, furnished the basis for most narratives of white, if not of black, student activism in the 1960s.

The 1980s had been a fertile time for academic studies of 1960s radicalism—perhaps paradoxically, in light of the prevailing political conservatism of the 1980s, or perhaps quite logically, given that in a conservative era, those with progressive sympathies may have wished to look for inspiration to a different time. The historical study of both black and white student movements in the 1960s had progressed by leaps and bounds when the 1980s had barely gotten under way. Sara Evans's *Personal Politics* (1979) and Clayborne Carson's *In Struggle* (1981) provided enduring frameworks for understanding the emergence of the civil rights struggle's youth wing, of anti-imperialist radicalism among American youth, and of radical second-wave feminism. Regarding the New Left, which in the 1960s was largely associated with the radicalism of white college-educated youth, the late 1980s saw a burst of books, by Todd Gitlin, Maurice Isserman, and James Miller (all 1987).[1] These works focused squarely on Students for a Democratic Society (SDS) at the national level, and what information they conveyed about campus activism was drawn from the northern rim described above. David Farber's important and original work *Chicago '68* (1988) broke new ground by offering a multivocal account of political and cultural conflict in 1960s America, using place as a frame to capture the clashing perspectives that marked the era. In short, for someone entering graduate school in history at the end of the 1980s, as I did, the study of 1960s radicalism seemed like an exciting frontier of scholarship, sure to produce lots of new and interesting work in the coming years.

There certainly has been some very fine work produced in the last 20 years. As I was finishing my dissertation, which focused on white radicalism in Austin, Texas, home of the main campus of the University of Texas, Van Gosse published *Where the Boys Are* (1994), a creative cultural and organizational history of U.S. solidarity with the Cuban Revolution. There have been more local studies published, too. However, the pace of production in this area of scholarship seemed to slow down at the turn of the century, specifically concerning white radicalism in the 1960s. The volume of work produced concerning the African American struggle of the 1960s—often placing that era's struggle in a broader frame of historical development and often focusing on the Black Power militancy of the era— far outpaced work on white radicalism. In the last ten years, substantial secondary literatures also have begun to accumulate concerning liberation movements by other groups of color in the United States during the 1960s, particularly the Native American movement and the Latino movements of the era (the latter emphasizing the Chicano *Movimiento* of the American Southwest). There has not been a lot of original work published on second-wave radical feminism recently. Alice Echols's overview, *Daring to Be Bad* (1991), is now 20 years old, and it remains, along with *Personal Politics,* the major primary-sourced history of that movement. What original work has been done concerning radical feminism recently has, paralleling historiographic developments regarding the history of 1960s youth radicalism in general, focused on women of color, seeking to expand definitions of second-wave feminism beyond the racial and class-specific conception with which that movement was burdened during its heyday.

For all the accomplishments of this recent work, there was a lot left undone. Very few scholars were bridging the racial divide of the emerging scholarship on 1960s activism. Rare were the historians who managed to bring white and black activists within the scope of a single project or to study the complex, but surely real, interactions between activists of different racial identities during the 1960s. Ironically, Evans and Carson had done more along this front in their early works than later historians did. Relatively few young scholars seemed to find the white left of the 1960s a worthy subject for studies at all. I don't wish to engage in special pleading for this subject. The work on movements of people of color was and is absolutely essential, for reasons that are, I think, too obvious to state. Nonetheless, when *The Politics of Authenticity,* which grew out of my dissertation, was published, I did not think I had had the last word about white youth radicalism in the 1960s—and not about the New Left in the South in particular. Bill Billingsley's book on Chapel Hill came out shortly after my book (1999), and I was overjoyed to see the publication of Gregg Michel's book on the Southern Students Organizing Committee (2004).[2] But it seemed to me that there was plenty more to say in this area, and I have to admit I was a little disappointed there wasn't more work being produced in it.

Last of all, I felt that a lot of work produced on 1960s militancy and radicalism in the first decade of the new century was slipping back into a celebratory or defensive mode. I saw nothing wrong with taking an affirmative view of 1960s radicalism. It was defensible in all kinds of ways, notwithstanding its faults. And I was not merely hoping for a "fair and balanced" assessment that would mix criticism with praise. Instead I had hoped that new work would get beyond the "for or against" frame of discussion and that it would venture new interpretive ideas that might help us understand the 1960s in a way we hadn't before. That kind of interpretive freshness was what I was looking for most of all.

I think the work showcased here is fresh indeed. The authors of this work are working to rectify some of the areas of scholarly neglect I've just mentioned, and I hope that they can help point us toward new areas of inquiry and new, higher levels of historical understanding. They are really digging in, doing the kind of archival groundwork that will lay the basis for future interpretive developments, and they are already pointing toward new interpretations themselves. I will not list all the fine individual essays here. The reader knows them already, and Robert Cohen, in his superb introduction to this volume, discusses them with great insight. But simply to note that between this volume's covers you will read about activism on historically black colleges and universities (HBCUs) as well as predominantly white universities; that you will learn about both campus environments and broader or different environments that nurtured student activism in the South, such as the Human Relations Project of the National Student Association or the Student Nonviolent Coordinating Committee (SNCC); that you will learn about events in public and private institutions of higher education; and that all of the essays published here concern the U.S. South—well, if anyone had predicted you would have such a volume in your hands even a fairly short time ago, you might have doubted it would come to pass. Yet here it is. We will all be learning from it (and no doubt from other works by the authors of these chapters) for years to come.

Before ending, I will take up a couple of the conceptual issues that these essays raise and that Cohen identifies in his introduction. These two issues are related. One is the question of whether we can usefully encompass both African American and white student rebellion in the 1960s in a single analytical category, in particular whether the concept of the New Left can serve this purpose. The second is the question of how to describe the activism chronicled in this volume's essays ideologically.

Cohen writes wittily that SNCC could be called "New Left–*ish*." There is much to recommend that view. It certainly was the case that, at least by 1964, SNCC activists were alienated politically from mainstream political liberalism, at least as it was represented within the national Democratic party. At the same time, I am not convinced that the New Left is a sustainable master category that can capture the breadth of black and white youth activism, even when it took on a radical or alienated form, in the 1960s. It's true that Jack Newfield, in *A Prophetic Minority* (1966), included SNCC as part of the New Left. It's also true that Carson, in *In Struggle*, discussed the intersection of SNCC and the New Left. Carson writes that "a convergence in the ideological evolution of SNCC and predominantly white New Left groups allowed them to share, for a time, a common radical vocabulary and anti-imperialistic perspective."[3] Carson portrayed this convergence as temporary, perhaps only obtaining in 1965 and 1966. Carson, who knew the collective mind of SNCC very well, understood that African American radicals and militants in the 1960s rarely identified themselves with the concept of the New Left. Starting in 1968, many youth activists of color—mainly outside the deep South, it should be noted in the context of this volume—began to identify themselves with what Max Elbaum, in a 2002 article, termed "Third World Marxism," for example during the student strike at San Francisco State College in 1968–69.[4] But even in those cases, the young firebrands carefully avoided saying that they were part of the New Left, which clearly connoted white radicalism to contemporaries. All this is merely to say that the lines of political identity separating white radicals from activists of color were quite real and important during the 1960s, and we elide those boundaries at the risk of distorting the past. At the same time, bringing the histories of black and white activism together, as this book does, is commendable and provides, at the very least, thought-provoking juxtapositions, highlighting contrasts as well as similarities. And we should not forget that black and white student activists did interact and work together, and not just in the early 1960s, despite the complexities and in some cases the ambivalence that marked those interactions. Some of the essays here do a real service by not letting us forget that.

In terms of ideological position, I think, once again, Cohen is on the mark in pointing out the relative moderation of activists in a southern context (especially in the deep South) and also in identifying them as—to quote Newfield—a prophetic minority in a broadly conservative environment. As far as the white student activists went, the early-model New Left—one hopeful about provoking reform in American society and politics and about merely opening intellectual and political life to radical perspectives, rather than fomenting a revolution—remained salient in the South when it had come to seem passé to a great many northern New

Left radicals. The southern New Left remained more a left-liberal movement than did their northern or west coast counterparts. This is a conclusion buttressed by Michel's book, *Struggle for a Better South,* and supported further by several of the essays in this volume.

Regarding African American activists, particularly those at HBCUs, the inappropriateness of classifying them as leftist radicals is equally clear. African American students who engaged in protest activity at Fisk and Vanderbilt Universities; at the University of Alabama; at various schools in South Carolina, North Carolina, and Mississippi had to devote far more of their energies, for a longer time, to fighting for their basic constitutional rights than white students did (although white activists sometimes had to struggle for these rights, too). African American student activists also, even when they came to voice their demands in the language of Black Power and radical antiracism, pressed an agenda of representation in college and university life that was not so different from the agenda of African Americans of older generations whose ideological and political position was definitely inside the U.S. political system. Just as SNCC, even as its perspective on American society became more radical, found a meaningful outlet for its efforts in traditional political organizing in Lowndes County, Alabama—and just as the Black Panther party by the early 1970s got deeply involved in city council and mayoral campaigns in Oakland—so too did southern black youth activists develop a political program and vision that was compatible with the traditional quest for empowerment within the party political system and governmental structure that absorbed the more "established" civil rights leadership, particularly in the South after the passage of the Voting Rights Act of 1965. The alienation of youth from the mainstream political system that became such a prominent feature for many white radicals in the late 1960s, even sometimes in the South, did not emerge in the same way in African American politics, despite the critiques of the civil rights establishment that militant African American youth sometimes expressed. If black youth activists were on the outside looking in on America's dominant political structures, they were trying to get inside, and it would be problematic to view them as revolutionaries seeking to replace one political system with another.

I'll end here. As I've noted already, these great essays give us ample food for thought and start to move us forward in the depth of our collective understanding of southern politics, youth politics, and the evolution of both the African American freedom struggle and white radicalism in the era of the 1960s.

NOTES

1. Todd Gitlin, *The Sixties: Years of Hope, Days of Rage* (New York: Bantam, 1987); Maurice Isserman, *If I Had a Hammer. . . .: The Death of the Old Left and the Birth of the New*

Left (New York: Basic Books, 1987); James Miller, *"Democracy Is in the Streets": From Port Huron to the Siege of Chicago* (New York: Simon and Schuster, 1987).

2. William J. Billingsley, *Communists on Campus: Race, Politics, and the Public University in Sixties North Carolina* (Athens: Univ. of Georgia Press, 1999); Gregg L. Michel, *Struggle for a Better South: The Southern Student Organizing Committee, 1964–1969* (New York: Palgrave Macmillan, 2008).

3. Clayborne Carson, *In Struggle: SNCC and the Black Awakening of the 1960s* (Cambridge, MA: Harvard Univ. Press, 1995), 175.

4. Max Elbaum, "What Legacy from the Radical Internationalism of 1968?" *Radical History Review,* no. 82 (Winter 2002): 37–64.

Afterword

DAVID T. FARBER

The history of southern student activism in the sixties era forces us to rethink the narrative of Movement politics. Few of us are surprised to read of the great diversity of actors and activities that characterized southern students' local responses to racial injustice and established social hierarchies, the war in Vietnam, institutional restrictions, and other concerns. But activists' diverse political responses should cause us to think harder about how to characterize and analyze the local nature of oppositional politics in the sixties era. We all know that institutional setting and conditions, local and regional structures of power, and the role of individual authorities and activists affected the dialogic nature of Movement political mobilization, overarching strategic goals, and protest tactics, but rarely have scholars of the sixties' "Movement of movements" explained how the so-called protest politics in the 1960s were both situational and interconnected, national and local, regional and cosmopolitan and transnational.[1] The history of southern student activism reveals these linkages and the challenges produced by such tensions between the specific, enacted forms that Movement tactics took in specific places and the general, overarching motives and principles that gave coherence and even international unity to the Movement of the sixties.

Historians of the 1960s-era social change movements have long debated how best to characterize and explain the political activism that transformed the United States and many other nations. Van Gosse, in his cogent but provocative scholarship, argues that the term *New Left* aptly describes not just the politics of the Students for a Democratic Society and narrowly like-minded organizations but also the Movement in general; for Van Gosse, the New Left movement, above all, was based on a radical democratic politics.[2] Sara Evans probably would agree with Van Gosse's general claim, but in her classic work on the origins and development of the women's liberation movement in the civil rights movement and the New Left, she offers a different focus, making the case for "personal politics," a style of engagement that she argues began in the civil rights movement and became central to women's liberation. To be a part of the "movement," she writes, "implied an experience, a sense of community and common purpose."[3] Doug Rossinow, one of the most astute scholars of the era, writes in a similar vein when he argues for "the politics of authenticity." Rossinow means that activists—and he is most concerned with white student radicals—sought not pragmatic changes in public policy or even the overthrow of the government as much as they wanted to find a way out of the atomized, alienated, and hyper-individualistic way of life that, they believed, characterized the United States at the advent of the 1960s.[4] During the 1960s, the sociologist Seymour Martin Lipset looked at those radical democratic personal politics of authenticity with consternation and dismissed them as expressive politics devoid of clear purpose and instrumental function and dangerous insomuch as activists refused to understand the need for civility and the importance of rules in the struggle for compromise between conflicting interests. The sociologist Wini Brienes, while not completely rejecting Lipset's claims, redeployed his analysis; she argued that Movement politics were not conventionally instrumental but were instead "prefigurative." The New Left movement, she wrote, "sought community as it sought to reunite the public and the private spheres of life."[5] All of these attempts to define generally the politics of the broad sixties-era Movement circle around a similar understanding: activists deeply involved in the racial justice movements, the student movement, the antiwar movement, the women's movement, the gay liberation movement, and other linked social change movements sought to model a new politics based on a more direct personal and lived involvement in a collective, democratic struggle for social change. Phrases like "beloved community" and "participatory democracy" are emblematic of this Movement politics and indicative, too, of the larger strategic vision that moved Movement activists to "put their bodies on the line."

So analysts of the social change movements of the sixties era, especially those sympathetic to these movements, have written many cogent characterizations of the activists' political struggle. In part in order to provide such cogent characterizations, scholars have paid less attention to the activists' continuing efforts to find and deploy useful political forms in those struggles to advance their causes. Tactics of dissent, in other words, have often been treated as less compelling subjects of historical description and analysis, except insomuch as they provide high drama, timeless inspiration, or obvious points of contention within movement circles. Rarely are movement tactics treated as key analytic sites, except perhaps for such climactic moments as the expulsion of whites from SNCC or the Weathermen's embrace of bombings. Lipset, in his classic criticism of Movement politics, spoke to this problem of effective forms of political struggle in "sixties" America when he complained that the activists' forms were, somehow, both inappropriate and ineffective. He seemed to believe that normative electoral politics were capacious enough to contain and respond to the concerns of activists. Like many critics of the sixties-era movements, he paid little to no attention to the problem of mobilization within these struggles (how to move individuals from complacency or apathy to engagement and action) or the means by which unpopular or non-majority political positions could or should be presented to the broader citizenry. Normative electoral politics, he and other critics of movement politics simply argued, would have better served the specific goals of the various movements of the Movement. The broad repertoire of protest that activists deployed in their politics of contention—to speak in the jargon of sociology—was certainly seen by many "Establishment" figures as dangerous and even un-American; certainly that was the view of figures as diverse as Bull Connor, J. Edgar Hoover, and Chicago Mayor Richard J. Daley.[6] Such blanket condemnation by such a range of authorities lends itself to a simple dichotomy—one repeated in historical memory as well as in scholarly accounts—between the activists and the Establishment. But a closer examination of social change politics in the sixties era reveals a very different view of activism and of the people and places affected by the Movement. The history of southern student activism is illuminative of that complex process.

Most basically and worth constantly repeating, especially when looking at the broad subject of southern student activism, Movement tactics were mandated by the problem of moving people in power from their comfortable, often self-serving positions to a different political and policy landscape in which their familiar beliefs and entrenched interests would be challenged or even overthrown. Those people in power in the South, as well as in the North or in a national context, varied according to the particular political problem being addressed. Racial justice activists had to contend with a generally complacent, self-regarding, and powerful white majority. Student rights protesters were fighting the near-absolute authority of university officials who were in some cases answerable to public figures and in other cases only to their boards of trustees and alumni. Antiwar protesters struggled to overcome a well-enshrined Cold War hegemony. The list goes on. Insomuch as activists joined hands in support of a broad movement for social justice, their opponents, too, multiplied and coalesced in opposition. Such coalition bloc building is the normative stuff of electoral politics and of legislative logrolling. But in the case of southern student activism, this dynamic obviously escaped the normative boundaries of electoral coalition building. For southern student activists, white and black, the problem of their enduring minority status in the face of an entrenched, passionately anti-Movement majority made their movement-building tactics and political resistance especially difficult and demanding. It also made their commitment to local electoral politics unlikely since it was so improbable a path to good results.

For most leftist or Movement student activists, electoral coalition building was, at a personal level and as a Movement cause, a nonstarter. Almost by definition, at least through the passage of the Twenty-Sixth Amendment in July 1971, a great

majority of students were not old enough to vote, and even those who could represented just a tiny, nearly powerless portion of the electorate. Without the vote,
money for lobbying, or powerful representation within legislative bodies, electoral
politics in the North and in the South was unlikely to produce short- or medium-
term results or to inspire new adherents. More fundamentally, the southern civil
rights movement grew and formed as it did in large part because African Americans in the region had been largely disenfranchised at least until the hard-fought
passage of the 1965 Voting Rights Act. The southern civil rights movement, to state
the obvious, had to develop outside of normative electoral politics. And as case
studies of the racial justice movement and the national student movement show,
even after the 1965 Voting Rights Act, the template for activism created by the
pre-1965 cohort continued to play an inspirational and axiomatic form even for
many who came after and could legally vote. Movement politics played to Americans' moral claims rather than to the majority's narrow self-interest; such a call
and commitment to high principle also moved some from complacency to support and from support to activism. This activism, in turn, offered people an opportunity to commit themselves to a worthy cause that was a subjectively transformative experience. Such a transformative experience—an existential commitment
to marking one's life through virtuous action, to speak in the cosmopolitan ver-
nacular of the era—was spiritually intoxicating for many activists. And like others
who had been rewarded with such an experience, they sought to share the good
news. Personal transformation was not the goal of social change movements but
was, given the larger political setting of Movement culture, especially in the largely
antagonistic setting of the South, an almost necessary aspect of the struggle. Personal transformation within and on behalf of a "beloved community" was part of
the reward of the endeavor and a bulwark against the violence and oppression that
was likely to be visited on the activist's body and soul.

For good historical reasons, scholars of the civil rights movement are increasingly dedicated to decentering the inspirational and canonical story of the
movement's march from the Montgomery bus boycott to "Bloody Sunday" outside Selma, calling instead, in Jacqueline Dowd Hall's term, for an accounting of
the "long civil rights movement" and, in Thomas Sugrue's case, for a Movement
history that also includes and even foregrounds the struggles and activists of the
North.[7] Such historiographical developments are worthy ones and better reflective
of the struggles undertaken by generations of racial justice proponents. At the
same time, such extensions of the historical record should not preclude scholars
from considering how the iconic and celebrated struggles of the southern movement in the 1950s and 1960s were seen at the time by activists as history-making
and as models of and for engaged struggle. We know that sit-ins were not a new

tactic in February 1960 for racial justice activists, and so did some activists at the time. But especially for young people, relatively disconnected from the long history of the racial justice struggle, in part due to the Cold War / McCarthy-ite erasure of the Communist Party's antiracist leadership and tactical inventiveness during the 1930s and 1940s, sit-ins were an attractive and inspiring form of protest at least in part due to student activists' sense that they were fashioning their own movement as they were creating their own forms of charismatic resistance. They could not vote, but they could march; they could not legislate, but they could sit-in. They could, then, use their bodies and their role in the market economy to make their claims on American public life. Like the white women who served as spearheads of reform in the Progressive Era, young student activists in the civil rights movement, in particular, used their outside-the-electoral-system status to self-consciously rethink democratic practice in the United States and become powerful historic actors in their own right. The visibility of their actions and the shock of their democratic creativity in a Cold War era grown politically complacent and oblivious of the meaning of democracy was both compelling for some and frightening for many others. But above all, southern student activists refashioned the repertoire of democratic political tactics—even if most of their forms of dissent were preexisting—and could and did take pride and pleasure in building a Movement political culture. While the instrumentality of that political culture was uncertain in the usual and conventional realms of American politics—legislative bodies, executive agencies, and courthouses—it was particularly effective in other institutional forums. Colleges and universities, not surprisingly for a student movement, were particularly efficacious settings for the nonelectoral tactics the student civil rights movement established as a template for contention and dissent.

Historians of the sixties era, somewhat surprisingly, have done relatively little work examining how and why student activism worked as it did on college campuses. Student activism on campuses is often treated as a kind of hothouse for an emergent national, rather than a regional (northern) or local, movement political culture that is then transplanted to more significant locations such as the Pentagon or the National Mall or the Democratic National Convention in 1968. Or, in a conceptually related fashion, the university-based student activism is treated as a somewhat odd corollary to antiwar activism better understood as a somewhat misguided and indirect means of changing national war policy. Southern campus-based activism is particularly useful for rethinking this approach to the site-specific student movement. For southern student activists, universities were not simply a practice field for a real political game to be played later; they saw their campuses as formative and fundamental institutional sites for social and political change.

Americans have long held ambivalent attitudes toward institutions of higher learning in large part because of the fundamental role colleges and universities play in producing and reproducing social hierarchy and cultural conventions. Most recently, many Americans have regarded colleges and universities above all as a critical locus of economic opportunity. In a more distant past, higher education was regarded as a pathway to elite status and community leadership. Academics and other proponents of the university as creator and upholder of a more, if you will, universalist and cosmopolitan ideal have often tried to balance these economic motives and notions of conventional elite formation with claims for the university as an ideal place for knowledge production and generative intellectual heterodoxy. Like other key building blocks in the American cultural matrix, universities and colleges have almost always been contested sites.

In the South, the official, often legally mandated segregation of schools made higher education an obvious target for civil rights activists. The U.S. Supreme Court's pre-*Brown* decisions, in positive response to NAACP legal challenges to the segregation of professional and graduate schools in Texas and Oklahoma, spoke to the unique service universities provide individuals as they seek equal access to the educational training that allows individuals to become practitioners in elite endeavors. Less well documented is the role student activists played in many southern colleges and universities as they struggled to stop these institutions from reproducing racial hierarchy, either through direct means of segregation or enforced accommodation to racism or less directly through the production and dissemination of race knowledge and racial practices that served to inscribe inequitable racial conventions. For southern student racial justice activists, and then later for campus-based student Movement activists more generally, part of their struggle was to confront alumni, trustees, and many administrators and students at key universities in the South who believed that the university served conventional social purposes, most especially the production and reproduction of elites in service to economic power in an established racial hierarchy. Activists faced this problem not just at white or historically white-only schools but also at historically black colleges, where the hope and idea of producing a local or regional elite—even if that black elite was broadly subordinated to local and regional whites—was a substantial factor, though by no means the only one restraining a racial justice–oriented campus political culture.

At the proudly parochial and traditional University of Mississippi and even the relatively more liberal and cosmopolitan Vanderbilt University, many still clung without apology or any apparent need for self-examination to an ideal of the university as a replicator of local or, at best, regional elites who were initiated through campus-based social networks (fraternities, football games, and so on). Many outside of the South saw the university similarly, but at the great state universities of the North and at the increasingly nationally oriented liberal arts colleges of the Northeast and Midwest, this narrow casting of the mission of higher education had long been seriously contested as these schools embraced knowledge production and competitive scholarship as ideals, offering students—and faculty and administrators—far greater opportunity for dissident practices based on the legitimating claim that universities were marketplaces of rigorously produced ideas that were supposed to produce intellectual heterodoxy and the overthrow of unsupported conventional thinking and received wisdom. As the famous case of the Free Speech Movement at the University of California at Berkeley proves, activists had to fight hard and long—well, for an intense semester, at any rate—to push the university to accept campus-based activism as a valid use of the university's marketplace of ideas claim. Nonetheless, Berkeley administrative leaders' claims about the proper function of the university gave dissident students and their allies intellectual room to maneuver and to make strong claims to legitimacy.

At universities and colleges in the South, historical case studies reveal that this view of higher education as a site for the production of intellectual and political heterodoxy was an even more contested practice. While no one has yet fully explored how and why southern universities, in particular, were less accepting of the ideal of the knowledge-challenging, convention-upsetting university, the pride of place of racial hierarchy in southern white politics and white society played a substantial role into the 1960s. To challenge conventional thinking and so-called traditional values in the white South was unavoidably to ponder the genealogy and legitimacy of centuries of white supremacy, and it also explains how and why ambitious and intellectually adventurous leaders at such southern schools as the University of North Carolina and Emory University simultaneously embraced antiracism and the ideal of the cosmopolitan research university.

Leaders at historically black colleges faced an even more challenging environment for allowing, let alone championing, the production and acceptance of unconventional or dissenting views and practices, especially as they related to local and regional racial culture and policy. Students at these schools were in much the same bind. For students, faculty, and administrators to turn away from the role of the historically black college as the prudent producer of local and regional black elites was to risk a great deal. Black activists who sought to use their campuses as sites of resistance rather than as avenues of accommodation to the established hierarchy faced direct or indirect white pressure and, in some cases, even violence, either of which risked those activists' present status and future aspiration. Such campus-based activism could also result in powerful whites choosing to rain down troubles on the entire school, damaging not just the life course of individual activists but also their fellow students' ambitions, their professors' jobs, and their school administrators' positions.

White and black southern student movement activists, then, faced daunting—though, as always, unequal—challenges in the use of the university or college campus as a site for political dissent. Yet those students also recognized that their schools were the very factories of their social reproduction and the shop floor upon which they worked daily. The immediacy of racial subordination and the palpable limits placed on dissent in most southern institutions of higher education put student activists in a difficult tactical position, even as it hammered home the need for continued resistance and expanded mobilization.

It is not surprising that after the remarkable—and the further removed we become from the early 1960s, the more remarkable that era appears to be—period of democratic creativity in the early sixties, southern student activists—literally young people of a different cohort—found themselves somewhat stymied as they searched for the means by which they could build upon their predecessors' struggles and successes. Especially given the very limited structural changes that had occurred at southern universities and colleges—token integration at most previously all-white schools and limited on-campus organizing opportunities—students had to generate a new set of democratic tools of dissent to move forward. To generate those tools in the specific, conservative institutional frameworks of southern schools, southern student activists turned, at least in part, to extra-local, extra-regional political linkages. Through organizational networks, personal connections forged in action, a growing alternative media, and the broadband of the national mass media, southern student activists began to draw tactically and even strategically on struggles that some, both inside and outside of the South, thought of as part of a national movement.

During the Progressive Era, politically active Americans looked internationally as well as domestically for inspirational solutions to the problems of a newly industrializing society. Implementation of those inspirational ideas generally then occurred at the local level—and only occasionally did some of those implemented policies and practices, a relatively small subset, become national policy or practice. Federalism, and not federal power, typified that particular age of reform. So too did the student movement, as well as the broader Movement of movements, take the form of a federated, often locally based set of democratic tactics of resistance and protest against social injustices as well as dissent from the nation-state's war in Vietnam.

Activists' ability to try out different tactics in service to a general strategy of resistance and radical challenge marked the sixties era of dissent. Southern student activists, building on a long-standing non-electoral movement culture, played a fundamental role in generating the democratically driven politics of dissent that the problem of white supremacy demanded, especially in the South. Given the more rigid institutional limits and conservative political culture of the South, it is not surprising that, especially in regard to the non–regionally based issue of the Vietnam War, southern student activists found inspiration and direction from activists based in other parts of the nation and from what was increasingly being perceived by activists and anti-activists alike as a national movement. Ironically, many of the first antiwar protests—those from 1965 to 1967—mostly followed the protest template established by the southern racial justice struggle. But as the antiwar movement went "from protest to resistance" in 1968 and after, Movement political culture did generally move away from that template, as activists developed new tactics and even goals. Some student activists in the South—as in the North—moved in these new directions, too, but never in the same numbers or (generally) with the same intensity as those outside the South. And just as many of the most militant turns of dissent in the North turned out to be counterproductive, so too did southern student activists' most militant turns turn out to be broadly ineffective.

Movement political culture, like the electoral political culture of the nation, moved unevenly across regions and locales, even as national frames of reference suggested broad turns and general shifts. Southern student activists moved always through multiple frames of reference as they worked in local settings structured by specific historical circumstances, even as they both created and reacted to regional, national, and even international conditions, opportunities, and challenges. Future synthetic and case-study histories of the Movement will do well to foreground how these multiple political influences and political landscapes affected Movement actions as they took place in specific places. Southern student activists, in particular, always marched through an unmapped political minefield as they sought social change. Too often historians of the sixties era, and I include myself in this, have failed to explain just how perplexing the politics of democratic change were for activists and non-activists alike in the United States in the sixties era. The economist Joseph Schumpeter used the phrase "creative destruction" to explain the difficult but necessary and regular process through which capitalist societies must pass. We have no similarly pithy phrase to explain how democratic societies move forward in the struggle toward greater social justice, but histories of the southern student movement and the broader Movement of the sixties era help us to see how hard but also how necessary it is for a democratic people to face their own social failures and find political solutions to them. That democratic process, alas, must also almost always involve a season of creative destruction.

NOTES

1. The phrase is from Van Gosse, *The Movements of the New Left, 1950–1975* (New York: Bedford / St. Martin's, 2005), 1.

2. See, for example, Van Gosse, *Rethinking the New Left: An Interpretive History* (New York: Palgrave Macmillan, 2005).

3. Sara Evans, *Personal Politics* (New York: Vintage, 1980), 102.

4. Doug Rossinow, *The Politics of Authenticity* (New York: Columbia Univ. Press, 1998).

5. See "Introduction to the New Left: A Critique of Some Critics," in Wini Breines, *Community and Organization in the New Left* (South Hadley, MA: J. F. Bergin, 1982), 6.

6. This theme is explored in my *Chicago '68* (Chicago: Univ. of Chicago Press, 1988), ch. 10.

7. Jacqueline Hall, "The Long Civil Rights Movement and the Political Uses of the Past," *Journal of American History 91, no. 4 (2005): 1233–63;* and Thomas Sugrue, *Sweet Land of Liberty* (New York: Random House, 2009).

ROBERT COHEN is a professor of social studies and history at New York University. His books include *Freedom's Orator: Mario Savio and the Radical Legacy of the 1960s* (2009); *Teaching U.S. History: Dialogues among Social Studies Teachers and Historians* (coedited with Diana Turk, Rachel Mattson, and Terrie Epstein; 2009); *Dear Mrs. Roosevelt: Letters from Children of the Great Depression* (2007); *The Free Speech Movement: Reflections on Berkeley in the 1960s* (coedited with Reginald E. Zelnik; 2002), which the *L.A. Times Book Review* named one of the hundred best books of the year; and *When the Old Left Was Young: Student Radicals and America's First Mass Student Movement, 1929–1941* (1997), named a Choice Outstanding Academic Book. Cohen is also consulting editor of *Emma Goldman, A Documentary History of the American Years,* the most recent volume of which is *Making Speech Free, 1902–1909.*

DAVID J. SNYDER is instructor of history at the University of South Carolina, where he teaches courses in American, European, and U.S. foreign relations history. A former Fulbright fellow, his articles and reviews have appeared in *Diplomatic History, The Journal of American History, Peace and Change,* and *The Journal of Cold War Studies.* He has also contributed chapters on public diplomacy and U.S.-Netherlands relations to several published anthologies. He is currently revising a manuscript addressing the Dutch response to American modernization policy in the early Cold War.

DAN T. CARTER is the Educational Foundation Professor of History Emeritus at the University of South Carolina. He is the author and editor of more than forty articles and six books, including *Scottsboro: A Tragedy of the American South* (1970); *When the War Was Over: The Failure of Self-Reconstruction in the South* (1985); *The Politics of Rage: George Wallace, the Origins of the New Conservatism, and the Transformation of American Politics* (1995); and *From George Wallace to Newt Gingrich: the Role of Race in the Conservative Counterrevolution, 1963–1994* (1996). Recognition for his work includes the Bancroft Prize in History, the Robert F. Kennedy Literary Prize, and an Emmy Award for the 2000 PBS documentary *George Wallace: "Settin' the Woods on Fire."* In 1961, Carter joined with other students in forming the South Carolina Student Council on Human Relations, the first integrated student group in South Carolina's history.

DAVID T. FARBER is professor of history at Temple University. His sixties-era publications include *The Sixties: From Memory to History* (1994); *The Age of Great Dreams* (1994); *Chicago '68* (1988); *The Columbia Guide to America in the 1960s* (coauthored with Beth Bailey and contributors; 2001); and *The Conservative Sixties* (coedited with Jeff Roche; 2003). Other books include: *Sloan Rules* (2002);

Taken Hostage (2004); and *The Rise and Fall of Modern American Conservatism* (2010). He has earned Choice Outstanding Academic Book recognition three times. His latest work is *Everybody Ought to be Rich: The Life and Times of John Raskob, Capitalist* (2013).

JELANI FAVORS is assistant professor of history at Morgan State University. He earned his PhD from the Ohio State University in 2006 with a dissertation entitled "Shelter in a Time of Storm: Black Colleges and the Rise of Student Activism in Jackson, Mississippi." In 2008–9 he was named a Mellon HBCU Fellow at Duke University. His research and teaching interests include U.S. history, African American history, student activism, the civil rights movement, and black popular culture.

WESLEY HOGAN teaches the history of social movements, African American history, women's history, and oral history at Virginia State University. Her book on SNCC, *Many Minds, One Heart: SNCC and the Dream for a New America* (2007), won the Lillian Smith Book Award, the Scott-Bills Memorial Prize for best work in peace history, and the Library of Virginia nonfiction literary award. She was the codirector of the Institute for the Study of Race Relations from 2006 through 2009. She is currently working on two books on twentieth-century freedom struggles.

CHRISTOPHER A. HUFF earned a PhD from the University of Georgia in 2012. His dissertation, "A New Way of Living Together: A History of Atlanta's Hip Community, 1965–1973," explores the New Left and the counterculture in the South's largest and most important city. His article "Radicals between the Hedges: The Origins of the New Left at the University of Georgia and the 1968 Sit-In" received the William Bacon Stevens Award from the Georgia Historical Society for the best student article published in *The Georgia Historical Quarterly* in 2010–11. He currently teaches history at the University of Georgia.

NICHOLAS G. MERIWETHER is the founding editor of the peer-reviewed journal *Dead Studies,* and his work on nineteenth-century Southern literary and cultural history, the 1960s, bohemianism, and the postwar Bay Area literary and cultural scene has appeared in a variety of popular and scholarly books and periodicals, including *All Graceful Instruments: The Contexts of the Grateful Dead Phenomenon* (2007) and *Reading the Grateful Dead: A Critical Survey* (2012), both of which he edited. He serves as Grateful Dead archivist at the University of California at Santa Cruz.

GREGG L. MICHEL is associate professor and chair of the Department of History at the University of Texas at San Antonio. His book, *Struggle for a Better South: The Southern Student Organizing Committee, 1964–1969* (2004), examines the turbulent history of the leading progressive white student organization in the 1960s South. His current work focuses on government surveillance of student activists in the South in the 1960s and 1970s.

KELLY MORROW earned her PhD in history from the University of North Carolina at Chapel Hill in 2012 with a dissertation entitled "Sex and the Student Body: Knowledge, Equality, and the Sexual Revolution, 1960 to 1973." She received the Spencer Foundation Dissertation Fellowship and has been awarded funding from the Center for the Study of the American South and the University of North Carolina at Chapel Hill Graduate School and History Department.

DOUG ROSSINOW is professor of history and chair of the Department of History at Metropolitan State University. He took his PhD in history from the Johns Hopkins University. He is the author of *The Politics of Authenticity: Liberalism, Christianity, and the New Left in America* (1998) and *Visions of Progress: The Left-Liberal Tradition in America* (2008) as well as numerous articles and essays. He is currently completing a history of America in the 1980s.

CLEVELAND L. SELLERS JR. is the eighth president of Voorhees College. He was active in the Mississippi Freedom Summer of 1964 and became SNCC's first program director the following year. In 1968 Sellers was convicted of rioting for his actions in what became known as the "Orangeburg Massacre" and spent seven months in jail; he was pardoned years later. He earned his EdD from the University of North Carolina at Greensboro and was the director of the African American Studies program at the University of South Carolina from 2001 to 2008. His publications include his memoir, *River of No Return: The Autobiography of a Black Militant and the Life and Death of SNCC* (1990). He has been recognized for his work by the National Voting Rights Museum and Institute; the United Negro College Fund; the City of Columbia, South Carolina; the University of South Carolina; and the Boy Scouts of America.

GARY S. SPRAYBERRY received his PhD in history from the University of Alabama in 2003. He is currently chair of the History and Geography Department at Columbus State University. His work has appeared in numerous publications, including *The Alabama Review* and *The Encyclopedia of Alabama*. He is currently revising his manuscript *Model City, Colored Town: Paternalism, Class, and Civil Rights in Anniston, Alabama, 1872 to Present* for publication.

MARCIA G. SYNNOTT is professor emerita of history at the University of South Carolina. She is the author of *The Half-Opened Door: Discrimination and Admissions at Harvard, Yale, and Princeton, 1900–1970* (1979; 2010). Other recent publications include "African American Women Pioneers in Desegregating Higher Education," in *Higher Education and the Civil Rights Movement: White Supremacy, Black Southerners, and College Campuses* (2007); "The Evolving Diversity Rationale in University Admissions: From *Regents v. Bakke* to the University of Michigan Cases" in *The Cornell Law Review* (2005); and "Crusaders and Clubwomen: Alice Norwood Spearman Wright and Her Women's Network," in *Throwing Off the Cloak of Privilege: White Southern Women Activists in the Civil Rights Era* (2004).

JEFFREY A. TURNER teaches history and is chair of the History Department at St. Catherine's School in Richmond, Virginia. He is the author of *Sitting In and Speaking Out: Student Movements in the American South, 1960–1970* (2010). Turner earned a PhD in history at Tulane University.

ERICA L. WHITTINGTON completed her PhD in history at the University of Texas at Austin in 2012; her dissertation is titled "From the Campus to the Globe: Race, Internationalism, and Student Activism in the Postwar South, 1945–1962." Her essay on the University of Texas YM/YWCA won the Texas Exes UT Heritage Society Essay Contest and appeared in the *Alcalde Magazine*. She is cofounder of the UT Gender Symposium and served as cochair of the Graduate Student Assembly. She has been awarded the Theodore Henry Strauss Student Award for Exemplary University Service. Whittington currently teaches American history at the University of Texas at Austin.

JOY ANN WILLIAMSON-LOTT is an associate professor in the College of Education at the University of Washington at Seattle. She has published chapters in edited volumes as well as articles in the *Journal of Negro Education, The History of Education Quarterly,* and *The History of Higher Education Annual*. She has published two monographs: *Black Power on Campus: The University of Illinois, 1965–1975* (2003) and *Radicalizing the Ebony Tower: Black Colleges and the Black Freedom Struggle in Mississippi* (2008). Her current research investigates the internal and external pressures experienced by black and white colleges across the South between the mid-1950s and the mid-1970s.